Critical praise for this book

This marvellous collection of essays is an important contribution to our collective understanding of the range of violence, mainly against women, that goes under the shorthand of 'honour crimes'. Like many such terms, it silen and conceals structures of domination, of violence and sexual regulation as much as it reveals the kind of defences that patriarchy summons to its aid. The contributors are passionate and analytical, legally informed and sensitive the dangers of culturalist and Eurocentric discourses. This book must find its way to the shelves of every concerned lawyer, activist and citizen.

Nandini Sundar, Professor of Sociology, Delhi University

An extremely timely and insightful book! The collection of essays in this volume will deepen our understanding of the many faces of violence against women. By challenging the invocation to justify crimes committed in the name of honour, the authors vocalise the silent but brave resistance of women worldwide whose lives are encroached upon with claims of dishonour. Combined efforts of activists, academics and women in their everyday lives in countering such social myths will amass in relocating the shame and dishonour from the victim to the perpetrators where they belong.

Yakin Ertürk, Middle East Technical University, Ankara,
UN Special Rapporteur on violence against women

'Honour crimes' are in fact among the most dishonourable of crimes involving the killing of others. While clearly condemning these outrageous practices, this book brings very welcome analytical balance, nuance and sophistication to the task of understanding and seeking to combat such killings. It is by far the best recent work on the issue and is indispensable reading.

Professor Philip Alston, Director of the Center for Human Rights
and Global Justice, New York University School of Law

This urgently needed volume provides invaluable insight on how we should understand the concept of 'honour crimes' as it impacts predominantly on women and girl children in different contexts throughout the world. The volume helps to debunk the view that 'honour crimes' are a 'Muslim' phenomenon, that they are separate from the issue of violence against women, and that the struggle for women's human rights is somehow 'alien' to non-Western or minority communities. Above all it offers an opportunity to develop strategies of resistance in the light of shared knowledge. Thoughtful and thought-provoking, the volume is an indispensable tool for anyone seriously committed to eradicating violence against women in all communities.

Pragna Patel, Southall Black Sisters

This is an excellent contribution to debates about 'crimes of honour', violence against women, and the politics of culture. Setting new standards for collaborative work between activists and academics, it is a major resource not only for those working in the field of legal studies, but also for social scientists and policymakers.

Professor Annelies Moors, ISIM chair,
University of Amsterdam

'HONOUR'

Crimes, paradigms and violence against women

EDITED BY LYNN WELCHMAN AND SARA HOSSAIN

SPINIFEX PRESS
Victoria

ZED BOOKS
London & New York

'*Honour*' was first published in 2005
by Zed Books Ltd, 7 Cynthia Street, London N1 9JF, UK,
and Room 400, 175 Fifth Avenue, New York, NY 10010, USA

www.zedbooks.co.uk

Published in Australia and New Zealand by Spinifex Press,
504 Queensberry Street, North Melbourne, Victoria 3051 Australia

www.spinifexpress.com.au

Designed and typeset in Monotype Bembo by Illuminati, Grosmont
www.illuminatibooks.co.uk
Cover designed by Andrew Corbett
Printed and bound in the EU by Biddles Ltd
www.biddles.co.uk

Distributed in the USA exclusively by Palgrave Macmillan,
a division of St Martin's Press, LLC, 175 Fifth Avenue, New York, NY 10010

A catalogue record for this book is available from the British Library
Library of Congress Cataloging-in-Publication Data available

ISBN 1 84277 626 6 (Hb)
ISBN 1 84277 627 4 (Pb)

Spinifex ISBN: 1 876756 61 6

Contents

Acknowledgements

Many people have been involved in the five-year process of the CIMEL/ INTERIGHTS Project on 'Strategies to Address Crimes of Honour' which has culminated in this publication. First, we would like to thank all the individual authors named in this book, for their engagement in a collective process of exchanging ideas and documenting experiences and critical reflections, for their patience with our editing processes, and for their friendship.

We would also like to thank all those named in individual chapters as having contributed to the research, and those working on the ground in organisations across the world whose activities formed the basis of the research papers or influenced our thinking, including the Association for Advocacy and Legal Initiatives, Ain-o-Salish Kendra, Centre for Egyptian Women's Legal Assistance (CEWLA), Latin American and Caribbean Committee for the Defense of Women's Rights (CLADEM), Kurdish Women against Honour Killings, Shirkat Gah, Southall Black Sisters, Women Against Violence and al-Badeel (working in the Palestinian community in Israel), Women's Centre for Legal Aid and Counselling (WCLAC), Women for Women's Human Rights, Lebanese Council to Resist Violence Against Women, the National Campaign to Eliminate So-called 'Crimes of Honour' in Jordan, the New Woman Research Centre and Nafisa Ibn, the Association Marocaine pour les Droits des Femmes and Centre Fama pour l'Orientation Juridique sur les Droits des Femmes.

Many people helped us through formal and informal discussions to gain further and valuable insights into the range of issues raised in this work and introduced us to new resources and information, including in particular Angelika Pathak, Javiera Rizvi, Gita Sahgal and Purna Sen.

All of those who contributed to the project over the years, including those at INTERIGHTS and at SOAS who have helped to administer it, require particular thanks, especially Maureen Goskin. We take this opportunity to credit the dozens of volunteers who have helped the project in different ways, including SOAS students and others working on the Annotated Bibliography, the Directory of Initiatives and the International Legal Materials, and who are acknowledged individually in those documents.

The project was supported by the Ford Foundation's Peace and Social Justice Programme in New York, through the good efforts and enthusiasm of Mahnaz Ispahani, then a programme officer. For subsequent years we owe thanks also to Fateh Azzam and most recently to Emma Playfair of the Ford Foundation's Middle East and North Africa Programme in Cairo, for continuing to support the project and to be engaged discussants in our work. Thanks are also due to Denise Dora of the Ford Foundation Brazil and to Aubrey McCutcheon, then of the Ford Foundation India, for the resources for exploring research and advocacy in Brazil and India, which are reflected in this volume.

Anna Hardman of Zed Books worked hard with us to get this publication out on schedule, and we thank her for her patience, support and flexibility.

On a personal level, Lynn's thanks go to Akram al-Khatib, for his love and for being everything that he is; to Elsie and Geoff Knights; and to friends including Laila Asser, Randa Alami, Urmi Shah, Aida Touma, Purna Sen, Emma Playfair and Anne Fitzgerald; and to Sara for her friendship and humour, for shared delights and despairs, and for teaching me so much. Sara's go to David Bergman for being there (and being with Laleh) and to Haneda and Kamal Hussain; to Gita Sahgal, Shohini Ghosh, Faustina Pereira, Beena Sarwar and Cassandra Balchin for conversations across the years, and lastly (and mostly) to Lynn and to Emma Playfair for being such good friends and mentors, for their insistence on building truly collaborative and transnational human rights initiatives, and never losing sight of political context at every level.

Finally, we would like to draw attention to the amazing input into the project from the women who worked as researchers on the project down the years. These include Samia Bano, who started it all off, and whose activist and intellectual critique of multiculturalism reinforced our approach to the work. Fouzia Khan was a bedrock through the middle years of the project; and the omnicompetence and enthusiasm of Moni Shrestha kept us all on track. Enormous gratitude is due in particular to Sanchita Hosali, whose timely arrival in the final phase of the Project, critical steering of and contribution to this publication, and ability to juggle research, writing and project organisation, ensured that there was method in the midst of the madness and finally a publication!

Lynn Welchman and Sara Hossain

We dedicate this book to all those who have been victims or survivors of so-called 'honour crimes', those who continue to challenge and combat such practices, and those who seek to build new structures, institutions and approaches which secure women's rights and liberties, not just to freedom from violence but freedom to determine their own choices and lives.

PREFACE

Violence against women
and 'crimes of honour'

RADHIKA COOMARASWAMY

In my work as the United Nations Special Rapporteur on violence against women, its causes and consequences, I soon came to realise that violence against women is closely linked to the regulation of sexuality. This is a sensitive but very important issue. In many societies the ideal of masculinity is underpinned by a notion of 'honour' – of an individual man, or a family or a community – and is fundamentally connected to policing female behaviour and sexuality. Honour is generally seen as residing in the bodies of women. Frameworks of 'honour', and its corollary 'shame', operate to control, direct and regulate women's sexuality and freedom of movement by male members of the family. Women who fall in love, engage in extramarital relationships, seek a divorce, or choose their own husbands are seen to transgress the boundaries of 'appropriate' (that is, socially sanctioned) sexual behaviour. 'Regulation' of such behaviour may in extreme cases involve horrific direct violence – including 'honour killing', perhaps the most overt example of the brutal control of female sexuality – as well as indirect subtle control exercised through threats of force or the withdrawal of family benefits and security. In these contexts, the rights of women (and girls) to control their own lives, to liberty or freedom of expression, association, movement and bodily integrity mean very little.

During my tenure as Special Rapporteur, I sought to address 'honour crimes' as a clear violation of human rights, and, given their gendered nature, as a manifestation of violence against women. Many of my reports (both annual and country visit studies) to the Commission on Human Rights, the foremost human rights body of the United Nations, included consideration of 'honour crimes'.[1] Through this work the incidence of 'honour crimes' – in countries including Brazil, Denmark, Egypt, Iraq, Israel and the occupied territories, Jordan, Kuwait, Lebanon, Morocco, the Netherlands, Pakistan, Qatar, Sweden, Syria, Turkey and Yemen – was brought to the attention of the international community.[2] In particular, my 2002 report focused specifically on gender-based forms of violence which constituted cultural practices within the family, including 'honour killings' and marriage-related practices.[3] These practices (and others) represent forms of domestic violence which until recently have escaped national and international scrutiny largely because they are frequently presented as 'traditional or cultural practices' requiring tolerance and respect. Thus, cultural relativism (or respect for multiculturalism) is often employed to excuse the violation of women's rights by inhumane and discriminatory practices in the community and family – despite such practices being clearly contrary to international human rights law. 'Honour crimes' may, depending on the exact circumstances, violate rights to life, liberty and bodily integrity, the prohibition on torture or other cruel, inhuman, or degrading treatment or punishment; the prohibition on slavery; the right to freedom from gender-based discrimination and sexual abuse and exploitation; the right to privacy, to marry and found a family; the duty to modify customs that discriminate against women; and the right to an effective remedy.

Although traditionally the international legal order has been premissed upon the public–private distinction, scholars and activists on women's rights have done much to break down this divide. In particular, the provisions of the Convention on the Elimination of All Forms of Discrimination Against Women 1979 (CEDAW, or the 'Women's Convention'), its interpretation by the CEDAW Committee, and the terms of the Declaration on the Elimination of Violence Against Women (a UN General Assembly resolution adopted in 1993), have reflected a fundamental shift in categorising violence in the family as a violation of women's human rights and rejecting justification of violence against women on the basis of custom or tradition. The development of the concept of state responsibility, including due diligence in preventing, prosecuting and punishing violence against women committed also by non-state actors, confirms that issues of violence against women are very much the concern of the international legal order.

Having been Special Rapporteur for nine years, I have come to advocate a dual approach to combating violence against women, including 'honour crimes'. First, we need to ensure that we draw upon existing international standards and laws in upholding state responsibility. As Special Rapporteur, I called upon states not to invoke custom, tradition or religious considerations to avoid their obligation to eradicate violence against women and girls. I recommended the development of national penal, civil and administrative sanctions to punish violence in the family and provide redress to women survivors/victims, irrespective of whether the violence was associated with a cultural practice. Penal sanctions are often necessary in such cases as 'honour crimes' may involve the commission of offences which, although criminal, remain unpunished or subject to extreme leniency. Criminal law measures to prevent, prosecute and punish 'honour crimes' thus need to be strong and effective and avoid the risk of being reforms on paper only.

Second, there needs to be a recognition that law-based strategies alone are not enough, and that there is a need for other interventions, including health and awareness-raising programmes, and in particular that states should seek to adopt appropriate education measures to modify social and cultural behaviours that sanction violence against women.

An important theme in my work as Special Rapporteur was the role of cultural relativism and the participation of women in the struggle to eradicate violence against women. The tension between the universality of human rights and cultural relativism is particularly complex, as women's identities are so integrally linked to their culture and community; women are thus wary of the arrogant gaze of critical outsiders. As Special Rapporteur I sought to develop the argument that women's rights must be asserted in a manner which allows women to be full participants in the communities they choose. There is a need to support women working within their communities at all levels, particularly women who are at the forefront of efforts to combat violence against women and struggle for women's rights – any other strategy risks creating a backlash. Where international attention and leverage are rooted in culturally sensitive strategies and locally supported, they can give strong underpinning to our situation-specific approaches and interventions on the ground.

It is within this framework that Sara Hossain and Lynn Welchman present the essays included in this volume. In an ambitious undertaking aimed at addressing both the academic and the activist audience, the volume brings together the practical insights and experiences of individuals and organisations in addressing 'honour crimes' in different geographical and social contexts, including abuses such as 'honour killings' and interference with the right to marry, as well as analysing relevant crosscutting thematic issues. It is distinctive in both approach and content, bringing together the experiences of activists, lawyers, academics and others working on 'crimes of honour' from the ground, in both North and South, rather than differently located actors writing *about* such activism. The result is a timely and useful resource for activists, policymakers and academics alike, and, as such, I commend it to the attention of the reader, and commend the CIMEL/INTERIGHTS Project, project partners and other authors in the volume on this contribution to the ongoing struggle to eliminate all forms of violence against women.

Notes

Radhika Coomaraswamy was United Nations Special Rapporteur on violence against women its causes and consequences, 1994–2003.

1. 2003 Report of the Special Rapporteur on violence against women, its causes and consequences, E/CN.4/2003/75; Addendum 1 to the 2003 Report: International, regional and national developments in the area of violence against women 1994–2003, E/CN.4/2003/75/Add.1; 2002 Report of the Special Rapporteur on violence against women, its causes and consequences, E/CN.4/2002/83; Annex 1 to the 2001 Report: Communications to and from Governments, E/CN.4/2001/73/Add.1; Annex 1 to the 2000 Report of the Special Rapporteur on violence against women, its causes and consequences: Communications to and from Governments, E/CN.4/2000/68/Add.1; Annex 3 to the 2000 Report: Mission to Haiti, E/CN.4/2000/68/Add.3; Annex 4 to the 2000 Report: Mission to Pakistan and Afghanistan, E/CN.4/2000/68/Add.4; Annex 5 to the 2000 Report: 'Economic and social policy and its impact on violence against women', E/CN.4/2000/68/Add.5; 1999 Report of the Special Rapporteur on violence against women, its causes and consequences: violence against women in the family, E/CN.4/1999/68; 1997 Report of the Special Rapporteur on violence against women, its causes and consequences, E/CN.4/1997/47; Addendum 2 to the 1997 Report of the Special Rapporteur on violence against women, its causes and consequences: Mission to Brazil, E/CN.4/1997/47/Add.2; 1995 Report of the Special Rapporteur on violence against women, its causes and consequences, E/CN.4/1995/42.

2. 2003 Report of the Special Rapporteur on violence against women, its causes and consequences, E/CN.4/2003/75: International, regional and national developments in the area of violence against women.

3. 2002 Report of the Special Rapporteur on violence against women, its causes and consequences, E/CN.4/2002/83.

INTRODUCTION

'Honour', rights and wrongs

LYNN WELCHMAN AND SARA HOSSAIN

This volume arises out of documentation and reflection by individuals and organisations across diverse regions, communities and cultures on existing and potential strategies of response to 'crimes of honour', seen primarily as a manifestation of violence against women, and a violation of women's human rights. It was catalysed in particular by the murder of two young women, Samia Sarwar in Pakistan and Rukhsana Naz in the United Kingdom, the reported responses of their families and the state, and the growing level of attention, regionally and internationally, to the issue of 'crimes of honour'. It discusses the actual and potential ground-level impact of this attention, which has grown substantially since 1999. It also considers the changing global context of work on 'honour crimes', which is affected by developments such as the attacks of 11 September 2001 in the United States and their aftermath.

The volume is an outcome of a collaborative, action-oriented research project aimed at mapping, disseminating information regarding and facilitating the development of strategies to combat 'crimes of honour'. Initially, the collaboration was between INTERIGHTS,[1] an international human rights organisation based in London, and CIMEL,[2] a research centre in the Law Department of the School of Oriental and African Studies of the University of London. However, it was conceived as, and developed into, collaboration with individuals and organisations in a number of different countries across the world over the five years of its operation.

At the time the project began, it was apparent that while there were interventions being made to combat 'crimes of honour' within many contexts, communities and societies, knowledge and understanding of these were often not shared across different cultures and regions. Thus, increasing regional and international concern with the issue was not necessarily reflected in a growing or shared understanding either of the nature and extent of the crimes, or of the strategies and needs, or even the fact, of locally placed actors already engaged in working in this area.

Through the project, therefore, we aimed primarily to exchange information regarding and to facilitate the development of strategies of response by activists, scholars, lawyers, community workers, policymakers and others committed to the elimination of these and related forms of violence. To this end, we supported locally based efforts by individuals and organisations to implement strategies of response in their own contexts, some of which are documented in the case studies included in this volume. Key elements of such strategies included interrogating the concept of 'honour' itself, as well as challenging its invocation to justify violence against women. In parallel, we set out to develop resources, in terms of information and analysis of the issue, which were made available initially to our partners, and later more widely through the project's website.[3] They include an annotated bibliography, which has been periodically updated, and which incorporates case summaries as well as annotations of books, chapters and articles.[4] A 'Directory of Initiatives to Address "Crimes of Honour"' was also compiled to facilitate networking and exchange between individuals and organisations from over twenty countries, and to provide a practical resource for those seeking expert information for legal or other purposes. A comprehensive and periodically updated compilation of key international human rights law materials sets out provisions of various international instruments relating to the rights implicated by 'crimes of honour', and resolutions and reports of the United Nations and its human rights bodies (this includes documents cited by authors in this volume, such as Jane Connors and Purna Sen). In addition, reports of major international or national meetings convened by, and other documents generated through, the project, are available on the website.

The project's framework is international human rights law, and both CIMEL and INTERIGHTS have a primarily legal brief. In particular, we situate 'crimes of honour' within an understanding of violence against women which, as Coomaraswamy and Kois (1999: 177) point out, 'accepts the fact that structures that perpetuate violence against women are socially constructed and that such violence is a product of a historical process and is not essential or time bound in its manifestations'. Our law-focused approach finds a certain resonance with various national and regional initiatives combating 'crimes of honour' around the world, as evidenced by the country-specific chapters in this volume. As Jane Connors sets out, international human rights law requires states to exercise due diligence in protecting women from such violations by private actors, while domestic legislation, court practice and informal legal structures vary in the level of protection and remedy they offer women, in particular where family or conjugal 'honour' is invoked. The impact of statutes, and efforts to change their provisions or application, are therefore central features of the research and advocacy efforts documented in this volume. At the level of society, informal codes mandating such conduct may be endorsed, to varying degrees, by some sectors of society, and challenged by others.

In this connection, the operation and hold of 'parallel legal systems' in relation to 'crimes of honour' is discussed in detail in this volume by Nadera Shalhoub-Kevorkian and Nazand Begikhani, while less 'formal' customary laws and social norms and the way in which the state legal system endorses, accommodates or challenges these latter are a theme in almost all the country-specific contexts. In addition, religious laws, and the attitude of religious authorities, may be critical in forming or reinforcing and also in changing opinion and practice in this area. The role of the religious right – political groupings that invoke religion and religious traditions as justifications for their activities, including those which seek to marginalise or obliterate the rights of women or minorities – is key here, as well as the role of those who challenge the validity of such positions.

It is abundantly clear that a narrowly legal approach, particularly one focusing on 'state law' and state legal systems as a stand-alone strategy unaccompanied by broader and deeper initiatives and understandings, is unlikely to change practice or to combat 'crimes of honour' effectively. In this regard we recognise the limitations inherent in the fact that our 'orientation towards circumscribed disciplines or subdisciplines remains strong' (Dobash and Dobash, 1998: 2). In particular, we look to the contribution of anthropologists in seeking to destabilise assumptions about 'honour and shame', sexuality, class, and the gendering process in specific contexts (Lindisfarne, 1993; Joseph, 1999). Nevertheless, by helping to 'surface' data and analysis from partners working in specific contexts, we hope to help dislodge the abstract in the debates on 'crimes of honour', allowing more thorough examination of context-specific variables and facilitating analysis of the socio-political and economic contexts of 'crimes of honour' and related forms of violence against women. For purposes both of research and of advocacy, the law – whether as articulated in statute, or as applied and interpreted by members of the judiciary, or as 'unwritten' law – describes a particular nexus of state, society and family, and gendering of relationships between these fields, and may be instrumental in the structuring of those relationships. Insisting on all these manifestations of the 'law', and those who form it and apply it, as instruments of change, means working on the law itself as an instrument in need of change.

This book reflects the primarily legal focus of most authors. In this introduction, we try to set out some of the themes that have run through the project as a whole, and indeed the ongoing work by project partners within their particular contexts. We look here at the uses and meanings of the term 'honour crimes', before proceeding to consider comparisons that are made with 'crimes of passion' and the issue of the partial defence of sexual provocation. We then consider the current popular association of 'crimes of honour' with Muslim-majority societies or communities, depite the widespread incidence of such crimes, and recent struggles to combat them, among Christian majority communities in Latin America or Southern Europe (see Silvia Pimental et al. and Maria Gabriella Bettiga-Boukerbout in this volume), as well as more ongoing efforts among Hindu and Sikh communities in India (see the paper by Uma Chakravarti). We also examine the complications that such associations bring for the work of local actors engaging in combating violence against women, and the particular challenges to addressing honour crimes occurring among religious minorities within multicultural societies. We go on to examine antecedents of the notion of 'honour' in colonial legislation and the latter's continuing impact. Finally we conclude by seeking responses to the questions which informed the beginning of the project, and which we believe are of continuing relevance in the struggle to eliminate violence against women.

'Crimes of honour'

The project uses the term 'crimes of honour' to encompass a variety of manifestations of violence against women, including 'honour killings', assault, confinement or imprisonment, and interference with choice in marriage, where the publicly articulated 'justification' is attributed to a social order claimed to require the preservation of a concept of 'honour' vested in male (family and/or conjugal) control over women and specifically women's sexual conduct: actual, suspected or potential.

The definition of 'crimes of honour' is by no means straightforward, and the imprecision and 'exoticisation' (in particular in the West) of its use are among the reasons for caution in use of the phrase. At its most basic, the term is commonly used as shorthand, to flag a type of violence against women characterised by (claimed) 'motivation' rather than by perpetrator or form of manifestation. Definitions tend to be by way of illustration; thus, in a highly significant article on 'crimes of honour' and the construction of gender in the Arab world, Lama Abu Odeh explains that

A paradigmatic example of a crime of honour is the killing of a woman by her father or brother for engaging in, or being suspected of engaging in, sexual practices before or outside marriage. (Abu Odeh, 1996: 141)

In her 1999 Report, the UN Special Rapporteur on violence against women records receiving 'numerous communications' on the subject of 'honour crimes' against women, 'whereby the family kills a female relative deemed to have defiled the honour of the family'. She continues with information on 'honour crimes' in Lebanon:

Honour is defined in terms of women's assigned sexual and familial roles as dictated by traditional family ideology. Thus, adultery, premarital relationships (which may or may not include sexual relations), rape and falling in love with an 'inappropriate' person may constitute violations of family honour.[5]

Chapters in this volume discuss the concept of 'conjugal honour' as well as 'family honour', and document 'honour killings' by husbands and sexual intimates who are not blood relatives of the victim, thus extending the range of 'paradigmatic' perpetrators. It is also argued that in some contexts, the range of female behaviour considered to violate 'honour' goes beyond sexual conduct (actual, potential or suspected) to include other behaviours that challenge male control (Aida Touma-Sliman notes 'staying out late and smoking', for example). At the same time, the contributions by Uma Chakravarti, Dina Siddiqi and Hannana Siddiqui clarify how these paradigms of 'honour' interfere with the right to choice in marriage across South Asia; forced marriage is one result, but other scenarios include being forced to remain in an unwanted relationship, or punished for leaving (or trying to leave) one, or exercising choice regarding whether to marry or not, and whom to marry. As well as the 'honour' invested in control over women and specifically women's sexual conduct, control over economic and social resources and property are often intimately linked in these equations. In addition, chapters in this volume (Nazand Begikhani, Aida Touma-Sliman, CEWLA, Nadera Shalhoub-Kevorkian) note the significance attached to female virginity and the resulting imposition (or attempted imposition) of virginity testing on females suspected of having 'violated' family honour, including through having been subjected to rape. 'Crimes of honour' may thus include violations of a range of rights as well as the more 'paradigmatic' 'honour killings'. The role of women family members in instigating or colluding with honour crimes, particularly in enforcing controls over marriage choices, and also in acts of violence, is also brought out in this volume (Dina Siddiqi, Danielle Hoyek et al., CEWLA, Purna Sen) as an issue that requires greater consideration.

Working on 'crimes of honour' as a form of violence against women does not imply that men are not also subjected to such crimes. For example, in the province of Sindh in 1998, the Human Rights Commission of Pakistan analysed the deaths of 97 men as well as 158 women in *karo-kari* 'honour killings' (Amnesty International, 1999a: 6). Again, in cases of forced marriage or interference with the right of choice whether or not and whom to marry, pressure from older family members over younger members will apply to men as well as to women. In the realm of fiction, the story of the 'honour killing' set by Gabriel García Márquez in a Colombian village, and given legal-sociological analysis by Teubner (1992) is of the murder by two brothers of the male seducer of their sister. However, women remain the majority of victims and survivors of 'crimes of honour', and have fewer available remedies, and thus development of strategies of support can effectively draw on the existing frameworks established to address all manifestations of violence against women. Where necessary, such strategies also involve challenging existing frameworks in order to secure women's rights and liberties; thus women's rights and human rights organisations have questioned the practice of placing women who have exercised their right to choice in marriage in 'protective custody' pending a judicial decision (see the chapters by Uma Chakravarti and Dina Siddiqi).

Among feminist and rights activists seeking to eliminate such violence, there is deep discomfort over the apparent meaning of the term 'honour' in the construction 'crimes of honour', as this seems to imply that women 'embody' the honour of males. There is also resistance to accepting a notion of honour that endorses or may indeed require violence against women, epitomised in the extreme example of an 'honour killing'. Thus in 1994, al-Badeel ('The Alternative'), established from organisations within the Palestinian community in Israel, called itself the Coalition to Combat the Crime of 'Family Honour' (see further Aida Touma-Sliman in this volume), encapsulating through quotation marks its own interrogation of the term. In its statement of purpose the organisation observed:

> it is not possible to give the term ['family honour'] a positive understanding, since it attributes all the maladies of society to women's bodies and individual behaviour, giving legitimacy to social conduct restricting women's freedom and development, using all forms of violence, the most extreme being murder.

In a round table convened by the CIMEL/INTERIGHTS project in 1999 (Welchman, 2000: 452), activists, academics, journalists and lawyers from different countries considered the use of concepts of 'honour' in strategies of response and resistance. It was pointed out that in Pakistan, activists have named the killers of women as dishonourable, in an attempt to destabilise the prevailing understanding of 'honour'. In the UK, women's rights activists argued that Zoora Shah, a British Pakistani woman convicted of the murder of a man after years of physical, sexual and economic abuse, had been in effect considered by the Court of Appeal to have no honour left to transgress; more recently, the slogan 'there is no "honour" in domestic violence, only shame' was invoked during the memorial of Heshu Yones (see further Hannana Siddiqui in this volume). Recovering or reclaiming the notion of 'honour' would reformulate it as attaching to women as well as to men, designating qualities of respect, tolerance and inclusivity. However, some participants sounded a note of caution, seeing risks (as exemplified in Zoora Shah's case) in seeking to recover a notion of honour as an attribute of women, given a context of court processes dominated by prevailing notions of honour as attaching exclusively to men or to male-headed families.

In the search for a better nomenclature, the majority of 'honour killings' appear to fit into the understanding of femicide defined by Radford (1992: 3) as 'the misogynous killing of women by men' and as 'a form of sexual violence'. She uses the concept of 'sexual violence' as a continuum in a radical feminist analysis:

> The notion of a continuum further facilitates the analysis of male sexual violence as a form of control central to the maintenance of patriarchy.... Relocating femicide within the continuum of sexual violence establishes its significance in terms of sexual politics. (Radford 1992: 4).

Further developing this notion, Nadera Shalhoub-Kevorkian (2002) argues for another continuum, in which 'femicide' would indicate a range of acts and situations including not only the physical killing of women because they are women but also threats and other components of the 'arduous process leading up to the actual death'. Shalhoub-Kevorkian situates her proposal solidly in the framework of her clinical experience in Palestinian society while recommending it also for analysis of other societies in light of the cross-cultural nature of the phenomenon of femicide.

It is clear that most 'honour killings' fit immediately into both the narrower and the wider understandings of femicide proposed above, while other 'crimes of honour' (such as interference with choice in marriage, physical abuse, intimidation, deprivation of liberty) might be covered either by the sexual violence continuum or by Nadera Shalhoub-Kevorkian's expanded definition of femicide. Such methods of naming have the clear advantage of unpacking the term and indicating the socio-economic and patriarchal frameworks in which such acts are committed and sustained, rather than reproducing the representation of that framework, with or without quotation marks around 'honour' to indicate the user's interrogation of the term. The assimilation of such crimes to a wider framework has the added advantage of avoiding the self-exculpation undertaken by some in the West who view such crimes as a problem of 'the other', risking paternalistic and ineffective interventions and the 'demonisation' of particular communities and, in particular, men within them.

The use of the term 'honour crime', or specifically 'honour killing', has at least two further risks: first, that it takes the description articulated by the perpetrator; and second, that reproducing the term may obscure (as may be the intention on the part of the perpetrator) the 'real motivation' (or at least contributing motivational factors) for the crime or attempted crime. In regard to the latter, sociological investigations of 'family honour' in different contexts indicate that 'the normative claim of honor often is mixed with social, economic, or political motives' (Araji, 2000) – that is, that 'family honour' is tied to social standing and mobility, and economic opportunities. For example, Nafisa Shah quotes Sardar Sultan Mugheri in Sindh as stating that:

> *Ghairat* (what is sacred and inviolable) is *izzat* (honour, dignity) and this comes with money and property. And if *izzat* is violated – then it is justified to kill and die for honour. (Shah, 1998: 239).

Besides the general and familiar association of women with property in the 'honour' paradigm, there are many instances in which the primary motivation for an 'honour crime' is more directly something other than 'honour' – a brother's arguments with his sister over inheritance, for example, or a husband's desire to be rid of a wife, with a murder not so much covered up as proclaimed as a matter of 'honour' in the expectation of a minimal punishment and less disapprobation from at least some sections of society than otherwise would have been the case.[6] The claims of 'honour' may be a contributing factor, but, as Nafisa Shah has commented, 'Vested interests … use the excuse of honour as a blanket cover for a multitude of sins.'[7] And mostly the voice of the victim in her own 'defence' is absent, as underlined by studies in this volume.

As to the problem of reproducing, even in quotations marks, the articulated motivation of the perpetrator or sympathisers in the family or society, we come up against the questions posed by Dobash and Dobash (1998: 4) in regard to the source of definitions of violence against women:

> Do we use the perspectives of victims? Of those who perpetrate the acts? Of researchers? Of the law? Of policymakers? Should researchers attempt to develop distinct, abstract, and definitive conceptualisations of these acts?

In this volume, Purna Sen suggests (in relation to the paradigmatic honour killings) six elements that could be used to distinguish 'honour crimes' from other acts of violence against women, moving us away from reliance on the perpetrator's articulation of motive. The CIMEL/INTERIGHTS project has tended to use a less methodical combination of definitions implied in the shorthand of the term 'crimes of honour' – those of perpetrators, of policymakers and to a certain extent of the law – from the perspective of challenges made to those definitions by advocates of change, including some of our project partners. For example, Uma Chakravarti argues against continued use of the term 'crimes of honour' because 'as feminists, we must discard the term in search of another that does not mask the violence in the killings and abuses', and 'because the violence becomes associated with the 'uniqueness of Asian cultures, with irrational communities and aberrant and archaic patriarchal practices refusing to modernise' (see also Purna Sen in this volume).

Still, problematic though it is, the term 'crimes of honour' has some uses in particular contexts. It is used in the project, as by some activists, to destabilise the notion of 'honour' as a received good when connected with crime. It is also used to extend an understanding of what might be called 'crimes of honour' beyond 'honour killings', one way of demonstrating the continuum of acts of violence on which 'honour killings' stand. It has obvious descriptive implications in its indication of the link that may, in particular contexts, be assumed in law, judicial process and societal practice connecting a 'crime' with a mitigating value, 'honour'. The idea of mitigation or impunity in statute or judicial practice for a 'crime of honour' is most immediately evoked in 'honour killing', but it also arises in other manifestations of crimes of 'honour'.

The most obvious advantage of the use of the term 'honour crimes' in an English-language context is the wide recognition of the term, but this is at the same time increasingly problematic. In this volume, Hannana Siddiqui criticises the 'loose use' of the term by the Metropolitan Police in their attempts to address a number of murders within minority communities in the UK. The association of phenomena of 'crimes of honour' with the 'East' (Abu Odeh, 1997; and see Uma Chakravarti in this volume) – and often with Muslim societies in particular – is one of the problems. In a *Guardian* report (5 July 2004) entitled 'Turkey Gets to Grips with "Honour Killings"' the one specific case example given was from an Amnesty International report which 'highlighted the case of a man who had a 24-year prison term for stabbing his partner to death reduced to two and a half years after producing photographs of the woman with another man'. In an explanatory memorandum for the Council of Europe's parliamentary assembly in support of a resolution on 'Crimes of Honour', rapporteur Ann Cryer (a British Member of Parliament) included in 'cases of so-called "honour crimes" in Europe' another Turkish case, that of a man who 'cut his pregnant wife's throat with a knife because he suspected that she was having an affair'.[8] On the bald facts, both cases might suggest use of a defence of 'provocation' rather than 'honour', were it not, apparently, for the fact that they happened in Turkey. Ann Cryer's report did include an attempt at definitions, which identified 'honour crimes' according to the claim of the perpetrator, and continued:

> The so-called 'honour crimes' should not be confused with the concept of 'crimes of passion'. Whereas the latter is normally limited to a crime that is committed by one partner (or husband and wife) in a relationship on the other as a spontaneous (emotional or passionate) reply (often citing a defence of 'sexual provocation'), the former may involve the abuse or murder of (usually) women by one of more close family members (including partners) in the name of individual or family honour.[9]

Besides the fact that this definition presents 'crimes of passion' as gender-neutral (in the face of the facts), it brings us to the issues of the link between 'crimes of passion' and 'crimes of honour'. Different positions have been taken regarding the utility of this comparison (see Purna Sen in this volume) but the juxtaposition at least underlines the argument that both are manifestations of femicide where culturally positive values legally/judicially mitigate the murder of women from, arguably, motivations of male control, whether named as 'honour' or 'passion'.[10]

Crimes of honour, crimes of passion

In her chapter, Jane Connors notes that among the disagreements at UN discussions of 'crimes of honour' from the year 2000 was the inclusion of 'crimes of passion' with 'crimes of honour' in resolutions on violence against women.[11] She notes the objection of the representative of Jordan, to the effect that 'How could states possibly exercise due diligence to prevent such crimes, if the crime in question is committed in a sudden spurt of rage?'[12] The significance of this intervention lies in the fact that most defences in criminal cases of 'honour killings' of women in Jordan argue that the crime was committed in a 'fit of fury', or indeed a 'sudden spurt of anger' in reaction to some (alleged) conduct on the part of the woman, allowing the court to rule on 'manslaughter' rather than premeditated murder and to reduce the penalty accordingly. The discussions on Jordan, Lebanon and Iraqi Kurdistan in this volume provide further evidence that it is rare indeed for a defendant to rely on particular provisions in national legislation that are the target of advocacy campaigns by those combating 'crimes of honour' (see the chapters by Reem Abu Hassan, Danielle Hoyek et al. and Nazand Begikhani). These provisions provide for a reduced penalty in the event that a man finds his wife or certain female relatives in the act of extramarital sex, and kills one or both of them on the spot. As Lama Abu Odeh (1997: 306) points out, in the case of 'honour killings' in Arab countries, 'the legal locus of these crimes is less the immediate legislation and more the general provocation rule found in almost every Arab Penal Code'. Sohail Warraich's discussion in this volume of the use by Pakistani courts of the 'grave and sudden provocation defence' in cases of 'honour killings' provides considerable comparative material in this regard.

There is a growing literature on the relationship and differences of crimes of honour and of passion. In the legal field, Abu Odeh (1997: 290) uses her earlier work on 'crimes of honour' in the Arab world in a comparative examination of the judicial treatment by US courts of 'the killing of women in the heat of passion for sexual or intimate reasons'. In focusing on how each legal system justifies its tolerance for the murder of a woman in particular circumstances, she demonstrates that the tensions in each system, 'although sometimes defined differently, have been surprisingly resolved in the same way' – in particular this comparison is made between the 'fit of fury' mitigation in Arab penal codes and practice, and the US plea of extreme emotional distress, which builds on the premiss that loss of 'self-control' reduces culpability. In-depth work on passion and the provocation defence in Western legal systems, notably Nourse (1997) on the USA, whose work is cited by Abu Odeh, but also Leader-Elliott (1997) on English and Australian law, reveals a 'steadily widening conception of provocation' (Leader-Elliott, 1997: 169) away from adultery, as 'the classic source of adequate provocation, enforcing rules of gender relations grounded in an older idea of property' (Nourse, 1997: 1341). The widening concept of sexual provocation in 'the West' appears to afford women (as wives and lovers) less protection even as their legal rights to choose and/or to leave a relationship are increased. In her examination of 'Modern Law Reform and the Provocation Defense', Nourse finds that 'Reform has permitted juries to return a manslaughter verdict in cases where the defendant claims passion because the victim left, moved the furniture out, planned a divorce, or sought a protective order' (1997: 1334).[13]

One difference that is often assumed between crimes of 'passion' and of 'honour' is the relationship of the perpetrator to the victim. The difference here lies in the murder of women by those who are or have been their sexual intimates (husbands, lovers) and those who have not been (close blood relatives). Other than the documented instances of the murder of women after incestuous rape in 'crimes of honour', as noted above, it is the case that not only 'family honour' but also 'conjugal honour' may be cited as a 'motivation' by the perpetrator. The term 'legitimate defence of honour' in Brazil (see Sylvia Pimental, Valéria Pandjiarjian and Juliana Belloque in this volume) refers to the wounded honour of a sexual intimate; how far this 'motivation' differs from the 'shame' experienced by a betrayed lover relying on sexual provocation as a defence is not immediately clear. Case studies in this volume indicate different findings as to what proportion of murderers were husbands of the victim. Commenting on research in Lebanon, Serhan posits that the greater number of husbands as perpetrators may reflect 'a change in the conceptualization of family honour' (Foster, 2001: 26). In Pakistan, figures from Sindh province from 1998 illustrate that the husband was the perpetrator in nearly 50 per cent of cases of *karo-kari* killings where the woman alone was killed (Amnesty International, 1999a: 6).

Even granted the paradigmatic family (as compared to conjugal) dynamic of 'honour', the response of courts in the 'West' faced with defences of passion or provocation can be examined for similarities with those of courts faced with 'honour' defences, at least in considering the implications of a passion/honour continuum that recognises, at some point, a justification for the use of violence against women as a part of control by family and intimates. As Leader-Elliott (1997: 169) asks in the context of law in the 'West':

> Is it not an unacceptable paradox that the progressive restriction of a husband's power to exert lawful control over his wife has been accompanied by a progressive enlargement of a partial excuse for killing her?

The complex background to such developments across the world includes rapid social change among and within different countries and communities, and 'globalising' cultural dynamics (for example, of 'modernity') that, as they are seen to open (some) women's choices, may be experienced by (some) men as threats. Such factors vary in their impact in different communities, but have to be taken into account in an assessment of family violence. Baker et al. (1999, 166) argue that 'honor should be part of any current concep-tualisation of patriarchy' in comparative and cross-cultural analyses and that 'honor systems are an integral part of the process of killing women by their families or intimates, regardless of where the woman lives' (1999: 164). Their theory includes three comparative areas related to honour systems – the control of female behaviour, male feelings of shame at loss of that control, and community participation in 'enhancing and controlling this shame'. In an article that draws on a large number of comparative illustrations, they are not arguing for a blanket use of 'honour' to understand 'intimate-perpetrated female homicides' in the USA and elsewhere in the English-speaking West, but pointing out that it may apply to some of those murders, despite the general weakness or absence of the community participation element (see Purna Sen in this volume), since it may be understood 'as an ideology held by those who seek to hold on to patriarchal power in a competitive arena by mandating certain behaviours by others, notably women. Here, the competitive arena may include the increasing demands for female equality' (1999: 173).

Questioning the stereotypical associations of 'honour' with the 'East' and 'passion' with the 'West' (Abu Odeh, 1997, 289), or 'reason' with the 'North' and 'irrational male violence and female passivity' with the 'South' (Baker et al.: 173), is important both to theory and to activism on issues of violence against women. It is important to identify commonalities as well as differences in the structure of violence. It is important to consider a gendered construction of self involving issues of ownership and control and their role in perpetuating violence; and generally to interrogate, in this regard, the application of the sexual provocation defence. At the most basic level of comparison, whether we are looking at the 'fit of fury' in Middle Eastern states, 'violent emotion' in a heat of passion in Latin America, or 'extreme emotional distress' in the USA, it is clear that societies across the world – through their laws and their courts – continue to countenance legal defences that overwhelmingly benefit males committing violence against females.

Crimes of honour and Muslim and minority communities

Issues of definition and terminology come to the fore in the current international focus on 'crimes of honour' and their consequent perceived association with Muslim societies. At the beginning of the year 2000, Asma Jahangir, United Nations Special Rapporteur on extrajudicial, summary or arbitrary executions, included the following careful statement in her annual report:

> The practice of 'honour killings' is more prevalent although not limited to countries where the majority of the population is Muslim. In this regard it should be noted that a number of renowned Islamic leaders and scholars have publicly condemned this practice and clarified that it has no religious basis.[14]

The remarkably increased level of international attention being given to 'crimes of honour' (however or whether defined) brings with it a risk both of crude stereotypes and associations, and of a reaction that may act (or be used) to undermine counter-initiatives and to complicate domestic strategies of response. Jane Connors notes in this volume the objections made at the UN General Assembly to the association that certain Muslim majority states felt was being made between 'crimes of honour' and Islam. Particularly in the post-September 11 climate, where many Muslim individuals and communities are under attack from Western powers, the potential of such risks is substantial, as discussed by Purna Sen in this volume. This does not mean that 'crimes of honour' cannot or should not be tackled by anyone other than 'insiders', but it does require particularly rigorous attention to the construction of equal and honest engagements and alliances, and conscious efforts to avoid this being or becoming, for the 'West' (sometimes representing itself as the 'international community'), a particular and isolated problem of 'the [already hostile] other'. Awareness of ways in which global politics has created a backlash, strengthening the forces of the religious right and increasing the spaces for their operation, and sensitivity to the changing geopolitical context, must not imply the silencing of the long-standing struggle of women against violence, including violence in the name of 'honour'.

In a number of countries, those investigating and challenging 'crimes of honour' in their domestic contexts have invested effort in challenging claims that there is support for such practices in the bodies of principles and rulings that make up Islamic law (see further Welchman, 2005). Members of the *shar'i* establishments in different countries have been invited to make public statements on the issue in efforts to persuade constituents against the idea of religious endorsement of violence in the name of 'honour'. On the other hand, a 'traditionalist' *shar'i* view advocating the implementation by the state of severe *hadd* punishments for extramarital sexual relations is not one espoused by civil society groupings currently joining efforts, nationally and regionally, to eliminate 'crimes of honour', nor by more general human rights initiatives. Indeed, civil society groups active in combating 'crimes of honour' tend rather to argue for the decriminalisation of consensual extramarital sexual relations (and of same-sex relations) and an end to the state's interest in the intimate relations of its citizens.

The broader referential framework of strict control over sexual relations is present not only in dominant interpretations of Islamic law but, at least officially, in contemporary Muslim (and other) societies. This is evoked immediately in internal and international debates over 'crimes of honour', demands attention from advocates for change, and entangles issues of culture and tradition with issues of religion. In his contribution to this volume, Abdullahi An-Na'im examines the nature of internal alliances that can, and in his view should, be sought in processes of intra-community dialogue aimed at challenging violence against women. His chapter builds on his earlier argument that efforts to eradicate such practices 'must take into account and address not only every and all types of justifications, but also the cultural circumstances and underlying rationales that might cause the practice to continue in the particular community.' (1994: 177). Suad Joseph has also addressed this question of strategies in the context of the Middle East in particular, arguing that 'We must identify, recognise, and understand the different constructs and experiences of rights in order to figure out how we can build the ground on which to stand together to advocate human rights and women's human rights' (1994: 9).

However, for others writing in this volume, as for many groups working on the ground, a key element of their actions is to address the negation, through honour codes and the resulting regulation of sexuality, of women's right to control over their body and indeed to sexual liberty (see Dina Siddiqi, Uma Chakravarti and Silvia Pimental et al.). Issues that are particularly complex to address include the diversity in social practice in different Muslim societies, and the related and specific contestation of sexuality rights. The chapters in this volume deal almost entirely with heterosexual relations and practice, although the threat or incidence of 'crimes of honour' against members of the lesbian, gay, bisexual and transgender (LGBT) communities has been noted by several authors, and is clearly an emerging concern for many. In relation to interference with the right to marry, for example, discussions held under the project's auspices, as well as the process of providing legal advice on such cases to government agencies, made apparent the fact that such interference in whether – as well as with whom and when – to marry, in turn created a space for discussion around the total denial of the rights of LGBT individuals in this sphere.[15]

In majority Muslim societies, 'crimes of honour' are found to occur among non-Muslim communities. In a May 2001 conference in Beirut, the organisers invited leading figures from both Muslim and Christian religious establishments to clarify the lack of religious endorsement for 'crimes of honour'. In this volume, Bettiga-Boukerbout notes the role of the Church in endorsing patriarchal values that lie behind the use of violence in controlling women's (particularly sexual) conduct. In situations where Muslims are a minority community, 'crimes of honour' occur across religions and cultures. In this volume, Hannana Siddiqui advocates the idea of a 'mature multiculturalism' that neither denies equal protection to women from minority communities nor contributes to the essentialising and 'othering' of minority communities. In a related argument, Bredal critiques immigration-focused approaches to tackling forced marriage currently being taken in Scandinavian states, both because they involve violations of human rights of men and women from minority communities in particular – to movement and to choice in marriage – and because they deny agency to women from minority communities (all of this in the name of protecting the rights of women). Hannana Siddiqui and Anja Bredal both argue that designing and implementing 'good practice' guidance for police, social support agencies and other authorities (including immigration authorities), and efforts to raise public awareness, must be pursued in a manner that does not contribute to further violations of human rights.

Colonial laws

Another relevant theme addressed in this volume is the continuing impact of the colonial legal heritage. Sohail Warraich traces in Pakistan particular challenges arising from the combination of the reintroduction of the partial defence of 'grave and sudden provocation' (derived from nineteenth-century British colonial law) with the application of the Qisas and Diyat Ordinance (enacted as part of late-twentieth-century 'Islamisation' measures under a military dictatorship). Case studies from the Middle East stress the provenance of the criminal legislation now governing 'crimes of honour' – in particular with regard to defences to charges of murder in cases of 'honour killings' – citing in this regard not only Ottoman penal law but the French Penal Code of 1810, identified as the source of certain Arab states' legislation on these issues.

These efforts are made, *inter alia*, in order to destabilise notions of such provisions being synonymous with 'traditional heritage' and something thoroughly 'indigenous' to particular societies, to be defended as such against outside influence. In Lebanon, the late Laure Moghaizel, as early as 1986, reviewed partial excuses for husbands who surprise their wives in adulterous acts or situations, and in some cases for the parents of daughters under a certain age, as provided in Spanish, Portuguese, Turkish, Italian and French law, either still extant or recently repealed (Moghaizel, 1986: 177). Bettiga-Boukerbout's chapter in this volume examines Italian legislation on the 'cause of honour', while the 'legitimate defence of honour' in Brazil and 'heat of passion' defences (with associated causes of violation of 'honour') in other Latin American states are considered by Silvia Pimental, Valéria Pandjiarjian and Juliana Belloque.

Parallels are also found in criminal provisions in countries of the Middle East and Latin America that (broadly) provide for reduced or suspended penalties, or suspension of prosecution, if a man accused of rape or sexual assault marries his victim. In Egypt in 1999 a change made to the law of criminal procedure repealed a provision under which, according to one article in the British press, 'in a case of rape, if the rapist and victim agree to marry then all charges will be dropped' (Negus, 1999). The law in question was rather more complicated, with a focus on the woman's abduction. Dupret (2001) traces the origins of the repealed provision to French law, and variations of it remain in the penal law of, for example, Jordan and Palestine. Nadera Shalhoub-Kevorkian (1999a, 1999b) examines the subject in her exposition of the dilemmas faced by rape victims in Palestinian society and the clinicians who seek to help them, and includes forced marriage to a rapist as within her definition of femicide (2002), giving a powerful illustration from her clinical experience involving a girl raped at the age of 10. The concern of the girl's family was to keep the crime secret and their solution was to have the rapist marry his victim when she came of age – the victim describes her mother speaking in terms of the rapist being forced into this marriage, with the agreement of his parents. Nadera Shalhoub-Kevorkian comments:

> The battle becomes one between families. The power of the idea of 'family honour', as well as the need to protect and preserve it, defines the victim's status and rights and frames the options that are open to deal with the problem – in this case, marrying her own rapist. (Shalhoub-Kevorkian, 1999a: 162)

Pimental, Pandjiarjian and Belloque in this volume note variations of this provision in the laws of a number of Latin American states. In Brazil, for example, a sexual offender cannot be punished 'when he marries the victim or when she marries a third person'. They find the legal reasoning here to be that 'since the sexual violence has not impeded the marriage prospects of the victim, the crime should be forgiven.' Their chapter also shows the similarities between the laws of Latin American and Middle Eastern states in the treatment of adultery, whether such penal provisions exist in current legislation or, as is often the case, have been recently repealed or amended.

Playing for the other side

Both the colonial heritage and contemporary global power structures (military, political, economic and other) necessarily complicate strategies of response to violence against women. In addition to the complexities noted above, there are the considerable challenges faced by activists accused of playing for, or at least into the hands of, forces ranged against the country or community by merely raising the issue of 'crimes of honour' as one requiring questioning and reform. For example, during one of the debates in the Jordanian parliament on amending the Penal Code, certain deputies charged that the then recent national campaign and efforts to repeal the relevant law were attempts by the West to infiltrate Jordanian society and make Jordanian women immoral.[16] Such perceptions, first, of endemic immorality in contemporary Western society and, second, of the dissipating potential on local cultural norms of a hostile agenda of cultural imperialism are widespread in many of the contexts considered in this volume. Activists, particularly those working on women's rights in their societies and on sexuality-related issues, are vulnerable to attack by 'conservative' and 'Islamist' groupings on grounds of 'inauthenticity', marginalisation and 'secularism'. On the other hand, as noted by Hannana Siddiqui in this volume, they may sometimes be criticised by progressive or leftist groups, as well as by more conservative elements of minority communities, for the proverbial washing of dirty laundry in public. Similar tensions can be read in Aida Touma-Sliman's narration of efforts within the Palestinian community in Israel. Nazand Begikhani describes how the dependence of Kurdish political movements in Iraqi Kurdistan on international support rendered them more responsive to advocacy for change promoted by international human rights groups such as Amnesty International, while at the same time noting significant internal resentment and resistance to the legal changes that followed. Abdullahi An-Na'im addresses this point directly, arguing that different types of advocacy work can and should be done by differently placed actors, but that these need to include 'agents of social change' located inside their communities engaging in 'intra-community dialogue' to contribute to social change from within, and pondering the development of appropriate discourses and capacities for such work. Strategies – and capacities – differ. As Deniz Kandiyoti notes, in a consideration of the related topic of advocacy on the issues of gender and citizenship in the Middle East,

> Some argue forcefully for the expansion of women's rights as individuals and condemn the stranglehold exercised over them by communal and religious forces; others argue for working through kinship and communal structures that may act to empower and disempower women simultaneously. (Kandiyoti, 2000: xv).

The activists who have written in this book work within their communities using the human rights framework, and set out, in their different interventions, the use they make of law. Many chapters provide examples of how such groups engage with their societies outside the processes of the law, seeking to challenge and change social attitudes that condone any form of violence against women, joining forces in order to strengthen internal voices of resistance.

As for the use by activists of external publicity and pressure, such as mobilising international public opinion, in many contexts complex and strategic choices are involved. In 2000, Farah Daghestani told a conference on 'Sexuality in the Middle East' that 'honour killings' of women 'have been responsible for the worst international attention Jordan has received':

Through the sensationalisation of the subject, the Western press has contributed to the issue becoming an even greater challenge for governments and religious leaders, pitting cultural identity and autonomy against cultural imperialism, at the expense of women. (Foster, 2001: 24)

It is of course the case that all types of governments tend to 'blame the messenger', particularly messengers criticising human rights records. It is also the case that local strategies of response and resistance can be complicated and undermined by external factors, which can include well-meant interventions as well as hostile (e.g. Islamophobic or racist) ones, and of course global events. These challenges have been illustrated recently by the controversy over Norma Khoury's story of an 'honour killing' in Jordan, *Forbidden Love*, withdrawn from sale in Australia by its publishers following challenges by Jordanian women's rights activists to the book's categorisation as a non-fiction 'memoir' (see further Abu Hassan in this volume). Other illustrations come in the particular challenges of combating violence against women in situations of conflict; in this volume, Nazand Begikhani, Nadera Shalhoub-Kevorkian and Aida Touma-Sliman all document the reduced attention that activists are able to give (and to attract) to these issues in times of military hostilities and threats to the particular national entity or community.

Strategising responses and creating alternatives

Thinking through the concept of 'crimes of honour' is one way of unpicking certain forms of violence against women. At the CIMEL/INTERIGHTS round table, participants agreed on the strategic importance of identifying the value and advantage of, on the one hand, separating out a 'crime of honour' as a particular phenomenon or form of violence against women, and, on the other, campaigning on the various manifestations of 'crimes of honour' solely within the broader spectrum of violence against women. Some felt that caution needed to be exercised in not collapsing too many forms of violence against women into the category of 'honour crimes'. Others felt that while we used the term for tactical reasons, and as a convenient shorthand to understand certain forms of violence, we needed constantly to be alive to our central concern, which was not an abstract exercise of disentangling or explicating the notion of 'crimes of honour' as such, but understanding how it contributes to violence and how both 'crimes of honour' and indeed the notion itself violate human rights.

The chapters in this volume, we believe, provide material that will help in finding answers to a set of questions regarding the phenomenon of 'crimes of honour'. Is the term 'crime of honour' at all applicable or useful across cultures, languages, legal systems? Are the manifestations of such 'crimes of honour' (as defined locally, by perpetrators, courts, police or survivors) comparable across time and place? What commonalities exist to justify designation of some crimes of violence against women as 'crimes of honour'? What variations challenge attempts to do so? Does the use of this category serve to essentialise certain forms of violence against women as being particular to certain cultures, communities or religions, thus facilitating further violations of the rights of such women and of other members of their communities? Or does the articulation of such a category, despite the many associated pitfalls, nevertheless assist in understanding the nature of such violence, and in further advocacy for the development of legislative, judicial and community-based strategies in response to such crimes? It is perhaps this last question with which the contributors to this volume are most engaged.

In the opening chapter, Jane Connors presents the international legal framework regarding violence against women and, in particular, developments at the United Nations in regard to 'crimes of honour'. Purna Sen then considers the current political context of action against 'crimes of honour', and the nature of alliances and coalitions that might be constructed around the issues involved. Abdullahi An-Na'im follows with a reflection on the human rights approach and the positioning of activists, arguing for specific and sustained attention to processes of intra-community dialogue in building consensus against 'crimes of honour'. The book then moves on to a set of context-specific studies from Europe, Latin America, South Asia and the Middle East. These studies analyse primary sources and data (including legislation, cases, court records, interviews) and consider the approaches and impact of advocacy for change in the various specific contexts. We believe that despite definitional and other difficulties in using the term 'crimes of honour', the chapters in this study illustrate at least two things: first, the entanglement of paradigms of 'honour' in a variety of manifestations of violence against women, and second, the willingness of a broad range of individuals and organisations from across the world to join their efforts to an undertaking aimed at presenting voices of resistance in a comparative context.[17]

Notes

1. International Centre for the Legal Protection of Human Rights, London, of which the South Asia Programme was primarily engaged in the project.
2. Centre of Islamic and Middle Eastern Laws, School of Oriental and African Studies, University of London.

3. The website is at www.soas.ac.uk/honourcrimes. One of the dilemmas faced by the project, in common with other such efforts, is whether and how to maintain such resources in a useful (updated) form in the future.

4. Originally the bibliography was hosted on the websites of two cooperating institutions, the International Women's Heath Coalition and the University of Minnesota's Human Rights Centre.

5. Report of the Special Rapporteur on violence against women, its causes and consequences, UN Doc. E/CN.4/1999/68 10 March 1999, para. 18.

6. Journalist Rana Husseini made these points to the CIMEL/INTERIGHTS round table: see Welchman, 2000: 442.

7. In Newsline, cited in Amnesty International, 1999a: 23.

8. AS/EGA (2002) 7 rev 2, 4 June 2002, para. 32.

9. Ibid., para. 3.

10. Compare, in the 'West', the popular perception of a 'cold blooded killer' to that of a man who kills in a crime of passion; as Leader-Elliott (1997: 162) describes the latter: 'The ordinary man is a sanguine man, a hot man, whose blood boils when his most vital interests are threatened.'

11. Note that in the UN General Assembly resolution, 'Working towards the Elimination of Crimes Against Women and Girls Committed in the Name of Honour' (UN Doc. A/C.3/59/L.25), adopted on 15 October 2004, reference to 'crimes of passion' was omitted. See further Jane Connors and Purna Sen in this volume.

12. Statement by H.R.H. Prince Zeid Ra'ad Zeid Al-Hussein, Permanent Representative of Jordan, Statement in Explanation of vote, Agenda Item 107: Advancement of Women, 55th Session of the General Assembly Third Committee, New York, 3 November 2000.

13. Leader-Elliott (1997: 169), in regard to whether sexual provocation should reduce murder to manslaughter, concludes that, 'given the disparity between the sexes in the matter of who kills whom, women may be far more likely than men to conclude that this particular claim to compassion is an anachronism.'

14. Report of the Special Rapporteur on extra-judicial summary or arbitrary executions, UN Doc. E/CN.4/2000/3, 25 January 2000, para. 78.

15. See report of the 'National Consultation on Women's Right to Choose If, When and Whom to Marry', organised by the Association for Advocacy and Legal Initiatives (AALI) in Lucknow, India, with support from INTERIGHTS and IWRAW-AP, in 2003; on file with authors. See also the project website.

16. *Jordan Times*, 23 November 1999.

17. We would like to draw attention here to the collection of papers in Mojab and Abdo, 2004, published after the current manuscript was submitted.

1

United Nations approaches
to 'crimes of honour'

JANE CONNORS

Over the last fifteen to twenty years, the approach within the United Nations (UN) to violence against women has been transformed from one centred purely on the advancement of women, crime control and criminal justice and addressed predominantly within the UN entities concerned with those issues, to one which incorporates a human rights perspective. Critical to this transformation have been the efforts of non-governmental organisations (NGOs) within UN forums, particularly the cycle of world conferences, to recognise all forms of violence against women occurring in all settings as an issue of human rights.

This chapter provides an overview of the approach to violence against women by the UN, indicating how specific forms of violence against women have been addressed within its framework. It describes developments in this area since the Fourth World Conference on Women held in Beijing in September 1995,[1] and traces the emergence within the UN of efforts to address 'crimes of honour' as a particular concern.

United Nations work on violence against women

With isolated exceptions, policy within the UN relating to violence against women initially concentrated on such violence within the family. The 1975 World Plan of Action adopted by the First World Conference on Women in Mexico did not refer to violence explicitly, but contained language relating to the dignity, equality and security of family and the need for the provision of assistance in the solution of family conflict. The Copenhagen Conference held in 1980, midway through the International Women's Decade, adopted a resolution on 'battered women and the family' and referred to violence in the home in its final report. However, it was not until the 1985 Nairobi World Conference, marking the end of the Decade, and especially at its non-governmental forum, that violence against women truly emerged as a serious international concern. The outcome document of that Conference, the Forward-looking Strategies for the Advancement of Women, linked the promotion and the maintenance of peace to the eradication of violence against women in both public and private spheres and identified a number of strategies to address violence against women in the family, in armed conflict, and against women subject to detention or penal law. It also called for measures to address the concerns of women victims of trafficking and involuntary prostitution.[2]

The impetus provided by the Nairobi Conference resulted in the first General Assembly resolution on domestic violence,[3] which, although not directed specifically at women, formed the background to the 1986 UN Expert Group Meeting on Violence against Women in the Family, and the 1989 study of the same name (Connors, 1989). These activities heightened the attention of the UN system and its member states to the issue of violence against women generally, thereby allowing the further contexts and manifestations of violence against women to surface. As the multifarious settings and manifestations of violence against women were revealed, and its association with gender roles increasingly appreciated, the approach to the issue shifted. Whereas earlier, violence against women in the family had been prioritised as an area of concern, this form of violence was now viewed as only one, albeit large, part of the phenomenon of violence against women. Further, the gender-based nature of violence against women and its linkage to the subordination of women to men, stereotypical patterns of behaviour, inequality between women and men and discrimination, led to its categorisation as a human rights concern, thereby allowing for a broader policy response to the issue within the UN and its associated entities.

At the forefront of efforts to identify violence against women as a human rights issue was the Committee on the Elimination of Discrimination Against Women, the UN treaty body established to monitor the 1979 Convention on the Elimination of All Forms of Discrimination Against Women ('the treaty' or 'the Convention').[4] This treaty, now ratified or acceded to by 178 States Parties,[5] sets out the legal obligations to eliminate discrimination against women and ensure they enjoyed no discrimination of political, economic, social, cultural and civil rights in the public and private spheres.

Despite attempts by delegations to include obligations relating to violence against women in the Convention during its drafting in the early 1970s

(Rehof, 1993: 91–92), no reference beyond trafficking in women and the exploitation of prostitution of women (Article 6), is made to violence against women in the treaty. As reports were submitted by States Parties to the Committee in accordance with their obligations under the Convention (Article 18), and NGOs also provided information on the situation of implementation of the Convention in various countries (for example, by submitting parallel/shadow reports), it became clear that violence against women was a central obstacle to the elimination of discrimination against women, and their achievement of equality with men. In response, the Committee adopted successive 'general recommendations',[6] within its competence under Article 21 of the Convention, based on the examination of reports and information received from States Parties. This series of general recommendations made clear that all forms of gender-based violence against women fall within the meaning of discrimination against women on the grounds of sex, as provided by the treaty. The first of these, General Recommendation 12 on violence against women, called for States Parties' reports to include information on the legislation in force to protect women against the incidence of all kinds of violence in everyday life (including sexual violence, abuses in the family, sexual harassment in the workplace), other measures adopted to eradicate this violence, the existence of support services for victims and statistical data on the incidence of all kinds of violence against women and on women who are the victims of violence.[7] General Recommendation 14 expressed concern at the continuation of the practice of female circumcision and other traditional practices harmful to the health of women, and recommended that states take appropriate and effective measures with a view to eradicating these practices, and include information on such measures in their reports to the Committee.[8]

The more substantive and detailed General Recommendation 19 on violence against women, prepared by the Committee as one of its contributions to the 1993 World Conference on Human Rights, indicates that gender-based violence is a form of discrimination that seriously inhibits women's ability to enjoy rights and freedoms on a basis of equality with men, identifying those rights and freedoms which are compromised by such violence.[9] Gender-based violence against women is defined as violence that is directed against a woman because she is a woman or that affects women disproportionately.[10] Such violence includes acts that inflict physical, mental or sexual harm or suffering, threats of such acts, coercion and other deprivations of liberty. Importantly, the general recommendation identifies the nature of state responsibility to eliminate violence against women and indicates that while the specific provisions of the Convention may not expressly mention violence, it predicates accountability for public acts of violence committed by the state and those connected with the state, as well as some acts committed by non-state actors.[11] It also makes clear that 'States may also be responsible for private acts if they fail to act with due diligence to prevent violations of rights or to investigate and punish acts of violence, and for providing compensation' (para. 9).

The Committee's linkage of gender-based violence against women to the international legal norm of non-discrimination on the basis of sex had a profound effect on parallel developments relating to violence against women within the political bodies of the UN. These included the development of a Declaration on Violence Against Women, prepared by the Commission on the Status of Women, and adopted by the General Assembly in 1993.[12] This Declaration defines 'gender-based violence against women' in terms of both site and manifestation, includes violence that takes place in both public and private life (Article 2), and sets out steps that states and entities of the UN should take to address it (Article 4). Importantly, it makes clear that states should not invoke any custom, tradition or religious consideration to avoid their obligations with respect to the elimination of gender-based violence against women, and should exercise due diligence to prevent, investigate and, in accordance with national legislation, punish acts of violence against women, whether those acts are perpetrated by the state or private persons (Article 4). Although there is no explicit indication in the Declaration that gender-based violence against women is a violation of human rights, Article 3 elaborates upon the human rights women are entitled to enjoy.

The final adoption of the Declaration was preceded by the Vienna World Conference on Human Rights in June 1993.[13] Coming on the heels of the Committee on the Elimination of Discrimination Against Women's General Recommendation 19, and the discussions surrounding the Declaration, the Conference also coincided with revelations of many incidents of gender-based violence in the former Yugoslavia. Women's NGOs from around the world had also focused on the Conference as a forum to air the international community's historical disregard of women's lack of enjoyment of human rights, and particularly its failure to recognise gender-based violence as a central human rights concern. An unprecedented number of women's human rights NGOs attended the Conference, and many activities, especially at the parallel non-governmental forum, concerned violence against women. Particularly memorable was a one-day tribunal where individual victims of diverse forms of violence gave testimony of their experiences and the frequent non-existent or weak state response.

In the outcome document of the Vienna Conference,[14] the international community went a significant distance to redress the disregard of women's limited enjoyment of human rights and asserted a vision of a world order which included the human rights of women. In particular, violence against women in some circumstances, such as armed conflict, was described as a violation of human rights and deserving of effective response and serious response from all parts of the UN.[15] The Vienna Conference welcomed the consideration of the creation of the first gender-specific human rights extra-conventional mechanism since the foundation of the UN in 1945, the Special Rapporteur on violence against women, its causes and consequences, and encouraged the GA to adopt the Declaration on Violence Against Women. The Conference also provided the first sign of encouragement at the political level for the development of a petition procedure to the Convention on the Elimination of All Forms of Discrimination, when it called on the Commission on the Status of Women and the Committee to examine quickly the possibility of introducing the right of petition through the preparation of an Optional Protocol to the Convention.[16]

By making clear that violations of the human rights of women, and especially gender-based violence against women, were a concern of all of the institutions of the UN, particularly those traditionally dubbed as the 'mainstream' human rights institutions, and not just a concern of the women-specific institutions within the UN, the World Conference set the stage for remarkable results. Some of these, such as the gender-sensitivity, especially with regard to gender-based violence, of the International War Crimes Tribunal with respect to events in the former Yugoslavia[17] and the Tribunal that was to be created with regard to Rwanda,[18] predated the closure of the Conference. Others occurred later, including the 1994 Commission on Human Rights (CHR) resolution which confirmed the creation of the Special Rapporteur on violence against women[19] and mandated the notion of gender integration into the work of the human rights system, and the inclusion of a gender perspective in the constituent documents of the Rome Statute of the International Criminal Court,[20] as well as the adoption by the Security Council of resolution 1325 on women, peace and security.[21]

At the Fourth World Conference in Beijing,[22] the international community built on the existing work on gender-based violence against women. Two of the twelve critical areas of concern identified in its outcome document (the Platform for Action)[23] as requiring urgent action in order to achieve the goal of gender equality concerned violence against women. These two areas – violence against women and women and armed conflict – are closely interlinked with another critical area, the human rights of women. Throughout, the Platform adopts the definition of violence against women contained in the Declaration on the Elimination of Violence Against Women, but also highlights specific forms of violence not explicitly mentioned in the Declaration. These include forms of gender-based violence which had become more apparent since the adoption of the Declaration, such as violations of the rights of women in situations of armed conflict, forced sterilisation and forced abortion, coercive or forced use of contraceptives, female infanticide and prenatal sex selection. Also, although making clear that women in all countries, irrespective of culture, class or income, are at risk of gender-based violence, the Platform indicates that some groups of women, such as minority women, indigenous women and women migrant workers, are especially vulnerable.[24] Three strategic objectives are established by the Platform for the elimination of violence against women: integrated measures to prevent and eliminate violence against women; the study of the causes and consequences of violence against women, as well as the effectiveness of preventive measures; and the elimination of trafficking in women, and the provision of assistance to victims of violence due to prostitution.[25] Recommendations to achieve these strategic objectives are primarily directed at governments, which are called on to condemn violence against women, exercise due diligence in prevention, investigation and punishment; implement existing international standards and support international mechanisms; adopt and effectively implement legal measures; introduce or strengthen awareness-raising of violence against women generally, and in specific sectors; and provide services for those affected by violence.

Beyond the Platform

It is almost ten years since the adoption of the Beijing Platform for Action, and there have been many initiatives at the national level to transform its recommendations into reality. The UN Secretary-General's report on the review and appraisal of the implementation of the Platform, which concluded in March 2000, describes policy and law reform, the introduction of services and assistance, education campaigns and advocacy campaigns to address values, attitudes and actions relating to violence against women which have been adopted in countries as diverse as Belize, Colombia, Canada, Germany, Israel, Turkey, Pakistan, Algeria and Poland.[26] Evidence of further progress is provided by responses to the questionnaire circulated in preparation for the ten-year review and appraisal, scheduled for 2005, by the Commission on the Status of Women of the Beijing Declaration and Platform for Action and the Outcome Document of the Twenty-Third Special Session of the General Assembly on Beijing + 5.

Within the UN itself, work on violence against women has continued, and become the concern of all parts of the system, with the Office of the UN High Commissioner for Human Rights, the Office of the High Commissioner for

Refugees, the World Health Organisation, the UN Population Fund, the UN Children's Fund and the UN Development Fund for Women being among those with specific policies or programmes relating to gender-based violence against women. The UN political bodies have continued to adopt resolutions on gender-based violence against women, and in particular those relating to specific forms of violence against women or groups of women particularly affected. Resolutions are adopted routinely on trafficking in women, violence against migrant women workers, and traditional practices affecting the health of women and girls, including female genital mutilation,[27] with the General Assembly calling for an in-depth study on all forms of violence against women at its 2003 session.[28] The Sub-commission on the Promotion and Protection of Human Rights, long seized of the issues of traditional practices affecting the health of women and girls and modern forms of slavery and slave-like practices, conducts studies on forms of violence against women which fall within the rubric of these agenda items, while decisions and resolutions on these matters are adopted annually. Where the treaty bodies are concerned, it is now not only the Committee on the Elimination of Discrimination Against Women which addresses forms of violence against women, but the Human Rights Committee, the Committee against Torture, the Committee on the Elimination of Racial Discrimination, the Committee on Economic, Social and Cultural Rights, and the Committee on the Rights of the Child, which frequently discuss forms of violence against women and girls in their dialogue with States Parties, their lists of issues and questions, their concluding comments/observations on the reports of States Parties, and their general recommendations/comments. The Special Rapporteur on violence against women has been a powerful voice within the human rights movement for the cause of gender-based violence, while other human rights special procedures, including other thematic and country-specific rapporteurs, now include the issue in their reports and other work.

Crimes of honour

The preceding survey has sought to show how the issue of violence against women is now conceptualised within the UN as a human rights concern. It has also sought to show that whilst the initial focus of its activity was on violence against women in the family, this focus has broadened. Violence against women addressed in the international sphere constitutes, in the terms of the Declaration on the Elimination of Violence Against Women, any act of gender-based violence that results in, or is likely to result in, physical, sexual or mental harm or suffering to women, including threats of such acts, coercion or arbitrary deprivation of liberty whether this occurs within the family, the community or perpetrated by the state. Moreover, such violence is not random, but is associated with inequality between women and men, and strategies to entrench and perpetuate that inequality.

In 1984, the Sub-commission on Prevention of Discrimination and Protection of Minorities (now the Sub-commission on the Promotion and Protection of Human Rights) established a working group to address all aspects of traditional practices affecting the health of women, which drew up a list of harmful traditional practices that would be studied. Although 'crimes of honour' were identified as requiring study, female circumcision was taken up first, with 'crimes of honour' yet to be studied. In 1988, the Sub-commission appointed Halima Embarek Warzazi to act as its Special Rapporteur on traditional practices affecting the health of women and girls. Ms Warzazi's reports have focused predominantly on female circumcision, or genital mutilation, although reports since 1999 have touched on 'crimes of honour'. This issue was taken up initially by treaty bodies, firstly by the Committee on the Elimination of Discrimination Against Women in its general recommendations and then in its constructive dialogue with States Parties presenting reports.

Human rights treaty bodies

In General Recommendation 19, the Committee on the Elimination of Discrimination Against Women indicated that legislation to remove the defence of honour in cases of assault or murder of a family female member was among the measures necessary to overcome family violence.[29] In 1997 the Committee discussed 'honour killings' with Turkey and included two paragraphs on the issue in its concluding comments, expressing the view that it was 'concerned about the provisions of the Penal Code that allowed less rigorous sanctions or penalties for "honour killings". That concept contravened the principle of respect for human life and security of all persons, which was protected by international human rights law.'[30] The Committee indicated that the 'practice of so-called honour killings, based on customs and traditions, was a violation of the right to life and security of persons and therefore must be appropriately addressed under the law.'[31] Similar concerns were raised in the concluding comments directed to Israel in the same year.[32] In 2000 the Committee expressed concern that several provisions of the Jordanian penal code 'continue to discriminate against women. In particular … that Article 340 of the Code excuses a man who kills or injures his wife or his female kin caught in the act of adultery.'[33] The Committee urged the government to 'provide all possible support for the speedy repeal of Article

340 and to undertake awareness raising activities that make "honour killings" socially and morally unacceptable.'[34] Again in 2000, the Committee expressed deep concern at the violence against women perpetrated through honour killings in Iraq,[35] and raised similar concerns in its concluding comments on several States Parties as diverse as Egypt, Netherlands, Uruguay, Yemen and Brazil[36] from 2001 to 2004.

Largely as a result of the lead given by the Committee on the Elimination of Discrimination Against Women in this area, the Committee on the Rights of the Child requested information on 'honour killings' in its 2001 list of issues to Turkey,[37] and included several paragraphs on the issue in its concluding observations.[38] The approach of these treaty bodies in their concluding comments/observations has been taken by other committees, including the Committee on the Elimination of Racial Discrimination and the Committee against Torture[39] in dialogue with States Parties.[40] The Committee on Economic, Social and Cultural Rights has also addressed the issue, welcoming the removal of legal recognition of crimes of honour in Tunisia,[41] and expressing concern about discrimination against women in Syrian society, in particular as reflected in the more severe punishment of women for adultery and honour crimes.[42] The Human Rights Committee has also taken up the issue, for example, in its 1997 concluding comments on Iraq[43] and those adopted during 2002 on Sweden.[44] Moreover, at its sixty-eighth session, in 2000, the Human Rights Committee adopted General Comment 28 on Article 3 of the International Covenant on Civil and Political Rights: equality of rights between women and men, which stated that honour crimes that remained unpunished constituted a serious violation of the Covenant and that laws that impose more severe penalties on women than men for adultery or other offences also violate the requirement of equal treatment.[45]

It is clear that in approaching 'crimes of honour' each treaty body has categorised these as human rights violations, despite the fact that they are perpetrated by non-state actors, usually family members, on the basis that state legislation and policy provide an environment in which such acts can occur, or that the state has failed to act effectively to eradicate the custom or practice. The treaty bodies have identified several rights in their respective treaties as being compromised where honour killings are concerned: the right to life; the right to non-discrimination; the right to equality before the law; the right to liberty and security of the person; and the right not to be subjected to torture, or other cruel, inhuman or degrading treatment or punishment. The Committee on the Elimination of Discrimination Against Women's General Recommendation 19, the Declaration on the Elimination of Violence Against Women, and the Human Rights Committee's General

Comment 28 also identify these rights as being compromised in the context of gender-based violence generally. Categorisation of an activity as a violation of human rights attracts state responsibility for that activity in international law. As the preceding paragraphs indicate, this may result in criticism by treaty bodies in the context of their constructive dialogue with States Parties and in their concluding observations or comments. Where the state concerned has accepted procedures allowing individuals to petition treaty bodies, as provided by the International Covenant on Civil and Political Rights through its First Optional Protocol to the Covenant[46] or the relatively recent Optional Protocol to the Convention on the Elimination of All Forms of Discrimination Against Women,[47] individuals who are victims of such violations may be able to claim relief through these procedures.[48] The Committee Against Torture and the Committee on the Elimination of Discrimination Against Women can also receive information on the issue which may trigger their *suo moto* inquiry procedures into well-founded indications that torture is being systematically practised,[49] or that grave or systematic violations of the rights in the Convention are taking place.[50] To date, the Committee Against Torture has conducted eight inquiries, while the Committee on the Elimination of Discrimination Against Women has conducted one, notably on questions of violence against women in Mexico.[51]

Extra-conventional mechanisms

The Special Rapporteur on violence against women has been consistent in locating honour crimes squarely within the rubric of human rights violations. Her interim report to the fiftieth session of the CHR drew attention to the issue, as did her report submitted to the fifty-second session of the Commission in 1996, the report on her mission to Brazil on the issue of domestic violence submitted to the fifty-third session of the Commission in 1997, the report on her mission to Pakistan and Afghanistan in 1999, her reports to the sessions of the Commission in 1998 and 1999, and in addenda to her reports in 2000 and 2001 including communications to and from governments.[52] Her report to the fifty-eighth session of the CHR in 2002, which concerned cultural practices within the family that involve violence towards women,[53] indicated that honour killings had been reported in a number of countries and were carried out not only by husbands, fathers, brothers and uncles, but frequently by under-aged males of the family to reduce punishment. She made clear that these crimes were based not on religious beliefs, but on cultural ideologies. The Special Rapporteur noted that there had been contradictory decisions with respect to the honour defence in several jurisdictions, including Brazil, and that legislative provisions exonerating completely or partially crimes related to honour existed in the penal codes of Argentina, Bangladesh, Ecuador, Egypt, Guatemala, the Islamic Republic of Iran, Israel, Jordan, Lebanon, Peru, the Syrian Arab Republic, Turkey and Venezuela. The Special Rapporteur also indicated that the Criminal Court in Amman had sentenced two men to death for killing their 60-year-old next of kin to cleanse the family's honour. The Special Rapporteur's report to the 2003 Commission at the end of her mandate, and particularly the addendum to that report, on international, regional and national developments in the area of violence against women,[54] also provides a wealth of information on the issue.

The Special Rapporteur on the independence of judges and lawyers,[55] the Special Rapporteur on freedom of religion and belief[56] and the Special Rapporteur on extrajudicial, summary or arbitrary executions have also discussed crimes of honour as part of their work. Where the latter is concerned, the Special Rapporteur considered honour killings in her reports submitted to the 1999 and 2000 sessions of the CHR and indicated that she had been working closely with the Special Rapporteurs on violence against women and on the independence of judges and lawyers, respectively, to monitor incidents of honour killings in which the state had either approved and supported those acts or provided the perpetrators with impunity through tacit or covert support. She also provided examples of states which had declared their opposition to honour killings, publicly condemning the practice, but she expressed the view that most states had taken little concrete action.[57] In her report to the 2000 session of the Commission, the Special Rapporteur indicated that she continued to receive reports of honour killings of women, and made clear that Islamic leaders and scholars condemned them. At the same time, she expressed concern that some governments placed potential victims of such killings in prisons or correctional homes. She also welcomed initiatives by Jordan and Turkey to address honour crimes. In an addendum to her 2000 report[58] and in her 2001 report[59] the Special Rapporteur noted that a constitutional body in Pakistan had categorically stated that honour crimes were not in conformity with Islam. She also addressed the issue of honour crimes in her reports to the Commission's 2002, 2003 and 2004 sessions.[60]

As with the treaty bodies, the rapporteurs link the actions of the family member, private, non-state actor perpetrator to the duty of the relevant state to protect, promote and fulfil human rights obligations, and, as articulated in Article 4(c) of the Declaration on the Elimination of Violence Against Women, to the obligation 'to exercise due diligence to prevent, investigate and, in accordance with national legislation, punish acts of violence against women, whether perpetrated by the State or by private persons.'

The United Nations political bodies

Attention by the human rights treaty bodies and the rapporteurs of the Commission of Human Rights to crimes of honour brought the issue into the political bodies of the UN. In resolution 2000/31 on extrajudicial, summary or arbitrary executions, adopted at its fifty-sixth session in 2000, the CHR noted with concern the large number of cases reported by the Special Rapporteur in various parts of the world of killings committed in the name of passion or in the name of honour, persons killed because of their sexual orientation, and persons killed for reasons related to their peaceful activities as human rights defenders or as journalists, and called upon governments concerned to investigate such killings promptly and thoroughly, to bring those responsible to justice and to ensure that such killings are neither condoned nor sanctioned by government officials or personnel.[61] A little over a month later, the twenty-third special session of the General Assembly, undertaking the five-year review of the implementation of the Beijing Platform for Action, called on governments to

> develop, adopt and fully implement laws and other measures, as appropriate, such as policies and educational programmes, to eradicate harmful customary or traditional practices, including female genital mutilation, early and forced marriage and so-called honour crimes, which are violations of the human rights of women and girls and obstacles to the full enjoyment by women of their human rights and fundamental freedoms, and to intensify efforts, in cooperation with local women's groups, to raise collective and individual awareness on how these harmful traditional or customary practices violate women's human rights. (69(e))

The special session also called on all stakeholders to 'increase cooperation, policy responses, effective implementation of national legislation and other protective and preventive measures aimed at the elimination of violence against women and girls' (96(a)). An indicative list of forms of violence followed, which included crimes committed in the 'name of honour' and crimes committed in the 'name of passion'.[62] Several NGOs that participated in the special session also highlighted these forms of violence against women'. Equality Now, for example, submitted a document detailing discriminatory legislation, including that excusing 'honour crimes', persisting in Member States of the UN,[63] and organised a well-attended side-event on the margins of the special session where the implications of these laws were portrayed by a highly talented performance artist. In his statement issued on 10 June 2000 relating to the special session, the Secretary-General indicated he was greatly encouraged at the progress made in dealing with new issues, such as honour crimes.[64]

The willingness of the international community to address 'honour crimes' in a preambular paragraph of a CHR resolution, and two paragraphs of the outcome document of the special session, encouraged the Netherlands delegation, which had sponsored a resolution on traditional practices harmful to the health of women and girls in the GA in 1997,[65] to circulate a draft resolution on 'crimes of honour' entitled 'traditional or customary practices amounting to crimes against women, including crimes committed in the name of honour'. Contemporaneously with the circulation of the draft resolution by the Netherlands, a documentary film entitled *Crimes of Honour* was shown at UN headquarters. The film, a large part of which takes place in Jordan, was perceived by some as an attempt to link Islam with violence against women, and with crimes of honour in particular.

The chairman of the Islamic Group submitted a letter to the Secretary-General, appending a statement of the Group, adopted at ambassadorial level, on 2 October 2000,[66] which indicated that

> member States of the Organization of the Islamic Conference, like other States Members of the UN, in keeping with their obligations under the universally accepted instruments on human rights, have all committed themselves to opposing any form of arbitrary or extrajudicial killing of any human being, particularly women, in the name of passion, honour or race. Conference member States have always been in the forefront of condemning the killing of persons, especially women and girls on any pretext, and have unreservedly raised. their voices in world conferences and in other relevant bodies of the UN system, condemning and opposing all forms of violence against women.

The statement reiterated that 'there is no linkage whatsoever between the killing of women and girls under any societal or communal banner, including in the name of passion, honour or race, and the teachings, practices and values of Islam.'[67]

The perceived linkage of the subject of the resolution recurred throughout discussions of the draft resolution, with further concerns arising as a result of lack of clarity with respect to the two concepts of 'crimes of honour' and 'crimes of passion' included in UN documents. Another draft resolution was prepared, entitled 'elimination of all forms of violence, including crimes against women'.[68] Action on both resolutions took place in the Third Committee (of the GA) on 3 November 2000, with complex procedural motions occurring as a consensus was sought on both resolutions, the first now entitled 'working toward the elimination of crimes against women committed in the name of honour',[69] and the second on 'the elimination of all forms of violence against women identified in the outcome document of the twenty-third special session of the General Assembly entitled "Women 2000: gender equality, development and peace for the twenty-first century".'

In his statement on 1 November 2000, introducing the former resolution, Ambassador A. Peter van Walsum, the Permanent Representative of the Kingdom of the Netherlands, noted that the Beijing + 5 outcome document was the first globally accepted instrument that explicitly acknowledges the occurrence of 'honour crimes', and that the draft had been renamed in order to reflect the fact that the elimination of honour crimes is a collaborative process requiring fundamental changes in societal attitudes, and the use of legislative, educational, social and other measures. Consensus could not be achieved on the resolution, with the delegation of Jordan introducing a number of oral amendments to the draft, which were not accepted by the representative of the Netherlands.[70] The resolution was adopted with 120 in favour and 25 abstaining, with many of those abstaining condemning 'honour killings', but expressing other concerns. For example, in his statement in explanation of vote, HRH Prince Zeid Ra'ad Zeid Al-Hussein, the Permanent Representative of Jordan, classified the crime as an 'odious phenomenon: a dreadful crime, a crime that has no bearing to any religion, nor any particular culture or tribal custom'. His statement also raised questions about the linkage of the issue with Islam which had resulted from the screening of the film. In addition he questioned the meaning of the term 'crime of honour', drawing a distinction between such crimes, and crimes committed in a sudden spurt of rage, or crimes of passion, with respect to which it is indicated that the obligation to exercise due diligence to prevent, investigate and punish cannot apply. To quote the Permanent Representative: 'if the crime in question is committed in a sudden state of rage? All states, wherein we find crimes of passion, would in due course leave themselves open to potential accusations of human rights violations for not having exercised "enough" due diligence to prevent the commission of this crime.'[71]

The companion resolution, introduced by Algeria, was adopted without a vote,[72] although several delegations indicated that they would have preferred a holistic approach to the issue of violence against women, and another expressed the view that it would have preferred to avoid a dichotomy between violence and crimes.[73] In its preambular paragraphs it reaffirms the outcome document of the special session of the GA which reviewed implementation of the Beijing Platform, as well as the call for the elimination of violence against women and girls in the outcome document that it transcribes. Among the forms of violence to be eliminated in the list contained in the resolution are 'crimes committed in the name of honour, crimes committed in the name of passion'. This list is repeated in an operative paragraph expressing deep concern at the persistence of various forms of violence. The resolution calls for the introduction or strengthening of legal, administrative and other measures to prevent and eliminate forms of violence against women; calls for the strengthening of awareness and preventive measures, including through public awareness campaigns; expressed appreciation for non-governmental activities to address violence against women and calls for government support in this regard; calls on states to fulfil their obligations under human rights instruments and UN policy documents, and to include information on violence against women in their reports to the Committee on the Elimination of Discrimination Against Women and other relevant UN treaty monitoring bodies; urges the UN system to assist states, upon their request, in efforts aimed at preventing and eliminating violence against women; and requests the Special Rapporteur on violence against women to devote equal attention to all forms of violence, including violence against women, in her work and reports.

Conclusion

Notwithstanding the controversy surrounding its adoption, Resolution 55/66 became the first General Assembly resolution specifically to address the elimination of crimes against women committed in the name of honour. The resolution explicitly identifies crimes against women committed in the name of 'honour' as a human rights issue and indicates that states have an obligation to exercise due diligence to prevent, investigate and punish the perpetrators of such crimes and provide protection to the victims. Calls are made on states with respect to implementation of international human rights obligations, and policy documents of the UN, with regard to legislation, awareness-raising campaigns, the involvement of public opinion leaders, such as educators, religious leaders, chiefs and traditional leaders and the media, in such campaigns, training for relevant law enforcement and other personnel, and the provision of support for victims or potential victims. The international community is also invited to work in this area, while treaty bodies are encouraged to address the issue as appropriate. As with its companion resolution 55/68 on the elimination of crimes identified in the Beijing + 5 outcome document,[74] the Secretary-General was requested to report on its implementation at the fifty-seventh session of the General Assembly in 2002.

The Secretary-General's report on working towards the elimination of crimes against women committed in the name of honour[75] makes clear that human rights treaty bodies, the CHR, its Subcommission and the Special Rapporteurs, particularly the Special Rapporteur on violence against women, have continued to address the question of crimes committed against women in the name[76] of honour. More importantly, the report outlines legal, policy and programmatic measures at the national level to prevent and penalise such crimes in countries which had submitted information on national-level implementation of the resolution. Following consideration of the report at its fifty-seventh session, the General Assembly again adopted a resolution on working towards the elimination of crimes against women committed in the name of honour, but without a vote.[77]

At the international level, therefore, 'honour crimes' are well on the agenda, and generally perceived as a matter of human rights. At the same time, the issue remains an uncomfortable one, with some delegations concerned that a focus on crimes against women committed in the name of honour is selective, rather than comprehensive in its treatment of violence against women.[78] The distinction between crimes of honour and crimes of passion is also questioned,[79] as is the appropriateness of mechanisms taking up such issues whose mandates are not women-specific.[80] Explicit recognition of the issue by the political bodies of the UN, as well as by the expert bodies and other mechanisms, provides a framework for the repeal of legislation sanctioning such crimes, as well as policy and programme interventions at the national level. The report of the Secretary-General on violence against women submitted to the 2004 session of the General Assembly[81] provides further information on legal and other reforms in this context, and it may well be that the discussion of the issue at international level has been among the factors behind these reforms. Where the broad human rights issue of violence against women is concerned, the Secretary-General's in-depth study on all forms of violence mandated by the General Assembly in Resolution 185 at its fifty-eighth session in 2003 provides a further opportunity for violence against women in all its forms, whether perpetrated in the private or public sphere, to remain a human rights issue.

Notes

The author is a Senior Human Rights Officer in the Office of the High Commissioner for Human Rights. This paper is written in a personal capacity.

1. See further www.un.org/womenwatch/asp/user/list.asp?ParentID=4001.
2. See further www.un.org/womenwatch/confer/nfls/.
3. GA resolution 40/36 (29 November 1985).
4. Convention on the Elimination of All Forms of Discrimination Against Women 1979, adopted and opened for signature by GA resolution 34/180 (18 December 1979). See Article 17 which relates to the Committee.
5. www.untreaty.un.org.
6. General recommendations are issued by treaty monitoring bodies to provide greater understanding on the nature of obligations associated with the human

rights articulated in the relevant treaty or to demonstrate how the treaty rights impact on certain thematic issues.

7. CEDAW General Recommendation 12 – violence against women (Eighth session, 1989), UN Doc. A/44/38 at 75 (1990).

8. CEDAW General Recommendation 14 – female circumcision (Ninth session, 1990), UN Doc. A/45/38 at 80 (1990).

9. CEDAW General Recommendation 9, UN Doc. A/47/38 (Eleventh session, 1993), para. 7: these rights and freedoms include '(a) The right to life; (b) The right not to be subject to torture or to cruel, inhuman or degrading treatment or punishment; (c) The right to equal protection according to humanitarian norms in time of international or internal armed conflict; (d) The right to liberty and security of person; (e) The right to equal protection under the law; (f) The right to equality in the family; (g) The right to the highest standard attainable of physical and mental health; (h) The right to just and favourable conditions of work.

10. Ibid., para 6.

11. Ibid., para 8 and 9.

12. Declaration on the Elimination of Violence Against Women, GA resolution 48/104 (20 December 1993).

13. See further www.unhchr.ch/html/menu5/wchr.htm.

14. Vienna Declaration and Programme of Action UN Doc. A/CONF.157/23 (12 July 1993).

15. Ibid., para. 38.

16. Ibid., para. 40.

17. See further, www.un.org/icty/.

18. See further, www.ictr.org/.

19. Commission on Human Rights resolution – Question of integrating the rights of women into the human rights mechanisms of the United Nations and the elimination of violence against women, UN Doc. E/CN.4/RES/1994/45.

20. UN Doc A/CONF.183/9; see also United Nations, 2002: Chapter IV, International Legal Framework.

21. S/RES/1325 (31 October 2000).

22. See further www.un.org/womenwatch/daw/beijing/.

23. UN Doc A/CONF.177/20.

24. Ibid., paras 113–16.

25. Ibid., paras 124–30.

26. The Secretary-General's Questionnaire to Governments on Implementation of the Beijing Platform for Action and the Responses of Member States and Observers are available at: www.un.org/womenwatch/daw.

27. See, for example, Violence Against Women, Report of the Secretary-General, A/59/281 (20 August 2004) paras 47 to 50, which catalogues the resolutions on violence against women adopted during the fifty-seventh and fifty-eighth sessions of the GA, those adopted by the Commission on Human Rights and relevant agreed conclusions adopted by the Commission on the Status of Women during 2003 and 2004.

28. A/RES/58/185 (18 March 2004).

29. CEDAW General Recommendation 9, para. 24(r)(ii).

30. Concluding comments on Turkey, A/52/38/Rev.1.

31. Ibid., para. 195.
32. Concluding comments on Israel, A/52/38/Rev.1, Part II.
33. Concluding comments on Jordan, A/55/38.
34. Ibid.
35. Concluding comments on Iraq, A/55/38.
36. Concluding comments on, respectively, Egypt, A/56/38, Netherlands, A/56/38, Uruguay, A/57/38, Yemen, A/57/38, and Brazil, A/58/38.
37. CRC List of Issues: Turkey, CRC/C/Q/TUR/1 (List of Issues).
38. Concluding observations on Turkey CRC/C/15/Add.152 para. 31; see also the Concluding observations on Lebanon, CRC/C/15/Add. 169.
39. See also the presentation of the Committee against Torture's Rapporteur on torture and gender issues on the outcome of Beijing + 5, where 'honour crimes' are discussed: CAT/C/SR.440, 43ff.
40. Both Committees discussed the issue in dialogue with Israel: CAT/C/SR/496 and CERD/C/SR.1251, respectively.
41. E/C.12/1/Add.36.
42. E/C.12/1/Add.63, paras 14 and 31.
43. CCPR/C/79/Add.84.
44. CCPR/CO/74/SWE.
45. A/55/40, Volume I (2000) 133, para. 3. The Committee indicates that Articles 6 on the right to life, 14 on equality before courts and tribunals and 26 on equality before the law and equal protection of the law may be violated as a result of unpunished 'honour crimes'.
46. GA resolution 2200A (XXI) (16 October 1966).
47. GA resolution 54/4 (6 October 1999). Optional individual petition procedures are also provided under the International Convention on the Elimination of All Forms of Racial Discrimination, Article 14; the Convention against Torture and Other Cruel, Inhuman or Degrading Treatment or Punishment, Article 22; and the Convention on the Protection of the Rights of All Migrant Workers and Members of Their Families, Article 77. The latter provision has not, at the time of writing, entered into force.
48. Although the petition procedures have not been used specifically in this context, the Committee against Torture's decision in *AS* v. *Sweden* (CAT/C/D/149/1999) concluded that a State Party has an obligation to refrain from forcibly returning a woman to her country of origin where she was likely to face torture for the crime of adultery.
49. Convention against Torture and Other Cruel, Inhuman or Degrading Treatment or Punishment, Article 20.
50. Optional Protocol to the Convention on the Elimination of All Forms of Discrimination Against Women, Article 8.
51. As of October 2004, the Committee has stated that a summary of its findings in relation to this investigation under Article 8 (Optional Protocol) will be made available at a later date, see further UN Doc. A/5938 paras 393–408.
52. E/CN.4/1995/42; E/CN.4/2000/68/Add.4; E/CN.4/1998/54; E/CN.4/1999/68; E/CN.4/2000/68/Add. 1. E/CN.4/73/Add.1.
53. E/CN.4/2002/83.
54. E/CN.4/2003/75 and Add. 1 to that report.
55. E/CN.4/1999/60, paras 41–42; E/CN.4/2000/61, paras 27 and 28.

56. E/CN.4/2002/73/Add.2.

57. A/55/288.

58. E/CN.4/2000/3/Add.1.

59. E/CN.4/2001/9.

60. E/CN.4/2002/74 and Add.1; E/CN.4/2003/3; and E/CN.4/2004/7.

61. E/CN.4/RES/2000/31.

62. A7S-23/10/Rev.1.

63. Available at www.equality.now.org. See now the report for Beijing+10.

64. Press Release SG/SM/77448 WOM /1214.

65. GA resolution 52/99; four reports on traditional or customary practices affecting the health of women and girls have been submitted to the GA since 1997, with a number of these containing information on honour crimes: A/53/354; A/54/341; A/56/316; and A/58/169.

66. A/C.3/55/4 and annex.

67. See also report of the Special Rapporteur of the Sub-commission of the Commission on Human Rights which draws attention to the well-meaning intentions of the sponsors of the resolution, and the projection of the film and the surprise of Muslim delegations at its tendentious nature: E/CN.4/Sub/2001/27/27.

68. A/C.3/55/L.13.Rev.1.

69. A/C.3/55/L.11/Rev.1.

70. A/C.3/55/SR/6; Advancement of Women, Report of the Third Committee, A/55/595, paras. 8 to 16; Third Committee adopts two draft resolutions on crimes against women – urging elimination of 'honour crimes' and of all forms of violence, Press Release, GA/SHC/3615.

71. Statement by H.R.H. Prince Zeid Ra'ad Zeid Al-Hussein, Permanent Representative of Jordan, Statement in Explanation of vote, Agenda Item 107: Advancement of Women, 55th Session of the GA Third Committee, New York, 3 November 2000.

72. GA resolution A/RES/55/68 on the elimination of all forms of violence against women, including crimes identified in the outcome document of the twenty-third special session of the GA, entitled 'Women 2000: gender equality, development and peace for the twenty-first century'.

73. A/C.3/55/SR.6; Advancement of Women, Report of the Third Committee, A/55/595, paras. 20 to 23; Press Release, GA/SHC/3615.

74. Report of the Secretary-General on elimination of all forms of violence against women, including crimes identified in the outcome document of the twenty-third session of the General Assembly entitled 'Women 2000: gender equality, development and peace for the twenty-first century', A/57/171 (2 July 2002).

75. A/57/169.

76. E/CN.4/2004/66.

77. A/57/549; A/57/PV.77; the GA also adopted a further resolution on the elimination of all forms of violence against women, including crimes identified in' the outcome document of the twenty-third session of the General Assembly, entitled 'Women 2000: gender equality, development and peace for the twenty-first century', A/RES/57/181.

78. See the comments of Jordan on the resolution presented in the Secretary-General's report on working towards the elimination of crimes against women committed in the name of honour, A/57/169, para. 15.

79. Ibid.

80. See GA Press Release, GA/SHC/3730 report of the debate on the resolution on extrajudicial, summary or arbitrary executions, which took place during the fifty-seventh session of the GA.

81. A/59/281.

2

'Crimes of honour', value and meaning

PURNA SEN

Growing international interest in honour killings has shown both the possibility of international collective working and the shortcomings of some such efforts. In particular, identifying Islamic cultures as deeply imbued with backward approaches to gender relations, associating Islam intrinsically with honour killings, and highlighting Islamic cultures as therefore inherently problematic have left a tangle of anger, moral superiority, urgency to act and defensiveness that complicate both conceptualising and acting against honour crimes.

What does it mean to talk of honour killings? The term is more widely known at the start of this century than in the previous decade and such killings are increasingly cast as emblematic of the problematic nature of one religion – Islam – and its treatment of women. In the post-September 11 climate, some Western concerns with honour killings so closely overlap the anti-terror discourse through exactly this recourse to almost knee-jerk condemnation of Islam that a Western anti-honour-killings agenda is in danger of being deeply mired in Islamophobic potential. In this context, any identification of the specificity and particularity of crimes and killings associated with honour codes is in danger of sharing this reception. But what if there are in fact features of crimes and killings of honour that *are* actually specific to given contexts and cultures? How can this be said in such an unfavourable climate? And if they are indeed specific to given cultural contexts, how, if at all, is it possible to have international cooperative work against such practices?

In this chapter, I recall a Western interest in codes of honour in the not very distant past and a continuing current interest from diverse quarters in the value of honour. I trace also the elements of colonial problematising of native gender relations, which made emblematic a number of specific practices, such as the veil and dowry. Through such discourses, colonial encounters cemented both the assumed moral superiority of the West over the rest and the existence of an intense eye upon 'other' cultures that were deemed to be in need of changing their gender relations to become modern and enlightened. Such discourses continue to shape and complicate the possibilities not only for international alliances but also for the safety and reception of indigenous voices that contest crimes of honour. Despite these difficulties, and perhaps illustrating some of them, the illegitimacy of crimes of honour has surfaced strongly within the human rights framework, the history of which I trace briefly. I explore these difficulties and a number of ways in which alliances address, and can profitably be forged to address, the practice.

In this chapter I also identify six elements that, I suggest, characterise honour crimes and that, I argue, do render them distinct from other forms of killing. Defining honour crimes in this way is a difficult task and I welcome a discussion of my proposal. Nevertheless, such crimes are absolutely within a broader continuum (Kelly, 1988) of forms of violence against women that, I suggest, forms the basis for effective international and extra-cultural alliances so long as certain conditions exist, such as the ability to hold a critical position with respect to one's own cultural location and a rejection of culture as the definitive shaping force of gender relations and as the ultimate divide.

The 'honour' motif

Contemporary preoccupation with the concept of honour has placed centre stage the problematic of codes of honour and their concomitant, crimes of honour. These are both primarily associated with Islamic and Middle Eastern cultures and with the killings of women. I shall return to these features but suggest that other locations and histories of the honour principle should be remembered at least, so that we realise the selectivity of Western memory in structuring the problematisation of Islamic practice.

Europe itself has been familiar with concepts of honour (Peristiany, 1966; Pitt-Rivers 1963, 1968; Bourdieu 1966; Brandes, 1980), especially as associated with medieval codes of chivalry and nobility. 'Noble' actions have been valorised through the concept of honour: duelling between men – that is, killing – formed an essential element of such codes of chivalry. Some of the matters over which men's honour could be tarnished, and for which they would duel to protect their honour, concerned the behaviour or favours of women. Such was the practice in Europe; a practice considered rightly honourable and proper among the elites in Western civilisations.

More modern times have seen the honour concept operate in southern Europe as the link between the individual and community. Honour in this context provides a moral framework for behaviour, norms or rules that provide a basis for acceptance in collective life. It is through the holding of honour that individuals find a place in their community, and thus the concept of honour is imbued with great power (Campbell, 1964, referring to Greece).

The concept of honour has not been entirely discarded in the West at the start of the twenty-first century. Examples from the UK alone show the breadth of constituencies, from the monarchy to 'national socialist' organisations, that claim the concept of honour, as defined in their respective fashions. The monarch is posited to be the 'fountain of honour'[1] who bestows tokens and rewards for 'distinguished service' that evidences chivalry or honour. This is done through the giving of titles,[2] which are themselves collectively referred to as honours, hence the 'honours list' of names thus endowed.

Another UK example is that of the neo-Nazi group 'Blood and Honour/Combat 18',[3] which claims a 'code of honour' such that 'to live by honour means that one is prepared to die rather than be dishonoured'. The scandal of behaviour that dishonours is considerable: an 'oath of honour means what it says − to break that oath is dishonourable, a cowardly act, and as such deserves death or everlasting ignominy' (Blood and Honour/C18, n.d.).

Perhaps use of the concept of honour by racists is less well recognised (Spierenburg, 1998), but historical grandeur or chivalry and the monarchy's 'honours list' are lodged in popular consciousness in the UK and perhaps in other parts of Western Europe. These are associations and aspects of honour that are widely celebrated as positive or seen as achievements. Even some who are anti-royalists accept the British monarch's bestowing of titles upon them as symbols of valuable recognition and reward. Thus honour retains positive meaning in the West in contemporary times, and in some quarters dishonour and death are strongly associated.

Dishonour of the 'other'

In other respects, though, the concept of honour has come to have a quite different meaning: backwardness, crime and 'otherness'. In the late twentieth century, Western-led international attention came to rest upon the use of the concept of honour in societies outside the West, particularly in Islamic societies. Unlike the use of honour in Europe, the concept was recast in a problematic frame via an Orientalist (Said, 1978) gaze that made the East in general, and Islam in particular, the focus of a knowing and superior Western eye. This lens sees honour as the motive that propels men to kill women for reasons that are deemed petty or unreasonable, and thus, as an extension of this reasoning, as barbaric or backward. This gaze also has a history, with colonial adventures setting the standards of judgement of native gender relations by the colonial power and of claims to moral superiority among the colonisers too. The Western viewer's eye thus seeks intervention that shapes the problematic society in ways that mirror practices in the West, in pursuit of a 'shared culture which may not always begin with the establishment of alien rule and end with the departure of alien rulers' (Nandy, 1997: 174).

The concept of honour has shaped the colonial encounter in many parts of the world, influencing claims to authority and rightness and defining appropriate sexual/marital relationships (see e.g. Lipsett-Rivera and Johnson, 1998; Dirks, 1992; Peristiany and Pitt-Rivers, 1992; Seed, 1988). Social constructions of sexuality and authority, although contested, served to uphold political hierarchies at the heart of unequal colonial relationships. In parallel, the treatment of 'native women' by 'native men' was singled out for attention and condemnation by missionary and colonial cadres, with religion forming a central divisor between colonials and colonised in struggles over gender relations (Krishnamurty, 1989; Lovett, 1989; Jayawardena, 1995; Walker, 1995). Polygyny in Africa, widow immolation and child marriage in India, veiling in North Africa and the Middle East were all traditions that were problematised by the metropolitan powers. Thus they became a key battleground wherein the *moral superiority* of the West was asserted over the backwardness of the rest; an important element of the enlightening Westernising zeal was the emancipation of native women from native men.[4] Modernisation theory posits gender relations as key indicators on the road from tradition to modernity; modernity that is exemplified by individualism and choice. Collective controls over individual actions through codes of shame and honour have been deemed remnants of backward cultures which have no place in contemporary societies and for those seeking to join the club of enlightened, secular and rational societies.

The treatment of women in societies and cultures outside the West has long been the marker for the judgement made of them in Western eyes (see, e.g., Mohanty et al., 1991; Ahmed, 1992; Said, 1978). The colonial legacy attaches to contemporary Western problematising of gender in southern countries (John, 1996, 1998; McClintock, 1995; Mohanty, 1997) and becomes seen by southern eyes as inherently cloaked in a discourse of superiority, moral absolutism and neocolonialism. As the veil, child marriage and widow immolation did in colonial times, 'honour' killings had at the end of the twentieth century become emblematic of the backwardness of oriental cultures that exemplify the oppression of women. Indeed, the veil still symbolises to some degree the same backwardness, characterising women as passive and oppressed. Resentment, suspicion and anger at this history undoubtedly illuminate the resistance that greets a (particular) Western critical gaze upon gender relations elsewhere. It complicates also the expression and perceived meaning of southern challenges to gender inequalities and gender violence in post-colonial states.

Muslims and the Islamic world are increasingly constructed in the early twenty-first century as the enemy of the West or of civilisation (Huntington, 1993); barbaric practices against women exemplify this disjuncture to those who argue incompatibility. In return it creates in the Muslim world a sense of being under attack (both culturally and literally) and thereby of being under siege. A siege mentality aids cohesion and masks heterogeneity, especially in terms of voices of dissent. This is centrally relevant to our consideration of Islamic responses to a particular construction of Western criticism of crimes of honour. The irony is that in responding to an absolutist interpretation of Islam the variety of Islamic voices are conflated into one and assume the very absolutist division along cultural or religious fault lines that has been used to assault them, in what Rouse (1999) calls 'orientalism in reverse'. The irony is that the hegemony of the West becomes the frame of reference for the Orient (John, 1996, 1998) and, as Spivak (1988) argues, subalterns reinscribe their subordinate position in society.

Focus on Islamic cultures also fails to recognise that the honour principle and killings associated with it may have parallels in non-Islamic cultures. I have mentioned above some European parallels; others can be found in Asia, where the concept of *izzat* (Chowdhry, 1998) is used in a similar way as honour elsewhere (see, e.g., Das, 1993: 214). In India the enforcement of honour can be the means of expression of power, especially violent power (Chowdhry, 1998: 333) and especially power as played out through gender norms.

Social and cultural themes that problematise womanhood can be observed across cultures and times. Central in this is the fear, control or shaping of women's sexuality. There are many varieties, though some patterns are clear. Women pass from the control of the father to that of the husband; marriage is the institution into which young women/girls are propelled around the time of puberty in culture after culture; monoandry and patrilocality confirm that the balance of power played out between families through marriage invests a great deal of de facto control of women among in-laws. Laws regarding the guardianship of children often formalise cultural patterns of belonging and ownership, vesting in fathers control over their children – affirming that women's duty is to reproduce and rear children but that authority does not follow obligation; as such her body and sexual encounters are sited within marital relations and are instrumental in the production of children for her husband/his family.

The starker version of such codes of control exists in the 'belt of classical patriarchy' (Kandiyoti, 1988), though similar direct or indirect constraints apply elsewhere. We can see controls on women's sexuality in many domains, such as the failure of many legal jurisdictions to grant women control of their sexual lives, even with their husbands, through the failure to criminalise (and even therefore to recognise) rape in marriage, based on the principle that once married a woman is deemed to have consented to sexual relations with her husband in perpetuity and is thus unable to express desire or rejection of him.[5]

Box 2.1   Schema of honour and dishonour dynamics

Honour

Vested in person (including conjugal honour] family, tribe, clan, community, collective.

Actions that can bring dishonour

Associating with male friends, having a boyfriend, attending college or going to work without permission, violating dress codes, choosing one's own marriage partner, and so on.

Actions that reclaim honour

Honour can be restituted through either the modification of the trangressor's behaviour (eg a forced marriage) or erasure of the carrier of the dishonour (killing).

Women's behaviour that upholds honour

Modest sexual behaviour, fidelity in marriage, no pre- or extramarital relationships with men, no unchaperoned rendezvous with men outside the family, meeting motherly obligations to children, meeting wifely obligations to husband, meeting daughter's obligations to parents, meeting daughter-in-law obligations to parents-in-law, and so on.

Gender, sexuality and honour

Women are undoubtedly the primary victims of crimes of honour. Their movements are restricted, their friendships and even conversations are monitored or controlled, their marriage partners are chosen for them, and they are clear targets of killings.

Codes of honour serve to construct not only what it means to be a woman but also what is means to be a man, and hence are central to social meanings of gender. Honour is thus intrinsically linked to norms of behaviour for both sexes and is predicated upon patriarchal notions of ownership and control of women's bodies. Social constraints regulate women's lives in ways that lie beyond statute and codified laws and have significantly more meaning attached. Women's sexuality is at the heart of concerns and social anxiety about women's behaviour in ways that inform prescriptions on their movements and relationships. The need to preserve a woman's virginity for her husband places limits not only and most obviously on her sexual behaviour but also by extension on any contact with men outside her immediate family in situations that may hold any sexual potential: 'women need to refrain from any sexual activity before marriage, and from any act that might lead to sexual activity and from any act that might lead to an act that might lead to sexual activity … every prohibitive demand she complies with constructs her simultaneously as female and a virgin' (Abu-Odeh 2000: 371; see also Abu-Lughod 1986).

Actions of men and women

Honour codes and crimes are not solely about individual men controlling the lives of individual women. They are about community norms, social policing and collective decisions and acts of punishment; these norms can also be applied to male behaviour to the extent that men can also be killed – *karo-kari* killings in Pakistan, for example, allow for the killing of both men and women suspected of illicit relationships. Not only men but also women play a central role in ensuring that women adhere to gender norms. Honour is asserted through killings – at one end of the scale – but also through constraints on movement, conversations, friendships, choice of marriage partners, and so on. Women are key in ensuring these limits and can also be party to decisions to kill women, including their own daughters; indeed in some cases they may be involved in the killings too (see chapters on Egypt and on Lebanon, in this volume). Lastly, these norms of control and killing are reflected in legal codes and judicial decisions that recognise, and offer scope for mitigation of sentence in cases of, violent actions used to reclaim honour, including killings (see Welchman and Hossain's Introduction in this volume; also chapters on Pakistan, Lebanon, Egypt, Palestine).

A particular feature in certain countries is that the state is complicit in crimes of honour and practices of violence against women. Complicity is evidenced by legal provisions and justice systems that explicitly offer perpetrators of crimes of honour exoneration for their actions, with the honour motif as mitigation. Such practices run contrary to the due diligence element of modern thinking on human rights, which places on states obligations to prevent, investigate, punish and provide compensation for violations of human rights (for application of the due diligence principle to violence against women, see Amnesty International, 2004). In countries from Lebanon to Iraq to Syria to Pakistan, legal codes and judicial practice allow mitigation against such killings, to be argued and given on the grounds of protection of honour or loss of control in the heat of the moment ('fit of fury' defences). Such state provisions therefore offer state legitimation of such killings and by implication of the values and codes that inform and underpin such behaviours. Women's transgressions of these codes, whether actual or perceived, thus become 'legitimate provocation' for criminal acts, mostly by men. Examples of such transgressions range from a woman refusing to participate in an arranged marriage to adultery. Such defences and continuities between the values of a killer and those of the judiciary are evidenced in the West by leniency shown by certain courts to male killers of women, which perceive, for example, 'nagging' by women, dating a new person, moving out of a shared home or failure to have dinner ready at a given time as mitigating circumstances (e.g. Nourse, 1997). Commonalities such as these indicate a thread that runs through cultures and contexts regarding the way social and cultural norms of gender seep from society to criminal justice systems to state agents and back again. These continuities are worthy of some attention and I turn to them below, but before that I offer a definition of crimes of honour.

Definitions of honour crimes are beset with difficulties. These can be avoided by limiting discussion to examples, as discussed by Welchman and Hossain in this collection. Colonial superiority and judgement cast a long shadow on the naming of any gendered practices as culturally or geographically specific to any post-colonial society/societies, especially so if there is no reflexivity in this process, as discussed further below. The challenge then is to be able to acknowledge if crimes of honour do have specific characteristics and to do so in ways that do not suffer the same traits of a Western, Orientalist gaze, as described above. It seems to me that crimes of honour share a number of features with other forms of violence against women, but also have a number of characteristics that mark them out from other practices. To posit a specificity that is flawed and that fails to see linkages is problematic; to deny specificity if it exists is also problematic.

I suggest here a definition of crimes of honour and an identification of key features thereof that seem best to capture commonalities in the range of recent and contemporary identification of such crimes. In summary, crimes of honour are actions that remove from a collectivity the stain of dishonour, both gendered and locally defined, through the use of emotional, social or physical coercion over a person whose actual or imputed actions have brought that dishonour; physical force may involve killing the transgressor of the code of honour. I suggest that crimes of honour have six key features:

1. gender relations that problematise and control women's behaviours, shaping and controlling women's sexuality in particular;
2. the role of women in policing and monitoring women's behaviour;
3. collective decisions regarding punishment, or in upholding the actions considered appropriate, for transgressions of these boundaries;
4. the potential for women's participation in killings;
5. the ability to reclaim honour through enforced compliance or killings;
6. state sanction of such killings through recognition of honour as motivation and mitigation.

These features in combination identify the particularity of codes and crimes of honour.

It is true that men kill women across cultures and across times for a variety of reasons, often benefiting from sympathetic judicial practices if and when they face justice systems. This is an overarching commonality but is not enough to describe the particularities that exist within this umbrella, such as crimes and killings that revolve around concepts and codes of honour.

The degree to which collective decisions and actions mark out crimes of honour and therefore mark their specificity is one that may be contested by the presence of killings that are argued to be 'fit of fury' killings, where the brother, husband or father is simply overwhelmed by anger, fury or passion and in the heat of the moment kills his sister, wife or daughter. Indeed, these defences are used and given as mitigation against murder charges, not only in killings associated with honour claims, but also in crimes of passion and in the provocation ground for mitigation in other jurisdictions, such as the UK. So, for example, in the UK, provocation is a partial defence to homicide (Homicide Act 1957), where the killing is said to have taken place as a result of a sudden and temporary loss of control.[6] Given the provision in a variety of legal jurisdictions of the possibility of a sudden, temporary, uncontrollable explosion of violence, it may be that the 'fit of fury' argument is one that neatly fits into available defences and that therefore explains in part the prevalence of such explanations of behaviour. I do not suggest that there are no killings that take place in uncontrollable and sudden anger, but I do propose two responses to the 'fit of fury' explanation of crimes of honour and other killings.

First of all, they are a defence that offers mitigation in law, and we may therefore see a higher proportion of these in court records than may actually be the case. The need to use available legal defences means they are likely to feature in statistics.

The second point concerns the nature of the society in which individual behaviours are embedded. In cultures where codes of honour operate, there is an overwhelming drive and motivation to collective morality, values and behaviours that conform with prevailing codes. What this means is that it is difficult for individuals to act in ways that challenge, contradict or contest (including by going beyond) these collective codes, and to do so incurs social costs. It seems likely to me that men who kill women in such contexts – that is, where women have transgressed the prevailing code of honour – act in ways that are accommodated and/or enabled by that code and benefit from so doing. Even if the law does not directly exonerate the killing, there is social advantage, recognition and possibly respect to be gained from the removal of the woman or girl who is considered to have stained the collective honour. The honour code thus reflects and contributes to socially legitimated constructions of gender norms that shape and reflect behaviours and are not separate from these.

I would conclude that where codes of honour dominate and are built upon collective values, behaviour and conformity with social norms, the individualistic 'fit of fury' argument offers an insufficient explanation of any pattern of killings that rests upon the values of such codes. That is not to say that men do not ever have a sudden fit of passion during which they kill a woman who has transgressed social norms; they do. I doubt, however, that such instances form the majority of honour-based killings of women. I also would see in such cases a continuity with femicides in many other countries and contexts. My case here is that there is something specific and particular about honour-based killings of women, and that one feature of that specificity is their being rooted in collectively monitored and policed codes of behaviour, the policing being in part carried out through killings. The prevalence of 'fit of fury' defences is in some proportion a reflection of the availability of that defence to a killer, rather than an adequate explanation of a socially based pattern of (predominantly) gendered killings. It is this social pattern that still needs an adequate understanding and explanation (to

which I seek to contribute), as distinct from the explanation of legal records
and legal practice.

I identify the lack of a clear definition of crimes of honour as a gap that
needs to be addressed, and suggest this definition as one that would benefit
from the experience and views of the many people who have worked on
and against such crimes. I also argue for both specificity and commonality
within a structure that allows alliances to be forged outside a colonial frame
of reference, and discuss this in the section on alliances below. However,
before considering alliances, it is helpful to recognise the contexts in which
crimes of honour are contested.

The return gaze

There are voices in post-colonial states that have consistently and clearly
fought violence against women, including crimes of honour, in their own
societies. But the history of the nature of colonial interventions on gender
provides great ammunition to detractors in their condemnation of women's
rights activists as Western influenced, untrue to their cultural traditions and
the unwitting or naive agents of a post-colonial project. The post-September
11 climate has strengthened these tendencies, as a polarisation of the West
against the rest[7] has played directly into such binary models that divide
absolutely.

At the same time, critical voices in post-colonial societies, including in
Islamic cultures, are easily able to turn their attention to gender relations in
the West, especially in those states that are seen to condemn Islamic cultures.
Evidence of violence against women in the West provides ammunition
for the accusation that there is hypocrisy in the Western agenda and for
the interpretation that societies without honour appear to have no limits
or principles governing human behaviour. Of course, in identifying the
problematics of such societies that are deemed to 'lack boundaries', attention
is paid to the behaviour of both men and women; nervertheless the bulk
of critical attention focuses on women – women having sex and children
outside marriage, women dressing immodestly, women living without men,
women living with other women, and men living with men (Independent
Centre for Strategic Studies and Analysis, Pakistan). What primarily fuels
such concerns is the absence of social and male controls upon women's
sexuality. In many cultures it is women's ostensible sexual misdemeanours
that undermine 'familial honour' (Geetha, 1998: 315).

The two sets of voices – one condemning 'backward' cultures and the
other defending them – appear to have no ground in common, on the basis
of which a conversation between them might take place: culture seems to

present here an absolute divide. Yet these two positions do in fact have a number of features in common: for instance, there is little, if any, recognition by either that cultures may themselves be either heterogeneous or intrinsically changeable; both problematise the other to an absolute degree; both focus on gender relations; and both identify honour and shame as problematic principles, due either to their existence or to their absence. But most importantly, I suggest, they share a failure to turn their critical eye inwards, to see and speak out against harmful gendered practices and relations within their own contexts. The failure to critique the widespread investment of powers of social control with men, including in the Western countries that condemn 'backward' societies and among those who defend those societies by attacking their detractors, disables a common analysis and therefore, I suggest, mitigates against a common agenda for action.

Such a pattern is not universal, however. Those who do have a common analysis can not only build a shared framework for understanding but can also join hands in collective action to address crimes of honour. Binary and accusatory approaches to crimes of honour, and to violence against women more broadly, disable the possibilities that might otherwise exist for common action. Actions to challenge and end harmful practices against women are essential in order to achieve change. Local voices exist and are central; effective alliances beyond these offer nourishment, support, ideas and solidarity.

Common frameworks

Women in 'backward' societies, like women elsewhere, have long contested the gender relations that obtain in their worlds. They are vocal, articulate and organised, especially so in relation to violence against women (see, e.g., Molyneux, 2000; Basu, 1995; Wieringa, 1995; Sen, 2003a). I have identified the strand of thinking that marks particular cultures as being resolugely problematic. I will now consider two alternative approaches that challenge honour crimes. These are ideal-type classifications that recognise that overlaps exist in practice.

1. One approach expands the concept of honour (i.e. that which is problematised) to incorporate practices in the West (e.g. crimes of passion; but also forced marriages in cultures with a less clear code of honour). Here, a variety of forms of violence are subsumed under the umbrella concept of honour. Honour is thus everyone's problem; it offers possibilities for alliances that forge a working solidarity.

2. A second approach attempts to find an alternative common language and framework within which to capture the various patterns of both gender inequalities and violence against women. Here the human rights framework and the commonality of violence against women provide the impetus for solidarity work.

Both approaches problematise non-Islamic cultures, thereby rejecting culture as the divisor, and seek a base from which inter-cultural coalitions and dialogues (An-Na'im, 1993) may be pursued. Similarities can be noted in relation to two key themes: the naming of a range of forms of violence as crimes of honour, and the locating of crimes of honour as part of a broader spectrum of violence against women. Both positions have been argued by feminists and human rights activists. For example, Human Rights Watch has observed: 'In countries where Islam is practiced, they're called honor killings, but dowry deaths and so-called crimes of passion have a similar dynamic in that the women are killed by male family members and the crimes are perceived as excusable or understandable' (Brown, 2002; cited in Mayall, 2002).

Let us begin by considering the first approach. At the heart of the principle of actions predicated on the concept of honour are a particular process and formation; these are worthy of some attention. I argue that it is possible to identify and analyse whether – and, if so, perhaps to what extent – crimes of honour remain distinct from or analogous with other forms of violence against women.

There are genuine commonalities in the ways in which the principles and values associated with the concept of honour are present in societies and cultures that do not employ this concept in the same way as do Islamic societies (Araji, 2000). The elements of control over women's behaviour, especially of women's sexuality, by men and to a degree by women, and the assumed right of men in their family and marital relationships to chastise, punish or kill them, find parallels in a range of cultures. In particular, crimes of passion and modes of gender relations that invest in 'machismo' a host of male powers over women in Latin America have been a commonly proposed parallel (Youssef, 1973), including in the UN (see discussion below and Connors in this volume). It is not only such behaviours and values that are common but also the formalisation and social sanction of crimes of passion conferred by the legal system (see CIMEL publications).

These features might suggest strong parallels between crimes of honour and those of passion. However, of the set of characteristics that I outlined earlier as identifying crimes and codes of honour, some are not present in crimes of passion. In the latter, the ongoing role of women in upholding codes of behaviour is not as clear. Of course women promote values that condemn and judge other women, but not of the same order as in societies governed by codes of honour. Nor are women key players in killings involving crimes of passion in the way they are in crimes of honour. Finally, crimes of passion tend to be individual acts of violence rather than collective punishments. The conflating of crimes of passion and crimes of honour is therefore a substantive error.

In the political dimension, there is motivation, I believe, to express solidarity with besieged Muslim colleagues and claim their travails as one's own. Sharing the horrific experiences of honour killings, a cornerstone of Western criticism, provides a hook for the solidarity being sought. This is a noble and understandable project, perhaps, but it does not stand up to rigorous scrutiny. There are alternatives.

The main alternative is the second approach outlined above: namely, framing crimes of honour as a particularity on a continuum of violence against women (Spatz, 1991; Sen, 2003b). The killing of women takes place in all societies; women are, statistically, in the greatest physical danger from men who are known to them; women's sexuality is widely feared and socially constrained, with male violence being associated with anxiety and the determination to control women's sexual lives. These factors have become increasingly recognised as crucial in the field of violence against women. Although the umbrella concept of 'violence against women' is extensive, it has the potential to capture both similarities (as described) and differences, for example in terms of dowry deaths being regionally or culturally located, and likewise crimes of honour (and indeed other harmful practices). The recent coming together of thinking and movements on violence against women with the human rights framework and its supporters suggests that commonalities can be accommodated without a consequent loss of recognition of diversity. Let us trace developments – and setbacks – in the UN's interest in this project.

The development of the UN framework on violence against women has been slow, with minimal recognition of violence against women in either the Mexico (1975) or the Copenhagen[8] (1980) outcome agreements (Sen, 2003a; Connors in this volume). The Nairobi forward-looking strategies (1985) named violence as a concern and began a process of elaborating strategies to address the problem. With the 1986 UN expert group meeting on violence against women, and a 1989 study on violence in the family, there began a shift from seeing women's experience of violence as simply a family problem to perceiving it as a larger problem and understanding such abuse as a human rights concern.

This timing unfortunately came *after* the drawing up and adoption of Convention on the Elimination of Discrimination Against Women, in 1979

(CEDAW, otherwise known as the 'Women's Convention'), which meant that violence was missing from this document. Indeed, the document now appears remarkable in this omission. However, this has to some extent been addressed in explanatory, interpretive statements made by the Convention's monitoring committee. The most significant of these, General Recommendation Number 19, states that violence against women is understood to be a form of gender-based discrimination (and thus under the scope of CEDAW) and that states are to be held accountable for violence against women, including by private persons. Many other developments followed in the 1990s, most importantly a Declaration on the Elimination of Violence Against Women in 1993 and the creation of the post of the Special Rapporteur on violence against women, its causes and consequences, who was appointed by the United Nations in 1994. The governmental Platform for Action arising from the Beijing world conference on women in 1995 had a section on violence against women as one of twelve critical areas of concern. In addition, the General Assembly has passed several resolutions on various forms of violence, including harmful traditional practices.[9]

UN initiatives that have specifically addressed honour as a theme in violence against women include a working group of the Sub-commission on the Prevention of Discrimination and Protection of Minorities and on Traditional Practices. The CEDAW committee has taken up issues of crimes of honour in its reporting and monitoring processes: with Turkey in 1997, Israel in 1997, Jordan in 2000, Iraq in 2000. Other bodies have also shown an interest in this issue – for example, the Committee on the Rights of the Child asked for information on honour crimes in its correspondence with Turkey. Several Special Rapporteurs have identified honour crimes as a human rights issue – including those on violence against women, on independence of the judiciary and on extrajudicial, summary or arbitrary executions. Together, these and other initiatives show clearly how crimes of honour have come to be seen as a human rights concern in the machinery of the UN.

At the same time, two other trends are perceptible: a growing tendency to link the notions of crimes of honour and crimes of passion; and, in some quarters, the association of honour crimes with Islam. These two tendencies appear to be contradictory – one accepting and the other rejecting religion as central to the problem. The latter is at the heart of contemporary troubles concerning crimes of honour, as the difficult passage of recent UN resolutions indicates. In 2000, the Netherlands sponsored a General Assembly resolution on 'traditional or customary practices amounting to crimes against women, including crimes committed in the name of honour'. This was contemporaneous with the growing level of international attention spotlighting crimes of honour, which identified these as a Middle Eastern/Islamic phenomenon, and indeed tended to conflate Islam with the crime. A documentary shown on television internationally and at the UN opened with the image of a Mosque and the sound of the call to prayer: thus was the essentialised link between Islam and crimes of honour cemented in the minds of many in the West. Such simple equations between religion and violence against women in this context have done considerable damage both to indigenous struggles against crimes of 'honour' (which can be strong, as in Jordan and Pakistan) and to international coalitions that seek to address the issue. At the same time the portrayal of Islam as a backward and problematic religion grew in strength (see Welchman and Hossain in the Introduction to this volume for further discussion).

The nature of the responses of those who feel attacked by such forms of problematisation and othering can be complex and varied, as indicated above. In the case of the 2000 resolution, the Organisation of the Islamic Conference rejected any association between Islam and 'the killing of women and girls under any societal or communal banner, including in the name of passion, honour or race' (Organisation of the Islamic Conference, 2 October 2000; see Connors in this volume). Debate and confusion over the meaning of the term 'crimes of honour', and their assumed link with Islam and/or with crimes of passion, generated great controversy. An alternate resolution, proposed by Pakistan, did not single out crimes of honour for special attention but linked them to the elimination of all forms of forms of violence against women. This resolution was adopted by a majority vote, with twenty-five abstentions (a very high proportion[10]). Nevertheless, the issue remains steeped in controversy (see Connors in this volume).

The UN is not a homogeneous entity that speaks with one voice. Disagreement and dissent are readily apparent, as was shown in the debate around the Dutch resolution.[11] On the one hand, high-level diplomats at the UN have made clear their perception that violence against women is in no way an issue that only affects a specific geographical (read 'cultural') region or othewise designated context. '[T]his is not a phenomenon of the North or the South, the East or the West. Violence against women takes place everywhere, and as much in Christian as in Muslim countries', observed the UN High Commissioner for Human Rights (De Mello, 2003). On the other hand, in March 2003 the Commission on the Status of Women failed to reach agreement on a resolution on violence against women because of intractable disagreements over the use of culture as a barrier to addressing violence.

The preference was then to conceptualise honour crimes as a form of violence against women that shares features with many other forms of violence. But the question is, are honour crimes the same as, or are they distinct from, other forms of violence? My six features, listed above, lean towards the particularity of experience of codes and crimes of honour. However, to declare as much in contemporary times risks the imputation of animosity towards those cultures with which such codes are associated. I have suggested that such a reaction is in many ways well founded. Yet, to oppose crimes of honour, including as a particular experience, is not always and necessarily to equate the practice exclusively with Islam; nor is it necessarily to accept religion or culture as an absolute divide. Arguably these two issues lie at the heart of the difficulty of particularising honour crimes. It is true that such criticisms can indeed be seen as an index of anti-Islamic times. Yet if one looks beyond this superficiality it is possible to determine whether there is an 'othering' informing this analysis.

Voices within societies that operate codes of honour have opposed honour crimes and have risked internal opprobrium for such resistance, not least because they are seen as siding with former colonial powers. This accusation of alliance with the metropolitan countries has functioned as a significant indictment by anti-colonial forces, including in post-colonial times. Yet women opposing these practices and those who have stood with them have actively struggled against *both* colonialism and local practices that oppress women. We need to be aware of this history when seeking to understand and to engage with struggles around violence against women, including crimes of 'honour', both in terms of the response from minority groups and more broadly from cultures in which such crimes are found.

Alliances

I suggest that there are four categories of response to crimes of honour. We can, to a degree, identify and explain their positioning with reference to the history outlined earlier. They are: (1) feminists and allies within societies with honour codes; (2) other social groupings within these societies; (3) feminists and allies in networks across these and other societies; and (4) progressives outside the societies concerned.

1. Feminists and allies within societies with honour codes

Feminist and other progressive voices from within the cultures in which honour crimes are practised are strong and unwavering in their condemnation of codes of honour that control and shape women's lives. There is a clear consensus that 'honour' crimes and killings are forms of violence that cannot be tolerated, and that legal provisions which grant 'honour' as a mitigating defence should be ended (e.g. Women for Women's Human

Rights, Turkey; Women Living under Muslim Laws, an international network; Kurdish Women Action against Honour Killings; Lebanese Council to Resist Violence against Women; National Jordanian Campaign to Eliminate 'Honour Crimes'). The CIMEL/Interights project has brought many of these groups and their campaigns together; accounts of such projects are included in this volume. Such voices may ally with feminists and friends from outside these localities; yet they are also likely to be critical of certain Western voices that oppose crimes of honour but fail to understand specific contexts, uncritically adopt an anti-Islamic position, or fail to recognise violence against women in their own locations.

2. Other social groupings within societies with honour codes

Broader social collectivities exist in cultures where codes of honour prevail, and speak out against such practices; these may be religious spokespersons or diplomats who represent the state. Scholars of Islam and religious leaders have in many instances stated that Islam does not authorise such killings, for example. While some religious voices have been unequivocal in their condemnation, indicating that crimes of honour lack any religious basis (see Welchman and Hossain, Introduction to this volume; Bardakoğlu, 2004) others have been noticeable for their silence on such issues (e.g. Afghanistan).[11]

3. Feminist and allies in networks across societies with honour codes

Feminists and other progressive forces (especially human rights activists) working at an international level, including the United Nations, have come together in a variety of ways to support and to work with feminists speaking from within cultures that practise crimes of honour. They share an analysis of a common oppression; their view of violence against women or crimes of honour links experiences across contexts, within a human rights frame.

4. Progressives outside societies with honour codes

Some of the interest from the West, including from those who consider themselves progressive, has been unhelpful, equating crimes of honour with Islam, in ignorance of or contrary to the pronouncements of Islamic schol-ars who have refuted such a religious basis. Such an equation may be a consequence of privileging cultural differences rather than commonalities. This approach is reflected in the history of academic disciplines too, with anthropology, for example, stressing inter-cultural difference but not ac-knowledging intra-cultural difference (see, e.g., Moore, 1994). More modern academic tendencies, such as cultural relativism and postmodernism, similarly fail to focus on commonalities and continuities across cultures and locations. This refusal to acknowledge a common basis for analysis is notably at odds with proposals for a universalist response. Universalism, and other approaches acknowledging commonalities, offer a better foundation and enjoy greater legitimacy. There is also greater potential in a common, shared analysis for shared and common solutions to be found. There is also little recognition in the relativist approach of internal dissent or contestation, or of analysis that counters the gender norms formalised in codes of honour.

I would include in this category of outside progressives certain Western voices that express outrage at crimes of honour in particular, and strongly disapprove of gender inequalities in such cultures, and consider the solution to lie in the abandonment of indigenous cultural values in favour of the adoption of more 'progressive' Western ones, whether this viewpoint be made known by inference or by explicit statement. Inherent in this approach is a moral or cultural superiority that meshes uncomfortably with the colonial legacy I have outlined above. Further, if it is coupled with discourses that further problematise such cultures, this approach can possess strong racist overtones. There is a tendency in Western societies to criticise minority cultures for gender discrimination and related violence, while failing to acknowledge that violence against women on the home front is of the same kind. Prevailing Scandinavian discourses exemplify this type of approach: the hosts continue to name their minority groups as 'immigrants', suggesting the absence of a settled and equal status with indigenous people, and honour crimes are framed as a cultural problem. Coupled with the Scandinavian reputation for gender equality, this suggests a hierarchy between cultures and, importantly, fails to acknowledge violence against women within local groups.

Collaborative work is problematic with those who deny the problem and with those whose words and deeds in some way appear to continue the colonial legacy described earlier. In contrast, the alliances with great potential are those that combine opposition both within and outside the contexts in which crimes of honour are to be found. In this way, those in the first group (feminists within) ally with the third group (feminists and others outside) on the basis of a common purpose arising from a feminist or other shared agenda.

The greatest potential for sustained and productive alliances around the issue of crimes of honour is among those individuals and organisations that occupy a crossover role within and outside the cultures at issue. At the heart of these alliances must be a rejection of culture as an absolute divide on issues of violence against women and acceptance of the fact that violence against women exists everywhere, albeit in a variety of forms. Furthermore, a central place that must be given to voices from within honour cultures. Hence a combination of the first three types of alliance, or categories of response, promises the most in the struggle against crimes of honour.

Conclusion

The concept of honour is neither a new nor a purely Islamic feature; nor is it a characteristic only of 'backward societies'. Western amnesia may lead to such conclusions, but the historical record tells us otherwise. Nor is honour associated exclusively with killings, although there does appear to be a strong pattern of causality. Colonial encounters have widely problematised non-Western gender relations and have constructed the metropolitan powers as the source of progressive and enlightening gender relations. Contemporary discovery of, and subsequent opposition to, crimes of honour in the West have meshed together the perception of a 'foreign' concept (honour), an alien and terrorist religion (Islam) and the bogey of violence against women into a politically potent mix. The serious problems of this construct have only become understood in the recent context.

I have suggested that, in order to understand and give social meaning and locus to crimes of honour, we should concentrate on six features that identify crimes of honour: (1) gender relations that problematise and control women's behaviours (especially women's sexuality); (2) the role of women in policing and monitoring women's behaviour; (3) collective decisions regarding punishment, or in upholding the actions considered appropriate for transgressions of these boundaries; (4) the potential for women's participation in killings; (5) the ability to reclaim honour through enforced compliance or killings; and (6) state sanction of such killings through recognition of honour as motivation and mitigation. Thus attempts to locate honour crimes either among or distant from other forms of violence can be based on a methodologically sound approach, thereby avoiding the charge that a given analysis may simply be politically motivated.

This approach, I suggest, enables recognition of a greater commonality between honour crimes and dowry-related violence and killings, for example, than is possible with the concept of crimes of passion. My conclusion, then, is that crimes of honour should be understood within a range of forms of violence – part of a continuum that spreads across time and place. Making culture the prime explanatory variable fails to account for the way cultural histories justify, excuse or formalise forms of violence against women in many places. To understand this, one has to be able to turn one's gaze inward and not only upon the 'other', enabling a critical self-positioning that recognises and challenges violence against women at home as well as elsewhere. It is precisely this that women in Islamic (and other non-Western) societies are able to do when they challenge honour crimes, In this, Western women in our fourth group, 'outside progressives', have a considerable amount to learn from them.

Making culture the divisor also renders those who inhabit the culture under scrutiny problematic per se, and suggests that their salvation lies in abandoning this culture and, by implication, adopting another. Almost invariably this Salvation is Western, Judeo-Christian culture. Is this really the answer? If the problem were Islam, or Islamic culture, it might be – but then only if Western culture and religion had eliminated violence against women. And, as we know, this is far from the case. If violence against women exists in the cultures that criticise the 'other', as it clearly does, then existing cultural practices do not determine the safety of women, as in no culture are women assured freedom from violence.

Notes

1. Monarchy Today; see further www.royal.gov.uk/output/Page347.asp.
2. Such as knighthoods or titles; for example, the Order of the British Empire (OBE).
3. Combat 18 is a racist, anti-immigration group based in the UK. It claims the history and title of National Socialism. See further www.skrewdriver.net/.
4. Adapting Spivak's remark that colonial discourses enmesh with the racialised and gendered project of 'white men saving brown women from brown men' (1988), we could note, as have others, that white women could be added to the category of saviours.
5. The majority of states fail to protect women from rape in marriage, those that do so include South Africa, the UK, Norway, the Philippines, France.
6. This understanding stems from an earlier case in which the following definition was given in court (*R*. vs. *Duffy* [1949 1 All ER 932]): 'provocation is some act, or series of acts, done by the dead man to the accused which would cause in any reasonable person, and actually causes in the accused, a sudden and temporary loss of self-control, rendering the accused so subject to passion as to make him or her for the moment not master of his mind'.
7. President George W. Bush's statement that 'you are either with us or against us' gave clear voice to this polarisation and is often quoted in the anti-Western heartlands of the Middle East and developing countries.
8. There have been four world conferences on women: Mexico in 1975, Copenhagen in 1980, Nairobi in 1990 and Beijing in 1995.
9. Traditional or customary practices affecting the health of women and girls, GA Resolution A/52/99 (12 December 1997); Report of the Secretary General 1998, Traditional or customary practices affecting the health of women, UN Doc. A/53/354 (10 September 1998).
10. High by the standard of UN processes of adoption of resolutions.
11. On 15 October 2004 the UN General Assembly passed an updated and amended version of the Dutch approach, a resolution entitled 'Working towards the Elimination of Crimes against Women and Girls Committed in the Name of Honour' (UN Doc. A/C.3/59/L.25), jointly sponsored by the UK and Turkey with eight new co-sponsors from the Organisation of the Islamic Conference.

This resolution makes no mention of crimes of passion and largely treats crimes of honour in isolation but does make mention of violence against women more generally.

12. On a recent visit to Afghanistan I was told by key informants that no religious leaders had made any such statements declaring crimes of honour to be un-Islamic.

3

The role of 'community discourse'
in combating 'crimes of honour':
preliminary assessment and prospects

ABDULLAHI AHMED AN-NA`IM

My objective in this chapter is to explore ways of engaging in an internal discourse within communities as one strategy among many to combat 'crimes of honour', as defined below. The term 'community discourse' is used throughout to denote discussion of every aspect of 'crimes of honour' within the local communities where they occur. The means include radio and television programmes in local languages, Friday sermons and discussions at local mosques, songs, formal and informal education in school, sports and youth clubs, and women's or other community associations. I use the term 'discourse' to indicate the widest possible range of activities and opportunities for discussion of all aspects of 'crimes of honour' within the community, at every level, public and private.

The approach in no way condones or seeks to justify these heinous crimes. Equally it makes no claim to be the primary or the most effective means of combating them. Rather, its aim is simply to explore every possibility of pre-empting such crimes to assess the options available for holding those responsible accountable for their actions. It is not enough to condemn the crimes without developing specific strategies to prevent their occurrence, and to deal with perpetrators and their supporters. If engaging in community discourse can help to prevent 'crimes of honour' and/or hold perpetrators accountable, as I suggest below, then those concerned with combating such practices should utilise and develop this approach.

In my view, transforming family and community attitudes towards these crimes by engaging in an internal discourse would contribute to their elimination by addressing the underlying causes, in addition to encouraging state officials and institutions to hold individual perpetrators and their supporters accountable for their actions. I maintain that this approach is an essential component of several complementary strategies to combat 'crimes of honour'. Though it can never be sufficient in itself to either prevent these crimes or punish their perpetrators, community discourse against 'crimes of honour' can be an effective means of denying them support. This internal discourse can also play a critical role in the socialising of children into totally rejecting any proffered rationale for these crimes. At another level, community discourse helps generate and sustain the political will to allocate resources and implement policies for combating 'crimes of honour', to punish perpetrators, and to deny them any moral or material benefit from their crimes. It is also a vital component in the process of transforming the institutional culture, and setting the priorities, of policymakers, police, public prosecutors, judges, prison officials and other authorities concerned with the social consequences of these crimes.

A more fundamental rationale for the proposed approach, indeed its *raison d'être*, I would suggest, is respect for the moral autonomy of individuals and families, and the self-determination of their communities. As a matter of principle, I believe, combating 'crimes of honour' cannot mean repudiating the human dignity and rights of all concerned, including the perpetrators of these crimes and their families and communities. Unless one subscribes to the patronising and authoritarian view that people should simply be coerced into 'doing what is good for them', it is necessary to gain their cooperation and support through an internal discourse within the community around cultural norms and institutions associated with these crimes. This is not to imply that one should postpone protecting women against 'crimes of honour', as I emphasise that practical measures should be taken immediately to safeguard the physical safety of women and hold perpetrators of 'crimes of honour' legally accountable. Rather, the question is one of long-term strategy – in addition to, not instead of, all that can be done immediately.

Even if one maintains that these crimes are so serious that an exclusively coercive approach to their prevention and punishment is justified, there is still the question of who is going to enforce their prohibition, and how. Since no one is suggesting that countries where these crimes occur should be colonised by more 'enlightened' powers or taken into the 'trusteeship' of the United Nations, all preventive measures, as well as punishment and rehabilitation of offenders, must be undertaken by national and local authorities. This is unlikely to happen in the first place, and cannot be sustained over time in any case, without the consent and support of the communities themselves. After all, the same local elite and state officials who are supposed to devise and implement the necessary measures are themselves a product of the same culture and context that produce the crimes. These critical actors are politically responsive to the same communities, even if they are not formally accountable to them in a democratic manner.

In emphasising the importance of this approach as an essential component of strategies for combating 'crimes of honour', I am not suggesting this is easy and always possible and useful, nor that all those concerned with combating these crimes should or can engage in actual community discourse. Rather, my limited objective is to argue for the critical importance of community discourse as an integral part of various strategies, and to call for a division of labour whereby some of those working to combat 'crimes of honour' do deliberately prepare for and engage in such an internal discourse within the community. In this process, I am also calling for a more realistic view of the nature and dynamics of the women's/human rights movements in the countries where these crimes occur, and their relationship to the community and the state in the present local and global context.

In what follows, I elaborate on the thesis of this chapter with particular reference to the role of the state and the relevance and implications of a human rights approach to combating honour crimes. I then identify some of the practical difficulties facing the proposed approach, and explore ways of overcoming them in order to facilitate the implementation of this approach whenever possible and useful. I draw in my discussions upon the results of a research visit to Istanbul in June 2001.

'Crimes of honour' and the state

The proposed approach is premised on the view that the state has the primary responsibility for combating 'crimes of honour'. However, it is also based on an appreciation of the fact that the state, in the final analysis, is the people who control and operate its political, legal and administrative institutions and processes. Whatever the state can or is expected to do – such as implementing administrative measures to prevent the commission of these crimes, effective investigation and prosecution of perpetrators, rehabilitation of and support for victims – is ultimately dependent on motivating and supporting officials, or pressuring them if necessary, to act accordingly. The same is true for holding them accountable for failing to take and follow up appropriate or necessary measures. For my purposes here, the question is: who is going to do that in a credible and sustainable manner, and how can it be done in practice? To address these issues, one needs to understand the basic nature of 'crimes of honour' and their context, the motivation of perpetrators and their supporters, the role of the family and community, and whatever else influences the behaviour of state officials and institutions regarding all aspects of this phenomenon.

What distinguishes 'crimes of honour' from other violent crimes is that they are usually perpetrated against women by close relatives, on the basis of allegations of sexual impropriety, in the name of protecting or upholding the 'honour' of the family. As clearly illustrated by cases from Turkey,[1] with regard to 'honour killings' the decision to kill the woman is taken in a family meeting, which also designates a young man within the family, usually a brother or cousin of the victim, to carry out the crime. By their very nature and alleged rationale, therefore, these crimes arise out of a collective deliberate decision that is to be executed in public, or at least publicised for the purported purpose to be achieved.

What does this collective, deliberate and public nature of the crime mean for the responsibility of the family and community at large? How can the prosecution and punishment of the immediate perpetrator be appropriate or sufficient where so many others are responsible for instigating or condoning the crime, and perpetuating a social and cultural system that 'demands' the offering of such human sacrifice? Other questions arising out of the nature and context of 'crimes of honour' include: whose honour is at issue, and why are women killed in the name of protecting it? Further questions are: do these crimes constitute human rights violations, and what practical difference can such a characterisation make? In other words, what distinguishes these crimes from other crimes from the human rights point of view, and what does this mean for strategies aimed at combating them?

Underlying these and related questions is concern about the limitations of an exclusively state-centric approach in this regard. That is, to affirm that the state has the legal obligation to protect the bodily integrity of potential victims, and to punish perpetrators of 'crimes of honour', whether as human rights violations or not, does not necessarily mean that the state will be willing and able to discharge this obligation. This is particularly true when state actors not only face strong and deeply entrenched cultural opposition in this regard, but are themselves sympathetic or indifferent to the moral outrage of these crimes. Another concern relates to the methods and costs/risks of state interventions in the realm of family and community. For example, is it safe to assume that state interventions at that level are going to be effective in combating 'crimes of honour'? How can one ensure that the power to take such intrusive measures will not be abused for other purposes?

Sexuality, family and community

One of the underlying questions raised by the specific nature of 'crimes of honour' is whether the family and community have a role in regulating the sexual behaviour of their members. If they do, consequent questions would include, for instance: what factors and processes determine or affect the way that role is played in different contexts, and what methods of social control are available to the family and community, especially during periods of transition and crisis? How are such methods to be judged, by whom and for what purposes?

Regardless of one's personal views about the extent and manner of such control in any given setting or time, the fact of the matter is that families and communities have played a role in regulating the sexual behaviour of their members in every human society throughout history. While the scope and methods of this regulation vary from one community to another, and over time within the same community, arguably social life would not be possible without a degree of control over sexuality. If one accepts this premiss, the question becomes one about the scope and manner of regulation, rather than of choice between regulation and no regulation at all.

The basic and most enduring means of regulation of sexuality happens through the organisation of the family and community at the collective level, and through early socialisation of children at the individual level. Both aspects are reinforced in a variety of ways, including action by the state through the legal regulation of marriage and sexual conduct, education, and even taxation and the provision of social services. Common experience indicates not only that these processes work effectively in the vast majority of cases but also that families and communities adapt their norms and processes to changing conditions over time. It is also clear that both the effective regulation of sexuality and adaptation of its norms and processes occur in subtle, spontaneous and unconscious ways.

In this light, 'crimes of honour' are a manifestation of the failure or inadequacy of familial and communal regulation of sexuality, rather than an indication that such regulation happens in those societies and not in others. The serious problem with these crimes is that they represent a violent and discriminatory response to the failure or inadequacy of traditional mechanisms for the regulation of sexuality. In other words, these crimes should be combated as excessive and violent methods of regulation of sexuality that usually target women alone, even though men are at least as responsible for the transgression as women.

While it is imperative to challenge this state of affairs, I strongly believe that it is counterproductive to suggest that the family and community have no right to regulate sexuality at all. Even the appearance of suggesting that will undermine the credibility of any effort to combat 'crimes of honour', thereby rendering the women of communities implicated in such practices even more vulnerable to violence in the name of protecting honour than they are at present. The emphasis must therefore be on asking why violence against women, or men for that matter, is never justified as a response to sexual impropriety, without appearing to imply that the alternative is abandoning all forms or degrees of regulation of sexuality. It is therefore wise to present opposition to 'crimes of honour' crimes explicitly in these terms to avoid any risk of undermining the effort by allowing supporters of the practice to misrepresent the position of its opponents as promoting sexual promiscuity and licence.

One of the tensions that needs to be resolved in this connection is the sense that some of those combating 'crimes of honour' may in fact hold a more liberal view of personal autonomy and sexual freedom that is unacceptable to the families and communities implicated in 'honour crimes'. Those who hold this view as a matter of principle would also totally reject the characterising of their positions as supporting sexual promiscuity and licence. Nevertheless, are those opponents of 'honour crimes' required to abandon, hide or misrepresent their own convictions, or change their personal lifestyle, in order to combat these crimes? I will return to this question and to related dilemmas and issues in the last section of this chapter.

'Crimes of honour' as human rights violations

A more liberal view of personal autonomy and sexual freedom than that accepted by the communities where 'crimes of honour' occur may be supported by current international standards of human rights. But it is also possible, in my view, to oppose these crimes as human rights violations without necessarily arguing for liberalisation of a community's approach to the regulation of sexuality as such. That is, one can object to 'crimes of honour' from a human rights point of view because they are excessively violent and discriminatory against women, without necessarily arguing that the community's view of sexual propriety is itself objectionable from a human rights perspective. Although these two positions are not mutually exclusive, I am more concerned here with the view that 'crimes of honour' can constitute human rights violations, even if one accepts the community's position on the regulation of sexuality in general. The question I wish to address at this stage is when a 'crime of honour' constitutes a human rights violation, and how useful such a characterisation is likely to be in practice.

The first point to note here is the importance of maintaining the distinction between the protection of human rights and other types of state obligations, including those in the general administration of criminal justice. The current expression of the human rights idea is intended to safeguard essential human dignity through the protection of a specific set of fundamental rights and freedoms against violation by the state and its agents. For this objective to be realised, the number and scope of these rights must be kept to an essential minimum core of rights. Otherwise, there is the risk that these rights will not be taken seriously by states, and the already weak mechanisms for their implementation will be even less able to cope with an extensive or open-ended list of rights.

Another related reason for maintaining a clear distinction between human rights and other types of state obligations is embedded in the idea of human rights itself. Since human rights are by definition intended to protect people against excess or abuse of the powers of the state, these rights apply only to those who act on behalf of the state or under the colour of its authority or approval. Consequently, crimes like homicide are not human rights violations unless committed by agents of the state, or with their approval. This point is usually made in relation to acts of violence against women like 'crimes of honour' in terms of the distinction between the public domain of state action and the private domain of the family and community.

Some women rights advocates challenge this distinction by arguing that the state should be held accountable for its failure to act with 'due diligence' in combating violence against women within the private domain of family and community. From this perspective, the state is responsible for its failure to prosecute effectively and punish those who perpetrate violence against women in the private domain, though their crimes cannot be attributed to the state as such. While I agree with this useful strategy for pressing the state to be more proactive in protecting women against abuse by non-state actors, I do not take it to mean repudiating the distinction between the public and private domains. This is wise because once the state is allowed to act within the private domain, it will probably abuse that power to violate human rights instead of protecting them. The point here is not that state intervention can never succeed in protecting women against 'crimes of honour' or domestic violence more broadly, as that can indeed happen. Rather, the concern is about the likely abuse of the power to violate the privacy of family and community.

In the final analysis, therefore, the question is still, what does state responsibility mean in cases of 'crimes of honour' that fall within the private domain? How can the state discharge its obligation to protect women against violence within the family and community without violating the integrity of the family and community, or the economic and psychological well-being of their members? For instance, how can the family cope with the stigma of visible state interventions, and what can the state do for the young men who are pressured by their families and communities to commit 'crimes of honour' against their sisters?

Exclusive reliance on the state-centric approach is further limited in that it tends to be *reactive* to already committed violations by the action or omission of officials of the state, rather than *proactive* to pre-empt their happening in the first place. This approach can also be problematic because it tends to be slow, costly and generally inappropriate for the task at hand. In view of the severe resource limitations of developing countries that might enable state agencies and officials to provide emergency housing, employment or social security, it is more likely that women who are vulnerable to violence from members of their own families will be placed in so-called 'protective custody' to ensure their immediate physical safety. What human quality of life would women in that position have, and who is to protect them from abuse by custodial officials, and how can the state have the necessary resources for a proper implementation of such a drastic measure?

Moreover, since no enforcement system can cope with massive and persistent violations, the state-centric approach will not work unless the violation of the normative system in question ('crimes of honour' here) is the exception rather than the rule. Only then can the system achieve and sustain the necessary political will for enforcement against a more manageable number of violators, and devote the resources necessary for implementation activities in general. In other words, a proactive approach that seeks to reduce significantly the scale and frequency of 'crimes of honour' over time is necessary for the satisfactory operation of the state-centric approach by enabling it to focus on its enforcement and implementation capacity on fewer crimes. That is unlikely to happen in practice, I suggest, without the sort of community discourse proposed in this chapter.

With due regard to all the preceding remarks and reservations, it is also clear that certain aspects of 'crimes of honour' do reflect patterns of human rights violations. In the more immediate sense, the persistence of these crimes indicates a failure of the state to protect the lives and bodily integrity of women, including the provision of effective remedies against these crimes. More broadly, 'crimes of honour' signify deep-rooted, multifaceted and endemic discrimination against women, which the state is obliged to redress under Article 5 (a) of the International Convention for the Elimination of All Forms of Discrimination Against Women of 1979, even when perpetrated by non-state actors.[2] However, it does not necessarily follow that a human rights approach is desirable and/or viable in all situations and settings. That is, one should carefully assess the advantages and disadvantages of this approach on a case-by-case basis, rather than automatically invoking it in all situations.

Accordingly, a human rights approach is relevant to combating 'crimes of honour', as a matter of principle as well as for tactical reasons, but should only be seen as one option among others, or as an element of a broader strategy, rather than the only possible and effective approach. Indeed, I would argue that the proposed community discourse is critical for the effective application of a human rights approach itself, as well as being necessary for supporting other strategies for combating 'crimes of honour'. In Turkey, for example, there has been significant growth in the women's/human rights movement since the 1980s. Feminist activists and NGOs have succeeded in opening shelters for battered women, research centres, and organisations that can lobby for legislative reforms and the adoption of administrative measures to protect the rights of women, with some considerable recent successes.[3] It is important to acknowledge and appreciate the significant work being done by these organisations in the protection of the rights of women.[4] The question that arose for me in Turkey is how to make these efforts more effective in achieving their objectives in rural areas where traditional patriarchal culture still dominates. What follows is about supplementing and supporting the initiatives of NGOs and others actors engaged in combating 'crimes of honour', and not displacing or discrediting them, or undermining their efforts.

Towards a 'community discourse' approach

A 'community discourse' approach is necessary, I suggest, as a means of transforming family and community attitudes about these crimes, as well as prompting and supporting state officials and institutions to combat them more effectively. For example, such an internal discourse within the community about 'crimes of honour' is critical for the early socialisation of children against cultural values that condone, even reward, 'crimes of honour', and for transforming the institutional culture and priorities of state officials concerned with various aspects of these crimes.

I also believe that including a community discourse component is required out of respect for the moral autonomy of individuals and families and the self-determination of their communities. To insist that even perpetrators of these crimes should not be denied their fundamental human rights does not in the least condone 'crimes of honour' or undermine efforts to combat them. On the contrary, failure consistently to uphold the human rights of all persons and communities constitutes a more serious risk to the essence of the principle itself. Like all principles, the concept of universal human rights is truly tested only when faced with a strong challenge, like the temptation to violate the human rights of perpetrators of violations in the name of protecting the human rights of their victims.

This principled position is supported by pragmatic reasons for respecting the moral autonomy of individuals and families and the self-determination of communities. No strategy for combating 'crimes of honour' can be implemented in practice, and sustained over time, without the consent and cooperation of the communities in question. Trying to imagine how 'crimes of honour' might be prevented or punished through purely coercive messages will immediately reveal how futile and counterproductive such an effort would be. Where are the human and material resources going to come from, and how long can they be sustained, without broad political support within the community? As clearly illustrated by the case of Turkey, in my view, it is neither desirable nor realistic to rely exclusively on state officials and institutions to combat 'crimes of honour', because they are part of the problem.

Recalling the earlier discussion about the possibilities and limitations of a human rights approach to combating 'crimes of honour', it may be helpful to elaborate briefly on the dynamics of human rights advocacy in Islamic societies, and developing countries in general (see further An-Na'im, 2001). The basic prevailing model of human rights advocacy can be described as 'mobilising shame' against offending governments by carefully monitoring and publicising human rights violations in the hope of generating pressure on those governments to respect and protect rights. This scenario assumes that there are constituencies that are ready and able to act on the information, and with sufficient power actually to succeed in influencing the conduct of offending governments. Due the realities of oppressive governments in developing countries and civil society organisations that are either unable to confront their own government or lacking the power to influence its policies, responses to information about human rights violations in those countries have tended to come from the governments and civil society organisations of developed countries.

This situation is obviously unsatisfactory and unsustainable for several reasons. First, reliance on external pressure tends to undermine the credibility of the human rights movement itself as a form of foreign intervention, thereby enabling oppressive governments to challenge it as a form of 'cultural imperialism'. Second, such charges are likely to resonate with local constituencies because foreign governments and civil society organisations have to be selective in their response, if only because they cannot possibly address all human rights violations everywhere in the world all at once. Another reason for selective response by foreign actors is that they will naturally act according to their own sense of priority and urgency, rather than to those of victims and local communities in developing countries. Whatever its reasons or justifications, this inevitable selectivity will further erode the credibility of the human rights movement in general, as well as diminish the effectiveness of foreign interventions when and where they do occur. Third, since foreign governments and civil society organisations have to balance their own competing interests and concerns at home and abroad, they are unlikely to mount or sustain a focus on any specific issue or place if that is deemed to be 'too costly'.

Moreover, recent developments in international relations seem to confirm these concerns about the credibility and sustainability of this model of international human rights advocacy. As the 'propaganda value' of championing human rights causes in international relations has diminished since the end of the Cold War, Western governments do not seem as willing to give such efforts sufficient priority in international relations. This diminishing interest has been compounded by a sense of deep insecurity in the aftermath of the terrorist attacks on the United States on 11 September 2001, which exposed the weak commitment of Western governments to upholding human rights standards, and international legality in general, in their own domestic and foreign policies.

The mounting limitations and the general unpredictability and unreliability of the present model of international advocacy clearly indicate, in my view, the need to invest in developing and supporting local constituencies for combating 'crimes of honour', instead of relying on foreign pressure. It is also clear to me that local constituencies cannot be developed and supported without a strategic long-term engagement in internal discourse within the communities about specific concerns like 'crimes of honour', in the broader context of gender power relations within the family and community. Although there are varying degrees of such discourse, as can be seen in the case of Turkey, what is lacking is a clear strategic approach to addressing the difficulties, assessing progress and failures, devising and implementing appropriate local plans for a 'division of labour' whereby various actors assume specific roles in the process. Since community discourse is neither easy nor effectively done by all those who are engaged in combating 'crimes of honour', there is need for careful preparation for different roles, continuous evaluation of efficacy and sustainability, and so forth, for the particular problem and locale in question. How can such a strategic approach be developed and implemented?

To begin with, all those working to combat 'crimes of honour' should really accept the need for internal discourse within the communities, instead of relying on international pressure for achieving their objectives at home. Part of that necessary reorientation, I believe, is to identify clearly and address the reasons why they have not taken community discourse seriously and acted on this more strongly or effectively in the past. In general, and subject to local contextual factors, there are two apparent reasons for the lack or weakness of serious engagement in internal discourse that are particularly relevant to enhancing commitment and helpful for the preparation process outlined below. One reason, it seems to me, is ambivalence about the appropriate scope of the human rights agenda in relation to the specific issues and/or region. As we asked earlier, for example, is the objective a narrow and specific focus on preventing and punishing 'crimes of honour', or a broader, more liberal understanding of personal autonomy and sexual freedom? The other reason appears to be an apprehension about conceding the terms of discourse about culture and rights to traditional or conservative segments of society. As I have briefly discussed elsewhere, secularised human rights advocates in Islamic societies are apparently reluctant to engage in an Islamic discourse about human rights because they worry about conceding the authority of that frame of reference while lacking sufficient knowledge of its concepts and methodology (An-Na'im, 1995). The same is probably true of a similar discourse in terms of local cultural values and institutions.

Whatever the reasons, active human rights and social justice advocates in Islamic societies, like those of other developing countries in general, tend to be educated intellectuals and professionals. It is also true, in my experience, that those active advocates tend to subscribe to values and lifestyles different to those of the communities whose rights and interests they seek to defend and promote. This is not to say, of course, that uneducated urban poor and rural populations are passive victims who have no awareness of their rights and interests. Rather, the point is that the realities of resources and power relations are such that those wider constituencies lack the ability to challenge state officials and institutions effectively for their abusive or inadequate policies or to hold them accountable for their failures to protect rights and achieve social justice. In fact, the ultimate purpose of the argument I am trying to make is to empower wider communities to mobilise whatever resources and skills are available to them in order better to protect and promote their own rights and interests. That is, the objective is to make 'elite representation' of the poor and uneducated segments of society redundant. Yet this cannot be achieved by denying the present realities of the situation.

Given these realities, in the short term at least, the question is, how can this empowerment happen in practice? Regarding the subject of this chapter, for example, how can the more active and articulate opponents of 'crimes of honour' help empower actors within local communities to combat these crimes more effectively? How can elite activists gain access to, and secure the confidence of, the families and communities where these crimes occur, in order to engage in internal discourse against 'crimes of honour'? In view of the likely differences of opinion over the role of the family and community in regulating sexuality, mentioned earlier, are elite advocates of human rights and social justice to abandon or modify their own views and personal lifestyle, for the sake of access to and credibility among local families and communities?

This set of questions brings me to the second element in the strategic approach to community discourse, namely a 'division of labour' whereby each group of actors plays the most appropriate role in a broader strategy. The basic idea here is that opponents of 'crimes of honour' from outside the communities in question should identify and support those local 'agents of social change' who are committed to combating these crimes and already have the necessary access and credibility to engage in internal discourse about the issues. As 'insiders' to the communities in question, local agents of social change are unlikely to agree fully with other campaigners from outside those local settings on the precise scope and rationale of what these two constituencies may cooperate in achieving. The question therefore becomes one of 'negotiating' the necessary level of agreement between insiders and outsiders, while respecting remaining differences. In other words, I am calling for a process of coalition-building around the core objective of combating 'crimes of honour', and a mutually acceptable set of methods or activities, while gradually working through differences over broader issues of scope and long-term objectives.

The main point here is that both sides find common ground for col-laboration, whereby each side makes its best contribution to the joint effort, without expecting or demanding full or immediate agreement on all aspects of the problem and its solution. To avoid any confusion, I am not suggesting that either side should abandon or modify their own views and action on human rights and social justice in general. Rather, it is a matter of agreement and cooperation over an agreed objective and set of activities, while keeping the right to pursue broader or different objectives in the field. However, it should also be emphasised that good faith and respect for the spirit of collaboration in such shared ventures would oblige both sides not to act in ways that undermine the shared purpose, at least without consulting and seeking an acceptable compromise over differences of opinion or strategy.

In conclusion, all aspects of this process must necessarily be understood and applied with due regard to local context and all relevant factors and con-sideration. Nothing I have said in this chapter should be taken as prescribing a rigid and static formula for combating 'crimes of honour' in any specific community, let alone all communities everywhere. All relevant factors must be taken into account in careful and deliberate planning for initiating and coordinating activities, testing ideas, and so forth, for community discourse as an integral part of strategies to combat 'crimes of honour', and not as a sole or even primary strategy.

Notes

This chapter was originally drafted on the basis of research in Istanbul in June 2001. I am grateful to Dr Feride Ciceoglu of Bilgi University for facilitating my research visit and to Alisan Capan for research assistance. I would also like to thank all the scholars and activists with whom I met and those who attended the concluding roundtable. The CIMEL/INTERIGHTS team edited the chapter for publication in this volume; for the full version of the text, including detailed consideration of the Turkish context and case studies, see the CIMEL/INTERIGHTS Project, www.soas.ac.uk/honourcrimes.

1. See the full text by An-Na'im on the project website, and see Sev'er and Yurdakul, 1999, and other sources on 'honour killings' and violence against women in Turkey listed in the Annotated Bibliography at www.soas.ac.uk/honourcrimes.

2. Article 5 of this Convention provides:

   States Parties shall take all appropriate measures:

   (a) To modify the social and cultural patterns of conduct of men and women, with a view to achieving the elimination of prejudices and customary and all other practices which are based on the idea of the inferiority or the superiority of either of the sexes or on stereotyped roles for men and women.

   I will return to how the state might fulfil these obligations in relation to 'crimes of honour' in particular, in the last section of this chapter.

3. For information on the campaign to amend provisions of the Turkish Penal Code and the outcome of these activities, including with regard to the defence of 'unjust provocation', see the website of Women for Women's Human Rights, www.wwhr.org [ed.].

4. Interview with Pınar Ilkkaracan, 26 June 2001, Istanbul.

'Honour killings' and the law in Pakistan

SOHAIL AKBAR WARRAICH

'Honour crimes' have been part of Pakistan's social and legal history for centuries, despite diverse legal approaches by the state. Nevertheless, the year 1990 is a landmark from the legal perspective: the Supreme Court Shariat Appellate Bench gave judgment in the Gul Hassan case,[1] the Law of Qisas and Diyat[2] was introduced, and Penal Code provisions on murder and bodily hurt were 'Islamised', most importantly, by the repeal of the provision for mitigation of sentence in cases of murder resulting from 'grave and sudden provocation'.

Rather than eliminating 'honour crimes', the new laws have themselves proved a barrier to justice for victims. Most significantly, by requiring the courts to follow 'the injunctions of Islam' in applying the Laws of Qisas and Diyat, they have contributed to retrogressive debate about 'honour crimes' and gender relations within the family. The courts' interpretation of the new laws, including conflicting interpretations of *Gul Hassan* and their reintroduction of the plea of provocation, has further exacerbated the situation.

This chapter does not seek to define 'honour crimes', largely because local understandings of this term vary depending on who kills whom and the perceived transgression of social norms which lead to a socially sanctioned murder. However, it uses the term 'honour crimes' rather than 'killings', given that responses to perceived or alleged transgressions of 'honour' do not necessarily result in homicide.

The first section of this chapter examines the historical and socio-legal context of 'honour crimes' in Pakistan, including consideration of the British colonial power's endorsement of patriarchal tribal values in the Penal Code of 1860 and judicial interpretations of these provisions until their repeal in

1990. The second section discusses the current provisions of the Pakistan Penal Code (PPC) and the Criminal Procedure Code (CrPC) 1898 applicable to cases of 'honour crimes', discussing problems in prosecuting such cases arising from the limitations of statutory laws and judicial decisions. This chapter does not deal directly with the Zina Ordinance 1979, but it should be noted that the introduction of heavy penalties for extramarital sexual activity undoubtedly contributed to an overall atmosphere that validates violent responses to women's actual and alleged sexual activity. This section highlights the problems in the investigation and prosecution of 'honour crimes', and the state's failure to utilise provisions in the new law proactively to prevent 'honour crimes'. The final section provides an overview of the responses to 'honour crimes' in civil society, and analyses state rhetoric and the continued duality of the higher judiciary on 'honour crimes' issues.

'Honour killings' occur in all four provinces of Pakistan and the tribal areas adjoining the border with Afghanistan. The practice has different names: in southern Punjab, *kalakali*; in Sindh, *karokari*; in Balochistan, *siyakari*; and in the North Western Frontier Province (NWFP), *taurtoora*. Traditionally, the practice has enjoyed social sanction, originating from social procedures for accusing and punishing individuals for extramarital sexual activity. Other than in instances where couples were caught in flagrante delicto or where a woman defied so-called 'social order and morality', such an allegation would generally be addressed by a local informal adjudication system.[3] Traditionally, 'honour killings' were committed or claimed to be committed upon discovering a woman family member indulging in extramarital sex. But over the years the claimed justifications have widened to include women's expressions of autonomy by, for example, exercising choice in marriage or a decision to seek divorce (Amnesty International, 1999). Additionally allegations of engaging in 'dishonourable' acts/behaviour have also become tools for extortion,[4] settling family feuds or exacting revenge upon an opponent (Shirkat Gah, 2002).

Analysis of the social aspects of 'honour crimes' indicates that they cut across class lines and are perpetuated by feudal structures intent on retaining their social and political hold over local communities (Ali, 2001). Although the wider social implications of 'honour crimes' are beyond the scope of this chapter, it is important to note that their impact extends far beyond the immediate woman who is killed, creating an atmosphere of perpetual threat, claustrophobic supervision and fear.[5]

The extent to which 'honour crimes' have become a national issue was reflected in July 2004 by the Federal Minister of the Interior presenting the following national statistics to the Senate, Pakistan's upper house (Table 4.1).

Table 4.1 Figures for 'honour killings', 1998–2003, as presented by Federal Minister of the Interior to the Senate, 9 July 2004

Reported total killed	Male victims	Female victims	Cases registered	Compromised	Pending in courts
4,101	1,327	2,774	3,451	2,028	1,262

Source: The News, 10 July 2004. These figures were published in Pakistan's four major national English-language dailies, albeit with slightly varying figures.

There is no reliable method to verify the incidence of 'honour killings'. Many cases are unreported; others are identified as such for the ulterior purpose of benefiting from lesser sentences. However, beyond the possibility of increased reporting, multiple sources indicate an increase in such killings. As the minister's statistics reveal, convictions in such cases remain nominal.[6]

The historical, social and legal context

There is no definitive local explanation regarding the origins of 'honour killings'. Some claim the practice originated with various Baloch tribes of Balochistan and spread to other communities as they migrated to different parts of the country. The Pathans of NWFP and Balochistan claim separate origins of the practice (Shirkat Gah, 2002; Ali, 2001). Colonial records on the then Balochistan[7] clearly mention the 'custom' of 'honour killing'.[8] They describe tribal codes[9] among the Baloch and Pathans detailing such matters as who could make an allegation against a woman, the proof required and the treatment of proven and suspected 'adultery'. There were certain patterns in the killings: only where a man and a woman were caught 'red handed' were both liable to be killed; where one of them, especially the male, escaped, their treatment then differed slightly from tribe to tribe. In some districts, the colonial record notes that although an 'unfaithful' wife caught in the act was liable to be killed, in practice the matter was often settled through cash compensation or a marriage exchange of women related to the accused man. If both the man and the woman were killed, no compensation was due. If both escaped, then the wife would be divorced by her husband. Other practices recorded divorce of a woman on suspicion of or proven adultery, and generally prohibition on marrying the man involved. Notably, tribal codes usually only mention the procedure for punishment for adultery by a *married* woman.[10] In contrast, in current practice women may become victims of 'honour killings' irrespective of their marital status. Statistics from 1999 show that of 303 women reported by national dailies as 'killed', 45 were minor girls and two-fifths of those killed were unmarried (Human Rights Commission of Pakistan, 1999).

Contradictory legal conceptualisations of women's sexuality

Upon independence in 1947, Pakistan inherited the legal system introduced by the British colonial rulers (Adoption of Laws Act 1949). In the colonial period, personal status law was based either on the personal law of the parties or on customs applicable to them.[11] The criminal justice system introduced in India after the 1857 Indian War of Independence was modelled on the English system.

The 1860 British Penal Code introduced the notion of 'modesty', and related concepts of 'chastity', 'enticement' and 'abduction', as part of a framework of collective 'honour'. Rather than safeguarding the rights of the affected individual woman, the law upheld the rights of third parties, be it the state, community or immediate family members. Effectively, in matters of legal adjudication, women became passive objects whose sexuality was to be controlled. Women's chastity and modesty were to be protected against violation by any male outside the relationship of a legally valid and socially accepted marriage, on the premiss of women's vulnerability and need for protection from men. Such protection could be granted only by placing women in the care, custody or guardianship of the father, husband or any lawful guardian – invariably a man. Women were not considered individuals – each crime in the Penal Code was classified in relation to the lawful protector or guardian. For example, under section 498 (Penal Code) 'enticement' was of a *married* woman, while under section 361 kidnapping or abduction was *from a lawful guardian.* Thus the 'removal' of women/girls through force or other means by any other male was a crime. This curtailed women's rights to personal liberty and freedom of movement since any association with a male outside the prohibited degree could be prosecuted as kidnapping or abduction and the woman restored to the male whose care or custody had been affected.[12] The nature of the crime was determined by two factors: first, the nature of the person from whose custody she had been removed; and second, the means used, whether force or deception. Although any injury to the woman herself added to the penal charges, the main concern was the injury to third-party rights.

In contrast to the provisions of the law on adultery (whereby an accused woman could not be prosecuted by the state), the Penal Code provided for the possibility of leniency where a husband killed his adulterous wife, through the exception of 'grave and sudden provocation',[13] which reduced a charge of murder to one of manslaughter. Cases of 'honour killings' were dealt with under this exception and judicial interpretation provided an even wider licence to killers. This concession was not confined to husbands but extended to other family members (see discussion below).

Pre-partition case law

Cases in various High Courts of India (pre-partition) clearly show that it was a well-accepted norm that a husband could benefit from the exception of 'grave and sudden provocation plea' if he killed his wife or her alleged lover on account of demonstrated adultery.[14] Where the circumstances involved a woman to whom the defendant was not married, certain differences appeared in the rulings. In a 1930 case the Calcutta High Court declined to extend the provocation defence where the accused was neither married to the woman involved, nor could be regarded as cohabiting with her.[15] On the other hand, in a murder appeal in 1932 the Madras High Court held that

> One cannot supply considerations of social morality to a purely psychological problem. The question is not that the appellant ought to have exercised control but whether he lost control over himself. When a man sees a woman be she his wife or his mistress in the arms of another man, he does not stop to consider whether he has or has not the right to insist on exclusive possession of her person as the case cited by the judge puts it. She is a woman, of whose person he desires to be in exclusive possession and that is for the moment, enough for him, he thinks of nothing else.[16]

It was the latter position that became established judicial practice, with the courts granting reduced sentences on the grounds of a broad interpretation of 'grave and sudden provocation plea'.[17]

Post-independence case law

Following independence there was much debate surrounding the form and content of the future constitution and its conformity with Islam. In the interim the Constituent Assembly adopted the Objectives Resolution, a set of guidelines to steer the committee drafting the Constitution.[18] To date, the purpose and scope of this resolution remains controversial within both parliamentary debate and the superior courts, notably because it raises the question of what law is to be supreme in Pakistan. This debate, more recently linked with issues of 'Islamisation', has been the context for numerous changes in Pakistan's laws since the mid-1970s, including the amendments to the criminal law in 1990 and consequently the prosecution of 'honour crimes'.

Pakistan's criminal laws remained unchanged until Zia ul-Haq introduced martial law in 1977 and began a process of political 'Islamisation'.[19] Changes based on the personal law of the Muslim majority were made applicable to all citizens. Under Zia's regime, the Constitution was amended through presidential orders and ordinances, which were later incorporated into the Constitution through the infamous Eighth Amendment.[20] The Objectives Resolution, hitherto a preambular part of all constitutions and thus non-justiciable, became a substantive part of the 1973 Constitution as Article 2-A. Additionally the Federal Shariat Court was created under Article 203C(1) of the Constitution with special authority to examine laws for their conformity with the injunctions of Islam.

Post-independence courts continued to hand down token sentences to perpetrators of alleged 'honour killings', ignoring the clear terms of the law, and granting male family members a virtual licence to kill their women on the pretext of 'honour'. Yasmeen Hassan (1995) discusses cases where the benefit of a provocation plea was extended not only to premeditated murders but also to cases where men were effectively given authority to monitor women's movements, and to kill them if they defied the social 'order'. In one such case, the court held that

> The appellant's admonishing his wife on her paramour's departure did not minimise the gravity of the situation or the provocation offered. In such a situation even if the wife begs pardon and asks for mercy, yet if he kills her, conduct would still be mitigated and he would not be guilty of murder.[21]

In another case, the Supreme Court held that a man who was looking for his sister on suspicion that she was meeting a man and who subsequently killed her was entitled to plead provocation because at the village level, and in many other social arenas, men's 'right' to control the actions of 'their women', particularly their sexual relations, is fully recognised and forcefully maintained.[22]

Post-1990: a new law but the problems deepen

The Gul Hassan case

Following the establishment of the Federal Shariat Court in 1980, various laws were challenged on the basis of their conformity with the Koran and Sunna, including those parts of the Penal Code dealing with murder and bodily hurt. The piecemeal changes to penal provisions dealing with such offences, commonly known as the Law of Qisas and Diyat,[23] were introduced in October 1990, following the directions of the Supreme Court Shariat Appellate Bench in *Federation of Pakistan* vs. *Gul Hassan* in 1989[24] to the federal government to amend the laws due to the Court's finding them repugnant to Islam.

The *Gul Hassan* judgment declared those sections of the PPC (and relevant sections of the CrPC) dealing with deliberate murder (*qatl-e-amd*) and deliberate hurt repugnant to Islam, because:

1. There was no provision for the right of *qisas.*
2. There was no provision for *diyat.*
3. There was no provision for compromise between the aggrieved party and the accused on payment of agreed compensation by the latter to the former.
4. There was no provision for the victim or heirs of the deceased to pardon the offender, whereas the government could issue a pardon without reference to or permission of the victim or the heirs of the deceased.
5. The provisions did not exempt non-pubert or insane offenders from the death penalty.
6. The provisions did not define the different kinds of murder and injury along with their respective punishments as prescribed in the Holy Koran and Sunna.

Equally, the court declared repugnant to Islam PPC (s. 109) and CrPC (s. 54), which provided that an abettor could be awarded the same sentence as the actual offender and that sentences could be commuted by the state.

The court's critique highlighted significant conceptual differences between the Muslim and common law penal systems in dealing with murder and bodily hurt. First, the PPC and CrPC contravened the basic concept of criminal liability in Islamic law; and second, they classified all murder and hurt as a crime against the state, rather than against victims or their heirs. In contrast, according to the Koran and Sunna, murder and hurt (of whatever kind) are viewed first as a violation of the rights of an individual and his/her heirs, and only then as a law-and-order issue and crime against the state.

Thus the judgment noted that under Islamic law it is the right of the aggrieved person and his/her heirs to demand *qisas*, and the state's right to prosecute is secondary. Nevertheless, the court added that in Islam the state can implement provisions for *tazir*[25] where the social order is disrupted, with no limit specified for such discretionary punishment. As the case law below shows, the state has rarely chosen to exercise this responsibility.

Changes introduced under the Law of Qisas and Diyat

From the outset the way the new law was introduced created confusion about its provisions. According to *Gul Hassan,* the penal provisions related to murder and hurt were to expire on 23 March 1990. The federal government filed a review petition, which the Supreme Court[26] disposed of on 29 August 1990, on the assurance that the Attorney General would shortly enact an ordinance to give effect to the *Gul Hassan* judgment. However, between August and 2 October 1990, three ordinances were promulgated, each amending the previous one, in some cases prior to the original's enactment. To this day, the precise date of application of the new provisions is disputed. This confusion was further compounded by s.338-H's PCC providing that s.309 and s.310 (relating to waiver and compounding of *qisas*) and s.338-E (relating to the court's discretion to apply a sentence even if the offence has been compounded) could be applied to pending cases, even though the concept of *qisas* had not existed for those cases.

The new law introduced several major changes. First, the concept of murder was completely altered: every unnatural death of a person at the hands of another was now considered murder, removing all previous categorisations such as manslaughter and culpable homicide not amounting to murder. Four new categorisations of murder were provided, of which only one, *qatl-e-amd* (intentional murder), is relevant to this chapter.

Second, different sentences for murder were introduced, depending not on the intensity of the crime, but rather on the form of proof of murder and the relationship of the offender to the deceased. This profoundly affected the treatment of 'honour killings', where the offender is invariably related to the victim and there are usually no witnesses. A murder is liable to *qisas* (retribution, i.e. the death sentence) if the accused confesses to the satisfaction of the court, or the requisite number of credible eyewitnesses are available.[27] Where the level of proof is not met, the murder is liable to *tazir* – a sentence of life imprisonment or death under s.302(b) PCC. However, s.306(b) and s.306(c) PPC automatically except certain relatives from *qisas* or *tazir* under s.302(b) – namely parents or grandparents who murder their child/grandchild, or where one murders their spouse and is survived by children from the marriage. Such offenders can be sentenced only to *diyat*, although the courts have discretion to impose a maximum sentence of fourteen years' imprisonment depending upon the facts and the circumstances of the case. Just how deeply this was to impact upon 'honour killings' was evident from 1999 figures, which show that out of 303 women reported by national dailies as killed, 269 were known to their killers, out of which the majority (198 out of 303) were killed by their brother, father, husband or son (Human Rights Commission of Pakistan, 1999).

Third, under s.307 PPC there are certain situations where *qisas* 'shall not be enforced'[28] and where 'according to the Injunctions of Islam the punishment of *qisas* is not applicable' (s.302(c) PPC). Significantly this latter provision does not contain any further explanation, thus leaving interpretation of 'the injunctions of Islam' to the court. Moreover, no lower limit for sentencing is set under this provision. This became central to the interpretation of the new law's applicability to cases of 'honour crimes'. Most 'honour crimes' are dealt with under this provision, with only light sentences awarded.

Finally, s.309 and s.310 PPC read in conjunction with s.345 CrPC, give the heirs of a murder victim, or the victim of any form of bodily hurt, the right to 'forgive' an accused or to enter into a compromise with them in return for compensation, known as 'compounding' the offence.[29] If the case is being heard under *qisas* or a *qisas* sentence has been pronounced, any one of the heirs may waive their right of *qisas* or accept a compromise. The courts are obliged to accept such a waiver or compounding even by a single heir, and the accused will be acquitted unless the court exercises discretion under s.311 PPC (discussed below). If the case is being heard under *tazir*, according to s.345(2) CrPC for a compromise to be effective it must involve all the heirs of the deceased and be held with the permission of the court; such a compromise amounts to the acquittal of the accused. As the perpetrators of women's murders or 'honour crimes' are frequently their close relatives, it is most likely that the victim's heirs will compromise with the murderer, and the crime will go unpunished (see Table 4.1).

It is difficult to determine which cases could be compromised under s.309 and s.310 PPC, particularly in cases where some heirs have compromised with the killers, common in 'honour killings'. Although the legal provisions refer to the waiver or compounding of *qisas*, both courts and litigants have tended to focus on the possibility of, or application of, the death sentence, irrespective of whether this is death as *qisas* under s.302(a) or as *tazir* under s.302(b). Judgments conflict over whether a single heir can waive or compound a case liable to *tazir* and confusion remains over which provision is to apply when all heirs have not pardoned an accused.[30] In 1997, amicus curiae appointed by a full bench of the Supreme Court differed on this point, concluding that s.309 and s.310 PPC are applicable only where the accused is sentenced under *qisas*, and that irrespective of the quantum of sentence all other cases can be compromised only by all the deceased's heirs under s.345(2) CrPC.[31] Thus if just one among the heirs refused to compromise, the perpetrator would still receive a heavier sentence. In practice, however, this decision did not settle the matter, as the judgment was itself variously interpreted until the Supreme Court subsequently clarified its 1997 verdict in two later cases.[32]

These new provisions caused serious injustices, including through prolonged litigation. There remains confusion over the application of s.309 and s.310 PPC and whether they relate to sentences under *qisas* and/or *tazir*. Moreover, trial courts have failed to check compromise deeds, sometimes accepting these where only the heirs of the deceased have signed, and failing to notice the contradiction between an accused denying the charges and a compromise apparently being made.[33]

In certain circumstances, irrespective of whether there is a waiver or compromise, s.311 PPC authorises the courts to impose a sentence of up to fourteen years under the concept of *fasad fil arz* (disrupting the social order). Equally, s.338E PPC grants the court vast discretion, irrespective of any compromise, either to acquit or, taking into account 'the facts and circumstances of the case', to 'award *tazir* according to the nature of the offence'. Notably, in preceding sections, wherever *tazir* is mentioned, a limit has also been prescribed; under s.338E PPC, however, no limit is provided for. However, these provisions have rarely been applied in practice due either to technicalities or to a lack of judicial application. It is illustrative of Pakistan's social, legal and political context that these progressive provisions of the new law have routinely been overlooked or ignored by the state.

The *Gul Hassan* judgment and 'honour crimes'

'Honour crimes' did not feature in the *Gul Hassan* judgment; nor were they the focus of any of the petitions challenging the old provisions. But, importantly, in the process of discussing what constitutes murder in Islam, the court made lengthy observations regarding 'provocation' using the example of extramarital sexual relations, *zina*, the main context and defence in 'honour crimes'.[34]

The Court stated, 'according to the injunctions of Islam, provocation, no matter how grave and sudden it is, does not lessen the intensity of crime of murder.'[35] Thus, 'from an Islamic point of view', a murderer could be exempted from *qisas* in only two situations: where the deceased was committing an act for which the sentence under Islam was death, and where the murder had been in self-defence. Justifying this opinion the court merely stated that Islam does not permit the murder of 'one who is *masoom ud dam*' (one whose life is sacred or whose blood is protected) – without further clarifying this protected category.[36]

Taking the example of a man committing murder after seeing his wife committing *zina*, the Court noted that the maximum penalty for *zina* is death; thus upon the condition that he provides proof in conformity with the required standards of evidence under Islam, he would be exempted from a death sentence under *qisas*.[37] Further, by taking the law into his own hands the accused had committed a crime against the state and could be punished under *tazir*. Subsequent judgments in 'honour killings' frequently ignored the conditional aspect of the exemption of *qisas* and the possibility of punishment under *tazir*, emphasising only the first point, that a husband killing his wife upon discovering her committing *zina* is not liable for the death sentence under *qisas*. This was to have serious implications for the prosecution of 'honour crimes'.

Finally, the Court observed that *qisas* would not apply in cases of self-defence, but without explaining what constituted self-defence, who had the authority to exercise it, and under what conditions it could be exercised. Case law discussed below reflects on how the courts' interpretation of self-defence 'with an Islamic touch' gave men of the family authority over women, enabling perpetrators of 'honour killings' to receive only nominal sentences.

Case law after 1990: reintroducing 'grave and sudden provocation'?

The following section examines case law post-1990 regarding certain 'honour crimes', specifically those where a plea of provocation was argued and accepted in mitigation even though the provision as such no longer exists in law. It should be noted that much of the reported case law relating to 'honour killings' involves the murder of men by men, although women are more commonly the victims of such killings, as shown *inter alia* by the figures presented to the Senate in 2004 and set out in Table 4.2. This may be because murders of women are more likely to be compromised and less likely to reach the superior courts and therefore be reported.

The unresolved question: who is *masoom ud dam*?

In *Abdul Waheed*,[38] the Supreme Appellate Court[39] examined the plea of provocation in the light of *Gul Hassan*. Both the prosecution and the defence relied on different aspects of the Gul Hassan judgment, evidencing its lack of clarity. The accused was convicted and sentenced to seven years' hard labour (s.302(c) PPC – murder where *qisas* is not applicable) on the basis of his confession that whilst he was attempting to shoot his sister, upon witnessing her in a compromising position with the victim, the victim interceded and was shot. The prosecution case collapsed due to non-credible eyewitness testimony, leaving the confession the sole basis of conviction. The trial court, referring to *Gul Hassan,* accepted the accused's account and regarded the victim as not *masoom ud dam.*

In the appeal (by the state to sentence the accused to death for *qisas* under s.302(a) PPC) in the Supreme Appellate Court, Justice Naseem Hassan Shah followed the conditional aspect of the *Gul Hassan* exemption from *qisas.* Although *Gul Hassan* did not specify the precise evidentiary requirements, Justice Shah referred to section 121 of the Qanoon-e-Shahadat,[40] noting that the onus of proof is on the accused when attempting to benefit from exceptions or special provisos. Further, the requisite evidence was the same as that for *zina* under *hadd*: four adult male Muslim eyewitnesses. In the present case, there was no evidence other than the accused's account. The Court also referred to *Mohib Ali* vs. *The State*, where the Supreme Court had observed: 'A mere allegation of moral laxity without any unimpeachable evidence to substantiate would not constitute grave and sudden provocation. If such pleas, without any evidence, are accepted, it would give a licence to people to kill innocent people.'[41] The sentence was enhanced to death as *qisas* under section 302(a) PPC.

However, a survey of case law reflects that in many subsequent cases of a similar nature, where the accused's confession and plea of provocation were the only basis of conviction due to rejection of the prosecution's evidence or a legal technicality, the court's positive interpretation in *Abdul Waheed* has not been followed. Three months after *Abdul Waheed*, a differently constituted full bench of the Supreme Court considered the same issues and applied *Gul Hassan* but reached an entirely different conclusion – all the more surprising as Justice Naseem Hassan Shah (who heard *Abdul Waheed*) and Justice Shafiur Rahman (who passed the opposing judgment) both heard the *Gul Hassan* case.

In *Mohammad Hanif,*[42] the accused pleaded provocation when charged with killing his brother, alleging that the latter had disgraced his wife by dragging her out of the house. The trial court sentenced Hanif to ten years' hard labour under section 302(c) PPC (murder not liable to *qisas*), imposing a fine payable to the deceased's heirs. The state appealed, arguing that the accused should be convicted under *qisas.*

On appeal, Justice Shafiur Rahman highlighted the shortcomings of *Gul Hassan*, noting its failure to define precisely *masoom ud dam*, in particular whether it meant someone entirely innocent, or someone whose acts would not invoke a death sentence. The Court opted for the former interpretation, excluding those who could possibly be prosecuted for any offence (such as entering a house), thus permitting subsequent murderers to declare their victims not *masoom ud dam* and receive lesser sentences. Moreover, *Mohammad Hanif* directly contradicted *Abdul Waheed* on the fundamental point of burden of proof. At no point were these strict standards of evidence set out in *Abdul Waheed*, again swinging the balance against justice for the victims of 'honour killings'.

This case reflects a typical pattern of South Asian criminal cases where the prosecution evidence is wholly rejected (often due to poor preparation) and the accused's statement stands without scrutiny. In effect, 'honour crimes' cases are dominated by the accused's account of the victim's conduct and the claimed motive for murder. Under the new *qisas* and *diyat* provisions, and given the definitional issues surrounding *masoom ud dam*, the victim's conduct is directly linked to the possible sentence. These factors invariably skew cases in favour of those who kill women and men and claim an 'honour' motive.

What offence has been committed?

A parallel question arising was whether, where *qisas* was not applicable, murders committed on account of *ghairat* (commonly translated as 'honour') fell within s.302(b) PPC (death or life sentence as *tazir* when proof for *qisas* is not available) or incurred a maximum sentence of twenty-five years under s.302(c) PPC 'where according to the injunctions of Islam the punishment of *qisas* is not applicable'. The new law does not precisely clarify the situations in which s.302(c) PPC would apply. Problems caused by this lack of textual clarity were compounded by the fact that s.338-F of the amended PPC guides the courts to follow the injunctions of Islam while interpreting the provisions of the Law of Qisas and Diyat.

In *Ghulam Yasin*,[43] the Lahore High Court considered whether murders committed on the pretext of *ghairat* deserve any concession. The case involved the murder of a man and the injury of an unmarried sister by her brother and paternal uncles, who claimed to have found her in a compromising position with the deceased. As motive was proved, the case turned on the nature of offence committed. The Court found that 'it is true that the provisions of this chapter relating to Qatl do not make any allowance for Qatl committed under *Ghairat*, but in view of s.338 F courts are bound to apply the provisions of law in accordance with the injunctions of Islam'.[44] In a particularly conservative and patriarchal interpretation, the Court mentioned various *hadith* (reported sayings of the Prophet)[45] and held that 'it is obvious that a murder committed on account of *ghairat* is not the same as *qatl-e-amd* [deliberate murder] pure and simple and the persons found guilty of Qatl committed on account of *ghairat* do deserve concession which must be given to them.'[46] The Court concluded that murder in such circumstances did not fall under section 302(a) PPC, and reduced the sentence to five years. The lower court's award of compensation was also set aside, apparently under the concept of 'one who is not *masoom ud dam*', the Court stating: 'in view of the fact that the deceased lost his life on account of his unlawful and immoral act, the present is not the case where the convicts could be directed to pay compensation to his heirs.'[47] This judgment has been cited in many subsequent cases to reduce sentences on appeal, especially in the Lahore High Court.

The unresolved question of defining self-defence

Muhammad Hanif was the first case to raise the issue of the exercise of self-defence in the context of provocation and exceptions to *qisas*. The Court took the accused's plea that his act was an exercise of the right of self-defence, and therefore not liable to *qisas*. The Court invoked the Koranic description of men as *qawam* over women,[48] explaining *qawam* as 'that person who is responsible for running the affairs of a person or an institution or system in correct manner, to safeguard and provide for the necessities of life.'[49] Thus a husband is considered to be responsible for protecting his wife from any disgrace. This use of verse 4:34 introduced yet another obstacle to the prosecution of 'honour crimes' and enabled increasingly wide interpretations in later cases.

The issue of whether a plea of provocation could still be taken after its legislative repeal finally came before the Supreme Court in *Abdul Haque* vs. *The State*.[50] The 'honour' element came from Haque's defence that he had murdered the deceased, in a courtroom, when the latter threatened to sexually assault all the women of Haque's tribe on his release. A three-member full bench of the Supreme Court requested the Chief Justice to constitute a seven-member bench to decide this 'fundamentally important' question of law, addressing a principle that 'has been well-recognised in the sub-continent for more than a hundred years'.

Ultimately, the five-member bench that considered Haque's appeal against the imposition of the death penalty,[51] after detailed discussion of *Abdul Waheed* and *Muhammad Hanif*, concluded that a provocation plea is not available if a murder is liable to *qisas*. It is, however, available as a mitigating circumstance for a murder considered under s.302(b) PPC (*tazir*). This had serious implications for the 'honour killing' of women, where most cases do not invoke *qisas* because they fall under sections 306(b) and 306(c) PPC (*qisas* is excluded on account of a relationship). The remaining cases invariably fall under section 302(b) (*tazir* when the level of proof required for *qisas* is not available), or section 302(c) (discussed below). By allowing the reintroduction of 'mitigating circumstances' for cases under section 302(b) PPC, this decision effectively ensured the impossibility of securing maximum sentences for the murder of women.

This case also illustrated the judiciary's reluctance to accept repeal of the provocation plea, one judge commenting 'notwithstanding the omission to incorporate exception [of 'grave and sudden provocation'] in the amended law, it still remains a relevant factor for deciding the question of sentence.'[52]

The above cases, and issues of *masoom ud dam* and *qawam*, the applicability of provocation, and the sentences for 'honour killings' were eventually discussed by a full bench of the Supreme Court in *Ali Mohd* vs. *Ali Mohd*.[53] The case involved the murder of a man, whom the accused claimed to have found in an 'objectionable position' with his wife (the latter having managed to escape). The trial court, apparently ignorant of the new law, had heard the case under the old PPC provisions and sentenced the accused to seven years, while the High Court deemed it a *qatl bil haq* (a rightful murder) and acquitted the accused.[54]

The Supreme Court concluded that *Mohammad Hanif* had overridden *Abdul Waheed* and, in an interesting take on 'fundamental rights', stated that

> the fundamental right to act as *qawam* conferred as it has been by the Holy Qur'an … must receive a construction most beneficial to the widest possible amplitude of that right.… There can be no doubt that included in the basic right of the man to act as *qawam* is the right to protect the honour of his women and to defend them from outrage, disgrace and insult.[55]

The Court, following *Abdul Haque*, found that in instances of 'provocation' sentences other than *qisas* would apply, adding that the courts were to decide which cases fall under s.302(c) PPC (which provides no minimum sentence in situations where, according to the injunctions of Islam, *qisas* is not applicable) and that *Gul Hassan* left no doubt that cases previously covered under the 'provocation' exception should fall within this section.[56] Ali Mohammed was sentenced to imprisonment already undergone (two years and one month) purely because he had exceeded his right of self-defence and used excessive force.

In a subsequent bail application for a 20-year-old accused of killing his 16-year-old sister and a man whom he suspected of having illicit relations with her, Justice Asif Jan of the Lahore High Court, referring to verse 4:34 of the Koran, said:

> A husband, father and the brothers are supposed to guard the life and the honour of the females who are inmates of the house and when anyone of them finds a trespasser, committing *zina* with a woman of his family, then murder by him whilst deprived of self control will not amount to 'qatl-e-amd' liable to *qisas* because the deceased in such a case is not a Masoom ud Dam.[57]

The merger of the concepts of self-defence and a victim who is not *masoom ud dam* thus appears to have resulted in the reintroduction of the 'grave and sudden provocation' exception. This brings 'honour crimes' full circle with the re-establishment of the century-long judicial tradition of providing lesser sentences for those who claim to have murdered for 'honour', albeit with a supposed 'Islamic' element to the interpretation.

However, there remained, as noted in *Muhammad Ibrahim* vs. *Soofi Abdul Razzaq*, 'various flaws and ambiguities' in the way *tazir* was to be applied, especially in cases of provocation based on *ghairat*.[58] This judgment stands out for its criticism of the situation following the introduction of the *qisas* and *diyat* provisions, and its acknowledgement that 'we are doing different experience on ad hoc basis', apparently an oblique reference to the cases above, which are heavily cited in the judgment. The case involved the murder of a woman by her husband after he discovered her 'in an objectionable position' with another man, and was rare in that the accused raised no defence and openly confessed to his crime. The general social atmosphere that had developed around such cases, and the prominence now given to the issue of *qawam*, were illustrated by the court's noting that 'The pivotal question to be resolved is whether an absolute right has been conferred upon a husband under Islamic Law to kill his wife on seeing her in an objection-able condition.'[59] After discussing numerous Koranic verses and *hadith*, the court referred to Federal Shariat Court judgments regarding *zina* which had concluded that 'It is a fundamental rule of Islam that doubt cannot be the basis for punishment but provides a ground to pardon',[60] and highlighted how the accused had completely failed to provide evidence of *zina*. Obliged to follow the Supreme Court in deciding the case under section 302(c) PPC, the Court nevertheless enhanced the sentence from three to five years.

Confusion over legal provisions applicable to 'honour crimes'

Whereas under the old PPC a single provision concerned 'honour crimes' (i.e. 'grave and sudden provocation'), jurists and legal professionals alike remain confused regarding the applicable new provisions and range of sentences. This has been compounded by conflicting judgments of the courts, including the Supreme Court, as illustrated by the prime example of *Faqir Ullah* vs. *Khalil uz Zaman*.[61] In this case, a husband killed his wife and injured her brother, claiming to have done so on account of *ghairat* and alleging that the brother was pimping the deceased, the accused's wife. As the deceased had a minor daughter, under s.306 (c) and s.308 PPC the murderer could only be sentenced to a maximum of fourteen years' imprisonment. However, the trial court sentenced him to death under s.302 (b) PPC. On appeal, the

Supreme Appellate Court retained the death sentence but converted it to one under s.302(a) PPC as *qisas*, without providing a reason. The accused filed a constitutional petition in the Supreme Court which held that the accused could not be sentenced to death either under *qisas* or *tazir* as the case was covered by s.306 (c) and s.308 PPC. The Supreme Court commented:

> The error committed by the courts in convicting the accused/petitioner under s.302 PPC and sentencing him to death is so serious that had the petitioner eventually been hanged to death, we are afraid it would have amounted to murder through judicial process. Needless to say that plea of good faith/bonafide/ignorance of law/incompetency is/are not available in such like cases.[62]

The father of the deceased filed a review petition against this decision in the Supreme Court, where a five-member bench overturned the earlier constitutional petition decision. The court agreed that *qisas* could not be imposed. However, it held that *tazir* could be imposed and, regarding the limit of such a sentence, stated:

> In cases where Qisas is not available, the Shariah has given authority to the state and the courts to award appropriate punishment to the offender keeping in view the circumstances of the case. Such punishment may reach up to life imprisonment or death by way of tazir. This kind of death punishment has been termed variously by the jurists but there is a general agreement that such a punishment is justified under the Shariah in special circumstances.[63]

The trial court's decision to award the death penalty under *tazir* was restored. The court did not comment on whether the limit set in s.308 PPC was to continue or stood cancelled.

This case is an extreme example of the complications arising from this law and the injustices it causes for victims, and in some instances also perpetrators; the two conflicting Supreme Court decisions were separated by a gap of almost five years.[64]

Judicial attitudes and 'honour crimes'

After a series of judgments where courts accepted a plea of 'provocation' in the context of men being 'in charge of women' and responsible for guarding women and for killing 'trespassers', the Lahore High Court ultimately declared such murders not to be an offence at all and acquitted an accused of murdering of two persons in the name of 'honour'. The accused had killed his daughter and her partner in the sugar-cane fields, after allegedly catching them in a compromising position. Medical evidence showed semen traces on vaginal swabs taken from the woman. The court held that in such a situation, the appellant, being the father of Mst X, one of the deceased, was overpowered by the wave of his family honour, *ghairat*, and killed both the deceased at the spot. In my opinion he has committed no offence liable to punishment.[65]

Such social attitudes permeate the decisions of the judiciary. In *Muhammad Ayub*,[66] a man allegedly killed his four-months-pregnant wife, claiming a *ghairat* motive, after seeing her in an objectionable position with another man – a statement the court took at face value. Although he was convicted and sentenced to twenty-five years' hard labour and a fine of Rs. 50,000 (payable to the deceased's legal heirs), the appeal court reduced the defendant's sentence to five years and set aside the fine. The court's sympathies with the accused were noteworthy:

> The appellant is an uneducated young man belonging to a tribe where no loose conduct of a female is tolerated and family honour is strictly guarded.... If he remains in jail for long time, there is possibility that he comes out as hardened criminal which is not desirable.[67]

This decision was added to the list of judgments cited by the defence in subsequent 'honour killings' cases.

In some instances, judges have made entirely speculative assumptions about the conduct of the murdered woman and the possible circumstances of the incident, granting reduced sentences and failing to provide justice for victims of violence. In *Amanullah*'s case a man and woman were killed as alleged *kalakali*. The accused pleaded innocence and demanded a trial, which resulted in conviction and a sentence of ten years' hard labour with a fine. The medical report had shown the presence of semen in vaginal swabs, but no cross-matching had been conducted; it appears that the mere presence of semen was sufficient for the appeal court to reduce the sentence. There were differing accounts of the incident, the bodies had been recovered at a distance from each other, and yet the judge referred to circumstances not mentioned by either the prosecution or the defence:

> keeping in view entire gamut of the circumstances and evidence of the case, I conclude that both the deceased had assembled in a thick place of garden for sexual affair. Somehow the accused persons became cognizant of their presence at the venue of occurrence, they reached the spot duly armed and found both the lovers a pari delicto position. The appellants lost self-control and acted on grave and sudden provocation. They fired at both the deceased and caused their death.[68]

The sentence was reduced to four years, which, given time already served, meant the appellants spent only a month or so more in jail.

There are also those cases where judicial endorsement of local practices and biases is visible, for example in *Imam Bakhsh*, where the accused killed his (much younger) wife and brother-in-law after catching them in a compromising position at home. The court did not criticise the practice of marrying young women to much older men, but noted it was not extraordinary or unbelievable that such a woman would *therefore* be likely to have gone astray.[69] Again, the court failed to be appalled at the customary conduct of the woman's own family – who had joined in the attack on her and subsequently disowned her body – rather considering this 'proof' of the 'disgrace brought by her to the whole family by her conduct'.[70]

In *Muhammad Ismail* vs. *The State*, a young man brutally murdered his mother after allegedly seeing her in a compromising position with another man. Yet again, a poor prosecution case led the accused to be sentenced on his own statement, although no evidence was established to support his assertions. Nevertheless, the judge stated that

> the appellant was a youngster at the relevant time, 18/19 years of age, and his father was *Hafiz e Koran* (having memorised the Qu'ran by heart) and blind by birth. His mother was earlier married to someone else and it is after getting divorce from him that she had contracted second marriage with the father of the appellant. The possibility that taking undue benefit of the disability of her husband, the mother of appellant had gone astray and developed illicit liaison with the deceased can't be excluded. The manner in which injuries were inflicted also shows that this was the act of the person in a state of frenzy. The appellant took plea of grave and sudden provocation from the beginning and reiterated before court.... His plea of grave and sudden provocation is accepted as such. The appellant has already served five years in jail and in my view the sentence already undergone will meet the ends of justice.[71]

Recent trends: a more positive direction?

Although the courts continue to validate pleas of 'provocation', perceptions of men being 'in charge of women' and the jealous guardians of women's sexual conduct, and the supremacy of 'family honour', since 1999 they have also adopted an opposing stance in a series of judgments. Two decisions of the Supreme Court are particularly encouraging. In *Abdul Zahir* vs. *The State* the Supreme Court considered the appropriate sentence in cases of murder where the plea of provocation was upheld and noted, 'by and large all cases of grave and sudden provocation would not *ipso facto* fall under section 302(c) PPC particularly those of wife, sister and other female relatives on the allegation of "siyakari".'[72] In *Muhammad Akram Khan* vs. *The State*[73] the

Supreme Court for the first time referred to the fundamental rights of the victim in an 'honour killing' case. The Court held that,

> Legally and morally speaking, nobody has any right nor can anybody be allowed to take law in his own hands to take the life of anybody in the name of 'Ghairat'. Neither the law of the land nor religion permits so-called honour killing, which amounts to murder (qatl-e-amd) simpliciter. Such iniquitous and vile act is violative of fundamental rights as enshrined in Article 9 of the Constitution of Islamic Republic of Pakistan, which provides that no person would be deprived of life and liberty except in accordance with law and any custom or usage in that respect is void under Article 8(1) of the Constitution.

Importantly, in these cases proper trials were held and the defence was unable to produce sufficient evidence to establish their claim that the deceased were killed for engaging in immoral acts. It is therefore yet to be seen whether the superior courts would similarly decide a case where the deceased had engaged in extramarital sex.

Equally encouraging, in terms of consistency in the application of the law,[74] is the Lahore High Court judgment in *Muhammad Siddique* vs. *The State*.[75] The case involved a man who had killed his daughter, her husband and their child following her choice marriage, claiming to have acted out of *ghairat*. The court proactively used its discretionary powers under s.338-E PCC to confirm the trial court's death sentence,[76] despite the fact that compromise had been reached during the High Court proceedings. In this case, for the first time, the court elaborated upon the circumstances in which such discretion could be exercised, including:

> criminal acts which are heinous on account of the number of people those are physically harmed or killed; or acts which are symbolic of a certain bias or prejudice against a section of society; or which are committed in the name of a creed or committed in reaction to the exercise of a fundamental right by the victim; or which cause general alarm and shock public conscience and acts which have the effect of striking at the fundamentals of a civil society.[77]

This judgment was clearly cognisant of the recent trend in 'honour crimes' where women are murdered after exercising their legal right to choice in marriage. The court went on to state that such offences require a judicial response, as

> A murder in the name of honour is not merely the physical elimination of a man or a woman. It is at a socio-political plane a blow to the concept of a free dynamic and an egalitarian society. In great majority of cases, behind it at play, is a certain mental outlook, and a creed which seeks to deprive equal rights to women i.e. inter alia the right to marry or the right to divorce which are recognised not only by our religion but have been protected in law and enshrined in the Constitution.[78]

The state's failure to utilise discretion positively

During the *Gul Hassan* case Justice Shafiur Rehman, commenting on the role and responsibility of the state in cases of murder and bodily hurt, noted that the decision to prosecute rests first with the victim or his/her heirs, a decision the state is dependent upon.[79] However, the final text of the new law did not absolve the state from its responsibility to prosecute violence against individuals, as murder and serious bodily hurt remained cognisable offences, obliging the state to act and prosecute. Equally, even where the heirs of the deceased have pardoned the perpetrator (with or without having received any compensation under s.311 PPC), under the concept of *fasad fil arz* (threat to the social order), the court still has the option of sentencing the perpetrator under *tazir* to a term of up to fourteen years' imprisonment. Similarly, s.338-E PPC grants courts wide discretionary powers to award a *tazir* sentence (no upper limit prescribed in law) for the offence of murder and bodily hurt, according to the nature of the offence and despite any waiver or compounding by the parties.

Yet a survey of murder appeals and revisions in the High Courts reveals that, aside from the cases of the early 1990s mentioned above, it is rare in 'honour killings' for the state to appeal against acquittal or for enhancement of sentence. Equally, where the right of *qisas* has been either waived or compounded, state counsel almost never press the court to use its s.311 PPC discretionary powers to sentence an accused. However, according to s.311 PPC, exercise of the discretion is conditional upon the lack of agreement between all heirs to waive or compound the right of *qisas* if the social order is threatened (*fasad fil arz*). Section 311 PPC states that 'fasad-fil-arz shall include the past conduct of the offender as being a previous convict, habitual or professional criminal and the brutal manner in which the offence is committed.' As many 'honour crimes' are particularly brutal, this section would seem to be available in many instances. However, the section also requires the court to consider 'the facts and circumstances of the case' while exercising its discretion, thus allowing social attitudes to influence implementation. This provision is further weakened by the possibility of the waiver of *qisas* and compromise; numerous cases never actually reach the stage where the court can examine the facts and circumstances of the case, as *qisas* can be waived or compounded at any stage, even at the start of the trial.

Further, the waiving or compounding of *qisas* halts all proceedings, so trial courts fail to record properly evidence relating to the facts and circumstances of the murder, making it difficult to establish a basis for the conviction of an accused under section 311's discretionary provisions. Even where the trial

Table 4.2 Figures for 'honour killings', 1998–2003, as presented by Federal Minister of the Interior to the Senate, 9 July 2004

Province	Total	Male victims	Female victims	Cases registered	Compromised	Pending in court
Punjab	2,253	675	1,578	1,834	1,412	422
Sindh	1,099	348	751	980	231	609
NWFP	448	188	260	361	185	167
Balochistan	301	116	185	276	41	23

Source: The News, 10 July 2004.

court convicts, the decision is likely to be overturned on appeal due to incorrect recording of the circumstances or other technicalities.

The trial courts' failure to follow basic procedures in such cases is further compounded by the High Courts' conflicting application of the law on compromise. For example, in *Nazar Ali*,[80] the accused had pleaded not guilty and requested a trial, but the heirs of the deceased claimed to have compounded the right of *qisas*. The trial court accepted this but sentenced the accused, under s.311 PPC, to five years imprisonment. On appeal, the Peshawar High Court acquitted the accused, setting aside the trial court's decision on the ground that discretionary *tazir* powers under s.311 PPC apply only where the murder committed was liable to *qisas* (unlike this case), and not when the murder is liable to *tazir*. This judgment was self-contradictory: while s.311 PPC certainly applies in cases of *qisas*, it is not clear how the court accepted the compromise (and consequent acquittal) because the accused himself did not accept that he had committed the offence and therefore had not been party to the compromise. This enables acquittal of the accused in 'honour killings' where the families of the deceased are all too willing to compromise.

In 'honour killings', the right of *qisas* is invariably either waived or compounded, as the murderers are often relatives of the victim, willing to forgive or compromise with each other. This therefore leaves no discretion to sentence such an accused. There have, however, been a few exceptions to this trend. In one case,[81] the trial court sentenced the accused to death for murdering his sister-in-law. She was survived by three children, her husband (the elder brother of her murderer) and her parents. While the appeal was pending, all her heirs, except her parents, pardoned the accused by waiving

Table 4.3 Figures for trial court decisions, 1998–2003, as presented by Federal Minister of the Interior to the Senate, 9 July 2004

Province	Decided cases	Sentences	Pending in appeal
Punjab	160 convicted	52 death 59 life 49 other	44 in High Court 1 in Supreme Court
Sindh	No details given	1 life 1 twenty-five years	No details given
NWFP	15 convicted 358 challaned/ under trial	No details given	No details given
Balochistan	Not mentioned	12 death 14 life	1 in High Court

Note: A challaned report is the final investigation report by the police, a 'pre-trial' report.
Source: *The News*, 10 July 2004.

their right of *qisas*. However, the court granted *diyat* to the parents and also ordered *badli sulah* (compensation in exchange for compromise) to the minor children, while the accused was sentenced to ten years' imprisonment under the discretion of *tazir* available to the court. This judgment, though positive, continues the confusion because there was no mention of the accused being convicted under *qisas*, so s.311 was apparently applied in a situation of *tazir*.

Overall, the state's failure to respond adequately to the problem of 'honour killings' is illustrated by the figures in Table 4.2, which confirms that, first, not all instances of 'honour killings' are registered and, second, a substantial proportion are compromised before reaching conviction, with most remaining cases taking years to drag through the courts.

The minister himself noted that because of certain legal complexities, the majority of pending cases would be compromised. Table 4.3 shows an even bleaker picture; out of a total of 2,253 'honour killings' in the Punjab since 1998, only 160 have resulted in trial court convictions. As the preceding discussion highlights, it can safely be presumed that a number of these sentences may be reduced or overturned on appeal. A survey of reported judgments over the period 1996–2003 shows only three cases involving murdered women reaching the Sindh High Court on appeal, all in 2002–3.

The state's failure to prosecute vigorously the murderers of women combines with the lack of interest shown by women's families in cases of 'honour killings'. In *Muhammad Mithal alias Waheed Bux* vs. *The State*,[82] the High Court passed a sentence of twenty-five years' imprisonment for the murder of the male victim, but only fourteen years in respect of the female victim, since neither her family nor the state pursued the matter of sentencing for her murder. Despite recent judgments condemning the brutality of 'honour crimes', the courts have been unwilling to move beyond applying s.302(c) PPC in cases of 'honour crimes', thus continuing to refuse to apply the maximum possible sentence (death, which can be applied in other murders).

Responses

Civil society

Civil society organisations, both in the larger cities and in smaller towns and villages, have for many years been engaged in combating 'honour crimes' and demanding official attention. Increasing media reporting, including the contributions of local and international filmmakers,[83] television serials[84] and theatre plays have all contributed to the often heated debate.

In April 1999 the killing of Samia Sarwar – allegedly for disgracing her family by seeking divorce without their consent – in the office of her lawyer, Hina Jilani,[85] particularly shocked the public conscience and catalysed both national and international responses. Reports by local and international human rights organisations (Amnesty International, 1999a, 1999b; Human Rights Watch, 1999; Human Rights Commission of Pakistan, 1999; Shirkat Gah, 2002), actions of the UN Special Rapporteur on violence against women, and the local press continue to highlight this inhuman practice, contributing to the increased visibility of 'honour crimes'. Civil society groups have launched dynamic campaigns against 'honour killings' through seminars, media campaigns and demands for law reform. They have also collaborated with certain governmental institutions, such as the National Commission on the Status of Women (NCSW), which convened meetings in the four provincial capitals with legal experts, human rights and women's rights activists, members of political parties, and religious scholars to discuss the loopholes in the law on murder and bodily hurt which benefit perpetrators of 'honour killings'.

In 2003, after lengthy consultations, civil society organisations drafted a legislative bill to combat 'honour killings and crimes'.[86] The draft bill seeks to amend the PPC and CrPC, adding a definition of 'honour killing', making this a non-compoundable offence and one for which ss.306(b), 306(c), 307(b), 309, 310, and 311 PPC should not apply. The bill proposes the addition of a new s.302(d) PPC. This provides that if *qisas* is not applicable under the injunctions of Islam, 'honour killings' should be subject to a maximum of twenty-five years' and a minimum of fourteen years' imprisonment. It also proposes the repeal of s.338-F PPC requiring the relevant provisions to be interpreted 'in accordance with injunctions of Islam'. 'Honour killings' are defined as follows:

> *qatl-e-amd* in the name of honour shall mean and include *qatl* on grounds or pretext of *karokari*, *siyahkari* or any other similar custom, or for the vindication of honour or *ghairat* under similar circumstances, or in anticipation of violation of honour or *ghairat* in similar circumstances, whether due to grave and sudden provocation or not.

State rhetoric

Successive administrations have so far only paid lip service to the issue. For example, despite public mobilisation over Samia Sarwar's murder, an attempt to introduce a resolution condemning 'honour crimes' in the Senate that same year could not even be heard (Siddiqui, 1999). More recently, although President General Pervez Musharraf has stated his unequivocal commitment to the eradication of the practice,[87] he has taken no concrete steps in this regard during his years of 'absolute power', other than isolated administrative measures in certain districts.[88]

A recently moved bill in the National Assembly, the Protection and Empowerment of Women Act 2004,[89] provides for prohibition of 'honour killings' and domestic violence, but has provoked widespread opposition from conservative forces, largely because it also seeks to repeal the infamous Hudood Ordinances (Asghar, 2004). Meanwhile, the efforts of certain members of the federal parliament and some provincial assemblies continue to be frustrated by the feudal attitude of the Treasury and opposition members. In August 2004, the Prime Minister was reported to be 'tak[ing] serious notice' of an increase in *karo-kari* cases after meeting two young doctors whose lives were threatened because of their choice marriage (*The News*, 18 August 2004); yet the same week Treasury members obstructed attempts by a woman member of the Treasury to inform the House of the need for state protection for this same couple. The disturbance led to the Speaker adjourning the session and expunging certain remarks from the parliamentary record (*Khabarain*, 20 August 2004).

In November 2003, when a resolution against 'honour killings' moved by a member of the Treasury benches was on the day's agenda in the National

Assembly, the Speaker would not allow him to present it. Further frustration followed when the item was rescheduled, and the mover was only given the microphone after he had walked out of the House in protest; he was later told by his colleagues to withdraw the resolution as those opposing it 'are, above all, Pathans and would not allow anybody to disturb their centuries old customs' (Habib, 2003; Haider, 2003). A comparable resolution met a similar fate in the Sindh Provincial Assembly the same month. A subsequent motion to enact a law moved in the Sindh Assembly by a woman member[90] also failed to attract support. However, efforts continued in the Sindh Assembly and a motion moved by a member of the Muthida Qaumi Movement was to be taken up in January 2004, but to date no law has been enacted by the provincial legislature (*Dawn, 22* January 2004). By contrast, particularly with regard to the stand of the provincial government, the Balochistan Assembly passed a resolution in January 2004 condemning 'honour killings' (*The News* 28 January 2004).

Over the past year, ministers, Members of Parliament, and retired superior court judges have participated in public forums and agreed to adopt measures of various kinds to combat the practice. In some instances this appears to be a response to pressure from progressive civil society groups, with participants remaining personally unconvinced of the need for reform. For example, an adviser to the government on education, Naseer Khoso, during a panel discussion, condemned 'honour killings' but said that he believed 'there are circumstances when men are so overpowered by what they perceive to be a slight to their 'honour', that they 'lose control' and are 'compelled' to kill their women' (*Daily Times*, 31 January 2004). In other instances, those who support law reform have been denied political space within their institutions to take effective action.

Courts

Although recent judgments do not yet reflect consensus on the issue, they do reflect increased attention to 'honour crimes' and related legal injustices. In 2003, the then Chief Justice of Pakistan took *suo motu* notice of the alleged killing of Shazia Khaskheli and her choice marriage husband Hasan Slangi on the orders of a tribal *jirga*. The Chief Justice sought an inquiry report from the subordinate judge concerned, and a police report. During the proceedings, a three-member full bench of the Supreme Court observed that the killing of young women and their husbands in the name of 'honour' is a considerable sin and that this practice should be terminated in Pakistan (*Daily Times* and *Khabrain*, 23 January 2004). Almost simultaneously, the Lahore High Court reached judgment in an appeal against conviction and sentence for the 'honour killing' of a man, holding that 'an accused in an 'honour killing' cannot be sentenced to death. He deserves concession. He cannot be acquitted either but death sentence is not justice with him' *(Nawa-e-waqt* and *Pakistan*, 13 February 2004).

Conclusion

The Law of Qisas and Diyat has been controversial from the start. As the cases discussed here demonstrate, human rights groups rightly opposed its 'privatisation' of 'honour crimes', and legal practitioners and judges rightly criticised its inherent anomalies.

Since 1990, debate has centred on whether murder and bodily hurt are now only crimes against the individual, or whether the state has any responsibility towards the victim and society in such instances. This question is directly related to the fundamental right to life as enshrined in Article 9 of the Constitution (1973), which the effective 'privatisation' of murder has substantially undermined. With the exception of a handful of progressive judgments, most fairly recent, the judiciary and the executive have both largely failed to protect this right, with the latter failing to take concrete measures to address either the practice or the law relating to honour 'crimes' or 'killings'. While perpetrators have enjoyed considerable judicial latitude in the courts, many others have never even faced the threat of legal action.

Under the new law, men who kill women for 'honour' cannot be brought to justice, given statutory limitations. Moreover, confusion continues over the applicable provisions, available sentences, their minimum and maximum limits, the criteria for compounding of cases and the availability of judicial discretion. More often than not, the exercise of wide judicial discretion, unfettered by any guidelines, in certain areas has been used to deny justice to women victims of 'honour killings'. The confusion created by the text of the law has in some instances also resulted in inhumane treatment of offenders, who have been subjected to conflicting judgments spread out over years regarding their death sentence.

Through these interpretations of the law, instead of systematically inter-vening to address violations of the right to life, judges have focused on the victim's conduct and have been influenced by and reflected customary attitudes condoning the control of and violence against women. Even in the most progressive judgments to date, when dealing with 'honour killings' the courts have continued to focus on the issue of 'provocation'. Although religion has been a reference point when debating issues of *masoom ud dam* and *qawam*, Muslim rules of evidence have been selectively ignored, revealing a convenient patriarchal bias in the application of religion.

Irrespective of the terms of the law, the general presumption both in the courts and in the popular imagination has been that the court's job is over as soon as a compromise is effected. The shabby judicial processes that have followed compromises reached in 'honour killings' have frustrated subsequent discretionary sentencing by the superior judiciary on appeal. But the superior judiciary is not fully absolved of responsibility. Aside from repeatedly failing to clarify interpretations of the new provisions, the High Courts and Supreme Court have themselves given judgments that have failed to provide justice for women victims of 'honour killings'. This is in contrast to the generally gender-sensitive nature of superior court judgments in, for example, family law cases.

Combined with the Zina Ordinance, the Law of Qisas and Diyat has reinforced the very notion of male control over women and the subordinated status of women in the family. In Pakistan's extended family context, this has meant women's continuing subordination to a wide range of male family members, who are seen as their 'protectors' and controllers. At precisely the point when the superior judiciary had begun to provide comparatively positive guidelines for the application of the Zina Ordinance, the Law of Qisas and Diyat was introduced, returning the debate on women's bodily autonomy and rights to square one.

Without the overhauling of existing provisions, and the framing of precise guidelines for application of the law, justice for victims of 'honour killings' will continue to be left to the interpretation of individual judges, subject to existing social biases. It remains to be seen whether the growing pressure from civil society, and certain judges, will push a reluctant government to take concrete and positive steps to address the situation.

Postscript

Immediately prior to the submission of the manuscript of this chapter, on 26 October 2004 the National Assembly of Pakistan passed a bill that purports to address 'honour crimes', which passed into law in January 2005. However, the measures contained in the legislation have been sharply criticised for failing to address adequately the concerns and demands of human rights groups. In particular the Joint Action Committee for People's Rights issued a press release on 1 November 2004 noting its 'strong exception to the Bill'. As the press release makes clear, the legislation does not address the basic problem of 'statutory concession' to the family members, who in the vast majority of cases are the perpetrators of 'honour crimes'. Nor does it provide a mandatory minimum sentence for 'honour killings' irrespective of the relation of the perpetrator to the victim. Worryingly, not only has the compounding of offences been retained, but any possibility of sentence in cases of compromises has been reduced by the amendment, which reads: 'An offence committed in the name of honour may be waived or compounded, subject to some conditions set by the court with the consent of the parties, keeping in view the facts and circumstances of the case.' In response to the bill the JAC demanded that the state assume its full responsibility under the law to register, investigate and prosecute all cases of 'honour crimes'; that the compounding of offences not be permitted in 'honour crimes' and a mandatory minimum sentence for such crimes be incorporated into the law; and finally that no 'legal concession' be granted to the family members as is available under s.306(b) and (c) of the Penal Code, and that a minimum mandatory sentence be incorporated in law (see also *Daily Times*, 4 November 2004). This legislation by no means represents a sufficient state response to 'honour crimes'; the critique contained in this chapter remains unaffected.

Notes

I would like to extend my thanks to Cassandra Balchin, Sara Hossain, Lynn Welchman, and particularly Sanchita Hosali for their assistance in producing this chapter. This chapter was submitted prior to the National Assembly passing a Bill on 'crimes of honour' on 26 October 2004. In this regard please refer to the postscript.

1. *Federation of Pakistan through Secretary, Law* vs. *Gul Hassan*, [PLD] 1989 Supreme Court [SC] 633, hereafter *Gul Hassan*.
2. *Qisas* and *diyat* are institutions in Islamic criminal law relating to deliberate murder and injury; *qisas* is 'exact retaliation' and *diyat* is monetary compensation.
3. Under which the local feudal leader and his companions determine the appropriate course of action, in a gathering known variously as a *panchayat* or *jirga* (traditional adjudication forums with an established composition, which today have no formal legal authority to decide on such matters).
4. A male who is co-accused with the woman has to pay in cash or kind or give a woman of his family in marriage to the family of the woman, in accordance with the findings of local 'adjudication' bodies (Shirkat Gah, 1996; Shah, 2002: 25).
5. When introducing the Criminal Law (Amendment) Bill – designed to address 'honour killings'- to Parliament in July 2004, opposition politician Aitzaz Ahsan said, 'We have paralysed our woman and sunk her into fear. We must liberate her from this fear' (*Dawn*, 21 July 2004).
6. According to one report, over the last three years 910 cases arising from such killings were registered, but only 293 (32 per cent) cases were completed, with only 25 (9 per cent) convictions and 260 (91 per cent) acquittals (Haider, 2003).

7. Today's Balochistan was then divided into 'British Balochistan' under direct British control, and the 'Balochistan States Union' with its own ruler.

8. During the British colonial period, District Magistrates/Collectors would compile gazettes to provide basic information about the area, its geography, history, climate, population, customary practices of the tribes, families in the district, etc. These gazettes served as guidebooks for the administration.

9. Practices which operated prior to the British occupation and which continued to be a point of reference during colonial rule.

10. Only the Zob district code mentions a widow.

11. Under s.5 Punjab Laws Act 1872 the rule of decision in matters of marriage, divorce, succession, and 'bastardy', would be any custom applicable to the parties, and the Muhammadan or the Hindu law if the parties were Muslims or Hindus. Other provinces and states had similar enactments governing the application of 'customary law' and personal law; e.g. the Bengal Laws Act 1876.

12. Under s.552 CrPC, a District Magistrate could order the immediate restoration of a woman or female child who had been abducted or unlawfully detained to her husband, parent, guardian or other person having lawful charge of her.

13. Section 304(1) PPC stated that to invoke this exception, the provocation must have been grave and sudden, which deprived the accused of self-control. It was no defence where provocation was sought by the accused, or was voluntary provocation received from anything done in obedience to law or by a public servant in the lawful exercise of his power or caused by another in lawful exercise of his right of private defence.

14. *Mangal Ganda* vs. *Emperor* A.I.R. 1925 Nagpur 37; *Dini* vs. *Emperor* A.I.R 1926 Lahore 485; *MD Zaman* vs. *Emperor* A.I.R. 1933 Lahore 165.

15. *Emperor* vs. *Dinbandhu* A.I.R. 1930 Calcutta 199.

16. *Potharaju* vs. *Emperor* A.I.R. 1932 Madras 25(1). Ibid., p. 25.

17. See also *Emperor* vs. *Jate Uraon* A.I.R. 1940 Patna 541.

18. See further the National Assembly debates as reproduced in *Hakim Khan* vs. *The Government of Pakistan* PLD 1992 SC 595; and Maluka, 1995.

19. The Penal Code was amended in 1979 when the Hudood Ordinances were introduced, while the Law of Evidence was amended in 1984.

20. The Eighth Amendment changed seventeen articles of the Constitution and affected sixty-five articles. See further Khan, 1995.

21. *Mohammed Sharif* vs. *The State* PLD 1987 Lahore 312, para. 7, p. 315.

22. *Mohammed Saleh* vs. *The State* PLD 1965 SC 446.

23. Sections 299–338 PPC, 1860, and sections 45, 337, 345, and 381 CrPC 1898.

24. See note 1. Appeals to the Federal Shariat Court (FSC) lie to the Shariat Appellate Bench of the Supreme Court, Pakistan's apex court. The FSC hears cases under the Hudood Ordinances (1979) and is empowered under the Constitution to examine the conformity of any law with the injunctions of Islam. All other legal matters are dealt with by Pakistan's regular civil and criminal courts. Cases under the Law of Qisas and Diyat are tried by Sessions Courts, with appeals generally going to the provincial High Courts and thereafter to the Federal Supreme Court.

25. *Tazir* is punishment other than *qisas, diyat, arsh or daman* (the latter being various forms of monetary compensation). Under the penal provisions, the quantum on punishment for *tazir* is in certain instances specified in law, while in other situations it is left to the discretion of the court. These are discussed below.

26. *Federation of Pakistan* vs. *NWFP Government* PLD 1990 SC 1172.

27. However, s.304 PPC and Article 17 of the Qanoon-e-Shahdat Order do not specify the number of witnesses and merely refer to the injunctions of the Koran and Sunna, which are subject to interpretation.

28. For example when an heir waives the right of *qisas* under s.309 or compounds under s.310 PPC.

29. The Law of Qisas and Diyat has rendered women vulnerable in other ways which are beyond the scope of discussion here. For example, when a woman's husband or blood relatives are killed, she is pressurised by the remaining members of the family or the murderer's family to compromise. See *Muhammad Arshad alias Pappu* vs. *Additional Sessions Judge* Lahore PLD 2003 SC 547 and *Muhammad Saleem* vs. *The State* PLD 2003 SC 512.

30. For example, *Muhammad Ashraf* vs. *The State* PLD 1991 Lahore 347; *Nazar Ali* vs. *The State* PLD 1992 Peshawar 176; *Muhammed Ishaq* vs. *The State* PLD 1992 Peshawar 187; *Nisar Ahmad and two others* vs. *The State* 1994 PCrLJ 1587; *Sadaf Ali* vs. *The State* PLD 1991 SC 202; *Javed Msaih* vs. *The State* 1993 SCMR 1574.

31. *Sheikh Muhammad Aslam* vs. *Shaukat Ali alias Shauka* 1997 SCMR 1307, at paras 22–24, pp. 1329–30.

32. *Muhammad Saleem* vs. *The State* PLD 2003 SC 512 and *Muhammad Arshad alias Pappu* vs. *Additional Sessions* Judge, Lahore PLD 2003 SC 547.

33. *Nazar Ali* vs. *The State*.

34. Under the previous PPC s.300 exception, read in conjunction with 304(1) PPC, an accused could rely upon the mitigating circumstances of the murder to obtain a lesser sentence by pleading the defence of 'grave and sudden provocation'.

35. *Gul Hassan*, p. 674, as discussed by Justice Taqi Usmani.

36. Ibid.

37. The Court referred only generally to the evidence required for conviction of *zina*.

38. *The State* vs. *Abdul Waheed, alias Waheed and another* 1992 PCrLJ 1596.

39. This was an appellate court hearing decisions against the specially constituted Anti-Terrorist Courts, and its decision was final. The case fell to this now defunct forum because an automatic weapon had been used.

40. Article 121 Qanoon-e-Shahdat [Law of Evidence] Order 1984: 'When a person is accused of an offence, the burden of proving the existence of circumstances bringing the case within any of the general exceptions in the Pakistan Penal Code or within any special exception or proviso contained in any other part of the same Code or in any law defining the offence is upon him and Court shall presume the absence of such circumstances.'

41. *Mohib Ali* vs. *The State* 1985 SCMR 2055 p. 2059.

42. *The State* vs. *Muhammad Hanif* 1992 SCMR 2047.

43. *Ghulam Yaseen* vs. *The State* PLD 1994 Lahore 392.

44. Ibid., para. 13, p. 396.

45. The judgment quoted several *hadith* in Urdu, ibid., para 14, pp. 396–7, including a *hadith* reported in *Sahih Bokhari* relating the story of Saad bin Abaadah and the Prophet's apparent endorsement of 'honour crimes'.

46. Ibid., para. 17, p. 398.

47. Ibid., para. 18, p. 398.

48. Koran 4:34.

49. Interpretation of this verse differs among classical jurists, as well as being contested by modernist proponents of women's rights in Islam. See Stowasser, 1998, for examples.
50. *Abdul Haque* vs. *The State* 1996 SCMR 1566.
51. *Abdul Haque* vs. *The State* PLD 1996 SC 1.
52. Ibid., para. 56, p. 33, and para. 8, p. 39.
53. PLD 1996 SC 274.
54. Ibid., pp. 279–80, para. 4.
55. Ibid. para. 25, p. 289.
56. Ibid., para. 29, p. 290.
57. *Muhammad Faisal* vs. *The State* 1997 MLD 2527 at para. 5, p. 2528.
58. *Muhammad Ibrahim* vs. *Soofi Abdul Razzaq* 1997 PCrLJ 63, at p. 276.
59. Ibid., para. 8, at p. 268.
60. Ibid., p. 276.
61. 1999 SCMR 2203.
62. *Khalil Uz Zaman* vs. *Supreme Appellate Court*, Lahore PLD 1994 SC 885; para. 10, 893.
63. *Faqir Ullah* vs. *Khalil uz Zaman* 1999 SCMR 2203; para.19 2214.
64. The first decision was pronounced on 3 August 1994, and the second on 10 May 1999.
65. *Sardar Mohammad* vs. *The State* 1997 MLD 3045; para. 13, 3049.
66. *Muhammad Ayub* vs. *The State* 1997 PCrLJ 2056.
67. Ibid., para. 10, p. 2060.
68. *Amanullah* vs. *The State* 1997 MLD 1402; para. 12 p. 1406.
69. *Imam Bakhsh* vs. *The State* 1999 YLR 19; para. 19(a) p. 25.
70. Ibid., para. 19 (j), p. 26.
71. 1999 PCrLJ 459; para. 9, p. 553. See also *Mukhtar Ahmad* vs. *The State* 2000 YLR 860 [Lahore].
72. 2000 SCMR 406 para. 19, p 413. *Siyakari* is a Balochi term for all sexual relationships outside marriage.
73. PLD 2001 SC 96; para. 3 p. 100. See also *Muhammad Khan* vs. *The State* PLJ 2001 CrC (Quetta) 978.
74. Please note, it is not the author's intention to advocate or support the death penalty; indeed, as the discussion below notes (third section, 'Responses'), civil society demands for the reform of the law do not include provision of the death penalty.
75. PLD 2002 Lahore 444. The court also referred to *Faqirullah* vs. *Khalil-uz-Zaman and others* 1999 SCMR 2203, p. 2214.
76. Following the provisions of 306(b) PPC, *qisas* and a death sentence under any other provision did not apply in the instance of the murder of the accused's daughter and granddaughter, but he received death as *tazir* for murdering his son-in-law.
77. *Muhammad Siddique* vs. *The State* PLD 2002 Lahore 444, paras 15 and 16, p. 454.
78. Ibid., para. 24, p. 457.
79. *Gul Hassan*, para. 4, p. 685.
80. *Nazar Ali* vs. *The State* PLD 1992 Peshawar 176.
81. *Muratab Ali* vs. *The State* KLR 1994 Criminal Cases 256.

82. PLD 2003 Karachi 655.
83. See, for example the BBC documentary 'Murder in Purdah' (1999) and its sequel, 'Licence to Kill' (2000).
84. See, for example, the television serials *Taquab* (2002) and *Ghairat* (2001) in Pakistan on PTV.
85. Now UN Special Representative for Human Rights Defenders.
86. The draft bill was prepared by women's rights and human rights organisations, along with concerned individuals including members of the Bar and several retired judges. The bill has proposed amendments in the PPC and CrPC and has been circulated to the major political parties.
87. 'The government of Pakistan vigorously condemns the practices of so-called honor killings. Such acts do not find a place in our religion or law. Killing in the name of honor is murder and will be treated as such' (Convention on Human Rights, Islamabad, 20 April 2000). 'I would like to urge all those in positions of authority to show that we are a tolerant, educated, progressive society and we do not tolerate honour killings' (BBC News Online, 10 February 2004).
88. For example, in November 2001, the district government in Larkana, Sindh (an area with a high incidence of 'honour crimes'), decided that to ensure the proper prosecution of *karo-kari* cases and to avoid relatives withdrawing statements, the local police station house officer would be the named complainant in such cases rather than the victim's relatives (*Dawn*, 12 November 2001).
89. The bill was introduced in the National Assembly in March 2004 as a private member's bill moved by Sherry Rehman of the Pakistan People's Party.
90. Ms Humera Alwani moved the motion on 12 December 2003.

5

Murders of women in Lebanon:
'crimes of honour' between reality and the law

DANIELLE HOYEK, RAFIF RIDA SIDAWI

AND AMIRA ABOU MRAD

The research on which this chapter is based forms part of a wider project on the part of the Lebanese Council to Resist Violence against Women, initiated after a conference convened by the Council on the subject of 'crimes of honour' in May 2001. The conference recommended *inter alia* the repeal of Article 562 of the Lebanese Penal Code. The term 'crimes of honour', in use in common parlance among the public and the media, does not appear in Lebanese law. However, Article 562 of the Penal Code is related to what are known as 'crimes of honour' and gives scope for the perpetrators of such crimes to escape the penalty set for the crime of deliberate or intentional murder. This research aims to provide a historical, legal and social analysis of Article 562 and the judicial treatment of 'crimes of honour' through an examination of case files and the jurisprudence of Lebanese courts.

'Crimes of honour' in Lebanon

In this part of the world, the ignoble phrase 'crime of honour' hides many tragedies. The prime reason for this lies in regressive intellectual discourses and the patriarchal order that still governs the region, resulting directly in the condoning of the killing of women under a pretext created by the perpetrators themselves (and serving their own interests) – that of 'defence of honour' or 'washing away the shame'.

A brief consideration of the two key elements in the phrase 'crimes of honour' is in order. The first, 'crime', is defined differently by various thinkers. Tarde defines is as 'violation of a right, or breach of a duty', while

Ferri defines it as 'unsocial action directed against a certain right'. Maxwell defines it as 'any action penalised in a particular political society, by virtue of written law or prevailing customs'. Garofalo distinguishes between actions considered violative of norms and customs agreed upon in one society and actions considered violative in all societies, times and climes. In Arabic, the second term, *sharaf*, is defined as exaltedness (*'uluw*) or glory (*majd*). The question is thus posed: where are 'crimes of honour' between these two concepts?

In these types of crimes, the victim is always a woman, related to the criminal by a blood tie up to the fourth degree – thus the mother, daughter, sister, paternal niece, paternal or maternal cousin, etc. – or by the marriage bond. The perpetrator is usually a man, very occasionally a woman raised on male values. The victim may be single, married, divorced or widowed. The crime attributed to her is having sexual intercourse with a man to whom she is not married. People call this forbidden relationship *zina*[1] and society's condemnation means that it is a source of shame (*'ar*) for the relatives of the woman concerned, tarnishing their honour (*sharaf*) to the extent that the only way to wipe away the shame – and restore the tarnished honour – is to remove the thing that caused it: that is, for a member of the woman's family to kill her.

Two things thus become clear. First, that sexual intercourse outside marriage impugns the honour of the female involved, not the male partner. Second, that a woman's honour is the property of her male relatives, not her own property; she is merely a custodian of this honour, bound to safeguard it for the man's sake under penalty of death by his hand. This is despite the fact that the woman's partner in such a relationship is a man, without whose participation – and likely initiative – no crime could occur. The woman faces the consequences alone.

Socio-historical context

Despite all the changes that have occurred in the situation of women in the East in the modern age, the relationship between men and women inside the family is still governed by the remnants of the idea of slavery. Slavery historically came about with the establishment of private property and then the patriarchal order, which made the man, the father, the owner of everything, with absolute authority *inter alia* over all the individuals of his family. Wife and children were a natural extension of the property of the head (*rabb*) of the family (the *paterfamilias*); indeed the use of the word *rabb*[2] denotes hierarchy, authority and ownership.[3] In the early stages of the 'patriarchal family', the father used to have the right to kill his wife and children just as he had the right to kill his slave.

The remarkable economic and scientific developments of the current age – which determine social relations between people – have not yet managed to erase once and for all the heavy heritage of this patriarchal order and the stamp it has left on how recognised rights are understood in Lebanese society, although it varies in intensity according to different geographical areas and particular affiliations of the various sectors of the Lebanese people. The remnants of these concepts derive their power and legitimacy from a variety of sources, notably the dominant culture, popular and religious heritage and the law. The dominant culture does not recognise a role for women apart from that of wife and mother. If a woman is permitted to pursue her studies or get a job, this is in order to improve her chances of marriage and is on condition that it does not conflict with her basic role in serving her husband and looking after his children. The upbringing of girls establishes this role and encourages them to emphasise their femininity in order to be desirable to men, while forbidding them to mix with men to the extent of 'criminalising' an emotional relationship with them. A woman's body is a tool for the husband's pleasure and for procreation; it is a 'shameful thing' ('awra)[4] that must be guarded by the family – and, beyond it, society – to which it belongs. While a woman is single, her body belongs to her father's family; when she is married, her husband and his family share this ownership.

Values, ideas, customs, morals and traditions change according to time and place, with changes in social and economic circumstances, type and level of civilisation and the level of religious adherence and duties. Religion was revealed – originally – for the benefit of people without discrimination between men and women. Nevertheless there are jurists (who are men) who are not ashamed to give erroneous interpretations of certain verses of the revelation in order to attribute divine legitimacy to their 'authority' (qiwama) over women on the pretext that God preferred men to women and thus gave men the right of control, possibly reaching the extent of ownership and disposal rights over mind and body alike. These range from the ancients, who held that a woman's husband was her 'Baal' (her lord and master), through the jurists, who held woman responsible for Adam's expulsion from paradise, through al-Ghazzali and others, who hold that 'a woman has ten sources of shame (awrat); if she marries then her husband covers (satara) one of them, and if she dies the grave covers all ten'. This heavy heritage is still very much in the minds of those who have yet to enter the twenty-first century and accept the idea of natural rights and the principle of equality, innate to every human being from birth to death, regardless of affiliations beyond his or her choice, including sexual affiliation.

The crime of woman murder under the pretext of 'washing away the shame' and protecting honour, which is owned exclusively by men, is entirely unacceptable. It should not be condoned in a country such as Lebanon, a founding member of the United Nations and participant in the preparation and promulgation of the Universal Declaration of Human Rights, a country which is bound by the texts of various international human rights conventions and treaties, having ratified them and given them precedence over domestic laws in case of conflict. Challenges on such grounds, and on grounds of the irrelevance of Article 562 to Lebanese court practice, were made by civil society actors from the early 1970s. The recent half-hearted amendment to the text came at a time when the article as a whole should have been repealed. We hope that an examination of the files on these crimes will shed light on this question and support the arguments for the abolition of Article 562 of the Lebanese Penal Code and the repeal of any other legal text that provides for discrimination between one citizen and another before the law and the courts.

The concept of 'crime of honour' in Lebanese law

Historical overview of Article 562

Today's Lebanon, as a state and political entity, achieved settled and established borders on 1 September 1920, when France, the mandatory power, returned the Beqaa valley to Mount Lebanon and declared the birth of 'the state of greater Lebanon'. The French Mandate over Lebanon began with the end of the First World War and the collapse of the Ottoman Empire, and ceased with the end of the Second World War when Lebanon achieved independence. Prior to that, from 1516, Lebanon had been part of the Ottoman Empire and was consequently subject to Ottoman legislation, drawn mostly from the Islamic *shari'a*. After the advent of Napoleonic codes and their spread through Europe and the West generally, the Ottoman state came under pressure from European powers and the peoples in the Ottoman domains to undertake its own process of codification. A set of modern secular codes were promulgated, drawn notably from French legislation with its roots in Roman law. Italian texts were also influential. Ottoman criminal law continued in force during the French Mandate period until the promulgation of the current Lebanese Penal Code in 1943.[5] On the subject of so-called 'crimes of honour', the Ottoman law provided as follows:

> Article 188: He who sees his wife or any of his *mahrams*[6] with another person in a situation of disgraceful *zina* and beats, injures or kills one or both of them

shall be exempted.[7] He who sees his wife or one of his *mahrams* with another person in an unlawful bed and beats, injures or kills one or both of them shall be excused.[8]

This text was derived from Article 324 of the French Penal Code of 1810, itself influenced by Roman legislation which sanctified the patriarchal order and considered paternal and marital authority to be absolute.[9] Article 324 was repealed from the French Code in 1975 along with other texts related to *zina*. In Lebanon, the secular laws issued from the beginning of the French Mandate period were drawn to a large extent from French law, including the equivalent provision in the Lebanese Penal Code of 1943.

Article 562 pre-amendment

Before its amendment the text of Article 562 of the Lebanese Penal Code provided as follows:

> Whosoever surprises his spouse[10] or one of his ascendants or descendants or his sister in a witnessed crime of adultery (*flagrante delicto*) or in a situation of unlawful intercourse and proceeds to kill or injure one of them, without deliberation, shall benefit from the excuse of exemption. The person who kills or injures on surprising his spouse or one of his ascendants or descendants or his sister in a suspicious situation with another person shall benefit from the excuse of mitigation.

In the first case the Lebanese legislator granted a complete exemption from penalty, while in the second the 'excuse of mitigation' required a considerable reduction in the legal penalty; both were binding on the judge, unlike 'mitigating reasons' provided for elsewhere in the Code. The granting of these excuses contradicted Article 549(3) of the Penal Code, which provides for the death penalty for intentional murder of an ascendant or descendant. Application of Article 562 required the combination of the following conditions:

The element of surprise

If the perpetrator already knew of the relationship between the victim and her partner, then the element of surprise is negated and the perpetrator cannot benefit from the legal excuse.

Caught in the act

The victim has to be caught in the unlawful act with her partner in order for the excuse of exemption to apply, or to be caught in a suspicious situation in order for the excuse of mitigation to apply. Being 'caught in the act' does not here require the perpetrator to actually see the victim at the moment she commits the act, but rather that all factors are present to make him certain that it has been committed. A 'suspicious situation' is one that creates in the perpetrator a belief (not certain knowledge) that an act of unlawful intercourse has occurred, was expected to occur, or was on the point of occurring.

Immediate commission of the crime of murder or injury

The excuse of exemption is granted the perpetrator by reason of his presence in a situation of spontaneous reaction as a result of the shock, which is gone once the immediate reaction passes. This is considered a subjective matter and is left to the discretion of the judge.

When all these elements are combined, the perpetrator may invoke the legal excuses provided for in Article 562. Those who are entitled to benefit from the excuses are the husband, ascendants and descendants and the brother or half-brother.

Attempts to abolish Article 562

Article 562 was heavily criticised by a number of Lebanese male and female jurists, including the late Laure Moghaizel and Abdullah Lahoud. Various civil society bodies and women's associations lobbied to have it amended with a view to its eventual repeal in full. In 1970 a socio-legal study by advocate Mona Zahil (1968) examining 118 judicial rulings on the subject issued by Lebanese courts 1958–68 was presented along with a memorandum setting out the reasons necessitating amendment to a number of deputies from the legal profession and to the ministers. The arguments can be summarised as follows:

- That the principle of equality between men and women is in the vanguard of human rights, a principle that Lebanon, as other civilised states, has called for. This principle prohibits distinction between the husband and the wife in situations covered by Article 562 and any other situation.
- That both spouses are bound to each other in marriage and each may be jealous and may react upon seeing the other violating this bond, being deeply hurt. A woman's psychological state in such cases is no less affected than a man's; both are bound by the duty of marital fidelity, which cannot be valid as a legal excuse for brothers, ascendants and descendants.
- That the leniency of court rulings in these matters does nothing to prevent such crimes.

The memorandum then proceeded to propose a text to replace the said Article 562, as follows:

> the spouse (male or female) who surprises his(/her) spouse in the situation of committing observed adultery and kills or injures without deliberation shall benefit from the excuse of mitigation. The fact that the husband or wife benefits from the excuse of mitigation shall not prevent the judge from granting mitigating reasons at sentencing, when required.

The proposed text differs from the original by (i) equating husband and wife as perpetrator of the crime or victim thereof; (ii) cancelling the excuse of exemption and maintaining only the excuse of mitigation; (iii) constraining the right to benefit from the excuse of mitigation – when applicable – to the spouses, to the exclusion of other family members; (iv) Canceling the excuse of mitigation in cases of 'suspicious situation'.

In 1975 Deputy August Bakhous, supported by organisations active in the field of human rights, proposed to the parliament an urgent law backed by a thorough legal study, aimed at repealing Article 562. The proposal did not proceed to become law. It was not to be until the late 1990s that an amendment was eventually passed.

Article 562 post-amendment

In 1996 Lebanon ratified the Convention on the Elimination of All Forms of Discrimination Against Women, and Lebanese NGOs redoubled their efforts for the amendment of Article 562. In 1998, at a meeting held in commemoration of the late Laure Moghaizel[11] by the Lebanese Women's Council, the Minister of Justice announced that he had referred to the parliament a draft law to repeal the 'excuse of exemption' from Article 562 of the Penal Code 'because it encouraged a form of private justice'. The draft text was ratified by the administration and justice committee on 3 December 1998, and subsequently by the parliament on 10 February 1999, when it became law.

It will be recalled that the original text of Article 562 had been, in effect, in Lebanese law despite the 1975 repeal of its source text in French law. However, the amendment introduced into Lebanese law in 1999[12] was confined to simply replacing the 'excuse of exemption' in the first paragraph with the 'excuse of mitigation' and deleting the second paragraph. The amended text thus reads as follows:

> Whosoever surprises his spouse or one of his ascendants or descendants or his sister in a crime of observed adultery, or in a situation of unlawful intercourse,

and kills or injures one of them without deliberation shall benefit from the excuse of mitigation.

The amendment did not state equality in treatment between the husband and the wife as perpetrator or victim, and retained the right of male ascendants and descendants to benefit from the legal excuse in the same way as the husband. As noted above, the Minister of Justice's explanation of the amendment was a desire to discourage 'private justice'. As commonly understood, private justice – that is, revenge (*tha'ar*) – involves the idea of retaliation on the victim by the perpetrator directly and without proceedings at court, in an act of revenge by the latter for violation of a *shar'i* right by the former. For this interpretation to apply to the crimes stipulated in Article 562, blind acceptance of the following assumptions would be required:

- that any sexual relationship outside marriage is a shame (*'ar*) and a sullying of the woman's honour;
- that this honour is the property of her husband or her male relatives, not of the woman herself;
- that the woman bears immediate and full responsibility for this sullying of her honour, whether it happened by her positive or negative will, or even if it occurred against her will, and she deserves the maximum physical penalty;
- that a woman implicated under the terms of Article 562 may be twice a victim of the man: first when she is assaulted by the man, and second when she has to pay with her life for what he did.

In effect, this means that the remnants of the 'patriarchal order' inherited from the ancient Romans still dominates the legislation of a country that considers itself in the vanguard of progress, civilisation and respect for human rights in the Middle East. Elsewhere, more advanced countries repealed all penal provisions related to adultery over twenty-five years ago. In such countries adultery is now considered a breach of one of the most important conditions of the contract of marriage and leads, upon request of the other spouse, to dissolution of the contract. As for other males of the family, they have no rights over a person who engages in an extramarital sexual relationship because the shame – if there be any – is incurred by the guilty party alone and does not extend to relatives. As for 'assault', it is the guilty party who must be interrogated, rather than his victim, upon request of the victim if she is an adult or by a guardian or custodian if she is a minor or lacking legal capacity.

Conflict between Article 562 and superior laws

In its constitution, Lebanon has committed itself to the principle of justice and equality for all Lebanese before the law. Paragraph (c) of the preamble provides that 'Lebanon is a parliamentary democracy based on ... social justice and equality in rights and duties between all citizens without discrimination or preference.' Article 7 provides that 'All Lebanese are equal before the law' with 'Lebanese' including women and men alike. The text of Article 562, along with certain other legal provisions, discriminates blatantly between men and women and therefore contradicts the letter and spirit of the Constitution. It is the lower text that should be overridden by the superior, rather than other way round.

Furthermore, Lebanon has voluntarily become a party to a number of international conventions and charters that invoke the principle of equality and require the abolition of all forms of discrimination between one person and another on grounds beyond their choice and will. By this, Lebanon has undertaken to be bound by the provisions of these instruments and to give them preference in application over the provisions of ordinary law in the event of a conflict between the two. The preferential application of the superior law in such cases is stipulated in Article 2(2) of the Law of Civil Procedure. Lebanon is bound by the most important international charter, the Universal Declaration of Human Rights, which rejects all discrimination on grounds of sex; while, by ratifying CEDAW, Lebanon is obliged to revise all legal texts that discriminate between men and women, starting with penal law because of its immediate and substantial impact on people's lives, freedom and dignity.

Legal analysis of the research sample

This section is based on a study of the files obtained from research into the judgments rendered in cases of murder committed against women under the pretext of 'defence of honour' in the records of the Court of Cassation, criminal courts and courts of first instance dealing with juvenile crime in the six governorates of Lebanon (Beirut, Mount Lebanon, Bekaa, North Lebanon, South Lebanon and Nabatiyya). They numbered twenty-five files, with the focus mostly on judgments issued 1998–2003. Two earlier studies preceded the current research into this subject. The first, by Mona Zahil (1968) and already mentioned above, covered a total of 118 judgments issued in the years 1958–1968. The second was carried out by lawyers Fadi Moghaizel and Miryella 'Abd al-Satir (1999) examining 36 rulings issued from 1995 to April 1998, before the 1999 amendment of Article 562.

For the purposes of our research, a data sheet was completed for each file, including the information required by the research, particularly information assisting in the identification of the social environment of the victim and the perpetrator, as well as the legal process – stages of investigation and trial, matters of legal text and interpretation. We experienced difficulty in obtaining these files due to lack of clarity in the recording of such cases in the court registers – these simply record 'murder', although we were enquiring about the possible existence of files related to murders committed against women by family members or relatives. This is indicative of the socio-legal problematic that the concept of honour (*sharaf*) goes unremarked in Lebanese law.

It is important to underline that the twenty-five files that we managed to obtain do not constitute a complete survey of all so-called 'crimes of honour'. This type of crime does not always come before the courts. Some are covered up by the family of the victim to avoid scandal and shame, and to protect the perpetrator from punishment, while in others the facts are distorted to portray a suicide or an accident, a matter of 'fate and destiny'.[13]

It was clear from the files that a number of crimes committed under the title 'crimes of honour' or 'washing away the shame' were not in fact such, although the perpetrator attempted to hide behind this pretext in order to benefit from the excuse of mitigation in Article 562 as amended. These include a husband who wanted to get rid of his first wife (the mother of his children) when she had gone to court to oblige him to pay maintenance after he had taken a second wife and found himself unable to maintain two separate households. Then there was a husband who used to beat his wife all the time for no reason; when she complained to her family, after putting up with his tyranny for years, he killed her along with her sister. This man acknowledged that his wife had been pure and chaste. A father killed his pregnant daughter recently divorced from her husband, because she was refusing to have an abortion to ease the burden of her pregnancy on him and his wife; this father had divorced the victim's mother when his daughter was 2 years old and entrusted her upbringing to her paternal aunt until she got married at 22. Another man killed his daughter-in-law because her husband (his son) was refusing to divorce her. And a brother killed his married sister because he didn't like the marriage...

These are real examples of the sort of personal reasons for the killing of women on the part of murderers who try in court to throw the easy (and in these cases standard) accusation at the victim of having 'brought shame' to him or his family. Here, those with personal interests may waive their rights in the trial, unconcerned with following the trial to defend the reputation of the victim and her innocence of the allegations made against her. The family of one of the victims in the files waived their right to claims against the accused, father-in-law of the victim, after the latter's sister married the victim's husband; in another, a father waived his rights against the husband of the victim after agreeing to a reconciliation involving a financial payment.[14]

Nevertheless, in the absence of personal claims, or if these are not pressed, the Lebanese courts tend generally to show compassion for the killer and to reduce the penalty through recognising 'mitigating reasons'. Most penalties in the files were reduced on the basis of Article 253, which empowers the judge to reduce the penalty if convinced that the perpetrator had mitigating reasons (not the 'excuse of mitigation').[15] Not one ruling was issued on the basis of Article 562 of the Penal Code. The crimes covered in the twenty-five files were by no means all similar, although all might be categorised as 'crimes of honour' as popularly understood, and despite constant attempts by the perpetrators to hide behind this phraseology in the hope of a reduction in penalty.

Therefore, maintaining Article 562 in the Penal Code is of no utility; rather, its repeal appears more necessary and urgent now than at any time in the past, since the damage it does is clear:

- it encourages the commission of crimes of murder against women, through giving the perpetrator the hope of benefiting from it after disguising the motivations for murder;
- it sanctifies the principle of sexual inequality between citizens before the law, in violation of Article 7 of the Lebanese Constitution and the contents of the various international human rights instruments by which Lebanon is bound;
- it is of no practical use as judicial interpretation is unconvinced of its utility and indifferent to its existence, so long as the terms of Article 253 enable the judge to take mitigating reasons into consideration when required.

Lebanese jurisprudence regarding crimes of woman murder

The twenty-five files in the research sample revealed that twenty-two of the perpetrators were transferred for trial on charges under Article 549 of the Penal Code, which provides for the death penalty in cases of intentional murder in certain circumstances,[16] and three under the terms of Article 547, which stipulates a penalty of between fifteen and twenty years of hard labour for intentional murder. However, the fact that the criminal act is classified in a particular way in the charge sheet when the alleged perpetrator is sent for trial does not prevent the court from reclassifying it if it considers this appropriate. Cases take a long time to come before the criminal court, after the preliminary investigations and the questioning; the accused may appoint a defence lawyer who presents the facts to the court as he sees appropriate, while the witnesses, usually relatives of the perpetrator, give statements different from those they recorded before the police or the investigating judge (*juge d'instruction*).

Thus we find that of the twenty-five cases, fifteen perpetrators were convicted under Article 549, seven under Article 547, one under Article 553 (which deals with assisting suicide[17]) and two under Article 554 (injury).[18] The courts did not apply Article 562, considering the act of the perpetrator to constitute the crime of murder as stipulated in Articles 547 and 549. They also generally declined to apply Article 193, which allows for sentences to be reduced in the manner set out in the text if the judge finds that the motivation for the criminal act was 'honourable' (*sharaf*), or Article 252, which provides the 'excuse of mitigation' to a perpetrator who committed the crime in an outburst of extreme rage[19] resulting from an 'unrightful' and dangerous act on the part of the victim. The accused did, however, benefit from 'mitigating reasons' under the terms of Article 253. Only two of the sentences applied Article 193 (with the accused stating that the motivation for the crime was pregnancy from illegitimate sexual relations)[20] and only one Article 252 (where the accused stated that his motivation was marital infidelity). These rulings can be compared to others where the same motivations were claimed but the court did not apply articles 193 or 252. The following extracts illustrate court practice in regard to these three articles (193, 252, and 253).

Jurisprudence regarding Article 193

The law requires that in order for an accused to benefit from article 193 regarding 'honourable motives', two elements must coincide: that the motive for committing the crime be characterised by chivalry and decency; and that it be free from the taint of selfishness, personal considerations and material gain.[22] This is illustrated in the following extracts from court rulings:

Case 1, where the motivation claimed by the accused was the illegitimate pregnancy of his daughter the victim:

> Whereas the court considers in accordance with the defence petitions and the charge sheet that the accused may benefit from Article 193 of the Penal Code as

he committed his crime driven by chivalry and decency[22] which were impressed upon him by customs in which he was rooted and traditions which were a constant and precious part of his daily life.[23]

Case 2, where the motivation claimed by the accused was the illegitimate pregnancy of his sister the victim:

> Whereas the court considers that the accused committed the crime with the motivation of preserving the honour and dignity of his family in a manner free of selfishness, which requires that he benefit from Article 193.[24]

Case 3, where according to her statement the accused, the mother of the victim, was motivated by the illegitimate pregnancy of her daughter, and where, although the perpetrator remained unknown, it appeared from the investigations that it was probably the victim's brother, with the mother admitting that she had committed the crime alone in order to take sole responsibility and protect her son from penalty:

> Whereas the role of the accused was confined to giving the perpetrator instructions consisting of telling him that the deceased had fallen pregnant through illegitimate sexual relations, in an environment with no solution except to wash away the shame by murder at the hands of those closest to her; further, her mother (the accused) helped the perpetrator with the acts preparatory to the crime by accompanying him to the place it happened.... And whereas the defence sought application of Article 193 on the basis that the motivation was honourable, and whereas the additional paragraph of said Article 193 stipulates that the motivation is honourable if driven by chivalry and decency removed from selfishness, personal considerations and material gain, and whereas the motivation for commission of the crime in question was not removed from selfishness and personal considerations, this request by the defence must be refused.[25]

Case 4, where the accused was the brother of the victim and stated the motivation as the bad behaviour of the victim and her engaging in prostitution with the knowledge and assistance of her husband:

> Whereas the accused when he killed his sister was driven by a passion for revenge on her because she would not obey his orders and his concern was the protection of his personal interest and that of his family, considerations that are personal and selfish and bear no relation to the qualities of chivalry and decency.[26]

An analysis of these rulings shows that the court takes into consideration the relationship between the victim and the perpetrator and the victim's social situation in considering whether the motivation was 'honourable'. Thus we find that judicial interpretation gives the right to protect the honour and dignity of the family to the victim's father and brother but not to the mother; at the same time, it withholds this right from the victim's brother if she is married as it goes first to the husband.

Jurisprudence regarding Article 252

Three elements must be present in order for an accused to benefit from the 'excuse of mitigation' under Article 252: that the victim has undertaken a wrongful act; that this act is potentially dangerous; that the perpetrator commits his crime in an outburst of extreme rage as a result of the victim's action. The following three extracts clarify the courts' interpretation of this provision. The rulings relate to crimes of murder on the grounds of marital infidelity. The courts have held that the brother may not benefit from the 'excuse of mitigation' while the husband may, as the victim's action affects his honour, dignity and manhood.

Case 1, where the husband of the victim was the perpetrator, the motivation for its commission marital infidelity; the victim had previously asked the perpetrator for a divorce and he had refused:

> Whereas the accused admitted that he had shot his wife under the influence of a fit of extreme rage provoked in him by a wrongful act by his wife – her adultery ... and the names she called him undermining his honour, dignity and manliness. And whereas the defence sought the application of Article 252 (Penal Code), which restricts cases in which a perpetrator may benefit from the excuse of mitigation, requiring the combination of three elements.... And whereas in applying these legal principles to the facts of the case in hand it transpires that: 1 – it is established that the victim committed a wrongful act in leaving her marital home and having an affair...; 2 – the victim undermined the honour, dignity and manliness of her husband in the manner set out in the relation of facts; the court holds the above-mentioned act by the victim to be wrongful and potentially dangerous in view of the accused mindset and mentality, especially given he is an oven worker; 3 – it is established that the crime was an immediate and spontaneous one committed by the accused in an outburst of extreme rage and that it would not have happened had it not been produced by the action of the victim.... Whereas the elements of the excuse of mitigation being present in the case, the accused shall benefit from the terms of Articles 252 and 251.[27]

Case 2, where the accused was the victim's brother, a juvenile, who claimed as motivation her engaging in prostitution. It was common knowledge that the victim used to help her father financially and provide for her young son after her husband had left her. However, her grandfather, who lived in Syria, bolstered the resolve of the accused to kill his sister if she refused to return with him to Syria. This ruling was the only one where Article

562 was mentioned by the court; the defence had asked that the accused's action be considered a defence of honour without specifically mentioning the article. The court held:

> Whereas the defence sought consideration of the accused action as a defence of honour, adding that the accused committed the act under the influence of a fit of fury and extreme reaction to the behaviour of his sister and therefore seeking the granting of mitigation circumstances in accordance with Article 252.... And whereas the defendant had several times threatened his sister that he would kill her if she did not change her behaviour; and whereas when he killed his sister he had not caught her committing the crime of observed adultery or in a situation of unlawful intercourse, but rather woke her up from sleep in a tent belonging to her father and talked to her, asking her to refrain from the immoral acts she was committing; then after about half an hour he came back and woke her up again and asked her to go with him to Syria, and when she refused he killed her; and whereas it can be concluded from the defendant's words that he was resolved upon his deed, arranged for the means of doing it and carried it out after consideration when the effect of anger had gone; and whereas the requirements of Articles 562 and 252 are [thus] negated.[28]

Case 3, where the accused was the victim's brother, the claimed motivation her marital infidelity:

> Whereas, even if it be correct to consider that the accused was in a state of fury and reaction at the time he committed the crime, it is not correct to hold that the remaining conditions necessary for the application of Article 252 are present, since the wrongful behaviour engaged in by the victim by destroying marital stability ... is not potentially dangerous and cannot by itself make the accused take his sister's life.[29]

In most of these rulings, whether or not the court applied Articles 193 or 252, it granted the accused mitigating reasons under the terms of Article 253.

Jurisprudence regarding Article 253

In contrast to the excuse of mitigation and the defence of honour, the law sets no specific conditions for the granting of mitigating reasons, leaving the question of whether to grant it to the discretion of the court. Accordingly we find that most of the rulings granted the accused mitigating reasons in accordance with the circumstances of the case and the facts. The following extracts set out expressions used by the court that indicate the position taken on crimes committed under the pretext of defence of honour.

Case 1, where the accused was the victim's brother and claimed as motivation her illegitimate pregnancy, although she had married after giving birth:

Whereas the court considers in view of the waiving of personal right and the circumstances that paved the way for and accompanied the commission of the crime…and whereas the court grants mitigating circumstances to the accused in accordance with Article 252 because his action was inspired by tribal customs which dominate his narrow and closed community…[30]

Case 2, where a brother killed his sister because of her illegitimate pregnancy:

Whereas the court in view of all the circumstances and the customs prevailing in the region and the circumstances that accompanied the deceased and consequently the crime, grants the accused discretionary mitigating reasons…[31]

Case 3, where a brother killed his sister because of her marital infidelity:

Whereas the accused was psychologically agitated and troubled when he shot his sister the deceased, and whereas in contrast to the excuses of mitigation and exemption the law sets no stipulation that has to be fulfilled in order for mitigating reasons to be granted, leaving this matter to the discretion of the court, and whereas the court, in view of the understandings of the accused, his family and his environment, and the fact that he is the father of three children, and the circumstances of the crime, grants him discretionary mitigating reasons…[32]

Case 4, where the accused killed his daughter-in-law because his son was refusing to divorce her – although her family waived their personal right after the sister of the victim married the latter's widow:

Whereas the court, in view of the circumstances of the case, the age of the accused, the waiving of personal right in the case and the social situation of the accused, considers that it has the discretion to award mitigating reasons…[34]

Case 5, where a father killed his illegitimate daughter aged 10½, after being away from home for nine years; he killed his daughter on his return on the pretext that she was not a virgin, although after her death it transpired that she was. The ruling was issued in 1998, the crime dated from 1988:

Whereas the court in view of the circumstances of the case and the date the crime was committed grants the accused mitigating reasons…[35]

Case 6, where a husband pushed his wife off a balcony because he was jealous and suspected there was a relationship between her and the son of her former husband; he admitted the crime to the police, only to deny it in front of the investigating judge, adding that he had no such suspicion. At the criminal court he insisted that he had not pushed his wife, but rather that she had thrown herself off; also in court, the son of the victim's former husband testified that he had not had an affair with the victim, but that she had brought him up. The record states:

> Whereas the court holds true to itself and to conscience, and in light of the facts … that at that dark hour of night and in a moment of great despair the accused pushed his wife off the balcony of their home … that the accused was desperately tried by his wife who was recovering from unconsciousness caused by pain and paralysis (she had partial paralysis of the foot) and he was visualising this healthy young man asleep in his bed that morning, or days before kneeling in the bedroom rubbing his wife's thigh while she lay in bed giving herself up to this massage.… Whereas the court considers not only the poor condition of his health but more particularly the reasons that pushed him to commit the crime in the manner set out above in granting him mitigating reasons…[35]

The expressions used by the Lebanese courts in such rulings show that they are still affected by the dominant discourse which links a woman's honour to her body and assigns ownership of this honour to her family and her husband.

Personal claims

In eighteen of the twenty-five files a personal claim was established. In nine of these eighteen, the personal claim was waived. Of the nine where it was not, three rulings bound the accused to pay the claimant personal compensation of between 50 and 100 million Lebanese pounds. No compensation was ruled in the remaining cases, despite the existence of personal claims, either because the person entitled did not seek personal compensation but sought only the imposition of the maximum penalty on the accused, or because they stopped attending the trial. The waiving of personal claims (or there being no such claim established) contributes to granting the accused mitigating reasons under Article 253, plus getting him released from detention, at which point he may stop attending hearings, prolonging the trial and therefore postponing the judgment. This in turn may contribute to the granting of mitigating reasons to the accused in light of the date of the offence by the time sentence is passed, as illustrated above.

Sentences

Where there were personal claims, sentences ranged from four-and-a-half years' hard labour[36] to the death penalty. In the other files, sentences ranged from two to seven years. One ruling which sentenced the accused to fifteen years' hard labour was dropped because the accused died before the conclusion of the trial. In another case, the death penalty was substituted by life imprisonment in accordance with Article 193, because at that time the court was prevented from granting the accused mitigating reasons by the terms of Law no. 302/94, which had temporarily suspended certain provisions of the Penal Code[37] and prohibited the courts from granting mitigating reasons in certain offences.[38] In three cases the court ruled that the elements of Article 549 were not established. In the first, the accused was charged under Article 554 (on injury) but the case was dropped because more than three years had passed and the personal claim had been waived. Another found that the offence had not resulted in the death of the victim but in injury, and passed a sentence of eight months. A third convicted the accused, the sister of the deceased, under Article 553, of having assisted her sister to commit suicide by poisoning, sentencing her to three years in prison. Where juveniles were convicted under Article 549 (intentional murder), mostly involving the brother of the victim, the sentence ranged from two to five years.

Social analysis of the research sample

This section examines the personal circumstances and social environment of both perpetrators and victims in the case files, with a view to identifying any common factors in the profiles of the twenty-five perpetrators and twenty-seven victims involved in the crimes covered in the case files[39] and dating from 1980 to 2002, as set out in Table 5.1. The perpetrators of these crimes were in eight cases the husband, in nine the brother, in three the father, in one the mother, in one the sister, in one the father's paternal cousin, in one the father-in-law, and in one the son-in-law.

Motivations

'Washing away the shame' or 'bad conduct of the victim' constituted the motivation claimed by the perpetrator in 78 per cent of the cases. Where the victim was single, this variously meant the victim's loss of virginity, pregnancy due to illegitimate sexual relations, or marriage without the knowledge and approval of her family. In the case of married women the perpetrators' statements referred to infidelity, even if this was a matter of groundless suspicion. In some of these cases it was the brother who 'punished' his sister, with or without the knowledge of or incitement by the husband.

We included the other 22 per cent of the research sample, where there were no claims of shame or misconduct by the perpetrators, who were all husbands of the victims, because the files showed that during the investigation the accused raised doubts over the conduct of their wives. At the same time, witnesses in the cases testified to various problems in these families, such as

Table 5.1   Crimes of honour in Lebanon, 1980–2003

Year of commission	No. of crimes
1980–82	1
1983–85	1
1986–88	2
1989–91	0
1992–94	7
1995–97	5
1998–2000	6
2001–03	3
Total	25

the wife being driven out of her marital home or denouncing her husband's violence against her by seeking divorce; the husband then sought to justify his crime by casting doubt on the wife's behaviour. In one case, for example, a husband stated that his wife would not have disobeyed him or left home had it not been for incitement by her family, who wanted to marry her to another man whom they had chosen for her with her consent. There was no mention in the case files of any of these perpetrators suffering from a psychological illness, which might have suggested rather their categorisation as 'crimes of passion' rather than 'crimes of honour'. Further, the manifest motivation for the crime was conforming to social rules, rather than feelings of abandonment and jealousy as a result of love, as would be assumed in 'crimes of passion'; witnesses (including grown-up offspring) related the ill-treatment these perpetrators meted out to their wives and their avoidance of family obligations.

Profiles of victims and criminals

The victims in the research sample were mostly married (75 per cent); 17 per cent were single, 4 per cent abandoned and 4 per cent divorced. They were also mostly young, with 44 per cent in the age group 20–24, as shown in Table 5.2. The educational level of the victim was not always shown in the files, but from those cases where mention was made of whether the victim was illiterate or educated we found that at least 33 per cent were illiterate. In

Table 5.2 Female victims of 'crimes of honour' in Lebanon, by age

Age	No. of victims
<15	1
15–19	4
20–24	12
25–29	3
30–34	2
35–39	3
40+	2
Total	27

addition, jobs held by some of the victims (such as seamstress and shepherd) do not necessarily require academic qualifications. The files gave the date of marriage in the case of thirteen victims, of whom 38 per cent were married before the age of 16.

The perpetrators in the files were all male except for two, a mother and a sister, and the majority (twenty) were illiterate or semi-literate. Most worked in jobs requiring physical labour, such as a concrete worker, agricultural labourer, or carpenter. Most were young: 48 per cent fell into the age group 15–26, with 26 per cent aged 27–39 and 26 per cent over 40. Minors under 18 accounted for 24 per cent of all the perpetrators in the sample.

Methods of committing the crime

The case files revealed that firearms were used in fourteen cases, and a further four cases specified that rifles were used. Other methods included knifing, throwing from the balcony, hanging and burning. Studies of domestic violence (see, e.g., Saidawi 2001: 16) have shown a concentration on bodily force by the perpetrator, while the use of a firearm in the case of a so-called 'crime of honour' appears as a guaranteed means of getting rid of the victim where – as in these cases – the intention is indeed to kill. In most cases more than one shot was fired at the victim – one file, for example, records that the victim had eleven bullets in her head and stomach – showing that the perpetrator was determined that the victim would not escape death.

Extracts from statements of perpetrators

'Honour' or 'washing away the shame' was the main pretext on which the perpetrators relied to justify their crimes against women of the family, as noted above. The following are some of their statements in the case files. From an accused, aged 16 years, who killed his sister and mother with several shots to the head:

> I repeat the contents of my statement ... admitting that I killed my mother and my sister because of their bad conduct. They were the talk of the town, particularly after my mother was arrested for prostitution and my sister, at her prompting, started down the same path.

From a father who killed his divorced daughter:

> Her repeated absence from home and not obeying me, as well as the fact that the neighbors would tease me about her bad conduct.... All that made me kill her out of honour, especially as she was pregnant by someone other than the man who divorced her.

From a young man of 21 who killed his sister:

> I regret what I did but at the same time I consider that I washed away the shame from me and my family, and in the end what is right is right.

From a young man of 18 who killed his married sister:

> My sister was degenerate, no good, unfaithful to her husband and cheating on him.

From a mother:

> I confirm that it was I who slit my daughter's throat without anybody else's help, to wash away the shame that her illegitimate pregnancy had brought on us.

And from a husband who killed his wife:

> When I found myself in the position of a cheated husband, after discovering that she was being unfaithful to me for a long time with a friend of mine.... I killed her to wash away the shame.

If the perpetrators relied on 'washing away the shame' to justify their actions, the following extracts from witness statements show how in some cases other family members supported them on similar grounds. From the mother of a minor who killed his sister:

> My daughter Najla was the talk of the town after becoming pregnant through sex out of marriage, and people used to tease her in front of my husband who used to come home fuming ... which provoked my son...

From a mother whose son killed his minor sister who was pregnant outside marriage:

> My daughter committed an ugly deed which affects honour and dignity...

It becomes apparent from the statements of perpetrators and victims, and sometimes from defence pleading, that in Lebanese society women still represent the honour (*sharaf*) and repute (*'ard*) of the family, and that the business of disciplining them is still the family's concern, because the woman's conduct can jeopardise the 'honour' of the entire family. From here one can discern the motivations that led two women in this sample to commit crimes on the grounds of 'honour'. Honour (*sharaf*) is a tribal/clan (*'asha'iri*) value that belongs to the family collective and relates to its reputation and social standing, while *'ard* is the honour that relates to women's sexual conduct (al-Khouri, 1993: 58). For them, a woman's entire value is represented in the hymen, and her virginity is the honour (*sharaf*) of the family; this means that the 'crime of honour' constitutes

> an act of reclaiming and deterring a woman who has tried to live for herself, or who was deceived, an act of putting her back in her place as a tool that is owned by the clan, an ownership that is transferred for an interest or a price from the father, brother or uncle to the husband. (Hijazi, 1998: 102)

One of the significant findings from the research sample is the identity of the perpetrators: the vast majority were members of the nuclear family (husband, brother, father) and only a small number (some 8 per cent) more distant relatives. This may indicate a decrease in the control of the wider circle of agnates over the extended family in the last three decades.[40] However, the other information in the files shows that this shift does not alter the sociological implications of honour crimes or the essence of the phenomenon in Lebanon, which remains essentially related to the male tribal value system with its connection of the concept of honour to female sexual conduct.

At the same time, the files showed that of the twenty-five perpetrators, not one was suffering from a nervous disorder or other kind of psychological illness. Criminal behaviour in 'crimes of honour' is not motivated by emotional factors alone; rather, this emotional reaction is learned and acquired. The killer learns the motivations, the justification, and the crime in such a situation is an expression of the force of certain values, a consequence of the standards and patterns of behaviour and the rules and norms that the individual has acquired through the social process of upbringing. These values and patterns prepare him as a person for the commission of this type of crime, justified within the socio-cultural context in which he lives. He is

Table 5.3 'Crimes of honour' in Lebanon, by district

Governorate	No. of crimes
Beirut	1
Mount Lebanon	5
Beqa'a	3
North Lebanon	12
South Lebanon	3
Nabatiya	1
Total	25

obliged to emulate the social rules or else be cast out and suffer alienation. It may be that here lies an explanation for why certain women and minors commit crimes to 'wash away the shame'.

Social and environmental context of victims and perpetrators

Most of the twenty-five crimes detailed in the files took place in the governorate of North Lebanon. The predominance in the research sample of cases from North Lebanon indicates the role of poverty and ignorance in providing fertile grounds for such crimes by reinforcing and maintaining male clan values. Official statistics show that North Lebanon has the highest levels of illiteracy (at 15.5 per cent) of all the governorates, and one of the highest percentages of families living below the poverty line[41] (Ministry of Social Affairs, 1996). The profiles that this study was able to produce of perpetrators and victims, particularly the variables of educational level and type of employment, suggest that the individuals in the research sample were from the poor and the lower middle class. This does not mean, however, that those factors alone affect the commission of 'crimes of honour'. Shame ('ayb) as a concept, in the name of which crimes of honour are carried out, is transformed, as Azmi Bishara puts it, into a morality system when the individual internalises it:

> If he makes it part of himself then it reduces the tension between the individual and the social, but at the expense of his ability to reflect, analyse, weigh things up and take responsibility – that is, at the expense of the development of his personality and that of those around him, particularly if this internalisation of the concept of shame ['ayb] turns him not only into oppressed but also into oppressor. (Bishara, 2003: 127)

The connection made between the concept of honour and women's bodies, as a source of shame, is at the heart of patriarchal culture. Particular practices and moral values linked to this concept may vary in severity and in the manner in which they are expressed, not according to particular social variables such as profession, education or income, but according to the interests of individuals and groups.

Conclusion

In light of the case files and previous studies, this study has shown that the Lebanese courts simply do not apply the terms of Article 562, because of the difficulty of establishing the necessary elements. The Article clearly serves no useful purpose. Further, it covers what people erroneously term 'crimes of honour'. Allowing it to remain in the Penal Code is not simply a matter of 'encouraging a sort of private justice, sanctifying direct retaliation, and using force to obtain a right', as was argued when the original article was amended in 1998. It also contributes to the founding of spurious cultural concepts that give a mistaken conception of the role and standing of women in society.

Today, after the amendment of Article 562, the Lebanese courts still tend to show leniency towards crimes committed on the pretext of 'defence of honour'. They do not, as shown by the rulings examined in this study, apply the terms of Article 562, and in practice only occasionally apply the terms of Articles 193 ('honourable motive') and 252 ('excuse of mitigation'), because of the difficulty of realising all the necessary elements. More commonly they apply Article 253 to recognise mitigating reasons. The question remains therefore, is it enough to call for the repeal of Article 562? Or does the problem lie in the dominant mindset of society as a whole, which ties the understanding of honour to the body of the woman, and considers it the exclusive property of men? And what role do the media play when bringing these crimes up as individual and personal cases rather than as an issue of general concern?

The repeal of Article 562 remains extremely important. For this action to have real meaning, however, it must be accompanied by a general plan of action for both governmental and civil society institutions, aimed at eliminating prevailing erroneous social and cultural assumptions and practices that lead to and support such crimes, through the raising of awareness, of men and women equally, of the role and standing of the sexes, in order to build a healthy society based on respect of mutual rights and obligations.

Notes

The original Arabic version of this study is being published and disseminated in Lebanon. This English text was translated and edited by the CIMEL/INTERIGHTS project and approved for publication by the authors.

1. Unlawful sexual intercourse, whether by married persons (adultery) or unmarried persons [ed.].
2. With meanings of lord; master; owner [ed.].
3. It seems that the word 'family', in its Latin original, came from the word *familia*, with the meaning of the number of slaves owned by one man. (In Arabic, the word *usra* (family) is from the same root as the verb meaning, *inter alia*, to capture or take prisoner [ed.].)
4. A modern standard Arabic–English dictionary (Hans Wehr) translates *'awra* as 'deficiency, imperfection' and the plural (*'awrat*) as genitals [ed.].
5. Penal Code of 1 March 1943, in force as of 1 October 1944.
6. Persons in a degree of relationship to the perpetrator that forbids their marriage [ed.].
7. Or 'pardoned' – *ma'fu* [ed.].
8. *Ma'dhur.*
9. Abu Odeh (1996: 144) gives the French text of this provision, translating as: 'He who catches his spouse, his female ascendant, female descendant or his sister in the act of adultery or illegitimate sexual relations with a third party and commits unpremeditated murder or wounding against the person of one or the other of them shall benefit from an absolute excuse. He who commits murder or wounding shall benefit from a mitigating excuse if he has surprised his spouse, female ascendant or descendant with a third person in a suspicious situation' [ed.].
10. Although the word used in Arabic could be translated as 'spouse', the fact that the word 'sister' is used (not 'sibling') indicates that it is the wife who is intended.
11. Laure Moghaizel died on 25 May 1997.
12. By Law no.7 of 20 February 1999.
13. *Al-qada' wa'l-qadar.*
14. The existence of 'personal rights' or 'personal claims' cannot prevent pursuit of a murder case, but if personal rights to compensation against the accused are waived by those entitled, the courts may take this into consideration at sentencing: see further below.
15. Article 253: 'If there are mitigating reasons (*asbab mukhaffifa*) the court shall rule: instead of the death penalty, for life hard labour or hard labour for 7–20 years; instead of life hard labour, for hard labour for not less than five years; instead of life imprisonment, for prison for not less than five years; and the court may reduce every other criminal sentence to three years if the minimum is more than that, and may reduce the penalty to half if the minimum is not more than three years, or may substitute by reasoned decision a penalty of detention for at least a year, except in repeat offences.'
16. Such as if the intentional murder was committed with prior deliberation, or against an employee in course of the latter's exercise of professional functions; or, as noted above, against and ascendant or a descendant (549(3)).

17. The penalty for assisting or encouraging someone in committing suicide carries a maximum penalty of ten years in prison if the suicide takes place.
18. Article 554 deals with causing injury or harm not of a nature to cause illness or to keep from work for more than ten days.
19. *Bi-thawrat ghadab shadid.*
20. *Sifahan.*
21. This explanatory clause was added to the Penal Code in 1983.
22. *Muru'a* and *shahama*. Wehr gives for the first: 'the ideal of manhood, comprising of all the knightly virtues, esp. manliness, valour, chivalry, generosity and sense of honour.' For the second he gives *inter alia* 'gallantry, noble-mindedness; decency, respectability' [ed.].
23. Case no. 284/1995 – decision no. 11/1995, Criminal Appeals Court of Beqaa.
24. Case no. 147/1994 – decision no. 18/1995, Criminal Court of Beirut.
25. Case no.41/2002 – decision no. 268/2002, Court of Cassation.
26. Case no.191/1997 – decision no. 192/1997, Court of Cassation.
27. Case no. 10/1999 – decision no. 85/1999, Criminal Court of North Lebanon.
28. Case no. 582/2001 – decision no. 413/2001, First Instance Chamber of Criminal Court of North Lebanon charged with juvenile cases.
29. Case no. 36/1998 – decision no. 11/1998, Criminal Court of North Lebanon.
30. Case no. 56/1998 – decision no. 1469/1998, Court of Crimes of Murder in Lebanon.
31. Case no. 124/1999 – decision no. 139/1999, First Instance Court in North Lebanon considering juvenile offences.
32. Case no. 36/1998 – decision no. 11/1998, Criminal Court of North Lebanon.
33. Case no. 356/2002 – decision no. 26/2002, Criminal Court of North Lebanon.
34. Case no. 10/1998 – decision no. 176/1998, Criminal Court of North Lebanon.
35. Case no. 161/2002 – decision no. 630/2002, Criminal Court in Mount Lebanon.
36. Articles 252/547, 251.
37. Articles 548 and 547.
38. Those stipulated in articles 547, 548 and 549. Law no. 302/1994 (of 21 March 1994) was issued to set a limit to crimes of murder occurring at that period. It was repealed in 2001 by Law no. 338/2001 (of 2 August 2001) after petitions from popular and civil society organisations.
39. The number of victims exceeds the number of perpetrators: one perpetrator killed his mother and his sister at the same time, and another killed his wife and her sister together.
40. Moghaizel and Abd Al-Sater (1999) found that the perpetrators of crimes of honour in the period 1985–1998 included only nuclear family members: father, husband, brother and son.
41. Defined as US$312 per month.

6

'Crimes of honour' as
violence against women in Egypt

CENTRE FOR EGYPTIAN WOMEN'S LEGAL ASSISTANCE

Background to the study

This study is based on various Centre for Egyptian Women's Legal Assistance (CEWLA) activities and publications from 1999 to 2004, particularly those associated with the organisation's project on 'crimes of honour'. Since its establishment in 1995, CEWLA has addressed issues of violence against women, taking as our basis the United Nations definition of violence against women:

> Any act of gender-based violence that results in, or is likely to result in, physical, sexual or psychological harm or suffering to women, including threats of such acts, coercion or arbitrary deprivation of liberty, whether occurring in public or private life.[1]

CEWLA's first engagement with violence against women was on the issue of female genital mutilation (*al-khitan*), one of the most significant forms of 'psychological, social and cultural' violence against women in Egypt. The work has now broadened, and in a recent training manual aimed specifically at equipping lawyers to deal with cases of violence against women, CEWLA focused on three manifestations of violence in the Egyptian family: female circumcision, incestuous rape and 'crimes of honour' (Abdul Salam and Sulaiman, 2003). These three forms of violence are linked by the conservative values of a male-dominated culture that constitutes the social background to their occurrence, empowering males at the expense of females and seniors at the expense of juniors.[2] All three are issues around which campaigning for elimination is challenged by social taboos and a cult of silence. The specific subject of 'crimes of honour' in Egypt has not been as much a focus of attention as it has been in recent years elsewhere in the region. There are no specific studies, and statistics are mostly lacking. CEWLA's research and advocacy project on 'crimes of honour' has sought to engage and encourage the community, and all those professionally concerned with the interests of the community (judges, lawyers, the media, and those working in civil society), towards an open dialogue about 'crimes of honour', which affect not only women but all of society in Egypt and elsewhere.[3] To this end we have produced and commissioned papers, prepared and distributed publications, held workshops, seminars and conferences, and actively engaged with the press.[4] Our thinking on ways forward for this work is set out at the end of this study.

Crimes of honour in Egypt

SIHAM ABDUL SALAM[5]

Crimes of 'honour' occur in societies where family relationships are governed by traditional customs, as in Egypt. The very few statistics that we have been able to find on the incidence of 'honour crimes' in Egypt include data from 1997 which suggest that honour-related crimes accounted for 5.4 per cent of all crimes in the country, according to a report from the Department of General Security. The 1995 report of the Department of General Security cited statistics from the National Centre for Social and Criminal Research to the effect that countrywide there were 843 crimes of intentional murder that year, of which 52 were 'crimes of honour' (*'ard*). In 2000, it was reported that 10 per cent of crimes of murder committed in Egypt in 1999 were 'crimes of honour (*sharaf*)' (Riziq, 2000).

The rules on honour/shame are associated on a very basic level with virginity and the hymen.[6] This traditional association – of honour and virginity as represented by the intact hymen – has led to the brutal killing of many young women on the basis of unfounded assumptions. It is for example an illusion to see an inexorable logic: virginity, hymen, blood on the sheets on the wedding night. Similarly we know of cases of girls with blocked hymens, their bellies swollen with menstrual blood, killed by family members who think they have fallen pregnant through illegitimate sexual relations; or girls whose stomachs swell with tumours, or girls whose periods stop due to anaemia – such conditions being revealed at the autopsy, along with the fact that the girl was a virgin (Riziq 2000).

A further basic concept is that women belong to their male family members. 'Crimes of honour' are crimes of murder committed against women judged by society to have violated the unwritten rules of honour and therefore to have brought shame to their families. A woman may do all sorts of things wrong in her professional or personal life and still hold her head up, so long as she follows the traditional conventions on sexual behaviour, even if only in appearance. These traditional rules on honour and shame dictate that a woman is not allowed to engage in any sexual activity outside the framework of a marriage that is approved by the men of her family.[7] They thus connect the traditional role of females in society – that of reproduction (child-bearing) – with the idea of honour and shame. In Egypt, the press have covered instances of women being killed not for having had sexual relations outside marriage, but rather for having married against the wishes of their families or even for having indicated that they would like to conclude such a marriage. Thus we read of a man who killed his 51-year-old mother because she told him she wanted to marry one of his friends;[8] of a man who killed his sister and her husband for getting married without the family's consent;[9] and of a father and mother who electrocuted their daughter because she had married a young man in a customary ('urfi) marriage against their wishes.[10] Divorce can also be considered a cause of shame for the family, as in the case of a student who killed his sister, who had divorced after only seven months of marriage, because his colleagues were ridiculing him.[11]

The honour/shame rules, as well as being connected with the traditional female role of reproduction, are based on a traditional female identity – the way in which society pictures women, even if this does not accord with reality – which assumes that women are by nature virtuous and thus that any transgression in their conduct is a violation of their deepest 'femaleness' or femininity. This is the source of the double standards applied to sexual conduct on the part of males and females; men are not considered virtuous by nature and by consequence their sexual excesses must be indulged, while a 'fallen woman' destroys her very self, tarnishes the honour of her family and deserves death (Morris, 1993: 31). In reality, of course, both males and females have sexual desires, and both have the rational ability to control their sexual activity – in this, they are equal. Assertions to the contrary arise not from serious studies of human nature but from the same male-dominated social discrimination that produced a law of honour and shame that judges the same behaviour by double standards, exonerating a man however much his misconduct in matters sexual proliferates, and convicting a woman for the smallest of faults.

The honour/shame law can be summarised as consisting in men's honour being measured by the sexual conduct of the women of their family. The rules assure the dominant male that the children his wife will bear him to inherit his wealth are indeed his offspring. Tribal and agricultural systems of social organisation consider sons a source of strength for the protection of the family's interests, as well as a source of cheap labour. Honour (*sharaf*) in this understanding is known as '*ard* (name, good repute); it is the men of the family who have this '*ard*, embodied in the sexual conduct of the women of the family. If a woman behaves properly, the men of her family or her tribe have honour (*sharaf*), while they are affected by shame if she misbehaves. A judgement that a woman has behaved badly does not necessarily involve some sexual deed on her part; laughing too loud in a public street or enjoying talking to a male stranger might be enough for a judgement that a woman has compromised her good repute ('*ard*), bringing punishment for her and shame for her family. Women have accordingly been killed on mere suspicion. Thus we read that the victim was talking to a young male colleague in the street;[12] that she was late getting home, albeit she was a child of 9;[13] that she used to leave the house a lot without her husband's consent;[14] or that she used to go out dressed in a manner that the killer thought inappropriate.[15]

Male-dominated society considers women who have reached puberty, or more generally who are of an age to be sexually active, as a danger to be controlled through segregation of the sexes, early marriage of girls, female circumcision, and preventing girls from engaging in such beneficial physical exercise as, for example, jumping and stretching in the belief that they may damage the hymen, which, according to traditional belief, is where female honour resides, and the loss of which thus scars a girl with shame, even if its loss has nothing to do with any sexual activity. Reproduction is the basis of gender division in society and this produces an exaggerated emphasis on virginity, which is seen to be a guarantee of paternity and the continuity of the paternal lineage.

Furthermore, '*ard* is more a matter of reputation than of fact. Rumours can tarnish the reputation of a girl. She may not have done anything that society would consider dishonourable, but nevertheless may be harmed by the men of her family to defend their honour (*sharaf*) against the rumours. A woman who commits a sexual violation is punished severely, perhaps even by death. In small communities unwritten customary law evaluates power relations between men on the basis of women; that is, loose sexuality on the part of women is considered a threat to the cohesion of their menfolk and their honour, and thus a man's honour (*sharaf*) depends upon his controlling the sexual conduct of the women of his family or tribe (Gilmore, 1987). This customary law is reflected in statute law on the question of crimes of honour, in that a man who kills in such circumstances is entitled to a reduced sentence.[16] Even when a woman is raped, she may be killed by her family on the pretext that she has shamed them. Although such behaviour on the part of men as harassment, assault and rape are usually to do with power relations among men, rather than arising from the way a woman looks or is dressed, society frequently convicts the woman who has been raped, blaming her for the rape – as if it happened because she was not modestly dressed, or simply because she left her house. Nor can most raped women have recourse to the state apparatus for redress against the perpetrator, as most do not even report the fact of the rape for fear of the scandal. This means that some 90 per cent of perpetrators get away with it (el-Dessouki, 1997).

Nor are men the only perpetrators of 'crimes of honour' (*sharaf*) in traditional male-dominated society. This society charges women with the task of supervising other women's conformity with traditional standards of behaviour to protect *'ard*. Older women gain status from their supervision of the conduct of younger women to guarantee the preservation of the honour (*sharaf*) of the family or tribe. Tools at their disposal for this task include gossip and may culminate in incitement to murder or indeed in its participation. Gossip is extremely damaging for women, capable as it is of destroying their reputations whether it be true or false, and also destroying the reputation of their female relatives; this may explain why some women encourage the killing of a female relative who violates the rules of honour (*sharaf*).

Unwritten rules of traditional Arab custom differentiate crimes of honour (*'ard*) – that is, crimes that impact on a woman's *'ard* – according to the marital status of the victim and her consent or refusal of the sexual act in question. Thus *zina* is a man having consensual sexual intercourse with the wife of another man; *sifah* is consensual sexual intercourse by an unmarried woman, whether she is single or divorced or a widow; and rape is having sex with a female without her consent whether she is married or not. Many women are killed by their families in today's Egypt in circumstances involving all these crimes of *'ard*. Perpetrators justify their actions by claiming that they are following ancient Arab custom; some even attribute what they did to zealous enforcement of the teachings of Islam. However, studies have shown that the killing of women who were victims or accused of crimes of *'ard* was by no means the norm among Arabs. In the pre-Islamic and early Islamic period the Arabs did not consider rape to affect the honour of the victim but as an insult to her husband or guardian, and their response was to kill the rapist or rape one of his female relatives to recover the status lost through the rape. Also, it appears that tribes in the south of the Arabian peninsula were tolerant of *sifah* (sexual relations outside marriage), while those in the north were much stricter and used to punish the female and her partner with death; this goes back to strong patriarchal traditions in the north influenced by ancient Eastern civilisations, particularly the Assyrians and the Hebrews, who would strictly punish both parties for sex outside marriage (*sifah*) (Zanaty, 1995: 220–34). By contrast, a foreign traveller in Oman at the beginning of the twentieth century noted the tolerant attitude of the Omanis towards crimes of *'ard* and reported them as considering honour killings (*sharaf*) barbaric and unacceptable (Zanaty, 1994: 24).

As for written laws, various Arab countries have legislation permitting a reduction in penalty in circumstances of 'honour killing'. The concept of 'crimes of honour' includes two conflicting ideas – crime and honour. Whenever there is leniency towards criminals under the pretext of defence of family honour, society and the judicial establishment are belittling heinous crimes against women within the family. Associating the crime with honour may mean not merely the pardoning but even the rewarding of a criminal for his action (Barthi et al., n.d.). The position in Egyptian law and legal practice is the subject of the next section.

Crimes of honour and the law

AZZA SULAIMAN

There is no provision on 'crimes of honour' in Egyptian legislation. Unlike certain other Arab states, Egyptian legislation constrains specific mitigation for a man intentionally murdering a female in a spousal relationship: that is, where a man surprises his wife in the act of adultery. This comes in Article 237 of the Penal Code:[17]

> Whosoever surprises his wife in the act of committing adultery and immediately kills her and the person committing adultery with her shall be punished with a prison [*habs*] sentence instead of the penalties set out in Articles 234 and 236.[18]

In her comparative examination of Arab legal provisions on this subject, Lama Abu Odeh has observed that 'the Egyptian provision adheres more closely to the idea of passion rather than that of honour; it limits the beneficiaries to that of the husband and only in cases of adultery, granting him merely a reduction' (Abu Odeh, 1996: 147–8). On the other hand, the commentary cited (and critiqued) by Abu Odeh in 'explanation' of the provision indicates the 'honour' rationale:

> The legislature has taken into account the psychological state of mind that hits the husband whose honour has been violated, the most precious thing that he possesses. At the moment that he catches his wife committing adultery he will no doubt lose his reason and kill his wife and her partner.[19]

The absence of a provision for other 'beneficiaries' (such as fathers, brothers, uncles) providing a reduction in sentence for the intentional murder of a female relative underlies Egypt's response to issues raised by CEDAW working groups on Egypt's third report and combined fourth and fifth periodic reports submitted under the Convention.[20] Asked to address 'the phenomenon of "honor crimes", where women are killed by male relatives for suspected sexual impropriety', the report presented by the National Council for Women states:

> In Egypt there is no 'honor crime' in law as in other Arab countries and those who commit such an act are penalized under the penal code and are treated as murderers.[21]

This does not mean, however, that family members who commit 'crimes of honour' are unable to benefit from reductions in sentence, according to circumstance. Article 230 of the Penal Code deals with premeditated intentional murder:

> Whosoever kills a person intentionally and with malice aforethought (/premeditation) or ambush [*tarassud*] shall receive the death penalty.

This Article makes no mention of any mitigating circumstances that might permit a reduction in penalty, regardless of the identity of perpetrator and victim. Nor does Egyptian law include a 'general excuse' of provocation, such as the partial defence available in Jordanian law for a crime committed in a 'fit of fury caused by a wrongful and dangerous act' on the part of the victim of the crime.[22] However, in Article 17 of the Penal Code the legislator gives discretionary authority to the judge to reduce the penalty in the event that there are mitigating circumstances for the perpetrator:

> In the provisions on felonies [*jinayat*], where the circumstances of the crime which is the basis of the prosecution require the compassion of the court, it is permissible to replace the penalty as follows: the death penalty with hard labour for life or for a fixed term; hard labour for life with a fixed term of hard labour or a prison sentence; fixed term of hard labour with a prison or detention sentence [*sijn* or *habs*] of not less than six months; prison sentence with a detention sentence of not less than three months.

It is this discretionary authority of the judge that is the core of the problem in these provisions. As a member of his society, the judge is inclined to society's view that a woman is the 'honour of the man' – whether this man is the father, the brother, the son – and thus may consider a woman becoming pregnant through sex outside marriage, or suspicions about her behaviour, to be among the circumstances inviting the compassion of the court for her murderer and thus permitting the reduction in sentence according to Article 17. The penalty for a felony (*jinaya*) can thus be reduced to the minimum of a *habs* sentence – three years – as illustrated by a ruling from the Criminal Court of Tanta on 15 December 1998:

> The brother of the victim was suspicious of his sister's behaviour and thought that she had fallen pregnant through extramarital sexual relations; her husband had been out of the country for a period. He asked her to abort her pregnancy and she refused, so he hit her on the head and then set her on fire. She managed to put out the fire and shut herself in the water closet. He then poured petrol under the door jamb, set it alight and she burned to death. The forensic report showed that the victim was pregnant, and with that the court issued a ruling of prison for three years for the man who murdered his sister.

It is evident from the crime and the sentence in this case that the court issued its ruling for the minimum sentence on the basis that the perpetrator had killed his sister in defence of the family's honour. The attitude of the judiciary in such cases thus reinforces the idea of social and legal tolerance for the deliberate murder of women in certain circumstances.

It has also been established that it is the 'court of fact' that has the authority to exercise compassion in the reduction of penalty under the terms of Article 17. Abu Odeh cites a commentator from 1964 as observing that

> The issue of extenuating circumstances is one that is left totally to the discretion of the court of fact, and it is up to this court to take it into account for the benefit of the accused even if he didn't plead for it ... and the Court of Cassation has no jurisdiction over the matter so that an appeal for considering the extenuating circumstances cannot be a cause for action before the Court of Cassation.[23]

Having examined the published rulings of the Egyptian Court of Cassation, Abu Odeh (1996: 163) points out that in practice

> honour killings that cannot be accommodated within the strict sphere of application of Article 237 are being relegated to the discretion of the lower courts of fact as cases requiring the sympathy of the judge under Article 17.

The way in which Egyptian courts deal with 'honour killings' under existing legislation can thus be revealed in any detail only through the examination of unpublished cases: those heard in the lower courts. The unpublished cases of lower courts collected by CEWLA during the course of our research into the legal treatment of 'honour killings' in the first instance criminal court of Qena are analysed in the following section. By way of overview, the following pleadings were accepted as mitigating circumstances in rulings at the court: that the accused succumbed (understandably so, in the eyes of the judge) to extreme psychological pressure; the notion that the victim, by defying prevailing traditions and customs (by, for example, dressing less conservatively, meeting a male friend alone, etc.) actually brought about her own death; and the notion that the defendant's act was a 'legitimate' attempt to restore his lost sense of honour and to rid himself and his family of the disgrace resulting from the female victim's alleged misconduct. The reasons put forward for killing women in the name of 'honour' are, in short, the result of prevailing social and cultural norms, which often result in vilification of the 'guilty' female victim who is presented – and may be regarded by the court – as having therefore deserved her fate.

Returning to Article 237, it is clear that the legislator has considered that the husband who finds his wife committing adultery is defending his honour, and that it is his right to kill her; if he does so, his penalty will be a prison (*habs*) sentence of between twenty-four hours and three years. This is a severely reduced sentence in the circumstance of intentional murder or manslaughter, and one would have thought it would be natural not to make an exception of wife murder in the general provisions, particularly given that there is already the mitigation provision in the law in the above-mentioned Article 17.

The wider treatment of adultery in the law is also worth noting, as it confirms differential treatment in statute as well as in practice of extramarital sexual activity by men and by women. Other articles relating to adultery in the Egyptian Penal Code include the following:

Article 274: The married woman whose adultery is established shall be punished by prison (*habs*) for a period of not more than two years. Her husband may stop implementation of this sentence by agreeing that she return to live with him as before.

Article 277: The husband whose commission of adultery in the marital home is established by a claim from the wife shall be punished by a prison (*habs*) sentence of not more than six months.

These provisions establish clear discrimination between the husband and the wife in the crime of adultery with regard to first the penalty, second the right of the husband (but not the wife) to grant pardon, and third the requirement for the establishment of the crime of adultery by the husband (but not the wife) that it occur in the marital home. In the year 2000, the response to questions on Egypt's CEDAW reports presented by the National Council for Women acknowledged the differing provisions on adultery and further noted that while Article 237 provided for reduction in sentence for a man who found his wife committing adultery, a woman who kills her husband upon finding him in the act of adultery would be subject to hard labour for life or for a fixed term of three to fifteen years under Article 234. The response noted that 'These provisions discriminate against women and are subject to discussion and review.'[24]

At the end of this study we set out a number of recommendations on law and policy for the attention of the National Council for Women and other agencies and institutions on the basis of the Egyptian government's responsibilities under domestic and international law. Internationally, Egypt's responsibilities derive from its adherence to principles of international human rights law. The international community considers violence against women to be an obstacle to women's complete enjoyment of their human rights. The United Nations Declaration against All Forms of Violence Against Women of 1993[25] calls for the elimination of all forms of violence to which women are exposed in the family and wider society. Included in its definition of violence against women are 'traditional practices harmful to women'. States are to exercise due diligence to prevent, investigate and punish acts of violence against women, whether committed by the state or by private persons,[26] and can be held accountable under human rights law if they fail to do so.

In 1981, Egypt became the first Arab state to ratify the Convention on the Elimination of All Forms of Discrimination Against Women (CEDAW), which was published in the *Official Gazette* and therefore became part of domestic law. Whilst Egypt has entered reservations to a number of CEDAW provisions,[27] these do not include Article 5(1), which calls upon states to

> take all appropriate measures to modify the social and cultural patterns of conduct of men and women with a view to achieving the elimination of prejudices and customary and all other practices which are based on the idea of inferiority or superiority of either of the sexes or on stereotyped roles of men and women.

There is also no reservation to Article 10(c) on education, which requires 'the elimination of any stereotyped concept of the rules of men and women at all levels and in all forms of education'.

Egypt's responsibilities under these and other instruments to protect women against violence thus require it to take various forms of action against 'crimes of honour' and other forms of violence against women. The conduct of the judiciary is also critical in this regard. The following section examines court rulings which offer no such protection to women, but rather condone, to varying degrees, murder of women on the grounds of the customary code of honour.

Crimes of honour and court rulings
AWAD AL-MORR[28]

In pre-Islamic times, news of the birth of a daughter would bring only gloom to the father. Fear of shame might lead him to bury her alive, and even if he kept her he would treat her as less deserving than a male child. Such practices are entirely at odds with the way Islam looks at the individual soul and imparts humanity equally to men and women.

To this day, however, men still control women's movements and constrain their behaviour. Many men mistreat women, harming them in word and deed. Come what may, women don't compromise their homes, many of them enduring endlessly for the sake of their children. Seldom are they treated justly, and the least rumour brings a range of unacceptable suffering, particularly since women have begun to mix with men at work, entering fields that are new to them. In our society, women are under the guardianship of men, which constrains them; it is as if women were less than men in their maturity and their intellectual capabilities.

Men and women may complement each other, but they are not in practice equal. Although the Koran honours women, the teachings of the Islamic *shari'a* remain distant from application in the brains of men who look at the guardianship (*qiwama*) they hold over women not as constrained by the relevant texts in the Koran, but as a sort of arbitrary authority and control, entitling them to prohibit women from doing certain things, for example depriving them of the right to work or even to visit close relatives; such men think they can be absolute in their orders, and regard women sometimes simply as chattels.

An examination of the rules on killing reveals that lawful killing consists of *qisas*, or killing in just and exact retaliation for a preceding murder: a life for a life. However, when a man kills a woman – especially in rural areas – it is not because she has murdered somebody else, but rather because of gossip about bad conduct on her part, or even, in the rulings discussed below, because of an entirely lawful relationship she has established with a man other than a relative, or in other circumstances. A man may stalk and kill a woman from his family; he may arrange and plan for the crime, calm and composed and cold-blooded; he may be a long time preparing it, and he may have others helping him. Killing in such a manner can only be held to include premeditation, and it may also be by way of ambush even if the perpetrator doesn't conceal himself behind a wall or in bushes or elsewhere but appears before her suddenly in order to hasten the blow that kills her.

In law the crime of murder includes the element of specific criminal intent on the part of the perpetrator, the intention to take a life, the evidence for which appears from the circumstances of the crime and tools the perpetrator used to carry it out. After intent comes the act of killing, whether the murder was in fact carried out, and whether the perpetrator killed the woman he intended to kill or mistook someone else for her, and whether he wounded her fatally or it was possible to save her. Murder is murder despite its motivations; these are reasons behind the killing that may not interfere with the law taking its course, nor with the judge passing his sentence. Murder is forbidden in all the holy religions. Allah prohibited all people from murder as an attack on life, even when that human life is still a fetus: the murder of a woman who has had illicit sexual relations and who is pregnant with an unborn child unable to live separately from her constitutes a brutal increase in the crime of murder. All crimes of murder with the element of deliberate intent end a life, and the punishment is the death penalty if the murder is premeditated or by ambush or with both. However, the judicial tendency in Egypt is to regard the crime of murder of a woman having unlawful sexual relations (even if she is unmarried – that is, not the wife of another man) as a crime of honour ('*ard*) requiring reduction of penalty under Article 17 of the Penal Code.

Furthermore, the judges may decide not only to reduce the penalty to the absolute minimum allowed, but then to suspend it. Thus they appear to be encouraging men to kill women affected by gossip damaging their reputations, even if there is no proof whatsoever for the rumours of illicit sexual relations; for the perpetrators, the gossip and rumours are like an emotional revolution which can only be stopped by the killing of the woman for this violation of honour.

We should reflect on the attitude that the murder of a woman as a punishment carried out by the man can be equated in terms of its consequences with her misconduct. *Qisas* – a right established in *shari'a* – presupposes the killing of one person for another. Leaving aside the matter of the imposition of the *hadd* penalty of stoning on an adulterous woman, when faced with a woman who has conducted herself badly and lost her way, the courts have to apply the rulings of the Penal Code. These, as noted above, consider murder with malice aforethought or ambush to be a deliberate crime, the penalty for which is death. However, as we shall see from the rulings analysed in this chapter, courts in Egypt ignore this penalty even in the case of the killing of a woman whose only crime was to marry a non-relative, or a woman who has not shamed her honour but whose mental illness has made her the object of ridicule in her village, or a woman surrounded by gossip affecting her reputation, even when there is no proof to support the rumours.

Case no. 1[29]

In this case, from 1998, the victim was a mentally disabled woman who suffered from a psychiatric condition and was killed by members of her family because she used to leave the house when her father and brother were not there and go begging for coins, and inside the house she would destroy the furnishings and food. After her mother died, her father and brother had no tolerance for her. They pushed her into a part of the house where no one would hear her screams, strangled her with a red shawl wrapped around her neck, then fell on her, punching her and hitting her with a stick on her back and stomach, and left her to die.

In court the crime was proven by witness statements and the autopsy report. There was no evidence in court that the victim had compromised her honour. The court was satisfied that the two accused had committed the crime of taking the victim's life and that the murder had been premeditated and planned. Nevertheless, it considered them deserving of the court's compassion under the terms of Article 17 of the Penal Code and sentenced them to ten years' hard labour.

It is hardly conceivable that a crime such as this would invite the compassion of the court! The victim had done nothing to incur dishonour, and had no awareness of or control over the things that she had done, in light of her mental disability and her psychiatric condition. Yet her father and her brother killed her in this brutal manner simply because they felt socially shamed by her; they killed her for fear that she would damage their reputation – not on the basis of a deed that had violated their honour, but merely on the prospect of such a deed in the future. Rather than extending its compassion to the murderer, should the court not have dealt severely with the perpetrators in light of the circumstances of the crime, and the brutality of the murder?

Case no. 2[30]

In the second case, a man committed murder with malice aforethought and by ambush of a young woman simply because she had married a man who was not a relative. The court heard that the accused had engaged his paternal cousin (the victim) in marriage, but that they fell out; she pulled out of the arrangement and against the wishes of her family married a colleague from work. She went with this man to his home town and from there to Cairo, where they were married. This provoked the conservative feelings of her family. The accused prepared a rifle and lay in wait for the victim on the road that she used to take to the school where she worked. He fired two rounds at her and then fled the scene and hid in a house nearby, where he stayed until apprehended by the police, still with the gun that he had used to kill his victim. Under interrogation, the accused said that he had killed the victim because of his desire to marry her and her refusal; that when he confronted her he shot her once from the front and again in the back when she turned in an effort to escape. The accused similarly acknowledged that the victim's flight to Cairo with her colleague and her marriage without the consent of her family had provoked his conservative feelings, after people abused him because of her shameful behaviour, so he resolved upon taking revenge upon her through lying in wait for her in the road and then killing her. The records of the ruling show the court decided as follows:

> Although the marriage of the victim was lawful [shar'i], the fact that she fled with her husband to Cairo and accompanied him there far from her family and clan and the place where she lived, went against the traditions of the rural areas, and without doubt brought shame to her family and left them socially reviled. The court takes into consideration the fact that the victim's brother (her *wali ad-damm*)[31] pardoned the accused in his statements in the record of the final session and thus applies the text of Article 17 of the Penal Code and sentences him to heavy labour for seven years, along with confiscation of the crime weapon.

It appears from this ruling that the court considered two elements when imposing the sentence: first, prevailing values among social classes in the rural areas, and second, the fact that the victim's brother (and *wali al-damm*) had pardoned the accused. The ruling thus mixes the application of statute law on the one hand with the application of Islamic *shari'a* on the other; these should not be mixed.

Case no. 3[32]

In the third case, in 1993, the accused ran up behind the victim in a banana grove after they had had a fight; the victim tripped over and the accused attacked her and inflicted the injuries shown in the autopsy report – he sat on her chest, grabbed her throat and choked her with the intention thereby of killing her. Then he took her body and threw it into an abandoned well near his house. He did this on account of her bad conduct, having learnt of this from her mother, and because she failed to follow his orders. The accused acknowledged the facts and the motivations for the murder.

The court found that the intention to kill was established, as the accused's intention by killing her was to get rid of his shame and to avenge his honour, which the victim had sullied by reason of her bad conduct, her licentiousness and her refusal to obey him. He therefore exploited the fight they had had to kill her. The court ruled for a sentence of two years in prison (*habs*) with labour, in view of the circumstances of the case, and relying, as in the other cases, on Article 17 to reduce the sentence to this level.

Case no. 4[33]

In the fourth case the accused man cooperated with others in killing a woman whose good repute had been affected by gossip. The court heard that the accused men had reviled the victim after she had fallen pregnant through unlawful sexual intercourse, and had agreed with each other that they wanted to kill her and her mother, the latter because she had concealed from them her daughter's immoral behaviour. So they lay in wait for the adulterous (*zaniya*)[34] woman; when she was brought to them in the car that had snatched her, one of them hit her with a cleaver on the head and neck and the others completed the deed; they also killed the victim's mother and then they cut the bodies up and threw them into an irrigation canal. The court sentenced one of the accused to prison (*habs*) with hard labour for three years. This was the sentence that the court considered appropriate in light of the victim's involvement in the crime of *zina* (unlawful intercourse) – her illicit pregnancy – which led her family to get rid of her after she had become the victim of the gossip in town and her family had been shamed by what she had done.

Case no. 5[35]

In the fifth case, the victim had fallen pregnant as a result of sexual relations outside marriage. When the accused learnt of this from his wife (the victim's mother), he threw dust on his face and refused to eat or drink for several days on end, distressed, grieved and humiliated by the shame that afflicted him as a result of what his daughter had done. On the day of the incident, the accused waited till everyone except the victim had left the house, then set her on fire, intending by this to kill her in order to wipe out his shame. He tied her hands and left the flames to swallow her and then went out to the cattle pen and stayed there until he was sure she was dead. Then he went to the police to inform them of his crime. Witnesses testified that he had tied the victim to iron pegs and then set fire to her. The autopsy report stated that the cause of death was burns all over her body, along with the shock of the flames that crept up and enveloped her. The report also stated that in her womb there was a fetus that had not gone to term, the death of which was caused by the death of the mother.

The court was satisfied that the intention to kill was established by the accused tying the victim to iron pegs which pinned her to the ground so that the fire would engulf her, and only leaving when she was dead. He had also locked the doors on her so that nobody could come to save her.

However, the court rejected the circumstance of premeditation, holding that the fact that the accused had stopped eating and drinking immediately upon hearing of his daughter's unlawful sexual activity, and throwing dust on his face, left him no scope for quiet thought to allow him to prepare for the perpetration of the crime. Rather, the opposite happened: the accused was a prisoner of enormous psychological pressures that precluded the ability to determine upon the crime and make the various preparations for it.

The court decided to show compassion to the accused under Article 17 of the Penal Code and ruled for a sentence of one year with labour, suspended for three years. The court justified suspension of the sentence, first because according to the Islamic *shari'a* 'the father is not taken in retaliation for the son' and, second, because the circumstances of the case made it clear that the accused would not repeat such an act.

It might be noted that the first justification for suspending the sentence is the *hadith* of the Prophet (peace be upon him) to the effect that 'the father shall not be taken in retaliation for the son'. This is the idea of quasi-ownership established in the matter as shown by the words of the Prophet 'you and your property belong to your father.' Thus if the child is owned by the father, should the father kill his son he is eliminating his possession. This is established for those who say that ownership is an impediment to *qisas* or creates a quasi-right. It was said also that the father is the cause of the child's existence and so it cannot be that the child becomes cause for the execution of the father. Some Hanbali jurists hold that the child's *wali ad-damm* is his father, and the father may not be killed if he kills his child by virtue of the blood guardianship he holds over his children. However, the Malikis disagree with the Hanbalis on this point and say that if the father lays his child down and cuts his throat, or kills him deliberately in another manner that could not have been a matter of discipline (*ta'dib*), then he is liable to *qisas* for that as it was an intentional killing and the general texts of *qisas* apply.

Case no. 6[36]

In this case, from 1996, the victim was a paternal cousin of the accused persons, some of whom had tried to kill her before. This was in view of the fact that her bad reputation was well known; she had left her home town with her mother to live in Ismailiyya, fleeing her family's pursuit of her. Then she came back to live in Qena, bringing her husband with her, which aroused the conservatism of the accused persons, who decided to get rid of her in order to wash away with her blood the humiliation and shame that had resulted from her deviant behaviour. They seized her by force from her house in front of her husband, put her in their car and took her to the place where the other accused persons were waiting. They took her to the scene of the crime, where one of them hit her on the head with a stone and another choked her, and they left her for dead. The other accused persons stood at the scene encouraging the killing, in the manner set out in the court papers.

During the investigation, the victim's sister stated that the murderers had themselves tirelessly defamed the reputation of the victim and that they had killed her unjustly. Counsel for the defence stated that the victim's husband was unknown and there was no evidence for the validity of his marriage to her, and in addition that the accused persons had had their confessions dictated to them by the investigating officer. The court held that the intention to kill was established and likewise both premeditation and ambush. The court exercised its compassion in respect of all the accused in accordance with Article 17 of the Penal Code and sentenced the two persons accused of killing her to hard labour for five years, and the rest of the accused, who had urgd on the killing, to hard labour for three years.

Case no. 7[37]

In this case the two accused persons (one male, one female) caused the death of the victim after she had become pregnant outside marriage. Enraged by the victim's pregnancy, they tied her feet and forced her to drink sulphuric acid from a beaker. This burned her insides and caused the death of her fetus. The court was satisfied that the two accused did not mean to kill the victim but only wanted to get rid of the fetus by causing the woman to miscarry. The court held that the intention to kill the victim had not been established, and that it was not convinced by statements of the police officer, since they were incomplete and based on inadequate inquiries, and on the words of others who did not testify to them before the court. It is not among the elements of the crime of causing a woman to miscarry that the pregnant woman should still be alive after the perpetration of this crime. The court accordingly amended the charge against the two defendants from murder of a woman to causing her to miscarry by forcing her to imbibe a noxious substance, an offence under Article 260 of the Penal Code. The court sentenced the man to prison with labour for a period of one year and the woman to the same penalty but suspended, on the basis that she probably would not repeat the crime.

It should be noted here that the ruling convicted the pair not of murder but of causing a woman to miscarry; accordingly this crime did not involve the intention of killing a woman who had been guilty of misconduct, but rather the intention of eliminating the evidence of the woman's fornication, since there were no papers to prove that she was someone's wife, and no one to testify to her marriage.

Case no. 8[38]

In this case, from 1997, the prosecution charged the mother of the victim with her deliberate murder by feeding her insecticide in a dish of brown beans. She had noticed a change in the colour of her daughter's face and had witnessed her repeated vomiting. The (unmarried) daughter confirmed that she had fallen pregnant. The enraged mother prepared the dish of beans for her; she then hid away the rest of the food and the insecticide. The court agreed with the charge made by the prosecution, not least because the accused admitted before the court that her daughter's illicit pregnancy had greatly upset her and that she had resolved to get rid of her in order to conceal the scandal and wipe away the shame. Having poisoned her daughter, she left her to die a painful death. Although the victim's father arrived and took her to hospital, she died from her injuries. The autopsy report duly confirmed the cause of death as the ingestion of insecticide, the remains of which were found in her stomach. This attested to the intent on the part of the accused, the victim's mother, who had committed the crime only to bury the shame. The court dismissed her not guilty plea and further dismissed a defence made on procedural grounds. Nevertheless it decided to show compassion to the accused under the terms of Article 17 of the Penal Code because the motivation for the crime she committed was to wash away the shame that the victim had brought upon her family.

In this case, the victim's dishonourable behaviour was established by her own acknowledgement. This was not so in all such rulings. This ruling is one in a series where the court extended its compassion to the accused in a 'crime of honour' ('ard), regardless of whether or not the illicit sexual behaviour of the victim was in fact established.

Crimes of honour in the press

The subject of 'honour crimes' in Egypt continues to provoke a range of opinions, including whether or not it is a phenomenon deserving of prioritisation. The noticeable lack of data on the frequency of such crimes substantially obstructs the preparation of appropriate interventions. In an effort to provide some indication of the extent of 'honour crimes' in Egypt, a survey was carried out of press reports of incidents in a number of Egyptian newspapers and magazines[39] over the period 1998–2001, in all some 125 items, documented by the Mahrusa Centre for Publication and

Press Services and CEWLA.[40] By far the most frequent reason (79 per cent) cited in the press reports for the perpetration of a particular crime of honour was suspicions about the conduct of the victim on the part of the perpetrator. The second most common reason (9 per cent) consisted of discovery of infidelity or the victim's acknowledgment of the same. Among other reported reasons (6 per cent) was the attempt to prevent the disclosure of an extramarital relationship with a female lover, whether the lover of the perpetrator himself or of one of his relatives. Here the lover of the perpetrator's father, brother, and paternal cousin fell victim to a crime of honour; in one case a man killed an employee discovered to be having a relationship with his daughter. Other reasons (6 per cent) reported included the mother wanting to remarry or having actually concluded a customary ('urfi) marriage; a brother's sexual assault on his sister (with the brother being killed); and a father's sexual relations with his daughter, with the victim then displaying signs of pregnancy. Where suspicions about the victim's conduct were cited as motivation for her murder, the killer was most often the husband, followed by the father and then the brother. It should be noted, of course, that these represent 'crimes of honour' that – mostly – ended up in court and that journalists chose to cover for the crime pages of their papers. It is therefore likely that they represent a minimum perspective on a wider picture that is, as yet, unknown to us.

Strategies of response:
together against crimes of violence and 'honour crimes'

During the course of our work on 'honour crimes', including receiving the feedback of participants at public meetings, workshops and conferences, CEWLA has identified a number of themes and proposals for strategies of response to 'crimes of honour' in Egypt. These include an emphasis on the need to problematise and challenge the patriarchal nature of society, which remains the most significant factor in the incidence of 'crimes of honour', reinforcing through culturally conditioned norms and traditions the subordination of women to the control of men. Here it is important to note that 'crimes of honour' are not restricted to the Muslim communities in Egypt; women in the Christian communities too are vulnerable.[41] Religion can be critical, and it is important to support the efforts of scholars and jurists who articulate a progressive and enlightened understanding of religious texts. At the same time, it is critical to emphasise in wider society the fact that the Islamic shari'a does not condone 'crimes of honour'. Lack of public awareness with regard to the shar'i position can be exploited by those opposing the campaigning and advocacy activities aimed at eliminating 'crimes of honour', who brand such activities 'anti-religious' and even 'un-Islamic'.

The attitudes displayed by members of the judiciary – notably in their exercise of discretion under Article 17 of the Penal Code – are a matter for considerable concern. The invocation of Article 17 for the benefit of perpetrators in cases of 'honour killings' is based on the idea that the perpetrator was under extreme emotional pressure to defend his honour, that the victim had 'deviated' from socially accepted standards of behaviour and that as a result the perpetrator was justified in his attempts to 'wash away' the shame that the woman had brought upon her family. Critical to the effort to prevent 'crimes of honour' is a strong stand by the judiciary and the legal profession against the accommodation and legal indulgence of these acts of violence against women, and for their greater protection in the family and in society at large. In Egypt there is a very positive precedent in terms of the impact that such judicial involvement can have in the historic decision of the Constitutional Court to enforce supervision of the electoral process. This decision was a real stepping stone in the promotion of democracy and constitutional practice in Egypt, and confirms the necessity of the judiciary's promotion of liberal values.

The media can also play an important role in promoting progressive social values. However, at the moment the Egyptian press does not appear to be challenging the phenomenon of honour crimes or presenting to society the paradoxes and contradictory values that are in play in its attitudes to the murder of women. Since the state controls a large proportion of the audiovisual media and press in Egypt, it could also play a more active role in achieving social change in this regard.

Education and training are obvious areas of focus for civil society institutions committed to ending violence against women. Besides awareness-raising among all strata of society, in particular among youth, specific training on domestic violence for NGOs and women's organisations would contribute substantially. Members of the medical profession might also benefit from a properly designed and targeted training programme.

With specific regard to state policy and the law, CEWLA has called on the government to condemn publicly all 'crimes of honour' as a violation of basic human rights and to revise all penal legislation that has the effect of affording protection to those who commit such crimes. In particular, the terms and application of Article 17 of the Penal Code stand in need of revision. Work to eliminate 'crimes of honour' should proceed with the benefit of a national plan of action to eliminate violence against women, and should figure among the priorities of Egyptian institutions and civil society organisations working in the field of women's rights.

The issue of 'crimes of honour' is the responsibility of all of society. To bring about real change there is a need to have an impact on social and cultural processes and the formation of political decisions. This can only come about if the legislative and executive branches become actively involved in a faithful application of the law and in securing the independence of the judiciary and the legal profession. Discriminatory laws and conflicting legal systems also need to be addressed, in order to ensure the provision of equal protection and a fair trial to men and women alike.

Notes

CEWLA would like to acknowledge the following, whose work contributed to this study and to the wider project: director Azza Sulaiman; president Yasir Abdul Jawad; advocate Hala Abdul Qadir; Dr Siham Abdul Salam; the late Counsellor Awad al-Morr, former Chief Justice at the Supreme Constitutional Court; Dr Karima Kamal, journalist at *Sabah al-Khair* magazine; Tahani Gabali, at the time advocate at the Court of Cassation and since appointed judge; Counsellor Shukri al-Daqqaq, president of the Alexandria Appeal Court; Dr Madiha Ubada, head of the Sociology Department at Junub al-Wadi University; and Ahmad al-Shuri. The current study has been edited for publication in this volume by the CIMEL/INTERIGHTS Project from Arabic materials produced by CEWLA, and approved by CEWLA for publication in English. Papers commissioned from authors outside CEWLA do not necessarily represent the views of the organisation.

1. UN Declaration on Violence Against Women, GA resolution A/RES/48/108 (1993), Article 1.
2. Ibid., p. 7. While traditional patriarchal societies organised socially by clan and ruled by customary law would accept female circumcision and crimes of honour, incestuous rape is not accepted in any traditional or modern society. However, it should be noted that a girl who has been a victim of incestuous rape may in some cases be killed under the pretext of 'washing away the shame' which has overtaken the honour of the family. Ibid., p. 9.
3. See 'Preface' by Yasir Abdel Jawad in CEWLA (various authors) 2002.
4. See for example el-Jesri (2004) and Fawzi (2004).
5. See full contribution in Abdul Salam and Sulaiman 2003.
6. See ibid., pp. 40–41.
7. Egyptian law does not require the consent of a woman's family to her marriage. However, as illustrated in this study, women have been killed for marrying without such consent.
8. Samir Hilmi in *Saut al-umma*, 31 May 2001.
9. Ibrahim Bilbaisi in *al-Ahram*, 30 December 1998.
10. Khalid Idrisi in *al-Wafd*, 14 August 2000.
11. Muhammad Mutari 'Allam in *al-Ahram*, 7 June 2000.
12. Tariq al-Dabagh in *al-Ahrar*, 10 June 1999.
13. Manal al-Ghamri in *al-Ahram*, 9 December 1998; Riziq 2000.

14. Mahmoud Barakat in *al-Ahram*, 30 June 1999.

15. Atif Da'abis in *al-Wafd*, 6 March 2000; Muhammad Mutari' 'Allam in *al-Ahram*, 5 October 1999.

16. The law takes this position despite the opinions of some *shari'a* scholars that it is not permitted to kill a woman because of suspicion about her behaviour – or indeed, even if someone catches a woman in flagrante delicto but does not have four witnesses with him to testify to the sexual act (Riziq, 2000).

17. Law no. 58 of 1939, as amended.

18. These provide, *inter alia*, for a penalty of between three and seven years for manslaughter with heavier penalties in the event of premeditation.

19. Abdul-Hamid Shawarbi, *On Aggravating and Extenuating Circumstances,* Dar al-Matbu'at al-Jami'iyya, Alexandria, 1986 p. 36; cited in Abu Odeh, 1996: 146. See the critique of Article 237 by Dr Shukri el-Daqqaq reported in Fawzi, 2004.

20. Annex to the Combined Fourth and Fifth State Periodic Report of the Arab Republic of Egypt on the Convention of the Elimination of all Forms of Discrimination Against Women, presented in October 2000 by the National Council for Women: CEDAW/PSWG/2001/I/CRP.2/Add.3.

21. Ibid., p. 16, response to Question 20.

22. Rauf Obaid, *The General Rules of the Egyptian Penal Legislation* (Matba'at al-Nahda, Cairo, 1964, p. 863; cited in Abu Odeh, 1996: 162). See further Abu Odeh, 1996: 157–61; and case study on Jordan: Hassan and Welchman in this volume.

23. Obaid, *The General Rules*, p. 864; cited in Abu Odeh, 1996: 163.

24. National Council for Women, to the Combined Fourth and Fifth State Periodic Report, p. 29, response to question no. 54 on Article 15 of the Convention.

25. UN General Assembly resolution A/RES/48/104, 23 February 1993.

26. UN Declaration on the Elimination of All Forms of Violence Against Women, Article 4(c).

27. Egypt has entered reservations to Articles 2, 9(2), 16 and 29 of CEDAW.

28. This paper was commissioned from Counselor al-Morr by CEWLA and is published in full in el-Morr, 2002. His Honour Counsellor Awad el-Morr was formerly Chief Justice at the Supreme Constitutional Court. His sad death in 2004 came before he was able to review this English version of his paper for publication.

29. Prosecution Case no. 831 of 1998 registered as 1035/1998 at the Criminal Court of Qena.

30. Prosecution Case no. 2333 of 1991 registered as 122/1991 at the Criminal Court of Qena.

31. In traditional Islamic jurisprudence, the *wali ad-damm* (literally 'blood guardian') is the male agnatic relative closest in degree to the deceased and entitled to waive on his own behalf and that of other interested parties and heirs the right to demand *qisas* (retaliation in kind for a murder: a life for a life) or the right to financial compensation (*diya*) [ed.].

32. Prosecution Case no. 3501 of 1993 (Dushna), registered as 576/1993.

33. Prosecution Case no. 4521 of 2000.

34. The adjective used is *zaniya*, from the same root as *zina* [ed.].

35. Prosecution Case no. 5158 of 1997.

36. Case no. 5145 of 1996 (Qena Central) registered as 802/1996 at the Criminal Court of Qena.

37. Case no. 981of 1996 (Farshut), registered as 342/1996 at the Criminal Court of Qena.
38. Case no. 830 of 1997, registered as 192/1997 at the Criminal Court of Qena.
39. *Al-Ahram, al-Ahram al-Misa'i, al-Wafd, Sabah al-Khayr, al-Gumhuriyya, Akher Sa'a,Ruz al-Yusef, al-Usbu'* and *Akhbar al-Yaum*. A few issues were missing.
40. CEWLA commissioned an analysis of the coverage of 'crimes of honour' in the Egyptian press from Dr Karima Kamal (Kamal, 2002) which could not be included in the current study for reasons of space. An English version of Dr Kamal's paper is available on both the CEWLA and the CIMEL/INTERIGHTS project websites.
41. CEWLA found in Upper Egypt that Coptic families were statistically as likely as Muslim families to commit 'crimes of honour'. El-Jesri (2004: 87) reminds her readers of the late Kamal el-Sheikh's film *El-Bostagi* ('The Postman'; 1968) 'which ends with a Coptic family taking the life of a daughter for having an illicit sexual affair'.

7

Researching women's victimisation in Palestine: a socio-legal analysis

NADERA SHALHOUB-KEVORKIAN

In *Rijal taht al-shams*,[1] Ghassan Kanafani tells the story of a group of Palestinian men being smuggled over the Iraqi border into Kuwait to find work. A truck driver hides the men in the big water tanks on his truck and drives into the desert towards the border. The sun is scorching, and the men have to keep absolutely still to avoid detection. At the border, the police, sitting sheltered from the sun, strike up a long and leisurely conversation with the driver. The chat over, the driver starts up his truck and crosses the border, driving for almost an hour before being able to stop and check on the men hidden in the truck. By the time he opens up the water tanks, they are all dead. The driver's first reaction is: 'Why didn't they bang on the tank?'

The study of domestic violence reminds me of Kanafani's story. The first question Western researchers studying violence against women ask is: 'Why do they stay?' Similarly, when we hear stories about child sexual abuse, wife abuse, or elder abuse, we ask, 'Why didn't they disclose their abuse?' In answer to this question, this chapter examines the power that the parallel legal system (the informal/tribal legal system) has on victims of domestic violence in the context of the occupied Palestinian territories. In some cases the parallel legal system is as powerful as the sun that burned the Palestinian men alive, while the victims are blamed by the question, 'Why didn't they ask for help?'

In the context of an ongoing struggle for the liberation and economic and political independence of Middle Eastern women, there are signs of resistance to socio-cultural norms that encourage violence against females and other vulnerable groups, particularly in the family (Afshar, 1993). Notwithstanding the sexism of certain legal policies and codes, the law is a tool that can work to support victims of domestic violence and aid their fight against abuse or neglect. In Palestine, during the politically formative period of state-building and of resistance to various forms of oppression, the question arises whether the Palestinian legal system (both formal and informal) can be reconstructed to promote legal and social human rights and protect victims of domestic violence from 'legalised' violence.

In discussing this question, I first raise some conceptual issues regarding domestic violence and the role of the informal/tribal legal system in dealing with violence against women and children, including violence related to concepts of 'honour'. I then present two field studies to illustrate the way these concepts are expressed in the legal system.

Conceptualising domestic violence

Historical factors

Despite a general tendency to attribute the Palestinian women's movement and activism to the male-led Palestinian national movement, historians and feminists such as Fleischmann (2003) and Dajani (1994) have established that women in Palestine were interacting with women elsewhere in the Arab world on cultural, political and intellectual issues long before the emergence of Palestinian or Arab nationalism. The activism of Palestinian women was thus beyond the frames of Palestine–British colonialism or Palestine–Zionism, beyond borders or nations. Fleischmann (2003) documents the initiation of women's charitable organisations as early as 1903, with elite Palestinian women creating liberal mores and modes of behaviour as active citizens in Palestine. British colonial rule manipulated the social and cultural structures in relation to women's issues to facilitate and reinforce social fragmentation and maintain control. In doing so, the British promoted a public–private dichotomy stressing women's role in the home and family as a method of preserving the 'authenticity' of Arab–Palestinian society. Such policy was not specific to Palestine. Subsequently the Israeli authorities empowered by British colonial rule followed the same path of 'letting the natives rule themselves' while at the same time facilitating, researching and maintaining orientalist approaches towards men and women. Israel's policies promoted and manipulated societal norms of 'honour', maintained clan and tribal leaderships and limited women's social and political participation. The various political, colonial and Zionist forces that stressed women's role in the home and private sphere blocked the process of transformation that Palestinian and other Arab women were going through, while creating a panic reaction in the region. This panic and fear of the 'Western' invasion, and the 'Western' insistence on 'modernising' women, empowered and affected men's perceptions of social and political transformation, threatened men's masculinity and virility, and endangered their role and status in society. Both powers – the external colonial/Zionist, and the internal patriarchal/masculine – brought about a reaction that turned women's bodies and lives into sites of resisting oppression. Colonisers and occupying powers aimed at 'modernising' and 'liberating' women, while patriarchal powers focused on 'protecting' and 'safeguarding' women from any external invasion. This turning of women's bodies, status and lives into a battlefield is ongoing. I hope the reader will consider the data discussed and shared in this article in this context.

Political factors

State-building patriarchy, and violence against women (VAW)

In the 1990s, Arab human rights and feminist activists began to address the abuse of women (primarily seen as 'crimes of honour') as an issue in need of re-examination at the social, political, cultural and legal levels. Other chapters in this volume consider efforts directed *inter alia* at the legal systems in this regard, for example in Jordan, Egypt and Lebanon (in the latter, these efforts had begun in the 1970s).

In Palestinian society, the struggle for women's right to defence against crimes of violence is taking place against a complex backdrop of state-building politics and resistance to oppression. Although the struggle against abuse of women began at the turn of the twentieth century, it peaked following the onset of the first intifada (uprising) at the end of 1987 (Dajjani, 1998). Various women's and human rights organisations began to address the issue of women's rights, scrutinising the existing legal code to determine its degree of congruence with the newly constructed socio-political atmosphere of respecting Palestinian national and human rights (Abdo, 1999; Al-Haq, 1989; Khadr, 1998). Rosemary Sayigh (1992: 19) has argued that women's issues were politicised within the Palestinian national liberation movement: 'Social changes adopted as part of national struggle are the main legitimating context for women's individual struggles.' Acceptance of Sayigh's thesis is related to the symbolic empowering image granted to females as the mothers of the nation – an image that has been reinforced by the cultural and political discourse of the Palestinian Authority (PA).

Women's status in the PA reflects the effect of traditional patriarchy and its manifestation within political structures. The PA's political appointments are motivated by party politics involving allegiance based on clan or tribal affiliation. Such appointments potentially endanger the status, liberty and equality of women. This factor overrides opposing tendencies arising from the political legacy of Palestinian society and context of occupation, including the ongoing political struggle giving the political precedence over the traditional patriarchal. Hence a breakthrough in women's socio-political and legal power does not appear to be on the horizon. Women remain 'hymenised' and subjected to the traditional structure of male domination and supremacy (Taraki, 1997).

The 1998 Proclamation of the Independent Palestinian State[2] declared national goals that are grounded in women's human rights. However, based on my previous examination of socio-cultural, patriarchal and political factors affecting legal treatment of 'femicide' cases (murder of females for the sake of 'family honour'), I question whether Palestinian reformists can actually begin promoting these same national goals.

Socio-cultural factors

Collective/patriarchal discourse and the family

The collectivist context of Arab society necessarily affects analysis of the role of the family in cases of domestic violence. It is difficult to identify one model that typifies all Arab families with respect to the status of the family in society, but certain core characteristics that impact on domestic violence can be generalised (Barakat, 1985; Shalhoub-Kevorkian, 1997a, 1997b). Despite the economic and political changes that have occurred in Arab society during the last three decades, the family is still considered the central unit in economic, social and religious life and a source of support, unity and cohesion that can support the individual socially, economically and politically. It plays a crucial role in providing assistance and services that are expected from formal social services in the modern state, such as mutual support in child rearing, mutual protection, financial support, employment, and so on. Family members are expected to be committed to the value of family protection, unity and reputation, which may require putting aside their own personal, needs, aspirations and desires. This is especially true for women, who are expected to protect their family's 'reputation and "honour"', and for mothers, whose own happiness is considered to be determined by their children's happiness, growth and success. Thus women's success or failure in marriage, child rearing, personal behaviour and life choices is considered as the failure or success of the family.

Women who are victims of domestic violence may receive support from their families, but they may also be blamed for their victimisation and may be perceived as sullying the family's reputation. This tendency to blame the woman when abused, or to demand the sacrifice of her life for the sake of her children, prevents women from seeking protection, shelter or support both within and outside their family.

Fear of disclosure of abuse is worst when the victim is a girl or young woman. Female children, girls or unmarried and young women fear seeking external help (Shalhoub-Kevorkian, 1999b) or disclosing any abuse inflicted upon them by family members. This situation clearly traps Arab women and girls, for while they are aware that their families are expected to help, protect and support them, they also know that in case of domestic abuse they may be pressured to maintain silence about their abuse, to return to an abusive husband, or to refrain from marrying for fear of disclosing sexual abuse by a father, brother or other family member. Such fear can increase women's and children's psycho-social vulnerability, personal anxiety, frustration, anger, helplessness, and reduce their alternatives in resisting domestic abuse.

Female vulnerability is aggravated by the patriarchal power structure of Arab families, which not only justifies inequality between men and women but also increases the ability of male family members to further control, misuse and abuse women. If abuse of women, girls and female children becomes known, it may be seen as indicating that their families failed to protect them, which in turn may threaten the power and masculine privilege of male family members. When men feel that their power is threatened, they tend to use violence to restore their dominant status (see further Haj-Yahia, 2000).

Legal factors

The traditional human resource and support system of the *hamula* (the clan or extended family) – which also controlled economic resources – was strengthened as a system of social control by various governing powers in Palestine who were unwilling themselves to deal with or intervene in social issues. Systems of control, leadership and local justice developed, based on central and powerful members of the society called the *jaha* (the 'face' of society). These leaders included Muslim religious leaders and 'wise men' (*hukama'*), who based their judgements on their life experiences and accumulated wisdom. They developed an unwritten system of tribal law comprising norms, customs and religious law (al-Aref, 1933; al-Abadi, 1986) claims that while most of these decisions were greatly influenced by Islam, the judges' lack of familiarity with the various interpretations of the Koran forced them to include their own opinions, which were based on social tradition.

After the establishment of the State of Israel, the population of the West Bank came under Jordanian rule while the Gaza Strip was under Egyptian control. In 1967, both areas were occupied by Israel and fell under Israeli military rule. There was anger and hostility at the Israeli occupation, and the justice system administered by Israel was perceived as discriminatory and oppressive. Palestinians in the Occupied Territories tended to use the informal system, including the tribal justice system, to solve their problems and conflicts. When, following the 1994 Oslo Accords, the Palestinian Authority (PA) took control in part of the Occupied Territories, it had to cope with different and sometimes conflicting systems of social control. Writing at the time about the weakened legal system under Israeli occupation, Bisharat (1989: 163) observes:

> The outcomes of court actions have become highly unpredictable, which reduces the appeal of formal institutions as avenues for dispute processing. Political favouritism and patronage have flourished, thereby undermining the value of legal expertise.

Bisharat (1989: 32) further explains how private disputes and confrontations in Palestine often rapidly become a community event: 'Gratitude is showered on the mediator who can produce a resolution on the spot and a boost is given to his status in the community. Conflicts that are not immediately resolved become the topics of discussion and speculation.' Corruption and *wasta*, the latter defined as 'the improper exploitation of official capacity for personal gain', affect the rule of law, and Bisharat concludes that

> Corruption and *wasta*, no matter the actor involved, are powerful solvents to the legal profession's claims to legitimacy based on mastery of technical expertise. Corruption and *wasta*, hence, constitute alternative systems of intermediation – mildly illicit and disapproved of in a formal sense, but no less functional for the fact – which often yield stronger guarantees of satisfaction than the legal routes proffered by lawyers.

This socio-cultural system, which affects the formal legal system and is reflected in what Bisharat (1989: 36) terms the 'infinite negotiability' of all social transactions, also applies to abuses inflicted upon women and children. In an analysis of a post-Oslo case of a 3-year-old girl sexually abused by a relative, I showed how the child's victimisation was turned into familial victimisation, and both were price-tagged and negotiated according to the status of the child's family. Here, the third and highest level in tribal adjudication was used, the *manshad*, who may deal with all manner of disputes but is specialised and uniquely qualified to view cases of *'ard* – offences against the chastity and purity of women.

When comparing the perception of offences by the formal court system – at the time administered by the Israeli occupation authorities – and by the tribal/indigenous system, Bisharat explains:

The formal court system conceives of offenses primarily in their material dimension, and its procedures assume a rational plaintiff who will take initiative to maximise a material or economic interest. In the ethos of honor, damage to the body or property, whether intentional or accidental, is an offense against the person, the proprietor, so to speak, of either the body or the property, in other words, against his or her honor ... the very sense of honor is, that it is of a different order of value than the material. (1989: 37)

In light of this uneasy fit between the formal legal perception of gender-related issues, sexual crimes and 'honour', it should not be surprising that informal modes for processing disputes coexist with the formal system. The institution of tribal adjudication, the parallel legal system, becomes an address for people to turn to in cases of sexual abuse. This institution has become further empowered due to the lack of political stability, and the failure in the post-Oslo period to entrench due legal process in the formal system.[3]

When discussing the sexual abuse of women and any related formal or informal procedures, one needs to examine both the formal legal apparatus and the parallel legal system. As yet, no studies have discussed the connection between the two systems of law enforcement, and how the existence of the two has affected their mutual evolution. I believe it is fair to say that while the newly established legal system of the PA was busy organising and establishing itself during a period of state formation, it left so-called 'women's issues' in the hands of the informal, tribal system, to which such matters had always been historically allocated. Since the process of transferring power from the tribal to the formal legal system is not an easy transition for the tribal heads and other notables within it, the PA was willing to give up or share part of its power with informal social control agents. The process of negotiation is clearly revealed in President Arafat's appointment of tribal notables as official advisors to the PA (Abdo, 1999).

After the arrival of the PA, three cases of sexual abuse (two in the West Bank and one in Gaza) were widely reported and provoked strong social reactions. The PA reacted by transferring such cases to the National Security Court, seeking speedy punishment of the offenders. At the same time the PA requested the intervention of the tribal system, asking their help in reorganis-ing and returning social stability (Shalhoub-Kevorkian, 1997b). The resultant judicial system has become a patchwork of secular, Islamic and tribal provisions that lacks harmony or consistency (Al-Rais, 2000; Dara'awi and Zhaika, 2000), a condition that is clearly apparent when dealing with the abuse of children and women. The question arises whether a dual (and in some cases triple) system of justice can lead to the promotion of women's rights.

It has been argued that the fine balance between the formal, public law and the informal, tribal systems of justice may be violated when women's victimisation is sexualised (Shalhoub-Kevorkian, 1999a; Mernissi, 1982) and female virginity, shame and honour direct the judicial cognition of legal practitioners (that is, the discretionary power of criminal justice personnel: see Abu-Odeh, 2000; Abdo, 1999; Shalhoub-Kevorkian, 2003). Although both systems have worked hand in hand to promote social stability, their cooperation with regard to gender related issues, such as the sexual abuse of women, discriminates against women and further oppresses them (Shalhoub-Kevorkian, 2000a).

To conclude, in contemporary Palestine attitudes towards the state and its law, the lack of political stability, the concept of honour and the moral panic reaction produced in cases of abuses inflicted upon women's purity and sexuality, the negotiability in transactions, and the alternative modes of dispute processing and intermediation (that are frequently more successful than actions through the civil system, and more in accord with patriarchal social values) represent formidable obstacles to the construction of humane victim-sensitive reactions to sexual abuse.

Gender factors: silencing as gender discrimination

Women and patriarchalism in Palestinian society

Many feminists today are beginning to understand that there is a relationship between patriarchal structures that increase women's inferiority, discrimination and inequality between men and women, and the historical and political context of women (Kandiyoti, 1996; Haj, 1992). In Middle Eastern society the political, cultural and social framework leads to the internalisation of unequal gender relations. Kandiyoti (1996) claims that the source of this inequality is not to be found in gender relations within the nuclear family where the male is the provider and the woman is dependent on him, but rather in the extended patriarchal family. In Palestinian society, particularly in rural society, classic patriarchalism facilitates the creation of cultural frameworks that internalise and strengthen the inferior status of women. Less classic patriarchalism is to be found in the towns, particularly among professionals of the middle class. Nevertheless, the power of the extended family and blood relations are still powerful forces. The power of a woman increases when she gives birth to sons, or when she marries or because she has a powerful father or has brothers (Haj, 1992).

The colonial past also influences issues of status and gender relations in Palestinian society. Haj (1992) holds that two issues have to be considered when analysing Palestinian patriarchalism, in addition to definitions of self and interaction between men and women: first, that Palestinian men are humiliated, depressed and lacking positions of power, and second, the social relationships and interactions that define these conceptions. The Israeli occupation in 1967 led to the creation of external orders and laws that governed the social, economic and political life of Palestinian society. Israel confiscated most of the resources of the population, particularly land and water. This economic oppression increased unemployment and dealt a 'death blow to the economic viability of the Palestinians as a community'. The position of women in the economy was harmed, if not abused. Due to social patriarchalism and the need to control them, women work in agriculture, factories (textiles) or in the tobacco industry, where their salaries are very low (Haj, 1992).

Beginning in 1985, and particularly with the outbreak of the first intifada in December 1987, women's movements involved in the national and social struggle arose. This politicisation of women led them to fight not only against the Israeli occupation but also against traditional rule and the patriarchal structure (Peteet, 1991). The onset of the second intifada in September 2000 increased the vulnerability of women and children, and destroyed most efforts to lessen the power of the PLS and the patriarchal monopoly over the vulnerable. Despite attempts by various women's organisations, the status of the woman in the family is still inferior to that of men, and inequality and discrimination still determine the efforts of policy makers.

Violence against women, family honour and the silencing of women

There are many techniques of silencing. One is tolerance of abuse (Shalhoub-Kevorkian, 1997a, 1999a). Another acceptable cultural method of silencing is 'femicide'. Femicide (euphemistically called 'killing for the sake of family honour') is defined here as the criminal act taken by an individual (generally male relative) in which the life of a female is taken as a means to cope with the perceived *'ar* (shame) her 'suspected' behaviour wrought on the family. The killing buries not only the victim but also the 'disgrace' associated with her. In essence, this cultural practice not only causes egregious injuries but also erases the most basic human right, the right to life. When enforced by traditions, culture, state, religion and the law, the politics of femicide move society to a condition whereby women are not considered human beings.

Recent research (Shalhoub-Kevorkian, 2002, 2003) shows that femicide is a major fear for girls and young women. They are willing to forfeit their liberty, the right to education, and choice of husband in order to escape it. Furthermore, if raped, women are obliged by cultural and legal codes to marry their rapist as a means to avoid being killed and prevent the shame that would stain the family if they refused to do so.

Although the system of tribal justice does not permit the honour murder of a woman (even if her actions were voluntary), prevailing tradition views such murder as lawful. In Jordan and in Palestine a man who commits such a murder is not charged with murder. In fact, if it becomes apparent that the murder was committed because of a violation of family honour, the murderer is considered 'innocent', someone who removed the shame attributed to the family and restored the family's honour.

Three considerations are involved when examining actions that violate honour. The first is 'safeguarding', involving the man who is expected not only to protect the particular woman but also to preserve the honour of all women in the society. The second is 'protection' and refers to the protection afforded to women if someone tries to harm them either verbally or physically. A lack of protection means that the man is considered shamed and as having brought shame on his family and on the entire *hamulah*. In addition, if a man does not protect women, others will refuse to protect his honour. Thus there is mutuality – each has rights and duties, and when duties are not fulfilled, rights are negated. The third consideration is 'punishment'. There is a call for severe punishment, including death (al-Abadi, 1986). If the woman agreed to the actions, she and the offending male will be killed together. The punishment is cancelled if it is agreed that the woman will marry the man in question.

Field studies

Over a number of years I directed a major action-oriented research project on femicide at the Women's Centre for Legal Aid and Counselling (WCLAC) on the West Bank (Shalhoub-Kevorkian, 2000a). The project included a variety of focuses and approaches, two of which are set out here. The first involved the gathering and analysis of official statistics on femicide and 'honour crimes' with a view to examining the utility of such data in exploring the problem. The second considered the effect of the parallel legal system in Palestine and its effect on female sexual abuse through interviews with police personnel, social workers and the judiciary; one of our focuses in these interviews was the practice of imposed virginity testing (IVT).

Field study 1: official statistics on femicide

Police data

Data from the Palestinian police on 'honour crimes' in the West Bank and Gaza Strip showed a total of 33 cases of femicide over the period 1996–98 (see Table 7.1). Table 7.1 shows that the prevalence of femicide decreased by nearly one half (46.7 per cent) from the base period of 1996 (but see

Table 7.1   Distribution of 'crimes of honour' by age and region (West Bank and Gaza Strip) as provided by the Palestinian police, 1996–98

Year	Total	Region		Age	
		West Bank	Gaza	Mean	Range
1996	15	5	10	20.5	13–32
1997	10	2	8	28.7	18–50
1998	8	3	5	30.6	14–50

Note: An additional five cases were documented during the first six months of 1999.

contrasting District Attorney data below). Femicide appears to occur in the Gaza Strip (69.7 per cent) with greater frequency than it occurs in the West Bank (30.3 per cent). Furthermore, the data depicted in Table 7.1 show that girls and women of all age categories (adolescents, young and middle-aged adults) are killed for reasons of 'honour'.

The police also supplied information about the relationship between the offender and the victim. The offenders were all close relatives of the victim (e.g., fathers, brothers, husbands, uncles). Furthermore, the data show that the crimes were sometimes committed by more than one offender.

District Attorney's files

Despite the full cooperation of the District Attorney (DA) in the West Bank, the researchers experienced difficulty in extrapolating data from the available documentation in the DA files on 'deaths resulting from suspicious circumstances and criminal acts'.[4] This was due, first, to missing information – for instance, the gender of the victim was frequently not stated and had to be inferred from the victim's name or by grammatical usage (when in doubt, the case was excluded). Second, there was also an ambiguous means of classification. Our review of the files did not yield a single crime classified as a 'crime of honour'. Rather, three categories were used: 'fate and destiny' (*qada' wa qadar*), 'murder' and 'unknown' (see Table 7.2).

The category of 'fate and destiny', which covered 86 per cent of the total number of female deaths in the files (N = 273), is enigmatic.[5] In interviews with the author, the DA and his deputy defined it as:

> an act that is not attributable to any premeditated or intentional human act, but is a result of, for example, old age, stroke or accident that was not caused by any person. Thus, in this category, there is no suspicion of a criminal act, or human interference or action. The DA's office or prosecutors are delegated to determine if the case is attributable to fate and destiny, mainly when realising that no party is liable.[6]

Table 7.2 Distribution of reported deaths (suspected femicides) in the West Bank, as extrapolated from the District Attorney's files, 1996–98

Year	Fate/destiny	Murder	Unknown	Total
1996	60	10	6	76
1997	74	11	3	88
1998	100	7	2	109
Total	234	28	11	273

However, in a workshop attended by both the author and the District Attorney, the latter stated, in the presence of the majority of prosecutors from the West Bank and Gaza, that 'This category is problematic. There is a discrepancy in the way various prosecutors use it.... It is more than possible that it was used to cover up legal or social hardship stemming from honour crimes.'

The elasticity of this category may stem from the Muslim belief that all events are ordained by God rather than willed by human beings. We could also assert that the concept is a legal one, because it is similar to such legal categories as 'death by misadventure' – that is, without criminal liability. The motive behind the use of such a broad legal classification scheme is worthy of further study. The interviewees (the DA and his deputy) defined the category 'unknown' as:

> Somebody committed a criminal act that caused the death of a person, but his identity is not known to the DA. Here there is a need to keep on searching for the offender so that justice can take its course. In such cases, the file is kept active and is closed only after ten years owing to the statute of limitations.

Thus, in this category, somebody is liable for the act, but the DA cannot determine the identity of the actor.

The DA's use of ambiguous concepts to characterise cases of 'suspicious deaths' of females contrasts sharply with the 'honour crimes' documented in police records. This discrepancy is compounded by wide differences in numbers: whereas police records pointed to ten cases in which females were the victims of 'honour crimes' in the West Bank, official DA files recorded 234 cases of female deaths from 'fate and destiny', 28 cases of 'murder' and 11 deaths for which the killer was 'unknown'. One can only speculate on the number of deaths actually related to 'crimes of honour'. It is clearly possible that cases of femicide are embedded in the other forms of documented or undocumented deaths.

Field study 2: interviews with police and tribal personnel and social workers

Methodology

The lack of previous research and the intricacy of the issue of female sexual abuse (including the issue of IVT) suggested that we use the 'Grounded Theory' methodology. Grounded theory stresses the importance of the continuous interplay between analysis and data collection, with a general method of constant comparative analysis (Glaser and Strauss, 1967). This methodology allows us to generate theory initially from the data if needed. If theory exists and seems appropriate to the area of investigation, the data can be used to elaborate on or to modify the theory (Strauss, 1987).

The necessary sensitivity and complexity of conducting research on the topic of female virginity and sexuality, and the inherent problems involved in opening a dialogue on sexuality with victims and social control agents, required us to be very careful in our interview procedures and protocols and when gathering data. We had to develop a methodology that was contextually nuanced, yet did not create panic or discomfort among the victims and social control agents. Opening a dialogue with victims, therapists, doctors and legal personnel, we tried not only to learn but also to search for methods that could decrease the victim's trauma. The use of our qualitative research methods emphasises that the study is historically positioned and locally situated, and its meaning is 'radically plural, always open and ... there are politics in every account' (Bruner, 1993: 13). The study lays no claim to being politically neutral. The positions taken by interviewees reflected their place in the social hierarchy, their degree of political involvement, and the ways in which their susceptibility to social pressures (particularly attorneys and judges) affected their analyses of each crime (Acker, Barry and Esseveld, 1983).

The tribal legal system

One of our salient findings with criminal justice personnel was their collaboration with community leaders to regain public order, primarily after the occurrence of a crime. In every case, prosecutors and police officers told us that they had requested assistance from a *Mukhtar* – a tribal head – to help them resolve the crime as well as to control any ensuing disruptions in the social fabric. If the *Mukhtar* asked them to leave the resolution of the case to the tribal heads, then prosecutors and police officers tended to comply. The justifications given by criminal justice personnel ranged from gender discrimination (a 'woman's crime' did not warrant official involvement), to the realities of the political situation in Palestine. As one prosecutor stated:

It is hard in this political situation to function, and closing the case ASAP is the best way. So, I personally impose the virginity testing on everybody.... I have no time for discussions and negotiations ... if I do not get the medical report by today, I might lose track of the case the second day ... mainly due to the uncertainty of the political situation (Ramallah might be under siege in no time). So, the community leaders bring the victim and the offender's family by force to us, and the police and the tribal heads work together, we on the criminal part, and the tribal *Mukhtar* on the social part. They force the man to marry his rape victim (and you should know that some men refuse to do so ... but we punish them by forcing them to marry their victims), they reach an *Atweh* [a temporary 'truce'], they visit the families, they talk to the victim's *Wali* [male guardian], and they come up with fast solutions. In some cases the women may be killed – most of the women killed are sinful women.

A police officer echoed almost the same sentiments, observing that he trusted the community tribal leaders' judgement and that 'We in the police do not have so much time ... we do not have the power either.' A prosecutor stated: 'We can't oppose community leaders, they help us in restoring security. We need them and they need us.' A tribal head who also works in the police force stated:

Dealing with sexual abuse is very dangerous ... we need to make sure that [the] women are not playing games ... some women, and from a very young age, use their sexuality to incriminate men.... I could tell you of so many cases of women who falsely accused older men of abusing them, and they were lying. This intifada raised so many cases ... and I think that the economic situation, the lack of money and the higher poverty rate made many men and more women use their sisters and daughters to gain money from rich or respectable men... the tribal law system is the only one that can control this trend and put an end to women's use of their sexuality.

This quotation erases the victim's voice, feelings and pain.

As we sought to identify alternatives to conducting virginity testing, two main strands of thought emerged. First, among the legal personnel there was clear agreement that the practice of IVT cannot be abolished. They also clearly perceived the test as a means of safeguarding the family's 'honour', or what they saw as the preservation of family unity and security – in short, securing patriarchal interests over the victim's safety. According to one police officer:

Men in the family are the main victims ... and any solution should take into consideration what men go through when their female relatives are sexually abused ... men lose their sense of direction, and this is why they tend to kill the victim and resolve the problem. As the Arab proverb states, 'nothing can help you to accept something bitter except something even more bitter'. IVT helps us give them answers and allows us to offer fast solutions.... You agree with me that one can't leave a wild animal inside his house or [to] play with his children ... and men turn into wild animals when their 'honour' is hurt.... I think that the main solution is to focus on the condition of the family's men rather than the victim.... If the men are under control ... women and victims are safe.

Not surprisingly, the women's voices present a markedly different view. All except one female social worker and all the female lawyers who participated in the focus groups suggested the total abolition of IVT, believing that it causes more problems for the legal system and social services than it helps resolve. One social worker voiced the following opinion:

I think that IVT is by itself a crime ... but [it] is a crime conducted by the criminal justice system ... They create the laws, they impose it ... and the 'they' are all men.... so IVT is only promoting patriarchy ... and I do not think it has anything to do with evidence.... It is a game by the patriarchal system to further control us.... Abolishing such practice is the best.

Another social worker stated: 'If we continue to live in this political atmosphere where no law and no order is possible ... we can't support the collection of medical evidence.' To this comment another social worker answered:

It is not only the political, it is also the gender biases that law enforcement personnel believe in.... Only when we work with them, train them, help them to see the victim and the offender in a more fair manner can we conduct such examinations.

Discriminatory practices by presiding judges

Courts tend to believe that victims are not free of guilt. One judge stated in an interview with the author: 'No smoke without fire; she must have done something wrong to get killed.' For instance, in one case, where a brother killed his sister as a result of rumours that she was engaging in adultery, his sentence was reduced 'because the accused's sister stabbed him in his manhood' (ta'an rujulatahu – i.e. her behaviour was an affront to his manhood), and 'what the deceased said is considered in our society to be beyond what is acceptable.' Obviously, the perpetrator's claim that his sister had confessed to adultery could not be contested, as she was not present to prove him wrong. No rigorous examination (e.g. psychological assessment) was made to ascertain if the conditions for invoking Article 98 of the Jordanian Penal Code[7] were met (e.g. that the accused was in a state of extreme rage). Thus the court manipulated the evidence in a gender-biased and discriminatory manner to reduce the sentence of the killer and even justify his criminal act. It failed to safeguard the right of females to a safe and secure life, and failed to deter potential perpetrators from committing similar crimes, conveying a message to society at large that it is easy to kill women and get away with it.

The courts deemed all 'sexual' violations committed by females not only as 'wrongful' but also as 'dangerous' for the stability and integrity of society. In the words of one judge who was willing to be interviewed for the study:

> When a man kills another man in a war, you do not consider it a crime, but an act of heroism. When a woman violates the most sacred socio-cultural code, she puts herself in a state of war where there are no winners, and the actor cannot be considered a criminal either.

This type of reasoning clearly affected the outcomes of court trials. Examples of this can be found in the references made by the court in a case where a father was charged with murder after striking his daughter on the head with a rock: 'when the father was told that his daughter was not *salima* (was 'damaged')'; 'when the father suspected that the neighbour had a dishonourable relationship with his daughter'; 'when the father learned that his daughter was not a virgin'. The words used by the court to explain the crime objectify the victim, making her a sexual commodity that must be kept 'pure' and 'honourable'. The court painted a picture that seems to suggest the real crime was committed by the girl (by engaging in a dishonourable relationship, by losing her virginity), and then concluded that 'the father acted to cleanse the shame (*'ar*) and to protect and safeguard his honour (*sharaf*).'

Similar use of patriarchal justification for femicide by the court was apparent in a case where a 16-year-old girl was killed by her sister after admitting that she was pregnant by her fiancé. Although an autopsy of the interred body (the victim was buried without a medical examination) revealed that suffocation was the cause of death – as a result of the sister placing a 10 kg bag of detergent over the victim's mouth and nose – the accused sister was convicted of involuntary manslaughter, under the rather strained assumption that she had not realised that her actions would kill her sister. One of the salient features of this case was that no one considered whether the victim might have been raped – by her fiancé or anyone else. No one was willing to question the pregnancy, as her being the victim of sexual abuse would not have relieved the girl of her guilt. Rather, the focus was on the need to end her life so as to save the 'family honour'. No one even looked closely at the age of the victim; at 16 years of age, she was legally a minor, and, theoretically, even a consensual act of fornication could lead to charges against her partner. Yet no one thought to accuse her fiancé of sexual abuse of a minor. None of these questions was raised because they contradicted cultural practices. Thus deliberate misinterpretation of the evidence not only relieved the accused of guilt and punishment but also released society (family members, the fiancé, the judges) from examining the social issues of sexual abuse stemming from the case.

External socio-political pressures on the judicial system

The discriminatory practices detailed above appear to have been reinforced by external social and political pressures exerted on the judicial system. The legal treatment of women is affected by the political process of constructing, deconstructing or reconstructing a law. The Palestinian case study is one clear example of the effect of colonisation, military occupation and other political hardships on legislation and the entire criminal justice system. When weighed against pressing political concerns, women's 'social issues' are considered secondary. In one interview a judge stated, 'There are more important issues to be discussed on the current Palestinian agenda than raising the problem of the killing of women.' Another prosecutor stated that political hardships prevented him from relating to crimes against women in the 'right legal way': 'When we Palestinians achieve a stable political situation and construct our own legal system, we will be able to talk about due process.'

There have been cases where the political affiliations of the accused earned him leniency. In one such case, a Bedouin man was charged with murdering his female cousin (who was his fiancé) because she had 'ruined his reputation'. Two of his brothers and his father were charged as accomplices. The tribe of the accused published a newspaper advertisement calling upon President Arafat to intervene:

> A.H. is the one who killed his fiancé, who did not preserve his honour or oath. This young man, sir, is one of the sons of the glorious intifada, a son of Fateh that will never abandon any of its men. He has sacrificed three years of his life in the cells and prisons of the Zionist enemy for the sake of beloved Palestine.

A presidential decree was relayed to the prosecutor to cease all criminal proceedings against one of the brothers accused as an accomplice and to try the killer under the rubric of crimes committed on the basis of defending family honour.[8] It is believed that the President was persuaded to take such action for three reasons. First, the accused (killer and brother) claimed to be active members in the Intifada and supporters of one of the leading political factions (Fateh). Second, the president did not wish to alienate members of a large Bedouin tribe. Finally, he accepted the tribe's claim that the brother did not act as an accomplice, but was arrested as he was running towards the scene of the crime after hearing the screams of the victim. The court ceased all criminal proceedings against the brother, although it proceeded with its trial against the alleged killer. Although he was convicted of premeditated murder (under Article 328 of the Jordanian Penal Code), his sentence was reduced owing to extenuating circumstances (Article 99).

This case demonstrates how sexist social and political pressures were used to influence legal proceedings. This pressure not only exonerated one of the alleged accomplices and reduced the sentence of the murderer; it also justified the crime and 'accused' the victim of a greater one − failure to preserve the 'honour' and oath of her fiancé, which was tantamount to her betrayal of the beloved Palestine. Hence the murderer was defending not only his 'personal' honour but also the honour of Palestine. The case risks setting an extremely dangerous precedent: politically active men who victimise their women could be 'exempted' from paying a penalty for their crimes. Serving a nation under a political banner becomes a licence to kill females in order to preserve the honour of those who claim to have been part of the larger struggle for nationhood.

Social and legal acceptance of tribal codes

Analysis of the various interviews with the agents of formal and informal social control revealed that it is the unwritten tribal code that dictates the range of possible reactions towards sexual abuse. The question of how to re-vision an existing and extensive patriarchal culture in a region torn by war and conflict is hardly demarcated into a clearly defined oppositional binary of right and wrong. If anything, this research reveals how the issues inter-relate, indeed depend on one another for their expression within the culture. In Palestine, there is no ready-made solution for judicial reform, since the parallel legal civil and tribal systems are also co-eval and interconnected.

Discussion

This chapter examines the relationship between social tradition, law, politics and violence against Palestinian women, providing an illustration of sexism in the Palestinian criminal justice and parallel legal systems in a specific historical context and war situation in Palestine. Notwithstanding a growing national resistance to all forms of oppression, the legal, social, political and cultural practices prevailing in Palestinian society (mainly the West Bank) are orchestrated implicitly to mute the voices of victimised females and hinder the construction of abuses against women as a social problem. In essence, the murderer and society are reconstructed as victims, and the victim is turned into the guilty party. The sexual, physical and social lives of women become 'hymenised' (Abu-Odeh, 2000), and acts of violence against females become constructed as legitimate 'protective' behaviour rather than criminal actions.

Analysis of the two field studies points to an interrelation between sexism, crimes against women, masculine–patriarchal gender biases, and the socio-political and cultural context of a given society (see also Crenshaw, 1991; Shalhoub-Kevorkian, 2000a; Smart, 1995). These problems are undoubtedly not unique to the courts of the Palestinian Authority nor to Palestinian society, nor yet to the Arab region; the uniqueness of the situation in Palestine lies in the momentum of state-building that opens up the chance to re-examine and reconstruct fair and just legal remedies. Whether the state-building period will allow re-examination of gender-biased legal structures, or further empower customary religious and patriarchal civil laws, is a question yet to be answered.

Currently there are indications of the perpetuation of masculine political domination. One striking example is the reinvention of the *hamulah* and the PLS as a state mechanism: such legitimisation of the *hamulah* has negative implications for women's legal status and especially for crimes inflicted upon women. On the other hand, Palestinian women have managed to 'de-hymenise' the political sphere, participating together with their male partners in resisting oppression and occupation. This opens a window of hope that crimes against women can be reconstructed and 'dehymenised' so as to be addressed in a humanitarian manner.

The process of state-building has required Palestinian society to adopt political strategies that empower the rights and needs of women from a human rights perspective. Recently there have been calls by Palestinian legal scholars and human rights activists for a dialogue on the challenges facing the legal system. For example, Al-Rais (2000) has stated that the failure of the Palestinian legal system to function in an independent manner is connected not only to the legal legacy that preceded the establishment of the PA, but also to barriers posed by the PA itself and its structural, social and political components. Dara'awi and Zhaika (2000), studying the 'exceptional legal system' of the PA, conclude that Palestinian people are no longer willing to accept political justification for the lack of fairness and justice. They argue that, following the construction of the Palestinian Legislative Council, the responsibility for justice and fairness in Palestine should be controlled by state officials.

I believe that the state-building period ought to raise the willingness of the courts and the criminal justice system to express, authoritatively and humanely, their opposition to legalised gender discrimination and to unacceptable practices such as accepting gossip and rumours as evidence. A clear statement would strengthen due process and preserve the legal rights of citizens. Failure of the courts to initiate social dialogue on this issue, in addition to their adoption of the dominant 'cultural' discourse, is a matter of concern.

The Palestinian people's resistance to abuse, be it political or social-structural, is closely connected with resisting personal abuse. Not only is the personal arena political, but a country's liberation cannot be separated from the liberation of the individual from all forms of oppression, including gender oppression. The belief that unjust laws and legal proceedings related to femicide should be modified is related not only to the denial of rights to women victims but also to the right of society to have healthy social, legal and political practices. To expect a sister, father, mother or brother to kill their female relative is immoral, unhealthy, psychologically traumatising and leaves long-lasting scars. Hence, modifying the law and other legal practices not only helps to preserve minimal human values; it can also serve as a therapeutic method to heal the long legacy of wounds inflicted by such crimes. Modification of the law and re-examination of legal proceedings could eventually reduce the acceptance of killing as a method of dealing with socio-cultural and political hardships and may create new insight and new discourses in the newly established state.

The analysis presented here imparts an important message: the criminal justice system, as reflected in our data, is failing to safeguard the legal and human rights of the victims of violence against women. Palestinian society is challenged to find the means to provide women with a sense of safety, fairness and respect of their rights whenever they are faced with such threatening situations. Unless a new political, social and legal order is constructed to help society find alternate methods of dealing with such crimes, women will continue to be killed – abused – and held responsible for their own abuse and deaths.

One of the policy implications of a study such as ours is the need to invest in training medical and legal personnel to be more sensitive to the victim's ordeal. This obvious solution is not one that can be easily implemented. I believe that we need to begin by exploring the culturally sanctioned themes of sexuality and gender and how such themes and accepted beliefs are translated into bodily rights, and what comes to constitute a corresponding violation of those rights. Only when such a discussion is under way can we begin to develop regional, national and international strategies for overcoming related human rights violations in the region with reference to law and social and political practices. Thus, in opening critical discussion, sharing experiences and identifying common concerns, we can perhaps begin the arduous task of deconstructing taboos around sexuality, and particularly around women's sexuality. The study of sexual violence cannot be examined separately from the gender-biased power dynamics that activate and tolerate such violence.

Sexual autonomy and bodily rights lie at the core of human rights, and notions of equality and empowerment cannot be applied to daily life unless sexual and bodily rights are fully realised. Working with representatives of the criminal justice system and sensitising them to the subject at hand is one means towards achieving change. In addition, law, especially in the form of civil codes, penal codes and personal status codes, has emerged as a central point of discussion, with a clear imperative for legal reform to be undertaken from a holistic perspective. When working to change laws and policies, the underlying philosophy and overall perspective of the law should be considered, and proposed changes should aim for comprehensive reform to the extent possible. The recent focus on penal codes in the region appears crucial in this regard.

Lastly, I believe that networking, not only within the region but also with counterparts in other regions such as South Asia and Latin America, is essential for developing successful strategies for promoting sexuality and bodily rights as human rights. The sharing of materials, resources, knowledge, information and experiences underlines the importance of such collaborations. We should not postpone the full realisation of the violation of sexual and bodily rights as a human rights concern; any procrastination causes pain and agony to many voiceless and invisible individuals.

Notes

1. Translated in English as *Men under the Sun*.
2. Issued by the 19th session of the Palestine National Council meeting in Algeria, 15 November 1998.
3. See further al-Rais, 2000. Sardar Ali and Arif (1998) argue that parallel legal systems do not necessarily violate due process.
4. The law applied in the West Bank differs from that applied in the Gaza Strip. We therefore decided to concentrate on the West Bank in the current study, and hope to deal with Gaza in the future.
5. Note that the number of male deaths attributed to Fate and Destiny ($N = 425$) was far greater than the parallel number for females ($N = 234$). It is possible that many of the male deaths resulted from occupational accidents. Palestinian men far outnumber Palestinian women in the workforce, especially in such hazardous occupations as construction.
6. The interview was conducted in Ramallah on 7 June 2001, with Mr Salah Mana'a, the DA's representative, as District Attorney Asa'ad Mubarak was on extended sick leave at the time. However, Mr Mubarak approved this definition at a later time.
7. Jordanian criminal law is still applied pending Palestinian penal legislation. Article 98 of the Jordanian Penal Code provides: 'He who commits a crime in a state of great anger resulting from a wrongful (*ghayr muhiqq*) and dangerous act on the part of the victim shall be liable to a lesser penalty [in view of extenuating circumstances].'
8. The court's final decision mentions President Arafat's order on 28 November 1996 to stop all legal proceedings against accused no. 2.

8

Culture, national minority and the state: working against the 'crime of family honour' within the Palestinian community in Israel

AIDA TOUMA-SLIMAN

In 1998, on the evening of Eid Al-Adha,[1] Mithal Khateeb, a 17-year-old girl from a Palestinian Druze village in northern Israel, was killed by her brother while her family prepared for the celebrations. Mithal's brother claimed he killed her in order to defend the honour of the family. In a public statement made to the media, the police characterised the crime as an 'honour crime'. At Mithal's funeral, a police representative disclosed that Mithal was still a virgin at the time of the murder.

Two days before Mithal was killed, she was taken to hospital by her father, who wanted to know whether she was still a virgin. Her family suspected her of having relations with a young man from the village. The physician who was asked to perform the test refused. As Mithal was a minor, he was prohibited from performing such a test without an order by the police or courts. He directed the father to bring such an order from the city police. Attempts to obtain such an order often signal to the police a risk of potential harm to the young woman in question, especially when it is her own family requesting such an order.

Upon requesting the order from the police, Mithal's father was told that he could only obtain one if he suspected rape and wished to file a complaint, which he refused to do. In the presence of her sister, Mithal stated that she was afraid of returning home with her father due to the threat of violence from him and the rest of her family. She was sent to her sister's house in a nearby village for one night to give her father time to calm down, and was ordered to be taken back to her father's house the next day.

In accordance with those instructions, Mithal was taken back to her family home the following day. She was killed that night. There was no intervention by professionals, including the police or social workers, to prevent her return to the house.

This case, and scores of others, are indicative of the failures of the police and the professional system to protect and save the lives of many threatened women and girls. Such failures occur even though the law in such cases is clear, especially in the case of minors, and even though there is an existing infrastructure of safe houses and shelters to which the police can refer women and girls at risk. In the case described, the police did not seek professional help, nor did they direct her to a shelter, despite her statement that she feared serious violence.

There are approximately ten cases a year of femicide among the population of Palestinian citizens of Israel. The community, the authorities and the media identify such cases as 'honour crimes'. The taboo regarding 'honour crimes' within Palestinian society in Israel was first broken in 1991 by Al-Fanar, a Palestinian feminist women's group, which organised a demonstration protesting the murder of a young Palestinian woman by her father and brother. Working against such violence in the Palestinian community in Israel means tackling a social problem with cultural roots in a multicultural context, and within the day-to-day reality of a national minority living in a complicated political and social situation, influenced by a hostile state system that seizes any and all opportunities to control the future of this minority.

The Palestinian minority in Israel is a small community of some one million inhabitants living in rural and urban towns and villages. The community has gone through substantial changes since the Palestinian *Nakba*[2] of 1948 and the establishment of the State of Israel. Palestinian society in Israel moved from the traditional leadership representing it before the state, to a more organised political leadership, developing the minority agenda and struggling for the collective rights of the group. In the context of such a political reality and a minority struggle seeking unity of the community at any price, women's issues – including 'crimes of honour' as violence against women – were marginalised and ignored for the sake of the general cause. Any effort to challenge 'honour crimes' was perceived as an effort to shatter the delicate balance between the different political and social groups inside the community.

The ways in which activists challenged the taboo, and the strategies we adopted to address the issue within our particular socio-political reality, are outlined below. This chapter examines how the Palestinian community in Israel, particularly the political, social and religious leadership, approach 'crimes of honour'; how the police deal with cases of Palestinian women whose lives are threatened; how the legal system, including the prosecution and the judiciary, deals with cases of femicide and 'honour crimes'; the nature and modalities of 'honour crimes' among the Palestinian community inside Israel, including an examination of the profiles of perpetrators; and the effects of activism by women's and human rights groups in the last decade on preventing such crimes.

This chapter draws on a variety of primary and secondary sources. The research team identified fifty-eight cases of 'honour crimes' between 1984 and 2000, from the electronic court files, the media and NGO archives. Permission was granted by the General Director of Courts to review and photocopy files from the archives of District Courts in different areas of Israel over the period 1984–2000. This effort yielded the records of only twenty-five cases, due to the poor filing system; some of the cases could not be located at all, and other files contained only the judgment. The results of our analysis of these twenty-five case files are set out in the section below.

The second section of the chapter draws on a review of one daily and two weekly Arabic newspapers[3] for the years 1994–2001, with a view to exploring the nature of press coverage of cases, victims and murderers, any statements made by public figures, and assessing the level of importance attached to the issue. The press review yielded more than a hundred items of relevance to our study, including news items of murder cases and their follow-up, coverage of activities by al-Badeel and others on the subject of 'honour crimes', and analysis of and features on the problem. A more limited review was made of the Hebrew press over the same period.

The archives of al-Badeel and of Women Against Violence were a further source of material. Al-Badeel started in 1993 as a coalition of organisations combating 'crimes of honour'; it is discussed further in the second section below. Al-Badeel's archives include not only minutes of meetings and activity reports and evaluations through the years, but also all its correspondence and interventions with the Israeli establishment and various agencies on specific cases and on operational responsibilities.

Case analysis

Profiles of the murderers

In all twenty-five cases for which records were accessible to the research team, the victim was killed by a relative, with the variable being whether only one or more than one relative participated in the crime. Nineteen of the murders involved a sole perpetrator, while six involved more than one. There were a total of thirty-three perpetrators in the twenty-five cases.

Tables 8.1, 8.2 and 8.3 show the brother to be the most frequent perpetrator of 'honour killings', with fathers, cousins and uncles following. Arab tradition generally accords 'ownership' over the woman to her birth family; relocation to her husband's family is seen as an element of a temporary contract that can be dissolved by divorce. It is therefore seen as the responsibility of close male blood relatives in the natal family to 'punish' women, and it is their family's honour that must be regained.

The case files showed that most perpetrators fell within the age group 18–25,[4] The most common profile of a perpetrator was the victim's youngest

Table 8.1   Relationship of murderer to victim in all twenty-five cases

Relation	No. of perpetrators
Brother	13
Father	5
Husband	3
Cousin	3
Son	2
Sister	2
Mother	1
Uncle (paternal)	1
Uncle (maternal)	1
Father-in-law	1
Nephew	1
Total (25 cases)	33

Table 8.2   Relationship of murderer to victim in cases involving a single perpetrator

Relation	No. of perpetrators
Brother	8
Father	3
Cousin	2
Son	2
Husband	2
Father-in-law	1
Unknown	1
Total (19 cases)	19

Table 8.3 Relationship of murderer to victim in cases involving more than one perpetrator

Relation	No. of perpetrators
Brother	5
Uncle (paternal)	1
Uncle (maternal)	1
Father	2
Mother	1
Sister	2
Cousin	1
Nephew	1
Total (6 cases)	14

brother, aged in his early twenties. Older family members are generally needed for the financial support of the family; in some cases, the youngest of the family may be persuaded to make a false confession to safeguard an older member who is the actual perpetrator in view of the family circumstances. Younger family members are also less likely than older members to be married and have children; once released, after perhaps fifteen years in prison, they are able to start a new life, including getting married and having a family.

The crime scene

In the past, most 'honour crimes' were either committed in public or carried out in the family home and then announced in public by the murderer to the village and the rest of the family. In this way, the participating members of the family were able to prove to society the ability of their men to control women's behaviour, and to deter other women family members from behaving in a way deemed dishonourable. By making the community aware of the crime, the honour and respect lost through the perceived acts of the victim were considered to be regained. However, the case files examined for this study suggest a move away from the home as the site of the killing to more distant locations, with no public announcement of the deed. One reason for this shift may be a growing fear of retribution from the state legal system should the killing occur in a manner so obviously connected to the family, for example by taking place at the family home. Thus, an attempt to avoid punishment might be one reason that some perpetrators chose to commit the murder in remote public spaces such as the beach or a forest. Nevertheless, in two cases we studied, the crime was committed during the day in the village square in front of passers-by, more in keeping with patterns in the past.

The reason claimed for the crime

In the majority of cases (those classified in the first six rows of Table 8.4) the 'reason' claimed by the perpetrator(s) for the murder was directly related to sexual relations outside marriage. There remain, however, a significant number of cases where this was not the case, supporting the notion that, over the years, the meaning of 'honour' has expanded to include any behaviour by a woman not approved of by family members, such as challenging male authority and taking responsibility for her own life. As women have gained mobility and freedom in decision-making, men in the family have increasingly felt their authority being threatened and have thus increased their control over women's lives, punishing them for any behaviour that

Table 8.4 Reasons claimed for murder

Reasons claimed for murder	No. of cases
Relations with man other than husband	5
Rumours of relations with men	3
Pregnancy outside of marriage	3
Losing virginity	2
Relations with men outside marriage	1
Prostitution	1
Dress code and living behaviour	2
Staying out late and smoking	2
Divorcing the husband	1
Leaving the house frequently	1
Refusing sexual relations in forced marriage	1
Complaints to police and professionals about violence	1
Inter-religious marriage	1
Unknown	1
Total	25

might be comprehended as expressing women's sexuality. The development of new values in Arab Palestinian society in Israel which are weakening the patriarchal system can thus provoke adverse reactions; Hassan (1999: 307–56) expresses concern at new patterns of honour crimes in which men try to stabilise a changing world by using violence against women.

Previous approaches made by the victim

The case files showed that five of the victims, aware of the danger they were in, had sought help from police/professional agencies and from other family members before they were murdered. It is of course likely that at least some of the other women were aware of the danger they were in, but did not find the courage to approach anyone. As for those who did, in none of the five cases did the families or the police or other professionals act to protect the woman who had approached them for help.

The lack of assistance by police in such cases is not uncommon. On at least two occasions al-Badeel provided the Ramleh police department with a list of women who had been threatened with death by their family and who were not being protected by the police – in 1997 through an official letter to the police and in 1998 at a special meeting of the Parliamentary Committee for Status of Arab Women headed by the then Member of Parliament Tamar Goansky, convened in Ramleh and attended by the police, women from the community and al-Badeel representatives. The list contained the names of women, known to al-Badeel and Women Against Violence (through their crisis centre) who were reluctant to report to the police their fears and the potential danger they faced; despite the rumours circulating inside the community, and the fact that the women were thus known to most people they were not confident that the police would protect them. On the contrary, for these women reporting meant increasing the danger. Al-Badeel and Women Against Violence subsequently documented at least five 'honour crimes' cases involving victims whose names were on this list. Their cases are not among the twenty-five examined in this section, due on the one hand to disorganisation in the Tel Aviv District Court archives compounded by a certain lack of cooperation on the part of the court, and on the other to the fact that most of the cases remained unsolved by the police; thus no suspects were charged and no cases reached court. The conduct of the police is examined further below.

The case of Mithal Khateeb (discussed above) and that of 21-year-old Massara Maadi are two among tens of cases known to Palestinian women's organisations where the police ignored the women's complaints and referred them back to their families or to well-respected figures in society, who in turn handed them back to their families, and thus sent them to their deaths.

Charges

The charges submitted to the courts in the twenty-five cases accessed for this study included fifteen counts of first-degree murder; five that began as murder charges but were subsequently reduced to manslaughter; two of grievous injury; one of attempted murder and one of causing death by negligence (the last involving the same charges for three defendants).

In most of the cases reviewed, and others followed up by Women Against Violence and al-Badeel, where the murderer confessed to the crime and was convicted of the murder, the police failed to pursue the investigation any further, including failing to investigate whether other members of the family were aware that the crime was to be committed. This approach to closing cases meant that many accessories to the murder escaped punishment.

In addition, concerns are also raised by the manner in which charges are modified in a number of cases. As an illustrative case study, we can look at the death of Leila Keis in 1989, which involved her two brothers and a sister. According to the court protocols, the charge sheets and the prosecutor's statements, Leila was forced to take poison on the understanding that if the poison did not work she would have to find another way to kill herself; some hours later her brother checked on her and she informed him that the poison had not worked and that she had tried to hang herself but had failed. He told her to wait for another three hours and if the poison had still not worked to take more. Five hours later he checked on her and found her trying to get out of a well three and a half metres deep into which she had thrown herself. He forced her to take more poison, asked their sister to watch Leila in order to avoid her accessing any medical help, disconnected the phone, and went and informed the other brother. The brothers visited the house in the afternoon of the following day, saw the suffering that Leila was in, and left her with their sister. Leila died at midnight, her body systems in total collapse.

In November 1999, the court laid charges of first-degree murder against the older brother (under Articles 300(a) and 301 of the Criminal Law 1977 (CL)), and manslaughter against the second brother and the sister (under Articles 298, 262, 322, 29 CL). However, in May 2000, the charges were amended. The elder brother was charged with persuading or assisting a suicide (a felony under Articles 302, 29 CL) and the other brother and sister with causing death by negligence (a felony under Article 304 CL). The brothers received prison sentences of between three and four years. The sister, however, was not imprisoned following the intervention of community religious leaders who asked the court not to send her to prison because of the disgrace it would cause the family to have a woman member in jail. It is also worth noting that the brothers of the perpetrators worked as prison officers in the jail.

The law and the courts

While there is concern regarding both the investigation of 'honour crimes' by the police, and the reduction, in some cases, of charges from murder to less serious offences, when charges of murder (or attempted murder) do reach the courts, the Israeli judiciary do not readily allow consideration of issues of 'family honour' to be pleaded in defence by the accused. In some cases we studied, the court, having examined all aspects of the crime and having pronounced its judgment, considered it necessary to address generally the question of 'honour killing', so that its decision could serve as a warning to others and prevent them from taking another person's life claiming justification in upholding the tradition of 'family honour'. Such judgments also make it clear that these murderers should have no claims on the mercy or sympathy of the judges. A useful example is provided by a statement of the Regional Court of Haifa:

> As a concluding remark in this judgment, we consider it necessary to state that one should never expect that in the juridical system of Israel we will recognise the issue of family honour as an extenuating circumstance, which could result in mitigating the charge in cases such as the one under consideration here at the moment from an intentional murder to a manslaughter. Such recognition would mean giving an official permission to each and every one to kill another person when 'family honour' is at stake. There is no way such statements can be recognised within the framework of our juridical system, and hence Israeli courts will not accept the claim of the defence that 'family honour' is an acceptable factor which should be taken into consideration when deciding on a judgment if the life of an innocent and unhappy person was taken.[5]

Intentionally causing the death of a person is classified as murder according to Article 300(a)(2) of the Israeli Penal Law 1997. The requirements for a conviction of murder include proving 'an intent to cause the death of a person'. Under Article 301(a), an 'initial intent' to kill is present if there was a decision to kill another person, preparation for the act, and if there was no provocative behaviour on the part of the victim that could have served as a motive for the murder. With regard to the last, the prosecution needs to prove lack of provocation in order to show there was 'an initial criminal intent' which shaped the murderer's decision to commit the crime. From studying the cases which served as a basis for this study we can conclude that the majority of defendants claimed that they did not have 'the initial intent' to kill; rather, immediately preceding the murder, the victim provoked them so much that they lost control of themselves.

Legal tests have been developed to prove the absence or presence of provocation. Two such tests are required in order to reach a final decision: a subjective test and an objective test. If both tests are satisfied and provocation is proven, the charge will be amended from murder to manslaughter, for which the maximum penalty is twenty years in prison (as compared to life imprisonment for murder).

The subjective test establishes whether or not the provocative behaviour did in fact influence the defendant to such an extent that it caused a loss of self-control on his part and made him commit the murder. This is a personal test that takes into consideration the specific circumstances of the event. It should determine whether the behaviour of the victim immediately preceding the moment of the crime caused the defendant to react in a violent way, thus establishing a cause-and-effect relationship between the behaviour and the reaction to it. To prove that subjectively there was provocation, it must be evident that the decision to kill the other person was spontaneous, and taken at a moment of loss of control. In the case of a man charged with killing his sister, the Regional Court of Haifa found that there had been no spontaneous provocation for the following reasons:

> He who claims that he had been provoked must be able to prove that at the time when the murder was committed, there was a teasing and provocative behaviour on the part of the victim, which made him completely lose control of himself and react spontaneously. There is nothing in the story of the defendant that would justify the claim of a subjective provocation, which requires that the defendant prove a loss of self-control that would make the killing a spontaneous act, not based on a previous consideration.
>
> In the case with which we are dealing here, the defendant went home and brought the knife, after he heard the deceased woman's words that provoked his anger. The killing of the victim was performed in cold blood and cannot be regarded as a spontaneous uncontrollable reaction.[6]

The objective test establishes whether or not it is possible to predict that a 'person from the specific settlement', were he in the defendant's place, would be likely to lose self-control and commit a murder. It is used to establish the kinds of behaviour acceptable in the given environment. The objective test is only applied once subjective provocation has been proven. So as to avoid unjustified mitigation of the charge from murder to manslaughter, the courts require a positive answer to the question whether a 'rational person' or a 'person from the specific settlement' would react in the same way in the same circumstances. Here, the courts do not allow provocative behaviour to be classified according to the norms of certain sectors of the society or according to people's sensitivity to the opinion of community leaders, as, for example, in matters of family honour. It has been held that 'the objective test does not grant the option of classifying provocation by different sectors of the population or by sensitivity for the traditions of [different] sectors, such as decreasing honour of women.'[7]

The penalty for murder is a life sentence, which may be mitigated by the court in a limited number of cases (Article 300(a)):

1. When a severe mental disturbance limited the ability of the defendant to understand what he was doing or how condemnable his deed was, or to refrain from committing the deed.
2. When the deed exceeded to an insignificant extent the degree of reasonableness required if pleading self-defence, necessity or coercion/duress.
3. When the defendant was in a state of extreme psychological distress caused by the deceased's severe and prolonged abuse of the defendant or a member of the defendant's family.

Following the 1995 amendment of the Penal Law, which included the above-cited article, it is possible to reduce the length of the maximum punishment for murder, but only in cases where the ability of the defendant to take decisions was damaged as a result of a severe psychological disorder or because of a mental disability which significantly limited his ability to understand what he was doing, or how condemnable his deed was, or how it could be possible to refrain from committing the deed. The courts tend to make limited use of this article, and in the judgment referred to above of the Haifa District Court explicitly asserted caution in regard to cases such as the 'honour killing' it was then considering.[8]

Where murder charges are brought in cases of killing in the context of 'family honour', the Israeli courts tend to impose the maximum penalty available in law. In imposing such sentences, the courts have expressed their clear objective of achieving not only punishment but also deterrence of such crimes:

The defendant decided his sister should die, even though she had not broken the law in any way. The defendant committed an act which is most condemnable and for which he deserves no pardon and no mercy. The defendant's use of the concept of an 'offence against family honour' as an excuse lacks any justification. It is the duty of the court to subject the defendant to the most severe punishment which the Penal Law reserves for cases when a human life was taken in an act of intentional murder, of which the present case is an example. Let it be known to every person that the argument of 'an offence against family honour' lacks any justification that could explain an act of violence of any kind whatsoever, especially the taking of a person's life. We regard the deed of the defendant as an abhorrent and detestable act of murder to be punished with all the vigour of the Penal Law, that is – with nothing less than a life sentence. This punishment should serve as a memorable discouraging example for both individuals and collectives. The sanctity of human life is not an empty concept, and whoever takes a human life should know that he will be punished with the utmost severity of the Penal Law.[9]

The Supreme Court, for its part, has expressed its support of the tendency to apply the maximum punishment for violent crimes in the name of preserving family honour, in light of the significant deterrent impact of such cases.[10] The Supreme Court has also related its role to non-legal educational and developmental efforts, as illustrated in its ruling in a case where a man was charged with the attempted murder of his sister and sentenced to seven years in prison. In his appeal to the Supreme Court the man claimed that his punishment should be reduced as he had acted in accordance with acceptable social norms. The court responded as follows:

> [W]e are of the opinion, which we also expressed in this judgment, that the deed which the appellant committed is of the utmost gravity, and the social norm of preserving 'family honour' through violent action, which is still acceptable in this sector of society, is a false norm, and all possible steps should be taken to eradicate it. Clearly, this objective is to be achieved not only through penalising, but also, and to a great degree, by taking action in the sphere of education and social development, and the implementation of more advanced ideas.
>
> Together with this, the Court whose function it is to preserve the rule of law in the state would fail in the fulfilment of its duty if it did not contribute to a change of these ideas, and an eradication of this false norm, by inflicting a preventive and exemplary punishment.[11]

In the case files that we reviewed, the courts declined to accept the various arguments put forward by lawyers for the defence, which included that the objective test was different for the Palestinians in Israel because of the pressure put on the defendant by traditions and culture; that the defendant was provoked by the victim's behaviour or lifestyle which caused loss of control; and the testimonies of social, political, and religious leaders explaining the traditions.

The victim's voice

What is clear in our review of the case files is a silencing of the victim's voice in court. Not only is the victim not physically present, but her narrative and her story are not brought before the court. For the most part, the details that emerge about the victim are those given by the defendant, or by witnesses for the defence. While it is, of course, the case that the two

sides in a criminal case are the state and the defendant, it remains the fact
that in the records of proceedings and in the judgments, there is nobody
to defend the victim's rights. In cases of attempted murder, a victim might
be brought to court by the defendant's lawyers to tell the court that her
relations with the defendant had improved, and that she had forgiven him
and to beg the court for mercy. Thus, when the victim's voice was heard
in court, directly or indirectly, it was used for the benefit of the defendant
to seek a lighter punishment, either by proving her bad behaviour which
had provoked him and 'forced' him to attempt to kill her, or by indicating
to the court that he had changed and regretted what he had done to her.
The social and family pressures exerted on the victim in order to achieve
such interventions is clear from their testimonies. On the other hand, the
systematic silencing of the voice of the murder victim, unable to defend or
protect herself, is a violation of her rights even beyond her death.

The Palestinian community:
from taboo to opposition

In 1990 the first demonstration against 'honour crimes' was organised by
the al-Fanar organisation to protest the murder of a young village woman
by her father, who claimed that he had to kill her after he realised that she
was pregnant outside of marriage. Investigations revealed that the pregnancy
was the result of rape by one of the woman's relatives, a fact known to her
father. At trial, the father's defence team called as a witness the head of the
Higher Follow-Up Committee representing the Palestinian minority in Israel.
The witness, also a local mayor, stressed that the father had had no choice,
that what he had done was the only way he could continue to live in an
honourable manner: 'these are our traditions, and that is how we act'.

   This was indicative of the dominant attitude towards 'honour crimes'
among the Palestinian community at that time. Al-Fanar and a group of
intellectuals and human and women's rights activists initiated a petition asking
for the resignation of this very public figure from his position. The petition
attracted a lot of attention and was published as a paid advertisement in the
newspapers. Although the called-for resignation did not follow, the effort
started a certain momentum and established the visibility of the challenge
to 'crimes of honour' that continues to this day.

   At the beginning of 1993, ten women and human rights activists established
al-Badeel, a coalition to combat honour crimes. Over the years the coalition
expanded to include more individuals and organisations, namely Women
Against Violence, the Arab Association for Human Rights, Kayan (a feminist

organisation), the Emergency Shelter in Haifa, Al-Siwar, the Movement of Democratic Women, the Crisis Centre for Support of Victims of Sexual Assaults–Haifa, the Emergency Line for Victims of Physical Violence, and several individuals, including social workers, lawyers and writers. Eventually, excluding the representatives of the various organisations, more than twenty-five activists were involved in al-Badeel, pursuing a range of strategies to widen the constituency of those condemning 'honour crimes' and working to raise public awareness in the community of their dangerous effect on society as a whole. A petition was circulated for signature and published, along with several articles on the subject; demonstrations and memorials for the murdered women were organised; and open lectures and workshops were held in public halls and in high schools. In addition, advocacy interventions were made to stakeholders, parliamentarians, ministers, police officials and others. Additional attention was drawn to these efforts when those in the community who disapproved of them sought to attack demonstrators. The fact that the petition was published as a paid advertisement forced the press to take note of the issue, and more critiques developed as to how the media dealt with 'honour crimes'.

In December 1994, al-Badeel held the first ever public meeting and study day on 'crimes of honour', focusing on the various aspects of the problem and seeking to educate the public. Although this event placed the problem of 'crimes of honour' firmly on the public agenda of Palestinian society in Israel, at that point no political figure participated in or took a clear position on the issue. Efforts continued with the Higher Follow-up Committee of Palestinians in Israel. A request by al-Badeel in October 1995 for the Committee to take an official position on 'crimes of honour' was ignored. In 1997, al-Badeel succeeded in getting the subject on the Committee's agenda but the resulting decision was very vague and the discussion included an intervention by a then leading figure of the Islamist movement (who was also a local mayor) to the effect that the women's movement should educate women in good behaviour.

However, changes in the positions of the Palestinians' political leadership were beginning to emerge. In 1997 the mayor of Nazareth participated in a memorial event organised by al-Badeel at the offices of Women Against Violence to commemorate the victim of an 'honour killing'. He told those present that '[w]e need to begin a serious discussion on these crimes ... to bring the largest popular forces to combat them. Such a struggle for serious social change needs the biggest forces from the people.' He called on the Follow-Up Committee to translate condemnation of 'honour crimes' into 'actual positions in each crime and into a viable plan of action' (al-Ittihad and al-Sinara, 2 February 1997).

Throughout 1997, members of parliament from the leftist Democratic Front for Peace and Equality addressed the issue of honour crimes by demanding clear positions from the religious leadership and assertive actions from the police. One Member of the Knesset, for example, 'demanded that the leadership from all the religions make every effort and work seriously against the problem of femicide against the background of family honour' (*al-Ittihad*, 22 May 1997). The Islamist political movement was also obliged to address the issue; in an editorial in their newspaper *Sawt Alhaq Walhuria* (7 February 1997) they condemned 'crimes of honour' but blamed immoral behaviour and women's dress codes, stressing that if religious rules were followed these crimes would disappear.

Fresh impetus was added when, in February 1998, the office of the President of Israel, Eizer Weizman, announced that in honour of Israel's fiftieth Independence Day, the President would grant amnesty to a number of prisoners, particularly those convicted in cases of 'honour crimes'. Al-Badeel initiated a petition to the President condemning his intentions and demanding that such plans be cancelled. Many people joined the initiative, which was eventually successful in stopping the plan for amnesties. In September of that year, a number of prominent political leaders from the Democratic Front and the General Secretary of the Altajamoua Alwatani Party joined a demonstration organised by al-Badeel in Nazareth. By this time, it was clear that Palestinian society in Israel was witnessing a change in the attitudes of the leading political parties. Different political leaders began to take a more active role in relevant discussions at various parliamentary committees, demanding more active efforts from the police and welfare authorities to protect Palestinian women from 'crimes of honour'. The Islamist movement in the meantime maintained its position of condemning the killings but blaming the behaviour of women.

As for the media, the turning point in Arabic press coverage came in 1995, after the murder of Ibtihaj Hasson, when the media reported that the people of the village gathered around the body clapping and cheering the murderer. This tragic and ugly scene was the impetus behind a wave of articles by intellectuals and human rights activists condemning both this murder and honour crimes in general. Prior to this, the press mostly ignored such crimes, and when it did cover them did so in the inside pages in short 'factual' reports presenting the news of the murder, the identity of the murderer, and the reason provided by the latter for the deed. After 1995, press releases issued by al-Badeel and women's organisations such as Women Against Violence were given more space in the newspapers; these press releases included details on the victim, bringing her otherwise forgotten identity into view.

Criticism of the dehumanising approach of the newspapers gradually produced a different approach. Newspapers began conducting interviews after each crime, presenting the attitudes of politicians and religious leaders, mainly focusing on the issues of adultery and sexual relations outside marriage. This at the same time reinforced the mistaken public perception that every victim of an honour crime was a woman who had committed adultery or led a very open sexual life. At the same time, the media could not ignore the activists from al-Badeel and women's organisations and were obliged to give space also to their voices. By 2000, different versions of each story of an 'honour crime' were being presented along with more details on the victim. For example,

> Hussein used to beat and insult his wife (the victim) since their first year of marriage fourteen years ago; many times she needed medical care after he beat her, and it is clear that he stalked his wife even when she went on the roof to hang out the laundry. (*Kull al-'Arab* 18 January 2002)

The Hebrew media, for its part, all but ignored 'crimes of honour' as an issue until the late 1990s. This approach can be explained only by assuming that it regarded such incidents as an internal Palestinian issue not related to the general public debate and not connected to femicide in particular or gender-based violence in general. Such coverage as there was tended to be by way of a short descriptive report providing the name of the victim and reporting suspicions of the crime having been committed against the background of 'family honour', with the murderer's stated justification. One outstanding exception to this pattern was a unique article published in *Haaretz* in 1990 by a Jewish Israeli columnist, Kobi Nieve. Titled 'Murder permitted, murder prohibited', the article considered the murder of Jamila Gaben by her father, the first case around which al-Fanar mobilised. The writer criticised the attitude of the Palestinian community in Israel and its leadership, arguing that

> the way they would have protested and screamed in the case of murder of Arabs for being Arabs – that's how they should have protested and screamed in the case of murder of women for being women.... Those who justify the murder of women in the name of any religion or tradition justify, in effect, the murder of Arabs also in the name of religion and tradition, and the murder of Jews in the name of religion and traditions, and Armenians.

This article was very much an exception, though. More generally, and in contrast to their coverage of the murders of Jewish Israeli women following domestic violence, the Hebrew media did not carry out any further investigation of the cases they reported, nor did they seek to look at the story from other angles. Similar to radio and television reports, the size and placing of news of such crimes indicated that 'crimes of honour' against Palestinian women were assigned lesser importance than the murders of Jewish women in Israel; the latter cases tend to be headline news.

The activities of al-Badeel and other groups had a certain impact on coverage of 'honour crimes' in the Hebrew media, noticeable in the late 1990s, including through presenting the internal discussion within the Palestinian community on this issue. The media began reporting on activities organised against 'crimes of honour', and from around 1998 the press began to approach women's groups such as Women Against Violence when cases occurred, seeking expert opinions, statistics and explanations. While previously the Hebrew media tended to present the problem as one of tradition, the inclusion of comments by and interviews with Palestinian activists led to the inclusion of criticism of police conduct and of the operation of other governmental agencies in relation to the issue.

Conclusions

This overview documents a long process of progress in the struggle conducted within the Palestinian community in Israel against 'honour crimes'. The efforts started with a small group, but through the years managed to create a public discussion on different levels – among broad sections of the public, among the community's political and religious leadership, among parliamentarians, ministers, the police, the judiciary and different state agencies.

If it is clear that the main catalyst was the creation of the coalition al-Badeel, with a set of high-profile and focused activities during the 1990s, it is also clear that the issues faded somewhat from general public debate after the year 2000. Two main reasons can be identified for this. The first is the political and military context which has produced an emergency situation, particularly in the West Bank and Gaza, since the outbreak of the second Palestinian intifada there in September 2000. Events since then included those of October 2000 when twelve Palestinian citizens of Israel were killed by the Israeli police force during demonstrations, the re-invasion by the Israeli armed forces of the Palestinian Authority areas (Palestine), and the growing humanitarian crisis in those territories. Against these events, the national political agenda has taken precedence over the women's social agenda. As has happened in the history of other conflict areas in the world, Palestinian civil society forces invested their primary efforts in the national issue and struggle in what is a crisis situation. The second reason is also comparable to experiences elsewhere. The experience of working in a coalition (al-Badeel) was new for all those involved, and brought together a range of organisations and activists. The challenges of organising and managing the processes of cooperation, coordination and facilitation were considerable, and at a certain point it became difficult for al-Badeel to continue to work as a coalition and to maintain the momentum of the work.

At the same time, the achievements of the active struggle of the previous decade are considerable, including the mainstreaming of the issue in the general activities of most civil society institutions and organisations, and influencing in some way the approaches of governmental and state agencies and the ways in which they engage with such crimes. 'Honour crimes' continue to occur, but those committed to their eradication, and indeed to the elimination of all forms of violence against women, now have considerable ground on which to build in designing and mobilising their interventions and strategies of response.

Notes

I would like to thank the following for their contributions to and assistance with the preparation of this chapter: Advocate Nasreen Eliemy-Kabaha, Rola Hamed, Naila Awwad, Suad Abed, al-Badeel, Women Against Violence, and in particular Joyce Song. The author is General Director of Women Against Violence and co-founder of al-Badeel.

1. The Feast of the Sacrifice, one of the two most important religious festivals in the Islamic calendar.
2. Literally 'disaster' or 'catastrophe'.
3. *Al-Ittihad*, *Kull al-'Arab* and *al-Sinara*.
4. None was aged below 18.
5. *State of Israel* vs. *Husam Kinaan*, 20 February 1996, Criminal Case No. 163/94 (Haifa), per Judges M. Lindshtraus, B. Gilor and S. Jubran.
6. *State of Israel* vs. *A'amir Hassun* Criminal Case No. 217/95.
7. *Azzam* vs *State of Israel*, Cr.M. 193/86, P.D. 41(3)343, 349.
8. *State of Israel* vs. *A'amir Hassun,* Criminal Case No. 217/95.
9. *State of Israel* vs. *Hussam Ben Salih* Criminal Case No. 163/94(Haifa).
10. *Muhammad Kango* vs. *State of Israel*, High Court Precedent, Vol. 92(2), 1992.
11. Supreme Court Case No. 233/85 Vol. B, 862.

Changing the rules?

Developments on 'crimes of honour'

in Jordan

REEM ABU HASSAN

AND LYNN WELCHMAN

Jordan is the country most intensely under the international spotlight when issues of 'crimes of honour' are discussed, perhaps along with Pakistan. This international attention can be supportive and can assist local strategies of response by giving a global context to the work and avoiding the impression that this is a peculiarly 'Jordanian problem' through placing the issue where it belongs, in the global framework of violence against women. However, it can also be problematic when – as is sometimes the case – links are made, inadvertently or deliberately, with Islam, or with some monolithic notion of 'Arab culture' or 'Jordanian culture'.

The title of this chapter, 'Changing the Rules?', alludes to the different bodies of 'law' that impact on the efforts to eliminate 'crimes of honour' in Jordan (and probably elsewhere in the world): the rules of legal texts, the rules of judicial interpretation in the courts, and the unwritten rules in different communities and sections of our society that have equal if not greater impact on the lives and freedoms of women and girls. 'Honour' killings that take place in Jordan and in other parts of the Arab world such as Palestine, Lebanon, Yemen and Egypt represent an extreme form of violence against women. It is thought that many cases of sudden female deaths presented as suicide are associated with honour crimes. Honour crimes are most usually committed by a male family member against a female relative suspected of adultery, extramarital sexual relations, pregnancy outside marriage, and so on. In such cases, the male murderer may benefit from a provision in the Penal Code allowing for a light sentence not exceeding a year in prison. These crimes are associated with Article 340 of the Penal Code, although this article may not in fact apply, as discussed further below. The explanations given for the continuing incidence of such crimes include their part in the broader pattern of male resistance to changing norms of social behaviour, the shifting power relations between the genders, women's increasing exposure to and involvement in public life, and the fact that Jordan remains an 'honour-based' society.

Issues of gender and women's rights became a priority in Jordan's political and social agenda in 1996, following the Fourth World Conference on Women in Beijing in 1995.[1] The democratisation process and the Beijing women's conference helped stimulate the creation of an environment where sensitive issues of women's legal status and equality before the law were discussed and challenged. People began to realise that violence against women exists as a social problem, and there is growing recognition that violence against women is not a private matter, but rather a criminal offence that merits a strong and swift response.

With specific regard to 'crimes of honour', activists in Jordan had been addressing 'honour killings' as one manifestation of violence against women since the early 1990s, but the profile of this work changed substantively at the end of the decade. Journalist Rana Husseini had been covering cases of 'honour crimes' in the English-language *Jordan Times* for some years, drawing attention in particular to the leniency of sentences given to convicted perpetrators in Jordanian courts. Her coverage attracted substantial local and international attention, and in 1998 she was awarded the Reebok Human Rights Award for her work. According to Nanes (2003: 119) it was this award that prompted interest from the CNN network, resulting in a short television 'segment' on 'honour killings' in Jordan. A civil society campaign was set up, the National Jordanian Campaign to Eliminate So-called Crimes of Honour, which Nanes considers to have been a 'unique civil society phenomenon' in the country (2003: 113) and to which Human Rights Watch gave its 'highest recognition' by way of an award in 2000, following the Campaign's high-profile efforts to collect thousands of signatures to a petition on the subject. Internationally, there was, as well as more general action on 'honour crimes' at the United Nations, described elsewhere in this volume, a substantial amount of attention devoted to the particular manifestation of this form of violence against women in Jordan, including from the Western media[2] and from international human and women's rights organisations and activists; there is thus a growing body of English-language literature on various aspects of 'crimes of honour' in Jordan, including a recent report from Human Rights Watch (2004) and a number of journal articles.[3]

Such material draws primarily on the efforts and experiences of organisations, agencies and individuals in Jordan who are in different ways engaged with developing strategies of response to 'crimes of honour'. Issues of particular focus that are addressed include the ongoing attempts to establish a shelter in Jordan for victims/survivors of domestic violence, including women at risk of 'crimes of honour', and the established practice of such at-risk women being placed in 'preventive' detention by order of a local administrative Governor.[4] Associated concerns include the police practice of imposing virginity tests upon women and girls at the request of their families, and more generally the development of capacities in police and other agencies to deal with domestic violence.

One major development in this regard is the promulgation of the Ordinance of Shelters for Family Protection (No. 48 of 2004) by the Council of Ministers. The Ordinance is a positive step in the relationship between women victims and the state, since it obligates the state to establish and render services to victims of domestic violence. The state has thus acknowledged its duty to provide its citizens, especially women, with safety and security, and recognised that the state is not a bystander but has a role in intervening when violence occurs in the private sphere.

Besides challenging the concept of 'honour killings' within different sections of Jordanian society, advocacy work among civil society activists – particularly the women's movement – has focused on legal texts and their application in practice. One of the aims of the National Jordanian Campaign to Eliminate So-called 'Crimes of Honour' was to secure the repeal of the above-mentioned Article 340 of the Penal Code, which provides as follows:

1. He who surprises his wife or one of his [female] *mahrams* ('unlawfuls')[5] in the act of committing unlawful sexual intercourse with somebody and kills, wounds or injures one or both of them, shall benefit from the exonerating/exempting excuse (*'udhr muhill*);

2. He who surprises his wife or one of his ascendants or descendants or siblings with another in an unlawful bed, and kills or wounds or injures one or both of them, shall benefit from the mitigating excuse (*'udhr mukhaffaf*).

In her important article on 'crimes of honour', Lama Abu Odeh (1996: 143) traced the origins of this Article to two sources, the Ottoman Penal Code of 1958 and the French Penal Code of 1810.[6] Its inclusion in the Jordanian Penal Code legalises a societal expectation that a male may – or perhaps should – kill his adulterous female relative in order to cleanse his family's honour of the shame that her extramarital sexual relations have brought. The first clause of Article 340 exempts the perpetrator from criminal penalty in the specified circumstances, which involve finding a person in flagrante delicto – catching the victim in the very act of extramarital sexual intercourse

– and the close family relationship between perpetrator and victim, which is such that they cannot lawfully be married to each other (*mahram*). This clause has rarely if ever been applied in the Jordanian courts.

The second clause of Article 340 allows for the granting of a mitigating or extenuating excuse, and the awarding of a reduction in penalty, which may result, in the event of a felony (such as murder with intent), in a prison sentence of six months to two years. The courts have interpreted the term 'unlawful bed' to mean a situation in which a woman is lying down with a man in a state which makes probable the existence of an illicit relationship between them. There is some jurisprudence on this clause, but it also is rarely invoked in practice.

Despite the little use made of Article 340 in the Jordanian courts, its repeal has been the target of sustained efforts by Jordanian human rights and women's rights groups, as well as by the government itself. Among the arguments raised by those who call for its repeal is the issue of constitutionality. Article 6(1) of the Jordanian Constitution provides that

> Jordanians shall be equal before the law. There shall be no discrimination between them as regards their rights and duties on grounds of race, language or religion.

The term 'Jordanian' refers to both men and women. In Arabic the male form of the adjective includes males and females. Numerous constitutional provisions guarantee the right of 'every Jordanian' to freedom of opinion, education, employment, political participation, and so on. These articles apply to men and women alike. Their application is not hindered by the fact that the constitutional guarantee does not specify discrimination on grounds of sex/gender. It has been interpreted that the grounds mentioned in Article 6(1) are examples of the forms of discrimination known by the legislator at the period of time when the Constitution was written in 1952. Therefore the constitutional provision is not restricted by these grounds and is open to govern any form of discrimination that may arise, including gender discrimination. This constitutional recognition of gender equality coexists with legal gaps in Jordanian legislation which fail to protect women's rights in some aspects.

At the end of 1999, against the background of the National Campaign's petition and increasing attention to these issues inside and outside Jordan, the government presented to the legislature a draft bill to repeal Article 340, following a request from the Jordanian National Committee for Women, the body officially charged with dealing with women's issues. This attempt failed when the elected House of Deputies twice rejected the draft, although the upper house, the Senate, approved the change. During one of the debates in parliament, certain deputies charged that the recent national campaign and efforts to get the article repealed were attempts by the West to infiltrate Jordanian society and make Jordanian women immoral.[7] This is only one illustration of the sort of challenges faced by activists on this issue, which underlines the need to present our advocacy as of internal motivation and initiative, even while we work within and claim as our own the framework of international human rights.

At the end of 2001, the government promulgated an amendment to Article 340 by way of temporary legislation in the absence of a sitting parliament. The Article as amended reads as follows:

1. Whosoever surprises his wife or one of his ascendants or descendants in the crime of adultery or in an unlawful bed, and kills her immediately or kills the person committing adultery with her or kills both of them or attacks her or both of them in an assault that leads to death or wounding or injury or permanent disability, shall benefit from the mitigating excuse.

2. The wife shall benefit from the same excuse if she surprises her husband in the crime of adultery or in an unlawful bed in the marital home and kills him immediately or kills the woman with whom he is committing adultery or kills both of them or attacks him or both of them in an assault that leads to death or wounding or injury or permanent disability.

3. The right of lawful defence shall not be permitted in regard to the person who benefits from this excuse, nor shall the provisions of 'aggravated circumstances' apply.[8]

The amendment replaces the excuse of exemption or exoneration with that of mitigation and extends the same possibility of a reduction in sentence to a woman who finds her husband committing adultery in the marital home. The terms of the third paragraph prevents the application in these circumstances of Article 341, which deals with legitimate self defence.[9] Article 341(1) permits self-defence in all crimes against one's own or another's person or honour ('ard), including abortion, rape, sexual molestation, kidnapping, prostitution, harassment and consensual sexual relations, provided that

1. the act of self-defence takes place at the time of the assault against person or honour;

2. the assault is unrightful;[10]

3. the accused could not put an end to this unrightful assault against person or honour except with the act of murder, injury or any other effective act (that is claimed as self-defence).

Once again, the progress of this amendment has been troubled. When parliament reconvened following national elections in 2003, it began the task of reviewing all the temporary legislation issued by the government (in accordance with Article 94 of the Constitution) in the absence of parliament.

The House of Deputies rejected the temporary law, including this amendment,[11] twice in the late summer of 2003, while the Senate approved it. The future of the amendment is thus still uncertain.

In the meantime, it remains the case that most perpetrators of 'honour killings' do not rely on any part of Article 340, pre- or post-amendment, in defending their actions in court. Instead, the vast majority of cases are defended on the basis of Article 98, which provides as follows:

> Whosoever commits a crime in a state of extreme rage resulting from an unrightful [*ghayr muhiqq*] and dangerous act on the part of the victim shall benefit from the mitigating/extenuating excuse.

This article is clearly of more general availability to a defendant than Article 340. Where the court finds the extenuating excuse to apply, it may reduce to a half the penalty for a felony, and to reduce any penalty for other crimes that have a minimum penalty of imprisonment for three years to a sentence of prison for a year.

Two components of Article 98 have been the subject of particular focus in the jurisprudence of the Jordanian courts: the perpetrator's claim to have been in a state of extreme rage (or a 'fit of fury' in the words of Abu Odeh, 1996), and the meaning of an 'unrightful and dangerous act' on the part of the victim of the subsequent crime. On the first, although the violent reaction does not have to be immediate, the courts have held that knowledge of the victim's act for a long period of time serves to reduce the effect of the anger on the perpetrator and therefore renders the extenuating excuse not available. According to the Court of Cassation, the fit of fury should have a severe impact on the accused, leading in that moment to him being deprived of any sense or perception, as well as of self-restraint, and thus becoming incapable of controlling himself (Court of Cassation Case No. 213/2004). The importance of determining the time period stems from the fact that the court differentiates between premeditated murder and murder resulting from a fit of fury, since the two cannot go together. Premeditated murder requires calm thinking and deliberation coupled with a period of time for that calm thinking to settle, as well as a premeditated intent to commit the crime. The mind, entrusted with responsibility and comprehension, is clear because of such calm reasoning and deliberation on what the person intends to do and reflection on the consequences. The fit of fury, on the other hand, means that the mind is confused and the self is agitated and therefore the person cannot think in a calm manner. The Court has stressed that no person could be in these two different states at the same time (Court of Cassation Cases No. 224/2000 and No. 979/2000). Consequently, the court engages in a debate on the time period between the accused gaining knowledge of the female's conduct and committing the crime. This debate shifts the attention from the killing itself to the absence of intent on the part of the accused, whom the court concludes as having acted spontaneously against an aggression on his honour, not his physical being. Thus the Court tends to overlook evidence of intentional homicide on the part of the accused and focuses instead on the behaviour of the victim and its alleged provocative impact.

The time period acceptable between the accused gaining knowledge of the female's conduct and committing the crime has fluctuated over the years. On some occasions the Court extended this period to one week, and at one point even to two weeks. However, recent judgments (1999–2003) have specified that reaction to knowledge of the victim's act by the perpetrator should be instantaneous and immediate in order to benefit from the fit-of-fury defence; the fit of fury should place the perpetrator in a state that negates any pre-arrangement or calm reasoning. In one recent case the Court held this to be no more than fifteen minutes (Court of Cassation Case No. 749/2002). The Court is thus shortening the time period during which the accused might be able to appeal to the defence of fit of fury.

Recent court rulings (e.g. Court of Cassation Case No. 1514/2003) have stated that in order to benefit from Article 98 the following is required:

1. the unrightful act committed by the victim should be committed against the accused;
2. this act should be dangerous, causing a fit of fury, and the crime should be committed before the effect of such fury lapses;
3. the act by the victim should be physical and not an utterance.

In one case, the Court concluded that the accused father knew of his daughter's misconduct five months before killing her (Court of Cassation Case No. 484/1999); in another, the accused knew of his sister's behaviour but the acceptable period of time had lapsed after the occurrence of the fit of fury (Court of Cassation Case No. 184/2000). Neither accused benefited from Article 98, although such knowledge could constitute an extenuating reason according to Article 99.

On the second issue raised by Article 98, that of an 'unrightful and danger-ous act', court cases show that the major reasons for committing such crimes are extramarital relationships, as well as suspicion of the victim's behaviour, committing adultery, prostitution, indecent behaviour and running away from the family home. In one case, the Court held that the victim, who was talking and pleading with her brother to believe her when he killed her, did not act other than in a rightful way with her brother, since she was talking to him in a manner which would not trigger his anger and lead him to kill her (Court of Cassation Case No. 453/1997). On the other hand, the courts have considered that an extramarital pregnancy on the part of the victim can constitute a wrongful and dangerous act on her part. Lama Abu Odeh (1996: 157–61) has examined a number of rulings on these issues from the Jordanian Court of Cassation from the period 1953–82, which shows that the court is lenient in accepting this tribal/legal criterion in such cases. This stems from the belief that the fit of fury can be triggered by the threat to the perpetrator's position which may be posed by infringements on the family honour. Thus, certain types of conduct by female members of the family could threaten the perpetrators' position and trigger a fit of fury.

It should also be noted that when the Court accepts such a defence, it is always connected with a waiver of the personal claim by the victim's family. Customs and traditions push the guardian of the female victim to waive the personal claim and drop charges. Waiving the personal claim by the guardian allows the court to use its discretion in applying extenuating reasons in accordance with Articles 99 and 100, allowing for lenient sentences even when Article 98 does not apply.

In general, however, it appears that the judiciary is beginning to take a firmer stand in such cases. Public prosecutors are now investigating such crimes more thoroughly, and such defences are no longer taken at face value. The investigations are being extended to ascertain whether the time period was instantaneous, whether the victim did indeed act in a wrong and dangerous way which caused a fit of fury, and whether it was the case that the perpetrator did not know previously of the victim's conduct. Hitherto the Court has not tackled the issue of conduct in a proper manner. A very recent case, from August 2004 (Court of Cassation Case No. 831/2004), is an example of the court's new position. The case record shows that the public prosecutor did in fact conduct a thorough investigation following the killing of a female by her brother because she expressed her refusal to marry her cousin. The court stated that the female's refusal to marry is a legitimate right guaranteed by the Islamic *shar'ia* and by the law. Notable is the fact that the victim's refusal was because she was in love with someone else; this was corroborated by the testimony of the victim's sister. The Court decided that the victim had not engaged in a dangerous act which might provoke the perpetrator; therefore he was not in a fit of fury when he murdered his sister and consequently could not benefit from Article 98.

Thus, while the concept of 'wrongful and dangerous act' remains challenging in the jurisprudence, the last few years have seen a number of rulings in the Jordanian courts that appear to indicate changes in attitude towards the perpetrator's claim to have been in a state of extreme rage or 'fit of fury'. These changing attitudes come against the background of increased domestic and international attention to 'crimes of honour', and the growing awareness in Jordanian society that violence against women is a phenomenon that needs serious attention.

In conclusion, a discussion (however brief) on developments in addressing 'crimes of honour' and violence against women in Jordan would be incomplete without mention of the controversy surrounding the book *Forbidden Love*, written outside Jordan under the name Norma Khoury and distributed by her publishers as a true account, a 'non-fiction *memoire*', of the 'honour killing' of the author's best friend in Amman. The book attracted considerable attention internationally; it is reported to have sold some 250,000 copies worldwide and Khoury's accounts and readings 'moved festival audiences to tears'.[12]

Readers familiar with the struggle against 'crimes of honour' in Jordan were taken aback at the hostility to Islam and to Jordanian society that they perceived in the text. In Jordan, activists who had worked for years on the issue identified a variety of errors and inconsistencies in the book, and, concerned at the possible impact, and at the image of the country they felt was being presented in the book, challenged the presentation of the work as non-fiction. Although the author maintained (and maintains) the truth of her account, in the summer of 2004 the Australian publishers withdrew the book from sale. In Jordan, the impact of the affair can hardly be overstated. The prominent journalist and campaigner Rana Husseini, mentioned at the beginning of this chapter, has been quoted as stating that it 'has ruined our cause'.[13] Those who oppose the advocacy of change, those who suspect a Western agenda to lie behind all such activism, are quick now to dismiss interventions on this issue as fiction and exaggeration, seeking to link the controversy over the book with the efforts of activists and reformers to protect Jordanian women from violence in general and from 'honour'-related violence in particular. Such positions pose challenges for those working in the field, but do not of course deter them from seeking and developing strategies of response to violence against women.

Notes

1. Jordan signed CEDAW in 1980 and ratified it in 1992.
2. See, for example, Griswold, 2001; and Jehl, 1999.
3. See, for example, Faqir, 2001; Ruane, 2000; Araji, 2000, 2001; Arnold, 2001; Kulwicki, 2002; Nanes, 2003; and see further the Annotated Bibliography on the CIMEL/INTERIGHTS project website at www.soas.ac.uk/honourcrimes.
4. Women are held in al-Jwaidah Women's Correctional and Rehabilitation Centre; for a recent report on this practice and on estimates of numbers, see Human Rights Watch, 2004: 25–7. The report cites cases of women being killed after

being released from detention into the care of their families after guarantees were given that they would not be harmed.

5. A *mahram* is a person in such a degree of relationship to the perpetrator that he would not be allowed to marry her under the rules of Islamic family law (sister, mother, daughter, aunt, etc.).

6. Respectively, Articles 188 and 324. Abu Odeh 1996: 143.

7. *Jordan Times*, 23 November 1999.

8. Article 9 of Temporary Law No. 86/2001, amending Article 340 of the Penal Code. *Official Gazette*, no. 4524, of 31 December 2001, 6026.

9. This defence is considered an exercise of a right in accordance with Article 60(1) of the Penal Code, which refers to defence of person and property, and is applied in reference to crimes of looting and robbery in certain circumstances.

10. *Ghayr muhiqq*: 'without right', or 'wrongful'.

11. Temporary Law No. 86/2001 also contains provisions amending the law on adultery, and certain other offences.

12. David Fickling in the *Guardian*, 26 July 2004.

13. Ibid.

Honour-based violence among the Kurds:

the case of Iraqi Kurdistan

NAZAND BEGIKHANI

In 1991, in the aftermath of the Gulf War and a mass exodus of Iraqi Kurds towards the Turkish and Iranian frontiers, the USA and the UK (the coalition powers) established a no-fly zone in Iraqi Kurdistan and implemented the 'Provide Comfort' programme, aiming to protect the population in the zone north of the 36th parallel against attack by Iraqi government forces. The Kurdish political parties that had been fighting the regime from the mountains came down to the cities and started governing the area.[1] In 1992, the Kurds held a general election, establishing a 105-member regional parliament and forming the Kurdish regional government. Women participated actively in this process, the first election in Kurdish history, and seven women were elected.[2] The Kurdistan Regional Government was not recognised by any state or international body, leaving it without significant economic support, but certain international non-governmental (NGO) and humanitarian organisations provided assistance to the population, helping to rebuild devastated towns and villages. In addition, the regional administration benefited, to a certain extent, from the 'Oil for Food' Programme established in 1995 by the United Nations.[3] However, since 1994 the two main Kurdish parties, the Kurdistan Democratic Party (KDP) and the Patriotic Union of Kurdistan (PUK), became engaged in fratricidal[4] confrontation, resulting in the division of the region into two separately administered areas,[5] one based in Erbil under the control of the KDP, and the other in Sulaimaniya under the rule of the PUK.

Before 1991, and under the rule of Saddam Hussein, honour killing was an issue that could not be discussed (Faraj, 2003). It was only after the establishment of the regional government that Kurdish women's rights groups began to highlight the problem. However, accompanying an increase in public and official awareness was a perceived increase in honour-based violence, and honour killing in particular. There are no exact or agreed statistics on the number of women killed in Iraqi Kurdistan in honour-related murders during the last thirteen years. Estimates range from 1,250 (Faraj and Shwan, 2003b) to some 5,000, according to the Independent Women's Organisation. Identifying the number of victims is complicated by, among other things, underreporting; victims frequently 'disappear' without any follow-up by the police (Faraj and Shwan, 2003b). Furthermore, honour-based cases are not categorised by the police and the courts as 'honour killings'. Although the cases are referred to publicly as such or as the 'purification of shame' (*ghasl al 'ar*), in the record they are classified as 'terror against women' or 'killings of women' (*qatl al nisaa*). In the last couple of years, especially since the 'liberation of Iraq', the Head of the Police in Sulaimaniya district has started to record and classify crimes in his constituency. There is a rubric that refers to 'killings of women or terror against women'. The record gives only the number of each case and the name of the police station responsible. The court record refers to the name of the 'perpetrator', the number of the file and the sentence. This situation complicates field research into honour killings.[6]

An 'honour crime' can be defined as any act of violence and abuse, actual or threatened, perpetrated against individuals, mainly women, by male members of the family and community in defence of their honour. Although paradigmatically men are the main perpetrators of honour crimes, women are not excluded from exercising oppression and carrying out murder. According to a study conducted by the Women's Information and Cultural Centre in Sulaimaniya, many women not only condone 'honour crimes'; they will often participate practically in carrying out the offence (Faraj and Shwan, 2001).

In Kurdistan, honour crimes take many forms, including 'honour killings', forced marriage, coerced marriage to an alleged rapist, and unlawful confinement and tight restrictions on women's movements. The supposed justification for such abuse is derived, in the first instance, from the perceived or actual behaviour or attitude of the victim, which is seen to have dishonoured their family, tribe or nation. Common 'provocations', although not exhaustive, include exercising freedom of choice in forming love/choice relationships, premarital sex, seeking divorce and suspicion of infidelity. Thus an honour crime is deemed acceptable when portrayed as a response to any behaviour that breaches social and sexual norms.

This chapter investigates 'honour crimes', in particular 'honour killing', in the context of the semi-autonomous zone of Iraqi Kurdistan. It draws to a degree upon the author's previous interventions in this debate (see References), but most of the material is based on field research carried out in

Iraqi Kurdistan in March and April 2004. This included fifty-two interviews with a variety of actors (judges, politicians, lawyers, police officers, women activists, as well as survivors and local witnesses), and sourcing of primary documentary evidence, including statutory provisions, court reports, police records and witness statements. In all I was able to review fourteen cases of honour killings and honour-based mutilations in the Criminal Courts of Dihok, Erbil and Sulaimaniya.

This chapter focuses on the permissive character of the legal framework inherited from the Ba'athist regime, moves towards reform of the law, and considers the forces of inertia that resist change and perpetuate crimes of honour. The first section introduces the statutory provisions that until recently (2000 in the PUK area; 2002 in the KDP area) explicitly provided leniency or mitigation in law for the perpetrators of honour crimes. The second section investigates the law in action through the illustration of a case study. The third section outlines the moves towards reforming laws governing 'crimes of honour' in Iraqi Kurdistan. Section four considers the social and political forces that render the reform process less than fully effective, and section five presents a further vignette to illustrate these obstacles. The chapter concludes with a consideration of the oppositional and reformist voices of Kurdish women in the context of strategies of response to honour crimes.

The law and honour

Despite the establishment of Kurdish regional government in 1992, the entirety of the preceding Iraqi legal provisions remained in force. These laws legitimise the subordinate position of women, emphasise a passive image of women, and reflect the belief that women are expected to embody collective morality.

The criminal justice system is Iraq is based on the Iraqi Penal Code (Law No. 111/1969) (IPC) promulgated after the Ba'athist regime came to power. The IPC replaced the Baghdad Penal Code introduced by the British military authorities in 1918. It was written in reference to the penal codes of Arab countries, because of the 'commonalities in social situations' and also driven by the nationalist ambition of constructing 'unified laws and terminologies' (al-Anbari, 2000: 172).

The preserving of women's honour, and thereby the 'family honour', is reflected in the IPC, especially those chapters and sections dealing with crimes against 'family' and 'morality and public decency'. The chapter dealing with 'crimes against morality and public decency' groups three sections ad-dressing the issues of 'rape, sodomy, indecent acts'; 'incitement to prostitution and fornication'; and 'immodest and shameful acts'. Although the provisions in these sections refer to both men and women, the focus is more on women, especially when it comes to punishment. In common with penal codes elsewhere in the region, some of which are examined in this volume, the IPC criminalises sexual relations outside marriage for both men and women, but takes a gendered approach to establishment of the crime and in some circumstances to penalty. Thus, according to Article 377, both men and women who commit adultery 'will be punished with imprisonment' for a period of between three months and five years. However, according to the same article, a reduced sentence will be imposed on a man if the woman with whom he has had a sexual relationship is married and he can prove his ignorance of her marital status. As for a husband who commits adultery, he is liable to punishment 'if he commits adultery in the conjugal home', while the same requirement does not apply to a wife. Similarities with other codes in the region can also be found in provisions providing for a reduced penalty for men who murder female relatives in certain circumstances. Article 409 provides that

> Whosoever finds his wife or one of his female unlawfuls (*mahrams*) in an act of adultery (*zina*) or in the same bed with her partner, and immediately kills one or both of them, or assaults one or both of them in an attack that leads to death or permanent disability, shall be sentenced to imprisonment not exceeding three years.

Other articles of particular significance for the judicial treatment of 'crimes of honour' include Articles 128 and 130–132, which come under the section dealing with 'legal excuse and legally extenuating circumstances'. Article 128(a) addresses conditions for the mitigating excuse:

> [Legal] excuses [have the effect of] either exempting from penalty or mitigating it, and there is no exemption unless defined by law. Besides these circumstances, the commission of the crime for honourable motives or based on grave (khatir) provocation by the victim without right shall be considered a mitigating excuse.

Article 130 IPC goes on to note the degrees to which sentences may be reduced in cases of accepted arguments for leniency, providing:

> If the mitigating excuse applies in a crime punishable with the death penalty, the punishment shall be reduced to life or temporary sentence or to imprisonment for not less than one year. If the punishment is temporary or a life sentence, it will be reduced to imprisonment for not less than six months, unless otherwise stipulated by law.

Article 131 regulates the reduction of lesser sentences, while Article 132 introduces a further possibility of reduction in sentence where the court finds that the circumstances of the crime or of the perpetrator call for the court's compassion. Reference should also be made to Article 41, which allows for the 'established right' of a husband or father to 'discipline' (*ta'dib*) his wife or children 'within the limits established by law or custom'. Hence violence in the name of correction is not only tolerated but is regarded as the exercise of a legal right.

The application of these articles is open to the interpretation of the courts and judges. In 1973 the Supreme Court issued a decision (no. 2147), which stated that '[i]t is legally excused for anyone who commits murder for the purification of shame' (*ghasl al-'ar*).[7] Although this decision is not referred to in the verdicts of the cases I reviewed, lawyers use it in the defence discourse. In current legal practice, Articles 128 and 130–132 of the IPC are utilised in court cases to support a defence that justifies or excuses killing for the sake of 'honour'. An inspection of Criminal Court records for cases heard between 1991 and 2000 in the three main cities of Iraqi Kurdistan – Dihok, Erbil and Sulaimaniya – reveals that in every case these provisions continue to be given prominence in defence submissions and form the justification for the application of unusually lenient sentences, including non-custodial measures, such as release on bail. As one prominent lawyer in Dihok noted during an interview, these articles 'are open to judicial interpretation and they have been used to provide leniency in honour crime cases'. Here, it worth noting that Article 409, which is directly related to honour killings, is not used in the court defence. In the twelve cases from the criminal courts of Dihok and Sulaimaniya that I studied, excuse or reduction in sentence is justified by 'honourable motive' with the support of Articles 128, 130 and 132. Reference is also made to Article 405, which provides for a life sentence or temporary imprisonment in cases of intentional murder.

Furthermore, interviews with the Ministry of Justice in Sulaimaniya confirmed that judicial consideration of a lenient punishment is considerably influenced by the withdrawal of the complaint by the complainant.[8] Although the public authorities cannot completely drop pursuit of a murder case, a withdrawal of complaint affects the judicial treatment of cases. In the case of Pela that I consider in the following section, the mother's withdrawal of her complaint paved the way for the release of the uncles, while the court pursued the case against the father and one of the uncles. In cases of honour killings, space for coercion over the complainant is left open. Subsequently, the court's verdict might be justified to the public as the result of the 'irresponsible behaviour' of the complainant, as happened in Pela's case when the mother was later blamed for the release of the two uncles.[9]

The law in action: the case of Pela

Pela, from Dihok in Iraqi Kurdistan, had been living with her family in Sweden since 1995, where she formed a relationship with a young Kurdish man from Erbil. Her father and paternal uncles (also living in Sweden) accused Pela of 'breaching Kurdish norms and customs'.[10] On 31 May 1999 Pela was sent back to the family house in Dihok with her mother on the pretext she was to be given away in an arranged marriage. Subsequently her father arrived in Dihok with Pela's younger sister, followed by her three uncles, two of whom had travelled from Sweden and the other from Australia. According to an investigating police officer in Sweden, 'the male members of the family had gathered initially in Sweden and planned to eliminate Pela'.[11] On 24 June 1999, while all the family members were downstairs, one of the uncles, RG, followed Pela to the first floor and shot her. Coming quietly back downstairs, he reported that Pela had committed suicide and forbade anyone from going upstairs. However, once the uncles had left the house the younger sister went upstairs to find Pela still alive. Pela told her sister that RG had shot her and asked for help, upon which her sister and mother tried to carry her out of the house. However, when they got downstairs, the uncles came back in; seeing Pela was still alive, RG shot her again several times.[12]

The local police took Pela's body away. The post-mortem report, dated the same day, noted that 'the hymen [was] broken a long time ago'. Pela's father and uncles were arrested. Two days after the crime, Pela's mother, FA, registered a complaint against her brothers-in-law and accused them of murdering her daughter. During the investigation, which lasted four months, the father insisted that he had killed his daughter after she had told him she was no longer a virgin and could therefore not go through with the marriage arranged in Dihok. The uncles denied their participation in the act, and, at the beginning of the investigation, two of them (SG and DG) were released. Later, on 8 August 1999, they were rearrested on the order of the Criminal Court. However, during their period of liberty they threatened FA, demanding she retract her complaint, which she did on 17 July, asking the court not to pursue the case because 'as a family, there has been reconciliation between us'. Nevertheless, a trial took place, with the defence relying heavily on the issue of 'honour':

> The father killed his daughter Pela as a consequence of her bad behaviour and her breach of traditional social norms in force in our society and according to which she was educated. She used to frequent bars as she was addicted to alcohol. In addition to that, she had left her parent's house in Sweden for more than a month and had illegitimate relationships.[13]

The Criminal Court in Dihok announced its verdict on 9 October 1999, introducing its decision as follows:

> The father killed his daughter after she told him that she could not marry in Dihok because she was no longer a virgin.... It is confirmed to the Court by the post-mortem report that the girl's hymen was broken while she was not married and this indicates that the girl was badly behaved and honourable motivation is reached in the case.

Pela's father and uncle RG each received a one-year prison term, suspended for three years on condition of good behaviour and guaranteed by a bail of 100 dinars deposited with the Court, to be forfeited in case of breach. The decision of the Court and the 'leniency' shown was justified by reference to the 'purification of shame', 'preservation of honour' and 'cohesion of the family':

> The Court has decided to impose a one-year imprisonment on each of the offenders, AG and RG, according to Article 405 of the Iraqi Penal Code and Articles 47, 48, 49 related to participation in the act, and with support of Articles 128 and 130 considering the motive of the murder was honourable and for purification of shame. Following this decision, AG's sentence will include the period of his arrest between 25 July 1999 to 8 October 1999 and RG's from 2 September 1999 to 8 October 1999. Given the honourable motivation and purification of shame (*ghasl al 'ar*) and as AG is the father and RG is the uncle, and for the sake of reconciliation between members of this same family and because of the absence of any past charges against either of the defendants, the court has decided to suspend the imprisonment for three years.

Reforming the law

For many Kurdish women, combating gender-based violence requires reform of the law. Thus, in the summer of 1992, soon after the formation of the Kurdish Regional Government, a group of Kurdish women representing women's organisations and parliamentarians presented a petition, signed by over 30,000 women, calling upon the Kurdish parliament to implement various reforms of the Iraqi Personal Status Code and the Iraqi Penal Code, including the abolition of all the provisions legitimising honour killing.

These demands were dismissed and ignored by the governing body. The fratricidal civil war not only divided the parliament and paralysed the government[14] but also diverted women from addressing gender-based violence. For many years during the war, women were preoccupied with normalising the situation and promoting peace initiatives, and the law reform proposals were not prioritised. At the end of the 1990s, with the increase in the number and force of women's organisations, and, above all, with the increase of honour crimes, the demand for legal reform was reactivated. Through marches, conferences and other public activities and interventions, pressure was placed upon the Kurdish authorities. The most effective campaign was organised in the Kurdish diaspora by a group of women from different parts of Kurdistan. The strength of this Kurdish women's network campaign, discussed further below, lay in its ability to access and help shape international public opinion, including the position of human rights organisations such as Amnesty International,[15] and to raise awareness among representatives of Western governments. As the credibility and survival of the Kurdish authorities depended in large measure on their relations with the outside world, the leaderships involved were particularly sensitive to the glare of international attention and opinion. The focus sharpened when a number of high-profile honour killings reached the courts and resulted in media attention in Western Europe. It is understood that, in January 2002, following the murders of Kurdish women whose families had taken refuge in Sweden, most particularly the killing of Pela and later Fadime Sahindal,[16] a Swedish government minister intervened personally to exert pressure on the Kurdish authorities in Iraq to take action against honour crimes.

The PUK were the first to commence the reform process, beginning with Articles 130 and 132 of the IPC. On 12 April 2000, Decree No. 59 was issued:

> Lenient punishment for killing women or torturing them with the pretext of purifying shame shall not be implemented. The court should not apply articles 130 and 132 of the Iraqi Penal Code no. 111 of the year 1969 to reduce the penalty of the perpetrator.

The KDP began legal reform of the IPC in June 2001, with the parliament voting for several law reforms to guarantee the rights of women and their protection. Law No. 14 of 2002, the most significant in relation to 'honour crimes', reads:

> Crimes against women with the pretext of 'honourable motivation' will not be legally liable for lenient punishment and Articles 128, 130 and 131 of the Iraqi Penal Code no. 111 of the year 1969 will not be implemented.

Despite vocal protests against the reforms from a number of judges, lawyers and religious authorities, discussed further below, a change has been registered in the approach of the courts. On May 2003, the Erbil Supreme Court reviewed a case by the Dihok Criminal Court and ordered that a one-year sentence against a man and his brother, who had killed the man's wife and her lover, be increased to fifteen years' imprisonment. The Dihok

Criminal Court had, in November 2002, justified the one-year sentence on the basis of Article 130, on the grounds that the crime occurred before the change of law in April 2002.[17] In Sulaimaniya, in November 2002, the Criminal Court sentenced to death a man who had killed a woman with whom he was in love. According to the Kurdistan Regional Government's Decree No. 180 of 30 August 2002, the death penalty was not implemented, but was automatically commuted to a life sentence.

However, the number of 'honour killings' cases reaching the courts is still very limited. There are many reasons that can explain this reality, including the persistence of *komelayeti* (see below) and the existence of two governing bodies with different judicial systems. This latter situation obstructs effective legal procedures, as a murderer can flee from the PUK zone to the KDP zone, or vice versa, without measures of pursuit being coordinated between the two. In addition, according to women's rights activists on the ground, the number of suicide cases among women, in particular self-immolation, has increased in the last few years (Faraj and Shwan, 2003b). Many are convinced that these are honour-based cases and that women are forced to commit suicide to 'save the family honour and avoid a prosecution'.[18]

The limits to reform

Unsurprisingly, Kurdish feminists and campaigners have heralded the reform of the laws governing 'honour crimes' as a major breakthrough. Within the governing parties, the reform process has provided significant legitimacy for the articulation of women's concerns. Prior to reform, there was a marked reluctance on the part of female members of the political parties to defend women accused of 'dishonourable' behaviour, because to do so ran the risk of tarnishing their image and reputation in the party and the wider community. Interviews with women in both the PUK and the KDP indicate that the change in the law and the 'initiative' shown by their leaders in enacting reform has provided them with far greater space in which to raise the issue of gender equality. However, optimism is limited. The reform of laws governing 'crimes of honour' is incomplete, open to evasion and the subject of vocal resentment from significant sections of Kurdish society.

For some legal representatives the reform falls short of protecting women adequately. They find the use of the word 'pretext' in the PUK's Decree No. 59 problematic, leading to potential ambiguity in the law. As a reformist judge noted in an interview, 'a man can still kill a woman if she is perceived as dishonourable, for example by losing her virginity.'[19] The issue of virginity (considered to be demonstrated through the status of the hymen) and the conduct of the (unmarried) victim retain importance despite the legal reforms. Where the hymen is broken it is taken as proof that the woman/girl has been dishonourable. Highlighting the ambiguity of the word, there is no 'pretext'; there is only the fact of the damage to the hymen and assumed loss of virginity (irrespective of how this may have occurred). Thus inspection of the hymen in cases where the victim of an 'honour crime' is an unmarried woman is still practised in post-mortem analysis and relied upon in court decisions; referring to the broken hymen suggests that there is 'cause' to 'justify' the murder, and the perpetrator may receive a reduced sentence.

The most open and vocal opposition to reform has come from religious leaders and the judiciary. They regard the reforms as not internal to Kurdish social transformation, but rather as an 'imitation' of the West. As one judge stated, 'Kurdish authorities have been under pressure following awareness of honour killing. The reforms have been made to give a positive image to the West.'[20] What is more, popular discourse appears to consider the reforms as an invitation for 'women to prostitute themselves without facing punishment'.[21] This resistance to change is significant and it would be inappropriate to dismiss it as no more than the expression of a 'backward' and 'false' consciousness. 'Honour crimes' in Kurdistan are rooted in the material realities of social structures and traditions, mediated by the specificity of the geopolitical dynamics of the national liberation struggle and the spectre of fundamentalism.

Kurdish social structure and tribal law

Historically, the principal basis for social and political organisation in Kurdistan is the tribe (*ashirat*). The Kurdish tribe 'is a socio-political unity and generally territorial and also economic, based on descent and kinship' (van Bruinessen, 1992: 51). The smaller entities of the tribe (*hoz*, *tira*, *taifa*, *binamala* and *mâl*) refer to the unities of clan, lineage and family.[22] Traditionally, 'the family' (*mâl*, *tâifa* or *binamala*) consists of an extended family group, sharing the same ancestors and living in the same household. The individuals belonging to this group are related by blood or through marriage. Power and property are transmitted through a patrilineal system. Newly married couples live in the home of the groom and this can extend to several generations. Central to the reproduction of this socio-political organisation is endogamy: marriage inside the same extended family, clan and tribe.

Traditionally, men have chosen their future wives from patrilineal kin; the father's brother's daughter (*amoza*) is the preferred choice. Among certain tribes, the first cousin has the obligation and the right to marry his paternal cousin, and if he does not intend to marry her, he has to make his position clear so that she can be given to another man. Women are married off at an early age[23] and often exchanged between families.[24] Marriage is not an individual choice but a collective affair, arranged and imposed by male members of the group. In so far as marriage outside of the family or clan is appropriate or permissible, the preference is for a man to marry a woman from the same territorial location as his tribe.

The system of endogamy is embodied in patriarchal structures; it is a form of control through which male domination is upheld, women's segregation enforced, and traditional and tribal norms and values preserved. Although there are many material and political factors behind this system, the main ones are the preservation of collective symbolic patrimony, 'honour' and tradition. As Delaney (1987: 43) puts it, endogamy 'is intimately related to the honour/shame complex, which is grounded in the theory of procreation'.

In the past, law has been defined and administered at the level of the tribe, overseen by a council of elders, *rishspî* (white beards), made up exclusively of men. However, the head of tribe is respected by all members of the group and has the supreme power over all. In this regard, an observation made nearly two hundred years ago still has relevance: the head's words 'are taken for law and he has the power of life and death' (Kinneir, 1818: 410). 'Honour killing' is one of the serious issues discussed and planned inside this circle.

Confronted by the forces of external 'modernisation', profound movements of population (due to internal displacement, forced migration and exile, and urbanisation), the tribal forms of organisation have been going through a process of disintegration. Hence, not all Kurds are embedded within the socio-economic structures of identifiable tribes or clans. Nevertheless, extended families remain powerful and important reference points in the definition and reproduction of the identities and material existence of individuals and groups, while the ideological legacy of clan and tribe continues to have a material force.

The legacy of tribalism is clearly pronounced in the reliance of many Kurds upon *komelayeti*, a structure run by elderly, religious, political and tribal representatives that assumes the responsibility for hearing disputes, passing judgement and enforcing sanctions and solutions. It is a tribally based procedure used to achieve reconciliation (*mesreti* or *solih*) between families or groups in conflict. Although *komelayeti* intervenes with the aim of peaceful reconciliation, to satisfy both parties, it may use force, including killing a woman on the demand of a powerful group; if one side is backed by an influential tribe, which asks for the death of a member of the other side, '*komelayeti* may accede and carry out the act of murder'.[25] In several cases concerned with alleged romantic/sexual relations that I was able to examine, *solih* was achieved by requiring both families/tribes to kill their own daughter or son, ending the affair and preventing further bloodshed. Without the intervention of *komelayeti*, it is assumed that an endless spiral of blood feud and revenge will ensure. What is more, by intervening, the *komelayeti* is able to ensure that disputes and matters of 'dishonour' are removed from community gossip, a crucial function in a context where gossip, groundless or otherwise, can provoke a series of 'honour killings'.

Fieldwork in Iraqi Kurdistan revealed the details of the application of this form of 'justice'. In one case a pregnant teenager faced death at the hands of her own family. *Komelayeti* intervened, imposing *solih* through obliging the lover's family to give a woman to the girl's family. 'The condition required by the girl's family was that their daughter had to leave the village and settle somewhere else',[26] severing all contact with her family. The young woman had to be excluded from her community and to die symbolically for her family, buried at a distance and forgotten. This symbolic death implies the removal of 'the dirty stain', which, because it has not been achieved by bloodshed, requires political power to protect the family from community gossip. If this is forthcoming, no one dare look down upon the family or talk publicly about the case. Hence, *komelayeti* does not achieve justice but rather through power relations imposes socially and politically accepted remedies. The courts, on the other hand, are viewed with suspicion because 'the court cannot establish justice nor find a remedy, it seeks to accuse one of the sides'.[27] This means cases never end, as public shame provokes further threats, future revenge and bloodshed. Thus, it is not surprising that in a society where tribal relations prevail, along with the associated patriarchal tenets of 'honour-based' values and customs, *komelayeti* is privileged over official judicial institutions.

The politico-military dynamics of national liberation

Alienation from codified law is further enforced by the politico-military dynamics of the Kurdish national liberation struggle. The fact that the Kurds are without a nation-state is highly significant, because without self-determination they have experienced the rule of law as a foreign and very often oppressive imposition. Central to the tradition of resistance is a disdain for the statutory regulation of social existence. By operating thus, traditional clan-based codes and values have been privileged. Furthermore, the veneration and reproduction of traditional values, norms and customs have served as a powerful motif within the discourse of Kurdish national identity, such that to challenge patriarchal conceptions of women and to erect legal protections from 'crimes of honour' is all too often derided as an assault on the nationalist cause.

Military power is central to Kurdish politics, a point further emphasised since the fratricidal civil war. Military strength has been the key determinant of the ability of the two main political parties to exercise governmental power within their own administrative territories. It is the key tool by which they have resisted the central power of Baghdad and maintained borders between themselves. However, both the PUK and KDP, while maintaining a nationalist rhetoric, have never been able to rely solely upon ideological commitment to the establishment of Kurdish national independence. Indeed, it is open to debate as to whether they are recognisable as nationalist parties, especially given their violent rivalry and capacity for collaboration with hostile state powers for the sake of fratricidal advantage. Nevertheless, what is clear is that the fragile power bases of the parties, especially during periods of violent rivalry, have been opportunistically seized upon by the party leaderships to court clan-based militias for the sake of establishing greater localised social weight and to bolster overall military strength. These alliances have been bought at a price. In particular, the need to ingratiate clan leaders has meant that the application of the law is uneven, as the decision to pursue a course of action is immediately politicised according to the relation of the accused to the pattern of military–political alliances. Thus indulgence of localised, uncodified systems of 'unofficial' justice, in the form of *komelayeti* for instance, is the cost of maintaining territorial control and ensuring a continued source of reliable fighters.

The spectre of fundamentalism

The unwillingness of the West to recognise the Kurdish regional govern-ments, the open hostility of the regional powers that govern different parts of Kurdistan – in particular Turkey and Iran – and their intrusions into Iraqi Kurdistan's internal affairs, have further undermined the ability of the Kurdish political organisations to redress the socio-economic situation of the population. Considered in conjunction with the recurring fratricidal wars be-tween the rival Kurdish factions, it is not difficult to appreciate that a fertile breeding ground has been created for the growth of elements committed to tradition and supposed religious orthodoxy, in particular groups operating as Islamic fundamentalists. Moreover, helped by states like Iran and Saudi Arabia, the Islamist groups have been financially strong and thus able to mobilise and offer resources to people who have been confronted by apparently unending deprivation. The ideology of these groups is both rampantly anti-Western and anti-modernist. The position of women is central to their platforms, but only so as to reassert the supposed need to disclaim notions of equality in the cause of defining the 'role' and 'duty' of women in accordance with old value systems (see further Begikhani, 1997). Thus, in addition to the war and its material consequences, the spread of fundamentalism has served as a dynamic to intensify and extend old practices and ideas.

The case of Soran

One night in the summer of 1998, 20-year-old Soran was walking home when he was shot. He survived but was badly injured and confined to hospital. Rumours that Soran was in love with a local woman had led the young woman's brothers to plan to kill them both. On the night they shot Soran, they also took their sister away and killed her. They considered Soran's survival an insult and a further source of 'dishonour' for them and their family. Thus, after leaving hospital, Soran was subject to 'protective custody' by the security forces under the control of the PUK, to 'protect Soran from the furious brothers'.[28]

The *komelayeti*, represented by elderly members of the community in the town, political representatives and religious men, intervened to seek a *solih*. After several months of consultation and negotiation, and as Soran did not have a sister, niece or cousin to 'exchange', the *komelayeti* obliged Soran's family to pay a large sum of money to the girl's family. Soran's family did not have this money and sought to reduce the amount. Finally, with the intervention of a very senior PUK politician, the levy was reduced and set at 90,000 dinars. Soran's family were forced to sell their house to provide the money, which was handed over in the presence of two male representatives from both sides, *komelayeti* members, several independent notables of the town and the top PUK politician. The money paid was compensation for the blood of the girl and reparation for the damage done to the 'honour' of her family, made all the worse by the survival of her supposed lover. Soran's family became homeless.

This case did not reach court. Many local people interviewed about the case regarded the 'settlement' as unjust.[29] However, the general opinion was that without the *komelayeti's* intervention, there would have been even greater bloodshed and Soran would never have been able to walk freely in his home town.

Yet Soran was the victim of a shooting. In interviews he was adamant that he never had a relationship with the young woman in question and that her brothers were acting purely on unfounded rumour and gossip. What is more, no action was taken to address the injustice visited upon the young woman by her brothers. Instead, it was the wounded survivor and his family who were required to make further sacrifices to avoid even more severe suffering at the hands of the men of violence.

The settlement was defined decisively by the political balance of forces prevalent at the time. The incident occurred in 1998, during the fratricidal war. The woman's family was affiliated to an influential militia tribe in the service of the PUK. The political leadership of the town, the PUK, had every reason to accommodate the demands of the aggressors because they depended upon their militia for military advantage and knew that the loyalty of clans to the party was changeable and could easily be transferred to rivals if specific interests were not met. When added to the fact that Soran's family had a background in the KDP, such that advantageous reciprocal relations were absent, the PUK had no compelling reason to alienate their allies in the name of objective justice for those who had neither history of paying tribute nor wares to exchange. When considering the political dimension of the case, we come to the conclusion that polarisation and fragmentation of the communities contributed to the context of perpetrating this particular human rights violation.

Against the tide: the voices of Kurdish women

Since the early 1990s, with the establishment of the 'safe haven' and the Kurdistan Regional Government, many new women's organisations were created, while pre-established formations were reactivated.[30] This was facilitated by several factors, including the creation of new political organisations such as the Kurdish Communist Workers' Party and the Kurdistan Islamic Union, the presence of international NGOs that sponsored certain activities, and the return of exiled women after years of life in the diaspora. Besides charitable work and literacy programmes, a number of these organisations have launched campaigns against 'honour-based violence'.[31] Through these campaigns, which include carrying out research on gender and violence, opening shelters to protect women against 'honour-based violence' and demanding changes in the Iraqi Penal Code, they have started to confront dominant patriarchal ideology and practices. The trend has been followed by the two main political organisations that had for so long distanced themselves from such issues.

However, the capacity of Kurdish women's groups to distance themselves from the dominant modes of patriarchy is not complete. A number of women's rights groups actually lend their support to and even participate in the *komelayeti* system. To a certain extent the involvement of women in the process of trying to achieve *solih* between families in conflict over 'honour' issues is a positive development in the campaign against 'honour-based violence', not least because it demonstrates that women have attained greater legitimacy in the eyes of the parties and the population. However, involvement by women's organisations in hybrid tribal justice forums is deeply problematic. Practically it has meant that they have been drawn into condoning and organising settlements that include, for instance, the exchange of young women between families (*jin ba jine*) or the giving of women in exchange for a child (*gawre ba bichuki*).[32] Thus, the capacity to invoke principles of universal human rights is severely diminished.

Of course, the complicity of women's organisations and the problems experienced in maintaining independence are a function of the extremely difficult circumstances of operating in the social environment of Iraqi Kurdistan. Although not entirely free from the gaze of the community and violence, the room for manoeuvre for some women is greatly broadened when operating in exile. Freed from the direct position of enclosure and armed with new communications technologies, Kurdish women from the diaspora have been able to assist in the strengthening of women and their organisations in the motherland.

At the beginning of the 1990s, against the backdrop of the fratricidal war, a group of Kurdish women from different European countries launched a petition against violence and criticised Kurdish leaders for their role in generating social violence.[33] From this initiative a series of actions took place and led to a campaign against 'honour-based violence'. In 1995, members of the network participated in the United Nations Forum on Women in Beijing where they raised the subject of 'honour crimes' and made their voices heard by a wider public. In March 2000, on the occasion of the first International Women's Day of the third millennium, the group named themselves Kurdish Women Action against Honour Killing (KWAHK) and launched a campaign under the slogan 'No honour in murder.'[34]

As a network campaign, KWAHK has been active in raising national and international awareness about 'honour-based violence' in Kurdish communities, in particular 'honour killing', both in Kurdistan and in the diaspora. With its strong link to women inside Kurdistan, KWAHK has been able to establish and consolidate an avenue through which women's voices can be heard internationally. A key KWAHK strategy has been to establish 'dialogue with human rights organisations, international NGOs, the United Nations and the Western governments who contribute to gender based violence by supporting regimes and parties who are violating women's human rights'.[35] Since its inception, KWAHK has pursued this strategy by actively promoting Kurdish women's rights and raising awareness about their situation through seminars and conferences, publications both online and in the press, and participation in local and foreign radio and television programmes. The same approach has also been used to increase the awareness of Kurdish women about their rights, their role in society and their importance in determining their own fate. In March 2000, when the campaign was launched, KWAHK opened a public debate about 'honour crimes' with members of the Kurdish community in London, where, 'in addition to the use of speeches and analytical papers, the community was called upon to commemorate, through a slide show and poetry readings, a group of women who were killed in Iraqi Kurdistan by their male relatives.' As 'honour crimes' have a clear political dimension, KWAHK has initiated dialogue and consultation with KDP and PUK party representatives in Iraqi Kurdistan.

On the international level, KWAHK has organised international conferences on the issue, participated in discussions and consultation meetings with governmental representatives of several European countries, including Sweden and the UK, and engaged with the United Nations in presenting an account of the situation of women in Kurdistan. Strategies of response among the members of the network (prior to consolidation as KWAHK) have also sought to address the lack of service provision for women at risk from violence from their families, including 'honour-based violence'. Thus in 1998 a women's shelter was opened in Sulaimaniya, which since its establishment has provided a safe refuge for more than a hundred at-risk women.

Finally, it should be noted that KWAHK is not the only Kurdish women's campaign against honour-based violence; others are also active on this issue both in Kurdistan and in the diaspora.[36] Factors that can militate against efforts to unite in one coalition or network all those organising against honour-based violence include the different positionings of groups linked to the left and those of politically autonomous women's groups. Particularly in the post-September 11 context, KWAHK seeks to avoid the risk of stigmatising specific communities, cultures or religions when developing strategies of response to 'crimes of honour'. There has, however, been a trend among several far-left women's groups to associate 'honour crimes' with Islam, an approach which inhibits productive dialogue and which I and others in KWAHK reject in preference to strategies of response rooted squarely within the human rights framework.

Conclusions

This chapter has explored 'honour crimes', in particular 'honour-killing', in the context of the semi-autonomous zone of Iraqi Kurdistan. As the chapter has shown, the political authorities in Iraqi Kurdistan were slow to depart from the permissive legal framework inherited from the Ba'athist regime. This law was framed to perpetuate the subordination of women and to regulate their conduct, perceived or actual, for the sake of preserving a 'masculine' conception of 'honour' and to attenuate 'shame'. The case of Pela clearly illustrates the social values that underpin 'honour crimes', the lengths to which people are prepared to go in order to avoid 'shame', as well as the law's tolerant interpretation of such violence.

Although women have been leading the call for legal reform, the process is incomplete. Not only is there resistance to change within the legal profession and judiciary; it is also apparent that the space for judicial tolerance of 'honour crimes' remains intact in parts of the relevant statutory provisions. Perhaps more importantly, the route to a more positive transformation is presented with deeply entrenched obstacles, forged within the heritage of tribal social structures (most graphically expressed in the reliance upon *komelayeti*), the continued centrality of militarism and the unresolved national question, as well as the presence of Islamic fundamentalism. Soran's case clearly demonstrates that reform is far from complete.

While grounds for disquiet are clearly evident, Kurdish women's organisations are maintaining pressure and making a difference. The reform process would not have got underway without their interventions. Yet it is also clear that protest is a perilous endeavour. Many women activists are extremely reluctant to raise the issue of 'honour crimes', because they too are entrapped in communities where the demand for silence is combined with the practices of rumour and gossip, in which there is an ever-present threat of destruction of reputation and physical danger. Nevertheless, voices of dissent are not confined to localised positions of enclosure. Exile has provided a relatively safe space for a number of Kurdish women to operate. By using established and new information communications technologies, networks have been built and sustained within and beyond Iraqi Kurdistan, able to communicate and organise in an unmediated fashion, to mobilise more readily and direct resources, to expose errant behaviours and to subject bearers of power to an alternative disciplinary gaze.

Yet these are mere beginnings. While the war and ongoing 'liberation' of Iraq have served to bring the issue of human rights into global view, it is apparent that even the modest reforms concerning 'honour crimes' may well be swept away within the rising tide of Islamist fundamentalism. Kurdish women are in the epicentre of a region that is undergoing a violent restructuring of global historic proportions. How the future is to unravel is unknown, but what is clear is that for women in Kurdistan the consequences are of life and death proportions.

Notes

1. At that time there was a united Kurdish Front comprising most Kurdish political organisations. However, the most popular and dominant parties were the Kurdistan Democratic Party (KDP) and the Patriotic Union of Kurdistan (PUK).
2. Five of the women represented the Patriotic Union of Kurdistan, and the two others the Kurdistan Democratic Party. Seven mullahs (religious authorities) were also elected, with five representing the KDP and two the PUK.
3. UN/RES/986/(14/04/1995).
4. The term 'fratricide' is a translation of the Kurdish *brakoji*. Both terms have strong patriarchal connotations, and many Kurds and in particular feminists refuse to use *brakoji*, instead using *shari nawkho* (civil war) or *khokoji* (self-destruction).
5. The military confrontation continued until 1998, when the leaders of the two parties signed a ceasefire agreement under the supervision of the Clinton administration in the presence of Madeleine Albright, then US Secretary of State.
6. During my own research I was fortunate to gain access to senior members of the police and other officials, who (although somewhat restrained) assisted me with valuable information and documentation.
7. Decree number 2147/Criminal/973, in *Majallat al-nashra al-qada'iyya* (Judicial Publication Journal), n. IV-year IV, Baghdad, 1973.
8. Interview with the Ministry of Justice in Sulaimaniya, April 2004.
9. Such blame has been articulated particularly by political representatives to justify the judicial system. Additionally, the failure of the judicial system to condemn murderers of honour killings is seen as the consequence of the Western world's failure to recognise the Kurdistan Regional Government and to procure for the Kurdish authorities the right to promulgate their own laws.
10. According to the witness statement of one of the uncles who participated in the killing.
11. Cited from a telephone interview with a Swedish detective inspector, Kickis A. Algamo, May 2004. Algamo not only investigated the case but was also involved in helping to save the life of Pela's younger sister and arranging her passage from Dihok to Sweden, where the case became public. The uncles stood trial and were later sentenced to life imprisonment.
12. Dihok Criminal Court, ref: 81/j/999. The case of Pela is narrated here as told by the younger sister and the mother in their court statements.
13. Cited from the lawyers' written statement in the court record.
14. The war made the elected government inactive, and in 1996 the PUK formed its own government based in Sulaimaniya. As there was only one Supreme Court located in Erbil, the PUK zone lacked a Cassation institution until 1998.
15. See, for example, Amnesty International, 2001a, 2001b.
16. Fadime Sahindal, a 26-year-old Kurdish woman from Turkey, was shot by her father in Uppsala. After refusing to accept an arranged marriage, she left home and lived with her Swedish boyfriend. Before she was killed, Fadime became an active campaigner for the rights of young women inside ethnic minority communities and gave speeches on radio and television and in the Swedish parliament. Her murder attracted worldwide media attention. Her father was arrested and stood trial in Sweden; he was found guilty and sentenced to life imprisonment. For more information see www.kwahk.org.

17. Dihok Criminal Court, ref. 283/j/2002.

18. Quotation from an interview with Ms. Tavga Abas, Head of the Centre for Social and Criminal Investigations, Erbil, 3 April 2004.

19. Quotation from an interview with judge Rizgar in Sulaimaniya, 8 April 2004.

20. Quotation from an interview with a judge in Erbil.

21. From an interview with a woman functionary in the Suleimaniya Criminal Court.

22. A series of terminology in Kurdish designates different unities and their anthropological signification, reflecting the complexity of Kurdish socio-political organisation and also the socio-cultural differences between different parts of Kurdistan. See Begikhani, 1997.

23. According to Talar Nadr of Women's Information and Cultural Centre, there are now in Iraqi Kurdistan 18,000 girls promised in marriage when they were children. See 'Women's Lives, Artistes' Views', a collaborative project by KWAHK, La Pluie d'Oiseaux and Women Information and Cultural Centre, at www.kwahk. org.

24. See 'A Study into Patriarchal Culture and its Effect on Certain Forms of Marriage in Erbil Governorate', carried out by Khatu Zin Centre for Social Activities, under the supervision of Dr Karim Sharif Qarachatani, August 2003.

25. Interview with Professor Abdul Fatah Botani, History Department at Dihok University.

26. Interview with Kurda Omar, the current governor of Koysinjak.

27. Interview with a lawyer in the court of Erbil.

28. According to a source in the town's security headquarters (*Asaish*).

29. The brothers bought a car with the money and after a few months had an accident. Local people commenting upon the case regard this eventuality as somehow a worthy and deserved fate, a consequence of the ugly (*haram*) affair.

30. Historically, Kurdish feminism was born and developed inside Kurdish nationalist organisations. As such, national liberation appears to be the main aim of Kurdish feminist groups. Until 1991, there was the Kurdistan Women's Union (KWU), established within the KDP in 1952, and the Zhinan Women's Union of Kurdistan (ZWUK), created inside the PUK in 1989. There were also Kurdish women activists working within the Kurdistan Women's Association, which was part of the Iraqi Women's Association attached to the Iraqi Communist Party.

31. Campaigns against 'honour crime' inside Kurdistan were first started by the Independent Women's Organisation, followed by the Women's Information and Cultural Centre. See *Yeksani* journal numbers published by IWO in the 1990s in Sulaimaniya; and *Jiyanawa*, which later become *Rewan*, published by WICC since 1998.

32. My field research identified this practice as a factor behind a number of crimes. In the case of exchanging sisters, when one of the sisters gets divorced, the other one has to leave her husband even if there are no significant problems in her family. In the case of giving a woman in exchange for a baby girl, if she later refuses to marry the man she is promised to, she will be in danger, the settlement will collapse and 'honour violence' is likely to follow.

33. The reaction to this action inside political elites was negative; one political leader condemned the women in question as 'whores'.

34. The group were members and activists from three London-based women's

rights groups: the Gender Working Group at the Kurdish Cultural Centre, the Kurdish Women Organisation, and the Kurdistan Refugee Women's Organisation. Later KWAHK established contact with several women's rights groups inside Kurdistan; since 2002, the Women's Information and Cultural Centre has been an active partner in KWAHK's campaign. The author is a founding member of KWAKH and continues to remain actively involved in the organisation. For more information, see www.kwahk.org.

35. For more information about this and other activities and positions described in this section, see www.kwahk.org.

36. For example, the Remember Fadime and Pela Organisation, in Sweden, and the International Campaign against Honour Killings, in London.

'Crimes of honour' in the Italian Penal Code: an analysis of history and reform

MARIA GABRIELLA BETTIGA-BOUKERBOUT

Criminal law is often used as an indicator of a country's values; whilst some forms of human behaviour, such as homicide, are universally condemned, the circumstances that are regarded as either aggravating or mitigating a crime provide insights into the fundamental values of a society. These circumstances change from place to place and time to time. The legal history of so-called 'crimes of honour' in Italy is a good example of how law and society exercise a reciprocal influence and provides an insight into the history of women's rights in the country.

Until fairly recently, women were excluded from several professions (either by law or more commonly by society) and legislators, judges and scholars tended to be men; laws were therefore made by men and interpreted by men. Ideas of women were often based on stereotypes and prejudices that long went unchallenged. Women themselves have contributed to this anti-feminist sentiment, for example by treating their sons and daughters differently.

Historically, Italian society has put enormous pressure on women to conform to certain values. An 'honest' woman was seen as someone who was married, did not work and took good care of her house and children. It was not necessary for her to be highly educated so long as she could take care of her family, and the Catholic Church's concept of Mary's role as virgin and mother contributed to this. Marriage was indissoluble until 1970; divorce was not possible[1] and separation was often impractical as it left women economically impoverished, and remained socially unacceptable for many years. Women thus often had to endure abusive or unfaithful husbands. Society condoned male adultery while, as discussed below, female adultery was a criminal offence; recourse to prostitutes was not uncommon – *case chiuse* (brothels, literally 'closed houses') were legal until 1958.[2]

It is within this context that the Penal Code provisions on 'honour crimes' are considered in this chapter. Today's society is very different, and, although full equality between the sexes has not been reached, the manifest discrimination that existed until quite recently has been greatly reduced. All references to the 'cause of honour' were repealed from the Penal Code (the Rocco Code of 1931) in 1981.

The idea of 'honour' in Italian law and society

Anthropological studies have shown that the concept of honour is deep-rooted in many cultures, as are the counter-concepts of shame and modesty. In the Mediterranean area, the concept of honour is multifaceted. While honour in a general sense can be gained through personal actions, 'sexual honour' can only be maintained or lost. According to Campbell (1987: 151), men are usually required by unwritten social rules to build a socially 'honour-able' reputation or maintain a reputation inherited by birth through brave and 'honourable' actions, while women have the duty to preserve their (and therefore their family's) 'honour' with passive conduct. Accordingly, as women are considered inherently weak, men have the right and duty to protect and shield them from their own weakness and the predatory intentions of other unrelated men. As noted by Giovannini (1987: 61)[3] boys and girls are encouraged to assume different roles from childhood: while female children are required to stay indoors and help with domestic chores, and are praised for a display of obedience and shyness, boys play outside with their friends and find adult approval in displaying an aggressive or dominant attitude.

Ten years prior to the enactment of the Rocco Code (in 1931), Italian scholar Mario Manfredini explained the first penal provisions that sanctioned crimes against modesty thus: 'the equivalent of modesty in men is jealousy and honour; i.e. the defence of their own personal value in society, the reaction to the endangerment of their own property and goods' (1921: 5). Acts that breached modesty were therefore initially sanctioned because they jeopardised the man's exclusive enjoyment of a woman, his right to possess her without interference.

The Rocco Code protects individual honour in both its general and its more specific meaning of 'sexual honour'. Honour in its general sense is protected by the provisions of chapter 2 (crimes against honour) in title 12 of the code (crimes against the person). The offence of insult[4] protects one's subjective honour, the intrinsic value of an individual, while the offence of defamation[5] protects the individual's objective honour or reputation, the idea that society has of a specific person (Fortuna, 2002).

Prevailing understandings of sexuality and honour can be seen in the provisions regulating crimes against public morality and decency and against the family. Sexual violence was considered an offence against public morality until 1996, when it became a crime against the person. The now repealed offence of 'seduction by promise of matrimony'[6] was subject to much scholarly debate, with many considering the provision to be 'an excess of protection' for women, not needed and not deserved (Pannain, 1957: 410). Pannain further argued that 'honest women can defend themselves against any kind of flattery ... [they] have an inhibitory power much stronger than that of men', and therefore, even when the woman does not 'make a move' clearly to seduce the man, it is still the woman who subtly ensures that the man seduces her, hoping that he will eventually marry her. In either case it was the woman who was considered to have enticed the man.

As noted by Maria Giuseppina Manfredini (1979: 303–6), marriage was considered the best thing that could happen to a woman. This explained the existence of Article 544 of the Rocco Code, which extinguished criminal responsibility for the crimes of rape, indecent assault and abduction where the perpetrator married the victim. This article was first introduced in the 1889 Penal Code (the Zanardelli Code) to allow 'the greatest amendment' on the part of the perpetrator to the woman he had dishonoured: marriage (M.G. Manfredini, citing the Ministerial Report to Parliament no. CXXXI). The intention was the protection of women who, having been subjected to rape, were considered to have lost their 'honour' together with their virginity and therefore had no other prospect of marriage. The provisions against adultery and extramarital liaisons reflected similar ideas.[7] Whereas adulterous husbands were guilty of a criminal offence only where it could be proved that they kept a mistress in the marital dwelling or openly elsewhere, wives were liable on the basis of the act of adultery itself, whether it was committed only once or consisted of an ongoing relationship (with an increase in penalty in the latter case). Husbands, however, were punishable only if their adulterous relationship caused a scandal and thus offended a wife's honour by becoming public knowledge. The differential treatment was justified by the idea that men and women committed infidelity for very different reasons. For example, Mario Manfredini (1921: 316) argued that 'when a wife gives herself to a man, she does not do it to satisfy a natural instinct, but out of love'. Therefore, a woman who commits adultery 'deprives her husband and children of the moral support and values that women give to their families. However, the husband can on some occasions follow his predominant sexual instinct and still feel the same affection and respect for his wife.' Mario

. Manfredini further relies on alleged physiological differences between men and women[8] to justify the idea that the 'sexual honour' of society is less offended by male adultery than by female infidelity. A significant reason underpinning the differential treatment was that male infidelity does not jeopardise one of the pillars of the monogamous family: the certainty of paternity.

In Italian society women were either seen as examples of modesty with no sexual desires, or as objects of exploitation. Prostitutes, at the exploited end of the spectrum,[9] were considered 'dishonoured', their human dignity was denied and it appears they were even denied spiritual assistance from the Church. Yet it seems that men were not required to confess their visits to the *case chiuse* because this was not considered a sin.[10] At the other end of the spectrum were the 'honest' women, seen as minors from the cradle to the grave, who – due to their alleged diminished capacity – needed to be protected by the men of the family. Such protection, particularly in the south of Italy, was a duty of fathers and brothers first, and then husbands (Gaudiano, 2000: 2). Until the reform of family law in 1975 women lost their surname upon marriage and took that of their husbands. They had to provide a dowry that was administered by the husband, and women who married foreigners lost their citizenship.[11] The husband was head of the family and had authority over his wife and children. He was allowed to utilise means of correction over his family members including the use of violence, such as beating, humiliation and even the temporary deprivation of personal freedom (Fortuna, 2002).[12] After such provisions were repealed by the family law reform of 1975, one view maintained that marital authority should not have been abolished:

> While on a moral level there is no doubt of the absolute equality of the spouses, the law should not have recognised the same equality with regard to the organisation of the family. In fact if family is a social institution, it must have an authority in charge, entrusted with specific powers, even corrective ones. (Bettiol, 1982: 329)

This extreme view does not appear to have been followed by the judiciary, and in fact the reform of the law had been preceded by statements of the Cassation Court[13] that the right to means of correction was not applicable where a husband abused his right against his wife, because the law did not grant him *jus corrigendi* (right to punish) over his spouse.[14]

The judiciary's more liberal view was in keeping with Article 29 of the Constitution, which maintains that 'marriage is based on the moral and juridical equality of the spouses'. Nevertheless, it is worth noting that, despite the enactment of the Constitution in 1948, it was not until 1975 that the discriminatory family-related provisions of the 1942 Civil Code were reformed.

'Honour killing', Article 587 of the Rocco Code

Article 587 of the Rocco Code enabled consideration of the 'cause of honour' in homicide or physical injuries, providing:

> Whoever discovers unlawful sexual relations [i.e. sexual relations outside marriage] on the part of their spouse, daughter or sister and in the fit of fury occasioned by the offence to their or their family's honour causes their death, shall be punished with a prison term from three to seven years.
>
> Whoever, under the same circumstances, causes the death of the paramour of their spouse, daughter or sister shall be subjected to the same punishment.
>
> If in the same circumstances, the perpetrator causes to the above categories of people a personal injury, the penalties provided by Articles 582 and 583[15] shall be reduced to one third; if death occurs as a consequence of the injuries the penalty shall be a prison term of two to five years.
>
> Whoever, under the same circumstances, commits against the above categories of people the crime regulated by Article 581[16] shall not be subjected to any punishment.

Historically, the legal differentiation of 'honour killing' from other forms of homicide is rooted in Roman law, under which no punishment was imposed on a father or husband vis-à-vis killing their daughter or wife and their paramour.[17] This was due to the *jus vitae ac necis* (power of life and death) that the *pater familias* (head of family) had over his family members (Fortuna, 2002).

Whereas the previous 1889 Zanardelli Code[18] had considered the 'cause of honour' as an extenuating circumstance to the crime of homicide (Article 377), the 1931 Rocco Code considered killing for the 'cause of honour' a separate crime, distinguished by its particular features from the offence of homicide. According to some scholars, the perpetrators of 'honour killings' were not socially dangerous individuals because they had reacted to an offence committed by the victim who had broken existing laws of morality (M. Manfredini, 1931: 504). The prison sentences prescribed by Article 587 represented a substantial reduction of the twenty-one- to twenty-four-year penalty for common homicide (Article 575 of the Rocco Code).

The existence of Article 587 is explained by the political context of 1930s Italy. Fascism was at its height and there were strict gender discriminatory rules to support fascist demographic policy, which encouraged families to have more children and pushed women who had just begun to gain a more active role in society back into the home.[19] Against the backdrop of the increasing authority of the *pater familias*, Article 587 effectively gave a 'licence to kill' to the heads of families whose 'honour' had allegedly been tarnished.

Under the terms of Article 587, the 'cause of honour' could be relied upon only where the perpetrator was either the victim's husband or wife, parent (father or mother) or sibling (brother or sister) and the victim was the specified relative of the perpetrator – spouse (husband or wife), daughter (but not son) or sister (but not brother) (Fortuna, 2002).

While the Rocco Code generally uses the term 'spouse', according to Maria Giuseppina Manfredini, the legislator extended the applicability of the 'honour defence' to wives 'without being entirely convinced' (1979: 293). The Ministerial Report to Parliament that accompanied the proposal for the Rocco Code justified the extension by stating that 'it has to be recognised that even women can perceive the offence to their honour and to their feelings' (M.G. Manfredini, 1979: 294). However, according to Manfredini, a woman killing her daughter or sister was only a theoretical (rather than realistic) possibility, as it was unlikely that women would act in such a way (1979: 294).

The jurisprudence of the Court of Cassation interpreted the elements required by Article 587 as follows. First, the 'unlawful sexual relations' had to be consensual, therefore did not include cases of sexual violence.[20] Second, 'sexual relations' required sexual intercourse to have taken place; mere licentious embraces and kisses did not count.[21] The 'discovers' element required the perpetrator to have been unaware of the relations until that moment. However, as opposed to the pre-existing position under the Zanardelli Code, it was not necessary for the perpetrator to surprise his family member in the act (in flagrante delicto); it sufficed that the culprit came to know for certain of the existence of such relations,[22] for example through a confession or finding an unequivocal letter. This important difference between the Rocco and the Zanardelli Codes vastly expanded the applicability of the 'honour cause'. Regarding immediacy, it was not necessary for the perpetrator to strike at the very moment he came to know of the victim's unlawful sexual relations; rather, Article 587 required that the perpetrator did not have time to calm down and reflect on the events, and was therefore still in a 'fit of fury'.[23]

During the Fascist period, strict censorship prevented newspapers from reporting local crimes, but soon after World War II many stories on 'honour crimes' began to appear. Such reports invariably came from the South of Italy. In the agricultural South the patriarchal and pyramidal structure of the family persisted much longer than in the richer and industrialised North, and values such as women's chastity and fidelity remained entrenched.

Perpetrators of 'honour crimes' were usually male family members of the woman who had been 'dishonoured' – killing the seducer was seen as necessary to restore the family's 'honour' and respectability. It was not, however, uncommon for women who had been seduced and deserted or for wives who had been abandoned by their unfaithful husbands to kill the man who had deprived them of their 'honour'. In both such examples, it is likely that the women absorbed the patriarchal ideology of society, particularly in the case of the woman who had been seduced, because as a non-virgin it would have been practically impossible for her to marry.[24] In some cases killing the seducer may have been a way for the woman to protect herself from her family's violent reaction; as such an action demonstrated her full agreement with the dominant values. Such a woman would not benefit from the provision of Article 587 but similar arguments, and/or the provisions of Article 62(2) – extenuating circumstances, discussed below – could be invoked by the defence, in seeking a more lenient sentence than for homicide. It was then up to the court to accept or dismiss such a defence. The decisions of the courts on these issues varied according to the geographic area of the country and the time at which they were taken. In Italy court decisions are not binding on future cases and, although the lower courts usually follow the orientation of higher courts, it is possible for different courts to have different decisions in different areas and different years. Judgments on 'honour crimes' slowly shifted from a total or partial acceptance of the 'cause of honour defence' to the condemnation by the Cassation Court, defined in 1972 as an anachronistic [and flawed] concept of honour.[25]

In the case of the rejected wife, according to societal norms, it was not strictly necessary for the wronged woman to kill her unfaithful husband to restore her 'honour', but again women may have absorbed the dominant culture and acted accordingly. In some instances the killing would probably fall within the concept of a 'crime of passion', but the woman's legal defence was likely to have been mounted as an 'honour crime' because Article 90 of the Penal Code did not recognise jealousy and emotional states as extenuating circumstances, whereas Article 587 granted favourable treatment.

Another type of case involved the family of a seduced woman killing the seducer but not acting against the woman herself. This scenario was not uncommon, as it was often easier for the family to blame and kill a stranger than a family member to avenge their 'honour'. Even where cases did not fall strictly within the requirements of Article 587, it was not rare for a sympathetic judge to acquit the culprit or impose lenient punishment because of the alleged 'honour motive' behind crimes (Moscon, 1961: 15).

However, not all judges showed sympathy towards 'honour killings', and as early as the start of the 1950s some courts and public prosecutors refused to apply Article 587 to cases that may have fallen within its limits. The legal recognition of 'honour killing' was also being debated in society, particularly following the 1961 film *Divorce Italian Style* directed by Pietro Germi, who adopted the comedy genre to ridicule 'honour crimes' and the approach of courts to this issue.[26] The film caused mixed reactions, but was mainly seen as a denunciation of ancient prejudices and clichés that allowed killers to go virtually unpunished. During the same period, Article 587 was also criticised by scholars for being anachronistic and contrary to constitutional values (Fortuna, 2002, citing Manzini, 1964). A further factor in the reorientation of the courts to issues of 'honour killings' was Law 66/1963, which admitted women to appointment as judges.[27]

In time, Article 587 began to be applied more restrictively and therefore defendants tried to invoke the generic extenuating circumstances of Article 62(1 and 2).[28] The Cassation Court consistently rejected the applicability of Article 62(1) to 'honour crimes' on the basis that 'the article cannot be applied if a fact of particular social or moral value does not exist objectively in reality but is only believed to exist by the perpetrator.'[29] The Article is applicable only when the motive determining the action is inspired by altruistic feelings[30] and not by feelings such as honour, jealousy and the like.[31] The Cassation Court further declared as early as 1972 that 'the social conscience does not accept the killing of the seducer on the part of the seduced woman or her family members, but it considers such a crime as a consequence of an anachronistic concept of honour'.[32] As noted above, the Italian legal system does not operate on the basis of binding precedent, thus there may be contradictions in the decisions of various courts. Gradually courts began to reject the 'honour defence', but it took time for a uniform view to develop among them.

The changed social values and the new orientation of the higher courts finally led to the abolition of the consideration of the 'cause of honour' as a defence to murder, by Law 442/1981; as one scholar put it, thirty-three years after the Constitution entered into force, 'a stain on our penal law and on our social conscience' (Volta, 1989: 959) was finally removed.[33] Subsequently the only allowance made by courts in judging on 'honour crimes' was either the application of Article 62(2) (the generic extenuating circumstance of provocation) or Article 133(1) ('surrounding circumstances/environmental influences'). With regard to provocation, the courts have interpreted the infidelity of the spouse to constitute an 'unjust act' which could cause a 'fit of fury' in the wronged party.[34] Applying Article 133 no. 1,[35] the Cassation Court stated in 1988 that 'a misinterpreted idea of honour could lead to the killing of a rival being seen as necessary in certain social environments' and therefore the judge shall take social and environmental influences into account when determining the penalty to be applied.[36] Both of these cases involved the killing of a spouse or their paramour. In recent years this occurrence seems to be more common than the killing of any other family member. This may reflect a changed society where the infidelity of women is regarded as the husband's problem and no longer that of other family members. At the same time, women's virginity has slowly stopped being seen as a value that the men of the family have to preserve, and premarital sex is no longer uncommon.

Relevance of the cause of honour
in other provisions of the Rocco Code

The Rocco Code also expressly referred to the 'cause of honour' in additional provisions regarding abortion, infanticide and desertion of minors.

The crime of abortion, categorised within the class of 'crimes against the integrity and sanity of the race', reflected the Fascist regime's demographic policy, which sought to control strictly the female body and specifically its reproductive functions.[37] Abortion was considered a crime against the state, sexual education was banned and the advertising of contraceptive methods was prohibited. The Church has a long-standing objection to contraception and the state did not allow the sale of the contraceptive pill until 1969; even then it could only be advertised as a cure for menstrual dysfunctions and not as a contraceptive method.[38] The Rocco Code severely punished the crime of abortion, allowing leniency in sentences only where it was committed in the 'cause of honour'. Article 551 provided that 'if the offences regulated by Articles 545 to 550 are committed in order to save one's own honour or that of a close relative, the penalties provided [by the above articles] shall be reduced to half or to two thirds.' The 'cause of honour' could therefore be applied to all the cases regulated by Articles 545 to 550[39] and constituted an extenuating circumstance in respect of the crime of abortion but not an autonomous offence.[40] This difference is important because, as a special extenuating circumstance, the 'cause of honour' did not modify the offence committed and its applicability was limited to certain subjects – the woman herself and/or her close relatives who acted exclusively to preserve her 'honour', but not their own.[41] The 'cause of honour' was a subjective circumstance and therefore could not be invoked by third parties who assisted in the abortion but were not related to the woman (e.g. doctors).[42]

Article 551 further required that the woman must have had 'honour' to protect and preserve, and was therefore not applicable to women already considered 'dishonoured', such as prostitutes or women generally known to conduct an 'immoral life'. The Cassation Court established that Article 551 could be applied to married women who acted to hide an adulterous relationship,[43] for example in cases where a pregnancy had begun while the husband was away,[44] but not in the case of women known to be 'loose'[45] or women who had already had an illegitimate pregnancy and continued to conduct an 'immoral life'.[46] However, in ambiguous cases, it was the duty of the judge to decide whether the extenuating circumstance was applicable to a specific case (Lattanzi, 1972: 721; M. Manfredini, 1921: 458). Article 551, together with the entirety of title 10 of the Rocco Code, was repealed by Law 194/1978, which finally legalised abortion.

Article 578 regulated infanticide for 'cause of honour'[47] and was motivated by similar demographic considerations as Article 551. However, in this case the 'cause of honour' did not operate as an extenuating circumstance but characterised an autonomous crime. In contrast to Article 551, the subjects that could invoke the provision were not only the woman and her close relatives but also other unrelated subjects who acted exclusively for reasons of 'honour'. Article 578 could not be applied when the woman was already 'sexually dishonoured'; nor could it be invoked if the infanticide occurred well after delivery, once society had already learned of the illegitimate filiation (Lattanzi, 1972: 579; M. Manfredini, 1921: 490). Law 442/1981 repealed Article 578.

The last reference to the 'cause of honour' in the Rocco Code was Article 592,[48] which provided for a very minor penalty in cases of desertion of an infant committed in order to hide an illegitimate filiation and preserve one's own 'honour' or that of a close relative. The provision reflected the common practice of abandoning newborn illegitimate children at the doorstep of convents. Law 442/1981 also repealed Article 592.

Conclusions

As this chapter has shown, despite the progressive Constitution enacted in Italy in 1948, which prohibited any form of gender discrimination, it was not until 1975 that the body of family law, with its patriarchal undertones, was reformed. Moreover, it was not until 1981 that the last references to the 'cause of honour' were repealed from the Penal Code. A main contributory factor to this delay can be seen as the unwillingness of most political forces to modify the status quo, coupled with their view that giving more rights to women would unbalance the structure of family and society.

It is interesting to note the apparent correlation between the reforms of gender-discriminatory laws examined in this chapter and the increasing visibility of women in the public sphere. Although universal suffrage was granted to Italian men in 1912, women were not granted this right until 1945. Whilst some parties encouraged women to stand as candidates for elections, there were only twenty-nine women MPs in 1968, their number having declined from the forty-nine present in the first Italian parliament in 1861.[49] The absence of women from the political scene and more generally from public life allowed legislators to turn a blind eye towards anachronistic legislation that suited most political forces.

In addition, Italy has been governed by the Christian Democrats[50] for over forty years, and the efforts of several opposition parties and groups to reform certain sectors of the law (including gender-discriminatory laws) often met with no success. However, social change, including the growth of feminism and the sexual revolution of the 1960s made women more self-aware. Since 1963 women judges have been admitted to the Italian bench and have contributed to the change in the orientation of courts to issues of gender discrimination. The 1970s saw a dramatic increase in the number of female students in higher education,[51] and increased education brought increased self-awareness and enhanced the position of women in the labour market. Certain opposition parties (such as the Communists and Radicals) were in the meantime actively promoting the participation of women in the political scene and lobbying for reforms that would grant them an equal status in society. New laws were eventually enacted, a process that, once started, proved to be unstoppable: in 1970 divorce became admissible despite the Church's opposition; Law 903/1977 ensured equal treatment at work; Law 898/1978 regulated abortion and maternity. And finally in 1981 all references to the 'cause of honour' were repealed from the Penal Code.

The process of reform continues today, under a momentum largely attributable to the ability of women MPs belonging to various parties to set aside their differences and come together to lobby for changes of law, as clearly demonstrated by the efforts to pass the Sexual Violence Bill in 1996.

Notes

A debt of gratitude is owed to Professor Francesco Saverio Fortuna, Professor of Criminal Law at the Law Faculty at the University of Cassino, Italy, in regard to this chapter. In particular, it builds on themes explored by Professor Fortuna in his presentation to the CIMEL/INTERIGHTS International Meeting on Strategies to Address 'Crimes of Honour', London, February 2002 (in Italian, unpublished, on file with the author).

1. Divorce became legal in Italy with Law 897/1970.
2. Law 75/1958, promoted by Parliamentarian Lina Merlin, was passed after many years of parliamentary debate, and the *case chiuse* were finally closed down.

Prostitution was still considered legal, but it was no longer possible to exercise it 'in houses, districts or any closed space' (Article 2 of the law). Today some NGOs and prominent women are backing proposals to reopen the *case chiuse* to decriminalise prostitution, and prevent health risks and exploitation by organised criminals of sex workers.

3. Giovannini conducted her fieldwork in the Sicilian village of Garre in 1974. Her findings, while representative of a certain rural society in Southern Italy, do not reflect the whole of Italian society at the time, as reality in urban areas and particularly in Northern Italy was markedly different. Moreover, the above-highlighted differences between the sexes that society encouraged in the past are now much less evident, although in some areas they have not completely disappeared.

4. Article 594:

Insult. Whoever offends the honour or decorum of an individual in their presence shall be punished with a prison term of up to 6 months or with a fine of 1 million lira [now calculated in euros].

Whoever commits the act by telegraph or phone or by written communication or drawings addressed to the victim shall be punished in the same way.

The penalty shall be a prison term of up to 1 year or a fine of up to 2 million lira if the offence consists in the attribution of a specific fact to the victim.

Penalties are increased if the offence is committed in the presence of more than 1 person.

5. Article 595:

Defamation. Outside the cases regulated by the preceding article, whoever offends somebody else's reputation in a conversation with others, shall be punished with a prison term of up to 1 year or with a fine of up to 2 million lira.

If the offence consists in the attribution of a specific fact to the victim the penalty shall be a prison term of up to 2 years or a fine of up to 4 million lira.

If the act is committed by publication in the press or by any other advertising tool, or by public act, the penalty shall be a prison term from 6 months to 3 years or a fine of a minimum of 1 million lira.

The penalty shall be increased if the offence is committed against a political, administrative or judicial body, or one of its representatives or against a collegial authority.

6. Article 526:

Seduction by promise of matrimony. Whoever seduces a minor female by promising to marry her and by misleading her on the fact that he is already married shall be punished with a prison term of 3 months to 2 years. Seduction means that there has been sexual intercourse.

This article was repealed by Law 66/1996 (law against sexual violence).

7. Article 559:

Adultery. The adulterous wife shall be punished with a prison term of up to 1 year.

Her paramour shall be punished in the same way.

> The penalty shall be increased to up to 2 years in prison in case of an adulterous relationship.
>
> The crime is punishable upon the husband's denunciation.

Article 560:

> Extramarital liaisons. The husband who keeps a mistress in the marital dwelling or notoriously elsewhere shall be punished with a prison term of up to 2 years.
>
> His mistress shall be punished in the same way.
>
> The crime is punishable upon the wife's denunciation.

8. For example, it was argued that women have long periods of sexual inactivity (e.g. due to pregnancy) and lose their sex drive earlier, as compared to men.

9. The contradiction of the existence of public brothels in the country that is home to the Pope and the centre of Catholicism has never been fully explained by the Church or the state.

10. www.cronologia.it/storia/a1959z.htm.

11. This provision of Law 555/1912 on citizenship was repealed by Article 219 of Law 151/1975.

12. Article 571:

> Abuse of means of correction. Whoever abuses their means of correction against a person subjected to their authority or entrusted to them for reasons of education, care, vigilance or custody or for the exercise of a profession or art shall be punished with a prison term of up to 6 months if their action jeopardises the physical or mental health of the victim.

13. The Court of Cassation is the highest appellate authority in the Italian criminal justice system. The Court is empowered to review decisions of inferior courts on point of law (not fact) and can remit the proceedings back to lower courts, indicating how to proceed.

14. Cassation Court, Section 6, Decision 5530, of 12 August 1974 (Beltrami and Petrucci, 2001: 1278).

15. Articles 582 and 583 regulate the crime of physical injuries and serious physical injuries, respectively, punishable by a prison term of 3 months to 3 years.

16. Article 581 punishes the crime of assault with a term of imprisonment of up to 6 months or with a fine.

17. Bullough (1997: 7) notes that a law of Romulus cited by Dionysius of Halicarnassus allegedly provided for the death penalty for adulterous women, and that both individuals could be killed if caught in flagrante delicto. Later, in 17 CE, Emperor Augustus passed the *lex Julia de adulteries coercendi*, which allowed a father to kill his adulterous daughter and her paramour when caught in the act in his or her husband's house. Christian emperors increased the penalties of the Lex Julia: Constantine introduced the death penalty and Justinian restored the husband's right to slay his adulterous wife.

18. For information on the Zanardelli Code and pre-Italian unification penal codes, see Fortuna, 2002.

19. From 1927 women's salaries were officially half that of men's; they were no longer allowed to teach in certain universities; and high school fees for female students were doubled. See further Previato: www.marxismo.net/idm/idm5/idm5_01.htm.

20. Cassation Court Section 1. 04.03.70 (Lattanzi, 1972: 778).

21. Cassation Court. 04.03.60 (Lattanzi, 1972: 778).

22. Cassation Court. Section 1. 27.04.65. (Lattanzi, 1972: 779).

23. Cassation Court. Section 1. 30.11.65 (Lattanzi, 1972: 779).

24. A woman who had lost her virginity or adopted 'immoral' behaviour was called *svergognata*, meaning shameless − that is, deprived of her shame and modesty.

25. Cassation Court, Section 1 02.02.72, *Rivista Penale*, 1989: 958.

26. The story is set in a Sicilian village. A married Baron, Fefe' Cefalu', is infatuated with his young cousin Angela but cannot marry her because divorce was not available. Inspired by a famous trial of a woman who had murdered her seducer, Fefe' consults Article 587 of the Rocco Code (which appears in a close-up on the screen allowing the audience to read it) and starts to plan the 'honour killing' of his wife. He pushes her into the arms of another man. Although initially things don't go according to plan, he eventually manages to kill her; he is sentenced to only three years in prison. Upon his return to his village he marries Angela. He is finally happy. However, the last scene of the film ends with his young wife flirting with another man.

27. Article 51 of the Italian Constitution states that 'all citizens of both sexes can work in public offices and be elected to public positions in conditions of equality'; however, women were prevented from joining the courts until 1963. In 1956 women were allowed to access the Courts of Assizes as part of the jury and the Tribunal for Minors, but this small concession was harshly criticised by scholars, judges and politicians alike, who commented on women being emotive and irrational human beings unable to exercise judgement during 'certain days of the month' (www.bibliolab.it/donne_web/allegato25_2htm). Once women gained full access to the courts, prejudices and stereotypes that had influenced the judiciary for many years started to be fought from within.

28. Article 62 no. 1 and 2:

    Generic extenuating circumstances. The following circumstances attenuate the crime in cases where they are not considered [by the legislator] as essential elements or as special extenuating circumstances of the offence.
    1. if the perpetrator acted for reasons of particular moral or social value;
    2. if the perpetrator acted in a fit of fury, caused by another's unjust action.

29. Cassation Court, Section 2. 12.01.60, *Rivista Italiana di Diritto e Procedura Penale*, 1960: 120.

30. Cassation Court, Section 3. 26.10.82, and previously in Cassation Court, Penal Section 4. 14.12.74 (both *Rivista Penale*, 1989: 958).

31. Cassation Court, Section 1. 13.12.78, *Rivista Penale*, 1989: 958.

32. Cassation Court, Section 1. 02.02.72, *Rivista Penale*, 1989: 958.

33. Repealing Article 587 erased the contradiction with Article 90, which states that 'emotional and passionate states do not exclude nor diminish the accountability of the culprit'. As maintained by the Cassation Court in 1976, jealousy does not impair the ability to understand; nor does it exclude intention, unless it constitutes a proper mental illness. Cassation Court, Section 1. 29.09.88 no. 12.863, *Rivista Penale*, 1989: 959).

34. For example, see Cassation Court, Section 1, Sentence 708 of 26.01.93 (Beltrami et al., 2001).

35. Article 133:

> Severity of the crime: assessment of punishment. In exercising his discretionary power indicated in the preceding article the judge shall assess the seriousness of the crime by looking at:
>
> (1) the nature, kind, means, object, time, place and any other characteristic of the action.

36. Cassation Court, Section 1, 29.09.88 no. 12.863, *Rivista Penale*, 1989: 959.
37. www.bibliolab.it/donne_web/allegato25_7.htm.
38. Ibid.
39. The 'cause of honour' was applicable to cases of abortion carried out on a non-consenting woman (545) or on a consenting woman (546), even if it caused her death or a physical injury (549); to cases where the woman herself induced an abortion (547); to cases of instigation to abort (548) and to cases where abortive procedures were carried out on a woman believed to be pregnant (550).
40. As opposed to Article 587, where 'honour killing' was characterised as a crime autonomous of homicide.
41. The formulation of the provision is not clear, but the view is taken in both scholarly comments and judicial decisions that the article is not applicable to cases where the person who committed the offence acted to save not the woman's honour but his own (Pannain, 1957: 581).
42. Judgments and the opinions of scholars are agreed on this point. See, for example, Cassation Court, 21.02.36 (Pannain, 1957: 579); Cassation Court, 24.05.47 (Pannain 1957: 579).
43. Cassation Court, 18.07.41 (Pannain, 1957: 583).
44. Cassation Court, 11.03.40 (Pannain, 1957: 583).
45. Cassation Court, 18.03.40 (Pannain, 1957: 583).
46. Cassation Court, 16.05.38 (Pannain, 1957: 583).
47. Article 578:

> Infanticide for cause of honour. Whoever causes the death of an infant immediately after delivery or of a fetus during delivery in order to save one's own honour or that of a close relative, shall be punished with a prison term of 3 to 10 years.
>
> Whoever concurs to the action with the exclusive purpose of helping one of the subjects indicated above, shall be subjected to the same penalty. In any other case, whoever concurs to the action shall be punished with a prison term from a minimum of 10 years.
>
> The extenuating circumstances of Article 61 are not applicable to these cases.

48. Article 592:

> Desertion of an infant for reasons of honour. Whoever deserts an infant immediately after its birth in order to save one's own honour or that of a close relative shall be punished with a prison term from 3 months to 1 year.
>
> The penalty shall be a prison term from 6 months to 2 years if from the action derives a personal injury to the infant and from 2 to 5 years if death occurs.
>
> The extenuating circumstances of Article 61 are not applicable.

49. www.bibliolab.it/donne_web/allegato25_2htm.
50. A party strongly linked to the Catholic Church.
51. www.bibliolab.it/donne_web/allegato25_2htm.

12

The 'legitimate defence of honour', or murder with impunity? A critical study of legislation and case law in Latin America

SILVIA PIMENTEL, VALÉRIA PANDJIARJIAN

AND JULIANA BELLOQUE

This chapter considers the legal treatment of 'crimes of honour' in countries across Latin America and the Caribbean, focusing in particular on Brazil. It outlines the gender-discriminatory aspects of laws and judgments of national courts relating to violence against women, analysed from feminist, socio-legal and human rights perspectives.

Major advances in securing the recognition and realisation of women's legal right to freedom from violence have occurred at international, regional and national levels. Nevertheless, today, at the start of the twenty-first century, prevailing laws and their interpretations by national courts across Latin America permit violations of women's human rights in the name of 'honour', by entrenching impunity for perpetrators of such violence and incorporating gender-biased myths and stereotypes against women subjected to violence. Such violations also result from legal theories, arguments and judicial decisions that create, use or apply the concept of the 'legitimate defence of honour' or the 'heat of passion' to justify the crime directly or indirectly, blame the victim and assure the perpetrator complete impunity or mitigation of sentence. This defence is applied in cases of bodily harm to or murder of women, in general committed by husbands, partners or boyfriends.

The first part of this chapter gives an overview of relevant statutory provisions and leading judgments related to 'honour crimes' in Latin America. The second part critically analyses the social and legal reality of Brazil, focusing on leading cases from the last decade in which the 'legitimate defence of honour' was invoked.

'Crimes of honour' in Latin America: overview

Legislation

As parties to the main international and regional human rights instruments securing women's rights to freedom from violence,[1] states in the region have committed themselves to guaranteeing equality and non-discrimination before the law. They have also committed themselves to ensuring the repeal of all gender-discriminatory laws, and to eliminating gender bias in the administration of justice. Nevertheless, across Latin America, national laws on violence against women – in particular on sexual violence – contain many gender-discriminatory provisions. These laws form part of the legal context underpinning the treatment and understanding of 'crimes of honour' (including 'honour killings') by the criminal justice systems in the region. Many countries have in recent years (particularly the 1990s) amended their Penal Codes in significant ways, while certain provisions continue to demand attention.[2]

One of the changes that many states in the region have made is to the way in which their Penal Codes classify offences of sexual violence. Bolivia, for example, changed its classification of sexual offences as 'Offences to Customs' to 'Offences to Sexual Liberty'; Peru has made the same change from its pre-existing 'Offences to Honour and Customs', while Argentina changed from 'Offences to Honesty' to 'Offences to Sexual Integrity'. Brazil, however, continues to classify sexual offences as 'Offences against Custom', while Uruguay maintains 'Offences to Customs and Family Order'.

Another issue that has been dealt with by some (but not all) states is that of the exemption from penalty, or cessation of criminal proceedings, in the case of sexual offences (including rape) where the offender marries the victim. Argentina, Chile, Colombia and Peru have all removed such exemptions from their penal legislation; Bolivia, Brazil, Guatemala, Panama, Uruguay and Venezuela maintain various provisions on this subject. In Brazil, for example, a perpetrator of sexual offences cannot be punished if he marries the victim or she marries a third person, exempting him of his criminal liability. The *ratio legis*, in that sense, is that since the sexual violence has not impeded the marriage prospects of the victim, the crime should be forgiven. In Argentina, although (as noted above) the exemption has been removed, the concept of *avenimiento* has been introduced; this is a type of agreement between victim and offender where there was a previous affectionate relationship between the parties. If the victim proposes such an agreement to the offender, the court may exceptionally accept it as extinguishing the criminal action or suspending the judgment if it considers this provides more appropriate resolution of the conflict and better protection of the victim's interests.

Adultery is still criminalised in some states, including Brazil and Mexico. In Venezuela, a woman who commits adultery is described as an 'adulteress' and liable (along with her partner in the offence) to a prison term of between six months and three years. If a husband is found guilty of adultery, on the other hand, he is described as a man who has a 'concubine', is liable to punishment only if the adultery is publicly known, and then only to a prison term of three to eighteen months, while the 'mistress' is liable to a term of between three months and one year.

Certain states also maintain laws that allow consideration of the woman's 'honesty' in crimes of sexual violence. In Brazil, the Penal Code still contains expressions such as 'honest woman' to describe the victims of offences of a sexual nature in crimes of violent abduction, as well as the expression 'virgin woman' for crimes of seduction; in Venezuela the expression 'honest woman' remains in the provision on rape, while Boliva for example has removed a similar reference.

Finally in this review, a number of states make provision for a 'heat of passion' or comparable defence. In Mexico, the Federal Penal Code provides for a reduced punishment for murder or bodily harm committed in the 'heat of passion', which is regarded as a mitigating circumstance. In Uruguay the 'heat of passion' caused by adultery is a factor that may be considered in granting a judicial pardon if one spouse surprises the other in the act of adultery and kills or injures her/him and the partner. The infidelity of one of the partners or the breaking up of the relationship[3] has also been accepted as a mitigating circumstance in defence of the offender. In Honduras, a person who finds his/her spouse or partner in the act of sexual intercourse with another person and kills or harms either or both of them stands to receive a sentence much lighter than would ordinarily be the case for murder or injury. Although this provision removed the pre-existing exemption from punishment applicable in such cases, it still reflects a culture that appears to look relatively favourably upon a person who kills or harms their spouse or partner after finding the former in flagrant sexual intercourse with the latter, rather than for any other reason. In Ecuador, the Penal Code holds that by virtue of the 'legitimate defence of the marital honour and self morality' no offence is committed when one of the spouses kills, hurts or strikes the other, or the 'correspondent lover', at the moment of finding them in the act of flagrant adultery. This provision remains in force despite the 1998 decriminalisation of adultery; although it is not used frequently as a defence, it continues to reflect a particular political (sexist) perspective on the idea of 'honour' and enables many offences, especially against women, to remain unpunished.[4]

Judicial application and interpretation

Gender-based violence is justified not only by certain aspects of legislation but also by legal arguments and judicial decisions that incorporate stereotypes, prejudices and discriminatory attitudes against women who suffer violence, negating their experiences and effectively treating them as the accused rather than the victims or survivors of crimes. Unfortunately, such arguments and decisions are still very common and are often to be seen in the conduct of prosecutions for sexual offences against women, especially rape (see Pimentel et al., 1998).

However, these discriminatory attitudes are generally most visible in the treatment of so-called 'crimes of honour' – that is, cases of battery and murder of women by their current or former husbands, sexual partners or boyfriends on suspicion of adultery/sexual infidelity and/or the desire of the woman to separate. Lawyers representing the accused in such cases use the 'legitimate defence of honour' by invoking 'conjugal honour' or the 'honour of the accused', in an attempt to justify the crime and commute or mitigate the sentence. They also resort to the defence of 'heat of passion' and other arguments to disqualify and blame the victim for the crime, by judging not the crime itself, but the behaviour of the woman and her sexual morality.

The following examination of the legal treatment of 'crimes of honour' in Argentina, Mexico and Uruguay illustrates the deeply rooted institutionalised gender discrimination present in the interpretation and application of law on crimes of violence against women. Following this, we move to a more detailed examination of the Brazilian context.

Argentina

Noted commentators Cristina Motta and Marcela Rodríguez (2000) argue that while in general the legal system does not formally incorporate gendered stereotypes, these remain clearly present in practice, and allow 'toleration' of harm and injury to women within the family sphere. Even where such an act of violence is treated as a crime and thus punished, 'there is a tendency to justify it, considering hidden stereotypes of gender and ancestral ideas about family and fidelity'. In this regard, Motta and Rodríguez affirm that 'Argentine case law related to the crimes of murder and bodily harm aggravated by the personal relations between offender and the victim offer expressive examples' (2000). In the reasoning of many judges, including decisions of higher courts, the private sphere is considered to be secret, and private violence is therefore to be treated with less severity. Jealousy, loveless feelings and non-compliance with conjugal duties are seen as reasons capable of justifying aggression and violence against women, and thus allowing mitigation of punishment in such cases.

In one case, the Supreme Court of the Province of Buenos Aires, when deciding whether a husband could invoke the defence of having acted under strong emotion in the 'heat of passion' in killing his wife, declared that 'ethics' and 'oppressed rights' are among the reasons used to support such a defence. The Supreme Court held that it should respect 'the rights protected by the legal system affected by the desire to murder, which is many times incited by a stimulus that is a provocation on the part of the victim'.[5] The Court held that in this case

> the facts that must be considered for the appraisal for the legal defence are: (a) 'the abandonment of the matrimonial home by the wife, taking the couple's children', conduct that causes the husband material harm (care of the house, kitchen, cleaning, etc.) and spiritual harm (solitude, deprivation of his children, and still more in this case the deficient sexuality and later fecundation) putting him under a surprisingly abnormal and difficult situation to overcome'; and (b) 'the reason for the abandonment', which it understood as one of the causes of separation between the wife and husband, namely the lack of sexual pleasure in their relationship; this fact by itself cannot be used from any point of view – religious, moral or legal – to justify that the wife leaves the matrimonial home, leaving her husband alone.

The Court reduced the punishment on the basis that 'the crime was committed for ethical reasons, conditioned by the previously mentioned circumstances, specifically [that the husband] found himself during the act in an intense state of emotional turmoil' (Motta and Rodríguez, 2000)

In another case, the judge reduced the punishment of a man convicted of killing his wife, on the basis that

> When the victim violates her legal and moral duties as a wife, in a serious and unusual – extraordinary – manner acting as the sole motive for his reaction ... the conduct of the victim works as an extraordinary mitigating circumstance, dismissing the idea of peculiar cruelty in the murder and of a higher degree of risk of dangerous behaviour. (Motta and Rodriguez, 2000)

In a 1988 case, another judge considered that

> the revelations, worries and humiliation suffered by the accused when confirming the wrongful conduct of the spouse, the drama which he had gone through which caused the crisis on the day of the crime in which he received the confirmation from her own lips that she had another man in her life and the fact that she intended to abandon the common life of the couple

were circumstances capable of supporting a plea of mitigation of sentence.[6]

Motta and Rodríguez (2000) hold that these cases illustrate a collective perception of the 'special' nature of offences committed in the family. They find this particularly shocking in light of the sociological reality in Argentina and elsewhere in the world where 'more than 90 per cent of the cases of violence inside the family are committed against women', and that the legal system appears to recognise and be more lenient to violence by individuals who harm their own relatives, thereby 'producing an erroneous message of impunity that incites insecurity of women at home'.

In 2003, a leading Argentinian newspaper reported that the court had reduced a life sentence to twenty-two years' imprisonment in the case of a man convicted of killing his wife, on the basis that he had been shocked by her asking for a divorce (*Clárin*, 25 June 2003). After having an argument with his wife, where she allegedly shouted and declared 'I want a divorce!', the offender hit her in the face, leaving her unconscious on the floor. After that he strangled her with a towel and a dress, put her body in a chest, drove to a wood and then set her on fire whilst she was still alive. It was claimed in this case that the 'heat of passion' constituted an extraordinary mitigating circumstance under the Penal Code. The court took the view that the perpetrator had acted in this way due to the disturbed nature of his personality, destroying what he loved the most, and therefore could not be appraised as if he were a person without these characteristics. It also considered that the murderer was not in a position capable of 'accept[ing] the family's disintegration'. The victim's family announced that they would appeal against the decision

Mexico

The Mexican courts continue to tolerate the murder of women where the killings are claimed to have been motivated by an attack on the 'honour' of their husbands. Gaspar Vargas Ríos, convicted for the murder on 22 April 2000 of his wife, lawyer Rocío Eugenia Mancilla Becerril,[7] was initially sentenced to only two years, ten months and fifteen days of imprisonment, after he claimed to have acted in the 'heat of passion'. The sentence was later reduced to one year and eight months by the Superior Court of Justice. In this case, the Court gave 'more value to the sexual act declared by the murder and the supposed adultery, without taking into account the evidence of a violent personality revealed in psychiatric tests on Gaspar Vargas' (Gonzales). It seems that the 'honour' of men is paid for by the death of women.

Article 293 of the Penal Code of the State of Oaxaca, Mexico, refers to homicide for 'honour'. According to Reyes Terán (CIMAC), 'homicide for honour, known in the other states as homicide in the heat of passion, guarantees a lesser punishment to individuals who kill their spouses on the ground of seeing him/her 'in sexual intercourse or close to its consummation'. The existence of such a provision reinforces impunity and the assertion of male proprietary rights over women.

Uruguay

In Uruguay, bodily harm and homicides committed mainly by men against their (ex-) wives (ex-) partners and (ex-) girlfriends are considered crimes of passion, committed under the legitimate defence of 'honour' as a spontaneous act (a 'thing of the moment') and are not seen as constituting domestic violence.[8] However, when women who have been subjected to years of domestic violence kill or harm their abusers, the courts have not allowed them to invoke this legitimate defence. As a result, such women have been convicted and sentenced to not less than ten years, the minimum punishment applicable in the cases of wives and 'concubines' who commit such crimes. In this situation, the courts have sustained arguments such as, 'if it is true that the woman has lived under real torture perpetrated by her husband, it is merely a case of a sick man and a homicide.'

According to Moriana, gender-discriminatory prejudices and attitudes, including about women's hysterical nature, serve in practice to perpetuate violence against women by men in the name of protecting male 'honour'. She also affirms that in the majority of cases, women who end up dead or grievously harmed, after having systematically protested the aggression, harassment and threats perpetrated against them, have not received an effective response from the judicial system.

The Brazilian legal context

Brazil is among the countries in Latin America with the longest and most extensive history of judicial decisions accepting the legitimate defence of 'honour' in crimes of homicide and violence against women by their partners or ex-partners, despite the absence of any specific legislative provision to this effect. This analysis is supported by sociological, anthropological and legal studies on Brazil carried out in earlier decades, which have demonstrated the prevalence of gender-discriminatory practices and attitudes relating to the administration of justice in crimes of violence against women.[9]

The feminist movement and women in general have through campaigns and other activities attempted to bring about a change in social attitudes. They have focused such efforts particularly on the Congress (legislature), the executive, the judiciary and all legal professionals, with a view to eliminating gender discrimination and violence against women.

The theme also reverberates considerably in the mass media, especially in cases where famous women have become the victims of so-called 'crimes of passion' by their present or former husbands, partners or boyfriends. Such reports have the effect of shocking society and making the news (though this may reflect the involvement of celebrities rather than the grievous nature of the crime itself or its claimed motivation). These occasions at least serve to highlight the issues and allow a debate to emerge. In other cases, however, media reports have from time to time focused on the theme independently of any particular crime, contributing to raising the visibility of the problem (see, e.g., Cotes, 2004).

Gender discrimination in the Brazilian Penal Code

The Penal Code (Decree Law No. 2848/1940, of which the General Section has been amended by Law No. 7.209/1984) is now more than sixty years old, and was clearly elaborated by and directed to a patriarchal society. Many of its provisions and underlying concepts reflect and incorporate gender discrimination, and are capable of producing a *systematic contamination* of Brazilian law more generally. Indeed, the failure of legislators to modify or repeal such provisions has enabled judges to interpret them in ways that wholly contradict human rights and violate principles entrenched in the Constitution of 1988.

Despite the 1984 reform of its general part, the Penal Code retains provisions that seem inconceivable in a democracy where equality between men and women is constitutionally enshrined.[10] These are also inconsistent with the state's internationally binding commitments to protect women from conduct causing death, harm or physical, sexual or psychological suffering, either in the public or the private sphere. These commitments include the duty to ensure the right of every woman to live free from violence and from all forms of discrimination.[11]

In the overview at the beginning of this chapter we referred to one striking example of a gender discriminatory norm in Brazil that violates constitutional and international guarantees of human rights. Article 107, Title VII of the Penal Code, allows commutation of punishment where an alleged offender marries his victim in cases of so-called offences to 'honour'. Such offences include rape and '*atentado violento ao pudor*', in which the offender, by use of violence or grievous threat, coerces the victim to commit a sexual act. It also permits commutation of punishment where the victim marries a third party, in respect of 'offences to customs' which are committed without real violence or serious threat, provided that the victim does not initiate criminal investigation or action within sixty days after the wedding. These provisions are clearly intended to protect the 'honour' of the victim and her family, rather than her right to physical integrity or her sexual freedom; according to this reasoning, the marriage 'repairs' the violation and restores the 'purity' of the woman.

For decades, such discriminatory legal provisions sustained the judiciary's understanding that coercion in sexual acts within marriage did not constitute rape or *atentado violento ao pudor*. Consequently, a husband's using violence to force his wife to have sex was considered for many years legally acceptable, supported by the regime of rights and duties governing the institution of marriage. It is only very recently that courts have started to reverse this scenario, convicting and sentencing men for rape and *atentado violento ao pudor* against their wives.

Similarly discriminatory attitudes infuse concepts and expressions used in the Special Part of the Penal Code that describe criminal offences, for example the classification of offences against sexual liberty, within the chapter entitled 'Offences to Custom'. The idea of 'offences to custom' is explained by commentators as protecting 'propriety, social rules established in the name of a specific "'social morality'" and "custom"' (Hungria, 1956: 88; see also Noronha, 1998). Custom here means habits of sexual life that are approved by 'moral attitudes', sexual behaviour that is adapted to social discipline and convenience (Hungria, 1956: 103).

Furthermore, several of the crimes defined in this section of the Code use discriminatory expressions in referring to the characteristics of a female victim. These are the so-called normative elements of the crime. For instance, Article 215 of the Penal Code punishes the act of having 'sexual intercourse with an honest woman by means of fraud', which is punishable by imprisonment of between one and three years, and, where 'the crime is committed against a virgin woman' aged between 14 and 18, imprisonment of two to six years. The expressions 'honest woman' and 'virgin woman' are normative elements of certain crimes, such as *atentado violento ao pudor* by means of fraud (Article 216), seduction (Article 217) and abduction by force or fraud (Article 219). Their use represents disrespect and denial of women's right to sexual liberty and reinforces a legal culture that continues to tolerate many forms of violence against a woman in her intimate, personal and family life. The following discussion of the acquittal of men who injure and kill their former or present wives, partners or girlfriends, and then invoke the 'legitimate defence of honour', is set in the context of this discriminatory legal culture.

'Legitimate defence of honour'

Under the Brazilian Penal Code, the 'legitimate defence' is a legal defence to a crime. Article 25 establishes that 'It is understood that it is a legitimate defence for anyone to use moderate necessary means to repel unjust aggression, present or imminent, to himself or somebody else.' Such a defence may be invoked only if the accused's response is *proportional* and *immediate* in respect of the 'unjust aggression'. According to legal doctrine, any and every legal right can be defended legally, including the right to protection of one's 'honour'. However, there is no consensus on whether the legitimate defence is applicable in cases of homicide or aggression committed in 'defence of honour' by the betrayed spouse or partner or boyfriend.

It is important to highlight the gendered use of this defence. It is rarely pleaded by women who kill or harm their (ex)spouse/(ex)partner on the basis of infidelity, perhaps reflecting the small number of cases where women use this degree of violence. The 'legitimate defence of honour' may therefore be seen as a legal defence that seeks to negate the punishment of husbands, brothers, fathers or ex-partners and boyfriends who kill or injure their wives, sisters, daughters, ex-wives and girlfriends based on or 'justified' by the defence of 'family honour' or 'conjugal honour'. However, it should be emphasised that in most instances there is no 'conjugal' or 'family honour' to be protected, since 'honour' is a personal and private attribute of one individual and cannot be ascribed to two or more individuals.

At the end of the 1970s and the beginning of the 1980s, the Brazilian women's movement united against the traditional invocation of the 'legitimate defence of honour' in cases of crimes of passion, creating a slogan that became famous throughout the whole country: 'Who loves does not kill.' However, in the last twenty-five years there has been little focus on this issue. Indeed, there is currently a distinct lack of extensive legal research evaluating the extent to which this legal defence is still being invoked or accepted by the Brazilian judiciary. It is in this context that the authors set out to review decisions of the Brazilian courts in relation to the 'legitimate defence of honour'. Our research is intended to serve as a starting point to investigate the current usage of the 'legitimate defence of honour' and as such is not intended to be an exhaustive anthology of judicial decisions relating to 'honour crimes' in Brazil. However, even this preliminary research has provided significant information about the subject. It demonstrates, for example, that judgments on the use of the 'legitimate defence of honour' are not unanimous: in some cases the defence is rejected outright; in others it is, in general, accepted although rejected because of particular factual circumstances; and in some cases, albeit with less weight, it is accepted and the perpetrator is released.

Over the last two decades this legal defence has continued to be pleaded, sometimes with success, in all regions of the country.

It is important to highlight that intentional crimes against life are tried, in accordance with the Constitution,[12] by a jury composed of seven laypersons. Because of the supremacy accorded to jury verdicts, the High Courts of Justice of the States – which have appellate jurisdiction – can overturn a verdict only if it is clearly contrary to the evidence of the case, and must then direct the holding of a fresh trial. Under no circumstances can the appellate judges substitute their decision for the jury's verdict. Thus, even if the jury's initial acquittal of an alleged murderer is overturned on appeal, it may be the case that the legal defence of 'the legitimate defence of honour' is invoked and allowed at a retrial, resulting in another acquittal.

There is currently a national debate across Brazil about the legitimacy of jury trial. For some it manifests the most profound spirit of democracy. For others it has limitations in that it is dependent on the knowledge and prejudices of the jurors. This debate notwithstanding, there is no doubt that many jury verdicts perpetuate and justify violations of women's rights.

Article 224 of the Platform of Action of the Fourth World Conference on Women, held in Beijing in 1995, establishes that violence against woman 'both violates and impairs or nullifies the enjoyment by women of human rights and fundamental freedoms'. It further highlights that '[a]ny harmful aspect of certain traditional, customary or modern practices that violates the rights of women should be prohibited and eliminated. Governments should take urgent action to combat and eliminate all forms of violence against women in private and public life, whether perpetrated or tolerated by the State or private persons.' The international community has made many legal recommendations in relation to the issue of 'crimes of honour'.[13] Specifically, it has criticised the use of the jury and even called for repudiation of cultural practices disrespectful to the human rights of women.

Methodology

For the purposes of this research we analysed fifty-four judgments of the higher courts over a five-year period (1998 to 2003), drawn from leading law reports and websites of the Brazilian courts. The study is limited by the lack of public access to the case law of all the states of the Brazilian Federation. In addition, to obtain a fuller picture of the application of the legal defence of 'the legitimate defence of honour', it would be necessary to analyse jury verdicts. However, trial court proceedings are not easily accessible in journals and websites, except where they have appealed. In the absence of such materials, this research cannot give a precise assessment of the extent of application of this legal defence, as it does not draw on all judgments delivered by the higher courts in such cases.

Despite these limitations, the research supports the assertion that 'the legitimate defence of honour', deployed to acquit men of the charge of killing their wives and ex-wives, is a cultural practice, as revealed by decisions of the Brazilian courts. This practice is based on the prevalence of gender-biased prejudices and stereotypes that require a critical analysis and response.

Our research aims to provide a *subjective*, and *not quantitative*, analysis of the issue. It seeks to demonstrate that even in the twenty-first century, and despite beliefs to the contrary, Brazilian society and culture continue to see men who kill or harm their (ex-)wives (ex)-partners or (ex-)girlfriends in the name of so called 'family' or 'spousal honour' as liable to be excused from culpability. It also highlights how Brazilian legal culture allows murderers to remain unpunished in certain cases. The legal defence in question bases itself on 'family' or 'spousal honour', which is not explicitly defined in legislation or jurisprudence, reinforcing a system in which the woman is oppressed by the man and by the values of a patriarchal society.

The decisions researched were grouped into four categories: (a) where the High Courts accepted the legal defence of the 'legitimate defence of honour' in cases of offences 'motivated' by the sexual behaviour of the victim with a third person; (b) where the High Courts rejected this legal defence due to the failure to meet the terms of the above-cited Article 25 of the Penal Code; (c) where a majority of judges of the High Court rejected this legal defence in absolute terms, with a minority dissenting; and (d) where the High Courts rejected this legal defence in absolute terms. A full listing, summaries and analyses of the cases are given in the full version of this text (see www.soas.ac.uk/honourcrimes). During the course of the research, we were struck by some of the gender-discriminatory observations of certain judges. We highlight some of these in the following critical comments, which focus on three cases in the first category.

Critical considerations

In three cases decided between 1990 and 2002, the Courts of Appeal of São Paulo and Acre accepted the 'legitimate defence of honour'.[14] One decision, from São Paulo, concerned the crime of bodily harm.[15] At trial in the first instance and on appeal, it was accepted that the defendant had used 'moderate' force in punching his wife several times, and that he had been motivated by his strong feelings arising from the victim's confession of her infidelity. The Court of Appeal noted:

Although nowadays it is possible to admit as an archaic prejudice the attitude of one who kills or harms an adulterous wife or partner, in this case the honour of the appellant was tainted by the declaration of his mistress with whom he had lived for many years that she was cheating on him with another man, and it was also impossible to ignore that the couple had four children, despite the unlawful union.

The second case from São Paulo involved a man killing his wife and her lover on finding them in flagrante. The Court of Appeal, affirming the jury's verdict, did not refer to the legal requirement of moderation in response to any aggression (see Article 25 of the Penal Code). Instead the Court saw the homicide committed by the 'betrayed' husband as his only option to avoid everlasting damage to his 'honour', declaring that 'If he had left that house without doing what he did his honour would be irretrievably offended.' It observed that

the defendant was raised in a different time, during the 1920s and 1930s, when morals and customs were different and probably more rigid than nowadays, which undoubtedly influenced his character, shaping his personality and future reflexes.

Noting that the subject of the legitimate defence of honour is 'controversial, in jurisprudence as well as in case law', the Court observed that

Adultery, in general, in all times, in all laws, from the most primitive to the most modern legislation, has always been considered a crime, an immoral and anti-social act ... [I]t is incontestable that, during a marriage, a spouse has the absolute right to fidelity from his/her partner and the right to demand it – a right that results in honour as a legal value to be respected and kept.

The reasoning here is of concern, as it moves beyond a *justification* to virtual praise for a homicide, as the court appears to consider the murderer to be 'a true defence instrument of his own society'. In this case, it was held that the homicide was committed in reaction to the crime of adultery – an offence which

does not only happen in relation to the individual but, also, in relation to the custom rules of a social group; the personal reaction is something that possesses and is motivated by a visible social weight. The individual reacts in respect to his dignity and in respect to the common sense of social values. He reacts because honour can only be understood and exist under a double aspect and under a duty towards him and towards society. In the defence of his right, he can have no other attitude or conduct as an individual and member of a specific organised social group.... Who acts in defence of his morals, in any aspect of it, acts as a true defence instrument of his own society.

In Brazil and much of Latin America, where there is a strong positivist legal tradition, there is an insidious effort to humanise the interpretation of these crimes. The expansion of the concept of legitimate defence to incorporate 'honour' ends up favouring men's, to the detriment of women's, lives. It is important to clarify that many subdivisions of jurisprudence in this century, including positivism in its various forms, represent in a sense efforts to protect better the rights of people, whether this takes explicit or implicit form. The major criticism of formalist positivism, though, is that in itself it does not guarantee protection of the rights of people. Therefore, to transcend established rights, to capture social and cultural values not constituted in the legal system, would be legitimate in cases where it would better protect people's rights.

Decisions such as these imply denial of the value of the woman and her life. Principles and rules of protection of human rights established by the UN and the Organisation of American States (OAS) are wholly opposed to such positions. The judgment violates, among others, Article 3 of the Universal Declaration of Human Rights establishing that 'every person has the right to life, liberty and security of persons'; and Article 5(a) of the Women's Convention,[16] which establishes that

> State Parties shall take all appropriate measures to modify the social and cultural
> patterns of conduct of men and women, with a view to achieving the elimination
> of prejudices and customary and all other practices which are based on the idea
> of the inferiority or the superiority of either of the sexes or on stereotyped roles
> for men and women.

It also violates Article 1 of the Belém do Pará Convention,[17] which states:

> For the purposes of this Convention violence against woman shall be understood
> as any act or conduct based on gender, which causes death or physical, sexual
> or psychological harm or suffering to the women, in either the public or the
> private sphere.

In the national sphere, Article 5, *caput*, of the Brazilian Constitution is also violated since it provides that all persons are equal before the law, being guaranteed the right to life, liberty, equality, security and property. The first subsection of that same article is also breached since according to its terms men and women are equal in rights and duties. There is also a violation of Article 25 of the Brazilian Penal Code, which establishes the conditions of the legitimate defence, since the legal requirements for the legitimate defence were not fulfilled.

However, the judgment was not unanimous and the dissenting opinion in this case presented well-founded arguments:

Honour is a personal attribute, independent from the acts of a third person, thus it is impossible to consider a man dishonoured because his wife is unfaithful.... The law and the moral do not permit that the woman prevaricates. But to deny her, for that reason, the right to live would be a refinement of cruelty.

These arguments were, however, dismissed by the majority of the judges, who preferred to favour prejudices to the detriment of the supreme right to life.

The third case was heard in Rio Branco, AC.[18] The accused was acquitted on the charge of attempted murder of his partner's lover, having found the lover in his bedroom, immediately after committing adultery with his partner. The circumstances of the case led the judge, during the first phase of the trial by jury, to acquit the accused based on the legitimate defence of honour, holding that

The accused, arriving home, found his partner with the victim in his bedroom, the adultery being perfectly revealed, which naturally inflicted a sense of inner wound, which made him react to protect his own moral integrity, as well as the moral integrity of his family and marriage, permitting the legal excuse based on the legitimate defence.

Significantly, there was no appeal from the office of the Public Prosecutor. The case was submitted to the Court of Appeal only because of the requirement for review of any decision to acquit an accused in the first phase of the trial by jury.[19] The Court of Appeal unanimously upheld this decision, finding that the accused had fulfilled the requirements of Article 25 of the Penal Code, because 'considering that the accused had acted in moderation, wounding the lover of his partner only with a stab of a knife, I do not see enough reason to condemn him for attempted murder'. The Court further made reference to a judgment of the higher court TACRIM/SP, where it was stated:

It is very easy to plead that the outraged honour is the honour of the unfaithful spouse and that this attitude does not harm the honour of the other spouse. However, this point of view is written in books, far from reality, especially among us Latins, for whom this is not the popular concept of honour: the outraged honour is the honour of the innocent spouse.

Such a unanimous decision in the Court of Appeal is particularly surprising for a decision taken in 2002.

Conclusion

The cases discussed above, and others contained in the full version of this text, demonstrate that the 'legitimate defence of honour' is still used to uphold the acquittal of men who kill or injure their partners. The defence is based on arguments that link the law to a patriarchal moral framework, and on concepts that are inconsistent with current legal theory. Such outmoded concepts include that of the male head of household protecting other family members, and of women's adultery being seen as affecting the honour of the husband and, through its effect on social morals, the state.

Many of the cases examined in our research show that the courts have adopted a position which tackles the problem neither with courage nor on any consistent principle. On the one hand, they have avoided applying the 'legitimate defence of honour' to commute sentences, given the absence of supporting evidence in specific cases. They have also refused to allow the 'legitimate defence' where there is evidence that the killer knew about the victim's sexual acts, and his acts were premeditated. On the other hand, they have also rejected the defence where the perpetrator and the victim were legally separated, holding that in this situation marital duties (including to sexual fidelity) would stand suspended.

In other cases the courts have taken a more principled position, consistent with the human rights of men and women, and rejecting absolutely the 'legitimate defence of honour' and its underlying concepts. They have denounced the 'primitivism' of the entire defence, and its incompatibility with current Brazilian culture. In these the courts emphasise equality between men and women, a right enshrined in the 1988 Constitution. They also underline that 'marital honour' is not a legal concept, as 'honour' is a personal attribute that cannot be transferred from one person to another. Therefore, if a woman is unfaithful to her husband or partner, her 'honour' may be harmed, but his is not. Finally, these decisions emphasise that, in the balance between the legal protection of 'honour' and life, the latter is undoubtedly the predominant value to be protected by the law.

Our pilot research has aimed to demonstrate that impunity for men who kill and injure women remains embedded in Brazil's law and jurisprudence, in the form of the 'legitimate defence of honour'. We need to identify the true dimensions of this problem, in order to end this form of gender-based discrimination. The present analysis has drawn on the values of gender equality and human dignity inherent to men and women. It is based on a legal framework which encompasses the Universal Declaration of Human Rights, the Convention on the Elimination of all Forms of Discrimination Against Women, and the Inter-American Convention on the Prevention,

Punishment and Eradication of Violence against Women, as well as the 1988 Brazilian Constitution.

Finally, it is important to emphasise that this is an activist–theoretical–practical study, and as such represents part of ongoing efforts for the recognition and realisation of the human rights of women. It is also intended to inform relevant actors in society – in particular the legal community – about the continuing prevalence within Brazilian institutions of certain attitudes and understanding which many people think no longer exist. It cannot be denied that, for many people, women's humanity is still undervalued or, worse, denied. Some Brazilian men persist in the view that women are possessions that can be discarded when no longer useful, at minimal cost to themselves. It is repugnant that judicial institutions, whose main constitutional role is to safeguard fundamental human rights, instead reflect and replicate such gender injustice, and myths and stereotypes regarding women subjected to violence.

Notes

The original paper in Portuguese was translated into English by Maria Eduarda Hasselmann de Oliveira Lyrio, lawyer, LL.M (Human Rights), University College London. The Portuguese and English texts of the full paper are available at www.soas.ac.uk/honourcrimes. The current summary was prepared for this publication by the CIMEL/INTERIGHTS project team, which is responsible for any errors or misrepresentations arising from the process of editing and summarising.

1. In particular the Convention on the Elimination of all forms of Discrimination against Women (CEDAW, UN, 1979) and the Inter-American Convention on the Prevention, Punishment and Eradication of Violence against Woman (Convention of Belém do Pará, OAS, 1994), both of which are ratified by the majority of countries in Latin America, and the Beijing Platform of Action, IV Woman's World Conference (UN, 1995). See, for example, paragraph 232(d) of the Beijing Platform of Action: 'Review national laws, including customary laws and legal practices in the areas of family, civil, penal, labour and commercial law in order to ensure the implementation of the principles and procedures of all relevant international human rights instruments by means of national legislation, and revoke any remaining laws that discriminate on the basis of sex and remove gender bias in the administration of justice.'

2. This section has been summarised from a more detailed overview in the original paper, which was based on information provided in the CLADEM sources cited in the References. The authors would like to thank the Documentation Centre of CLADEM (CENDOC CLADEM); Susy Garbay, coordinator of CLADEM Ecuador; and Moriana Hernández Valentini, coordinator of CLADEM Uruguay, for the information they provided.

3. According to information provided by the national coordinator of CLADEM Uruguay, Moriana Hernández Valentini.

4. According to Susy Garbay, coordinator of CLADEM Equador. Amendments to the Penal Code in 1998 removed an article which had allowed 'honour' to exempt from criminal liability.

5. Decision of the Supreme Court of the Province of Buenos Aires, 12 December 1989.

6. CN. Crim e Corr. 5 February 1988.

7. Román Gonzáles, *Vetusto el Codigo Civil vigente que regula las relaciones familiares: perspectiva machista justifica la violencia de género en Edomex*. CIMAC, Mexico (Ciudad de México: CIMAC, in www.cimacnoticias.com/noticias, accessed 10 September 2002).

8. According to the information provided by the Uruguay national coordinator of CLADEM, Moriana Hernández Valentini.

9. See full report for sources cited, including Human Rights Watch, 1991.

10. Article 5, chapter I, of the Federal Constitution of the Republic of Brazil, 1988.

11. Articles 1 and 6(a) of the Inter-American Convention on the Prevention, Punishment and Eradication of Violence against Woman (Convention of Belém do Pará), approved by the General Assembly of the Organisation of American States (OAS) on 9 June 1994 and ratified by Brazil on 27 November 1995.

12. Article 5, Chapter XXXVIII of the Federal Constitution.

13. See International Legal Materials on the CIMEL/INTERIGHTS website; and see Human Rights Watch, 1991: 26–9, on the role of juries.

14. Criminal Appeal n. 633.061–7, 6 December 1990 (Court of Appeal of São Paulo); Criminal Appeal n. 137.157–3/1, 23 February 1995 (Court of Appeal of São Paulo); and Recurso de Oficio n. 01.001650–3, Rio Branco, 1 March 2002 (Court of Appeal of Acre). Note that *recurso de oficio* is the automatic submission of a case to the Superior Instance for possible reversal. Such cases are determined by law.

15. Criminal Appeal n. 633.061–7, 6 December 1990

16. Brazil ratified CEDAW on 1 February 1984.

17. Inter-American Convention on the Prevention, Punishment and Eradication of Violence Against Woman.

18. Recurso de Oficio n. 01.001650–3, Rio Branco, 1 March 2002.

19. In accordance with Article 411 of the Criminal Procedure code.

13

'There is no "honour" in domestic violence, only shame!' Women's struggles against 'honour' crimes in the UK

HANNANA SIDDIQUI

On 29 September 2003, in what came to be described, particularly by the media and the police, as an 'honour killing', Abdella Yones, an Iraqi Kurd, admitted to murdering his daughter, Heshu Yones, for having a boyfriend and for being 'too Westernised'. In 1998, Rukshana Naz, a Pakistani/British woman, was killed by her mother and brother. Convicted of her murder in 1999, Rukshana's mother justified the killing, saying 'it was in her *kismet*' (fate). The brother attempted to make a 'cultural defence', arguing in mitigation that he had been provoked into killing his sister because she had brought shame and dishonour on to the family by refusing to stay in her marriage to a cousin in Pakistan and by becoming pregnant by her lover in the United Kingdom.

An 'honour killing' is murder in the name of 'honour'. An 'honour crime'[1] is one of a range of violent or abusive acts committed in the name of 'honour', including emotional, physical and sexual abuse and other controlling and coercive behaviours, such as forced marriage and female genital mutilation, which can end, in some extreme cases, in suicide[2] or murder. Southall Black Sisters (SBS) have, for many years, argued that cultural defences are used by men from minority communities to justify violence against women in the name of religion and culture. 'Honour', in this context, is essentially about defending 'family honour', although this is often extended to reflect the 'honour' of the community. Women who transgress traditional forms of acceptable female behaviour are accused of having brought shame on their family and so besmirched its 'honour'. Failure to be a 'virtuous' woman, such as an obedient and dutiful wife, daughter and daughter-in-law, leads to condemnation by the extended family and the community at large. In particular, women's sexual conduct comes under strict scrutiny and surveillance. Women are expected to remain chaste or 'unstained' by adultery (and to observe the norms of heterosexuality). Even a hint or allegation of 'immoral' female behaviour is enough to destroy a reputation.

'Honour' is used as a motivation, justification or mitigation for violence against women as seen from the perspective of the perpetrator, often with the collusion or active involvement of the community. It is essentially a tool to police and control a woman's behaviour. Transgression results in her 'punishment', often in the form of social ostracism, harassment and even acts of violence. Extreme cases in the UK have led to murder, while some women have been driven to suicide. In one of SBS's cases, for instance, a South Asian woman (A) hanged herself in 2000 after finding out that her husband intended to divorce her to marry a younger woman. Her husband had subjected her to domestic violence and made false allegations of adultery against her. In family and community perceptions, this would reflect badly on A's moral character and family 'honour', which, together with the stigma of divorce, would have ruined her two daughters' prospects of marriage. It appears that A may have committed suicide, in part to preserve her 'family honour' and protect her daughters' future.

While 'honour' is essentially used to control female sexuality and autonomy, to some extent men also may come under pressure to conform to prescribed forms of male behaviour, such as those ascribed to the good and dutiful son, in order to preserve the good reputation of the family. However, whilst certainly homosexuality incurs severe stigma and condemnation, in general heterosexual men face no or less severe consequences when compared to women regarding 'honour crimes'. While 'honour crimes' may be committed over general family reputation or status (such as feuds over land and property), and lead to male-on-male violence, most disputes centre on the control of women. Thus, even where a man is killed in a dispute, the reasons often rest on the fact that he or his family had ruined the woman's reputation by refusing to carry through a promise of marriage or that the man had an actual or perceived sexual relationship with her.

Notions of 'honour' have existed in most societies, including in Britain. In the case of the aristocracy the term conjures up images of a duel at dawn where gentlemen defended their honour, often because of a slight against a woman's moral character and reputation. Its prevalence has somewhat diminished in many Western countries, although the notion of personal 'honour' and even family reputation appears still common, particularly in Italian (Bravo, 2001; Pelaja, 2001) and Greek society.[3] However, these notions have a much reduced controlling impact on the lives of white British women and indeed many non-white British women. In 2003, a consultation document by the Law Commission of England and Wales reviewed partial defences to homicide, including provocation, finding that the defence of provocation is historically rooted in male notions of 'honour' (Law Commission, 2003: 19). Although in Britain white men continue to use cultural defences in the context of perpetrating domestic violence where they eventually kill their partners, they do not refer to 'honour' as a motivating factor. Instead, although not always explicit, the underlying justification is the legitimate use of violence to maintain patriarchal power and control over women's behaviour. The notion of women as men's property remains, and men's excuses for murder often rest on 'nagging and shagging' defences – that it is the woman's socially unacceptable behaviour in the form of nagging or actual or perceived 'adultery' which caused them to 'snap' and kill out of anger. While these excuses are shared by men in all communities, a stain on their 'family honour' is no longer given as the motivating factor by white British men. The explicit use of 'honour' to justify murder or domestic violence is therefore now specific to certain black and ethnic minority communities in the UK.

'Swallowed her whole'

Most of the reported cases of 'honour killings' in Britain involve women from South Asian (Indian or Pakistani) or Middle Eastern, and mainly Muslim, backgrounds. However, our experience at SBS shows that 'honour killings' or crimes cut across racial, religious and cultural divides. The case of Surjit Athwal, for instance, involves a Sikh British woman who went missing in 1998 on a visit to her in-laws in India, where her natal family believe she was killed in an 'honour killing' (BBC Online, 12 November 2003).

Notions of 'shame' and 'honour' are strong and influential in tight-knit minority communities propped up by orthodox and conservative cultural and religious values. In such situations, the community often condones or perpetuates 'honour killings' or crimes, where a conspiracy of silence can hamper justice. Tasleem Begum, for instance, was killed in 1995 after being run over three times by her husband's brother, Shabir, as she waited for her lover. Shabir was angry at the prospect of Tasleem bringing 'shame' and 'dishonour' onto the family. A local newspaper wrote the following about the community's response:

> Religious leaders at Bradford's central mosque said they did not condone the killing, but pointed out that 'according to the Koran, killing this woman was correct'. A shroud of secrecy descended. Many knew the answers to police questions, but no one told. It was as though the pavement in Lepage Street, close to the supermarket

where Tasleem worked, had opened up and swallowed her whole, leaving no trace of her, her crime or her punishment. Det. Supt. Brian Steele, leading the murder inquiry, met a wall of silence everywhere he turned. He asked local people to 'search their souls' and 'recognise their obligations' to assist the police. But he became convinced that while many local women knew, they were too frightened to speak out, and that while many local men knew, they secretly agreed that Tasleem had brought disgrace and dishonour to her family and had to be eliminated. More than a year later, her sisters, her cousins, still refuse to tell, keeping their silence in the name of Allah. (*Yorkshire Post*, 5 October 1996)

For some sections within minority communities, however, notions of 'honour' may have more positive connotations, and are not about sexual control, but about respecting a sense of 'personal honour', dignity and integrity. Therefore, for many in the community, violence in the name of 'honour' is in fact a highly 'dishonourable' act, which requires social condemnation of the perpetrator, not the victim. These views were expressed in the early 1980s during a campaign following the death of Krishna Sharma, an Indian-origin woman, who hanged herself after years of domestic violence from her husband (Gupta, 2003a; McFadyean, 1992; Bedell, 1992). SBS organised a women's demonstration which marched through Southall and picketed outside the husband's house. The aim was to break the silence on domestic violence within Asian communities and to subvert the traditional notions of 'shame' and 'honour'. We argued that it was not women who should be condemned by the community for bringing 'shame' and 'dishonour' on them by challenging male violence, but rather men who perpetrate the abuse.

It's different for women

Women's groups in the UK have been dealing with 'honour'-related or motivated crimes for over two decades now. Our experience has shown that domestic violence is often justified in the name of 'honour', and that 'honour' is the reason why many women in minority communities are unable to leave abusive situations. It acts as an extra constraining factor in preventing them from leaving. Not only are women afraid of bringing 'shame' onto their family and community and destroying their 'honour', but they also fear the resulting social ostracism and harassment. 'Honour', therefore, has a different meaning for women than for men within the community. Male perpetrators use it to justify or excuse their violence, often supported by the conservative elements within the community, while women are trapped by its confining nature, which exerts control over their sexual freedom, preventing many from leaving abusive situations and sentencing them to pariah status if they do.

The state has failed to recognise this crucial difference, and has created a system which can reward violent men using cultural defences – often as a plea in mitigation by claiming provocation after killing their spouse, partner or family member in a context where the men have perpetrated repeated abuse – by accepting their excuses. In contrast, it fails to understand the pressures on women when they are unable to leave violent situations. Thus women kill or harm men not because, like men, they are attempting to preserve 'honour', but because they are driven to do so out of anger, despair or fear as a result of the violence they experience. Take, for instance, the case of Shabir Hussain. Although convicted of Tasleem Begum's murder in 1996, Shabir successfully pleaded manslaughter on the grounds of provocation when a retrial was ordered following appeal against his conviction. His sentence was cut to six and half years.[4]

Conversely, Zoora Shah, a Pakistani/British woman, is serving life for killing a violent man, Mohammed Azam, with whom she had a long-term relationship. Zoora, a non-literate working-class woman, killed Azam after he subjected her to twelve years of rape and sexual exploitation, including forced sexual relations with other men. Zoora had sought help from Azam's brother, a prominent member of the community, but he said he was unable to do anything. Finally, feeling depressed and desperate, and especially after Azam showed a sexual interest in her teenage daughters, Zoora poisoned him. At trial, Zoora did not admit to the killing and was convicted of murder. However, after she had met SBS, and following a period of counselling, Zoora confessed. She said she had been unable to explain her actions earlier because of the 'shame' and 'dishonour' which would have befallen her if she had admitted to a history of sexual violence, particularly in an area like Bradford, where she lived, and where the Asian community is deeply conservative. Although she was now telling the truth, Zoora's appeal against conviction was dismissed. The Court of Appeal ruled that her story was 'beyond belief' and that, considering her sexual history, she had no honour left to preserve.[5]

Zoora, it appears, did not fit the stereotype of a respectable, passive Asian woman, as had been the case with Kiranjit Ahluwalia, an Indian/British woman, whose release from prison was secured by SBS, together with her legal team, in 1992, following an appeal against her conviction for the murder of her violent husband. 'Honour' had also acted as the cultural factor in preventing Kiranjit leaving her husband. But, following expert and legal representations, and a public campaign, the Court of Appeal eventually understood the cultural context in which she had acted.[6] In comparison to Zoora, however, Kiranjit was not considered to be 'flagrant' – coming as she did from a respectable middle-class background with no allegations of sexual misconduct against her. It seems the legal system punishes women who do not fit the image of a virtuous woman, and colludes in the communities' perceptions of the 'dishonourable' woman.

This collusion has been apparent in other cases, including in family, immigration/asylum and suicide cases. For instance, at the inquest into A's death (discussed above) SBS argued that A killed herself because of the need to preserve 'family honour', and that her husband had threatened divorce, knowing full well the repercussions for A and their daughters, and as part of the pattern of his abusive behaviour. The coroner dismissed SBS's arguments and ruled that A committed suicide because of depression brought on by the prospect of divorce. He held that the notion of 'honour' had no specific meaning or consequences for women in minority communities, noting that even King Edward VIII had been compelled to abdicate to avoid dishonour to the monarchy and country resulting from a king marrying a divorcee! By failing to acknowledge the role of 'honour' in A's death, the coroner failed to understand or explain the impact of cultural pressures on women experiencing violence in minority communities, or to take any action to challenge or remedy the situation.

SBS have challenged these responses not only by fighting individual cases but also by raising these issues in the wider political arena through campaigning and policy interventions. For instance, the campaigns to free Kiranjit Ahluwalia and Zoora Shah sought to highlight how women within minority communities are constrained by notions of honour within abusive situations. Our submissions to the Law Commission's 'Review on Partial Defences to Murder' and the Home Office Review of 'Rules for Coroner's Courts' have called for the legal system to introduce measures to prevent violent men being able to use cultural defences in order to excuse murder, and for state action to prevent women being driven to suicide as a result of domestic violence and oppressive cultural practices. While these interventions have produced debates within government, in the courts and among the public, which have in turn produced greater awareness and pressure for change, there is still some way to go in ensuring the state effectively tackles the problems manifested in the cases of A and Zoora Shah.

From forced marriage to honour killings

In recent years, particularly following the death of Rukshana Naz, the issue of forced marriage has hit the headlines. Although Rukshana's case also represented the issue of 'honour killings', the media defined it as one concerning forced marriage (e.g. Chohan, 1999; BBC News Online, 5 August

1999). There was a public outcry about this and other high-profile cases of forced marriage. SBS demanded a public inquiry and the issue quickly gained the attention of the government, which, in 1999, established the Home Office Working Group on Forced Marriage. Now, however, 'honour killings' have captured the public imagination and become the new 'popular' issue, drawing column inches from the media and social commentators. Indeed, cases of deaths involving women from certain minority communities, which were once defined as resulting from pressures to have a forced marriage, are now redefined as 'honour killings'. For instance, in early 2003, Sahjda Bibi, a 21-year-old Pakistani/British Muslim woman, was killed by a cousin for refusing to marry a blood relative,[7] and the media used this as another opportunity to discuss forced marriage. In late 2003, however, following the high-profile case of Heshu Yones, the media immediately reclassified Sahjda's murder as an honour killing (e.g. *Birmingham Post*, 2003; cf. M. Cowan, 2004; *Sircar*, 2003; cf. Hill, 2004).

In Heshu's case, the Metropolitan Police Service, for the first time in its history, labelled a murder as an 'honour killing' (BBC News Online, 30 September 2003), although, unlike Rukshana's brother, Abdella Yones did not explicitly argue 'honour' as the motive. The media followed suit, and the case received similar, although not as great, media attention as that of Rukshana Naz. However, unlike in the aftermath of Rukshana's death, the government was slow to respond to the issue of 'honour killings'. The climate is different now. Post-9/11, some in government seem cautious to comment or respond in such cases, as many of the reported cases involve women from Muslim communities, while for others these issues remain marginal and not part of mainstream concerns. Also, Mike O'Brien, who had formed the Working Group on Forced Marriage while a Home Office Minister, and who had shown a particular interest in addressing the problem of forced marriage, is no longer responsible for this portfolio. The current Home Office Ministers, who have expressed concern over 'honour killings' in public meetings and debates, have not so far made any public announcements or taken specific initiatives to address the issue.[8]

The Metropolitan Police, however, have used the media to profile and research cases of 'honour killings' under the leadership of Commander Baker.[9] In 2003, the Metropolitan Police held a seminar on honour killings.[10] This aimed to consult women's groups on the issue, and the police stated that they also planned to hold seminars with the media and faith leaders. During the debate on forced marriage, the police, along with the government, had been vocal in their determination to tackle the problem. However, both prioritised the need to consult community and religious leaders. The solution, they argued, was to end forced marriage by educating the community.

We criticised them for failing to consult survivors of forced marriage and women's groups, and for ignoring the state's responsibility in addressing the problem. It was only as a result of campaigning led by SBS that the government and the police acknowledged that they had a role, which resulted in an improved response from the Foreign and Commonwealth Office in cases of British nationals being forced into marriage overseas, and in the establishment of the police guidelines on forced marriage.

Similar arguments have now arisen in relation to 'honour killings' and 'honour crimes'. The police, by consulting community and faith leaders, are still clinging to the argument that educating the community is a priority, although now they also give the impression that women's groups are just as (not more) important in the consultation process. They have been keen to involve South Asian and Middle Eastern women's groups and scholars in the newly established Metropolitan Police Working Group on Honour Killings. However, despite this development, in the view of SBS questions remain regarding the police's agenda.

'Mature multiculturalism'

At their seminar on honour killings, the police showed a clip from a documentary on 'bounty hunters', broadcast on Channel 4 in the 1980s. The 'bounty hunter' highlighted in the film was a man hired by certain South Asian families to track down women who had left home, intimidate and force them to return. In this clip, South Asian male relatives of a woman who had left home were seen instructing the bounty hunter. They even suggested killing or injuring her in the name of 'honour'. The police pointed to this clip as highlighting the collusion of the family and community in 'honour killings'. We stated that we raised this matter with the police just after the documentary was broadcast and were equally concerned that the police had failed to pursue any criminal charges against these men!

We said that it was no surprise to us that these men felt so free to make such horrific threats and comments on camera with impunity and pointed to how multicultural assumptions had prevented the police from acting. Such assumptions include the view that it is intolerant, or even racist, for a majority community to interfere in minority cultures. Thus, respecting cultural difference means allowing the minority community to govern or police itself. It also seems to mean that any intervention is determined in consultation and agreement with self-styled community and religious leaders, who are seen as gatekeepers and who, historically, have represented the most powerful patriarchal and conservative forces in the community. Multiculturalism, which aims to promote racial harmony *between* communities, fails to address problems *within* communities, such as oppressive practices against women and other less powerful groups. The leaders rarely challenge the status quo, and the state colludes with them to deny protection to women within the community for the sake of maintaining good community or race relations.

However, in the debate on forced marriage, the government has shifted its traditional position on multiculturalism. This approach was symbolised by the words of the Home Office Minister, Mike O'Brien, who talked of a 'mature multiculturalism' when discussing forced marriage. He added that 'Multi-cultural sensitivity is no excuse for moral blindness' (*Hansard*, 10 February 1999).

Mike O'Brien supported the long-held view of SBS that the state must intervene in minority cultures in order to protect women and girls from forced marriage. However, despite this recognition, the new concept of 'diversity', which calls for more *equity* of treatment between different dis-advantaged groups, rather than *equality* within these groups, still silences women's demands, which are considered as equal to, but not carrying more moral authority or rights than, those of community leaders. Thus, once again, the more radical voices of women are compromised by the more conservative forces within the community. Interestingly, in a climate of religious revivalism, such forces are also being increasingly represented or fronted by women.

This development became evident in the forced marriage debate. The Home Office Working Group on Forced Marriage advocated mediation in cases of forced marriage as one option in tackling the problem. SBS, who were part of the Working Group, opposed this recommendation, arguing that it compromised protection because it created pressure for the victim to accept promises made by her abusers, usually her parents and other members of the family, that they would not force her into marriage. This means victims were often reconciled to live at the home through a process of mediation by agencies – a practice formally adopted by social services and often informally by other agencies, such as the police. SBS argued that promises made to reform are often broken and are difficult to enforce – placing women and girls in dangerous situations. We pointed to the case of Vandana Patel, who, in 1991, was stabbed to death by her husband in the supposed safety of the Domestic Violence Unit in Stoke Newington Police Station in North London after the police had acted as 'mediators' in bringing the couple together.

Our arguments, however, were not accepted by the Working Group (Home Office, 2000: 20), which, as part of its membership, included a religious women's group that, along with the Joint Chairs to the Working Group, Lord Ahmed and Baroness Uddin, supported the more conservative elements within the community who argued against too much interference from the state. Mediation and reconciliation meant that the state did not need to break up families, thus preventing women from leaving home. This limited state intervention in minority communities and did not undermine the status quo. This policy creates a differential approach to women in minority communities because it is not advocated for women in the majority community when tackling domestic violence.[11] The recommendation enabled the Working Group to pursue a policy akin to appeasement, which amounted to allowing the discriminatory and morally blind approach of multiculturalism in through the back door.

Reinventing old 'solutions'

Shifts in political leadership have added another twist to the tale. David Blunkett, appointed Home Secretary in June 2001, supported the views of some Labour MPs such as Ann Cryer (Keighley), who have called for more immigration controls to tackle issues such as forced marriage:[12] a 'solution' often proposed for problems concerning black and minority communities. Following the race riots in northern cities (including Oldham, Burnley, Leeds and Bradford) involving South Asian youth in 2001, David Blunkett argued that the riots were caused by the lack of integration by young male South Asian immigrants, who are unable to speak English, and who hold 'backward' attitudes towards and perpetrate oppressive practices against women, such as forced marriage. The solution, for him, lay in their 'adopting British norms of acceptability' and imposing greater immigration controls on overseas marriages and conditions of entry into the UK (BBC News Online, 10 December 2001). He advocated that people from South Asian communities should find a marriage partner in the UK to assist with integration, and that citizenship and English tests should be introduced for immigrants applying for British nationality. Although the tests have yet to be introduced, from February 2004 new citizens were required to swear the recently introduced pledge of citizenship, in addition to the long-standing oath. In addition, the Home Office has extended the probationary period for overseas spouses from one year to two years and raised the age at which an overseas spouse can join their British spouse from 16 to 18 years of age on the grounds it reduces bogus or forced marriages.[13]

SBS, however, criticised the government as this 'solution' failed to tackle either forced marriage or the race riots. While it is important to acknowledge that forced marriage, and gender violence more generally, are supported by value systems which condone the control of women's sexuality and autonomy, these values do not differ much from 'British values', where domestic violence is also justified on the same grounds. Thus, it is not 'British' or 'Western' values that hold the solution to the oppression of women in minority communities, but rather the struggle for women's human rights waged by the South Asian and other minority women's movement in the UK and abroad. Furthermore, the riots were led by alienated young South Asian men born and brought up in the UK with a good command of English and, in many cases, a strong British-Asian identity. Neither forced marriage nor the riots could be resolved by more immigration controls, but by tackling poverty, deprivation, racism and sexual oppression. However, instead of resolving these underlying problems, it appeared the state was now using the demand for women's rights in minority communities to impose immigration controls and justify a racist agenda.

These recent developments follow initiatives taken in Scandinavia. Denmark, for instance, has introduced an age limit of 24 years for overseas spouses. There is little proof that the policy prevents forced marriage. Instead, it has reduced migration into the country, thus undermining civil liberties and the rights of migrant communities. It has also created a backlash in the country because it affects white indigenous households who marry overseas. In the UK, too, there is little evidence that changes to the immigration rules have benefited abused women. Instead, despite some improvements in immigration policy in cases of domestic violence, the extension of the probationary period in fact works mainly to entrap women in violent relationships for much longer periods and prevents many from leaving home for fear of deportation (Jooshi, 2003). In addition, increasing the age limit for overseas spouses has, in the experience of some agencies, and as predicted by many women's rights groups, led to a prolonging of the time young women or girls are left abroad prior to or after marriage. This measure also does little to help the many women and girls subjected to a forced marriage inside the UK.[14]

In addition, many women seeking asylum or protection in the UK are returned to abusive situations abroad, resulting in gender persecution such as domestic violence, forced marriage and, at the extreme, 'honour killings'. In one of SBS's cases, an Indian-origin woman died after consuming poison when her husband had failed to regularise her immigration status. Her friends state that she was terrified of returning to India as a twice-divorced woman (this was her second marriage) because of shame and dishonour, and the resulting social ostracism and harassment she would experience. Ironically, despite the 1999 landmark House of Lords cases of *Shah* and *Islam*[15] recognising gender persecution as a ground for asylum, and at a time when the state has condemned practices such as forced marriage and 'honour killings', the state still remains reluctant to give protection to many women escaping these abuses from abroad by granting them full refugee status.[16]

Negotiating the space between race and gender

Black and minority women's groups, such as SBS, have often been criticised by sections of the anti-racist left for 'washing our dirty linen in public' and undermining the anti-racist struggle. The racist backlash, to some extent, is evident from the use of immigration controls to tackle forced marriage (and, it should be added, race protest and uprisings). However, at the same time, the backlash from the conservative and religious elements in the community ensured that mediation was accepted by the Home Office Working Group as an option in the fight against forced marriage. This is the dangerous and shifting ground on which black and minority women have to raise issues of gender violence, negotiating the space or the intersection between race and gender. Despite these drawbacks, however, black and minority women have made some gains. Forced marriage, for instance, has been acknowledged as an abuse of human rights and some progress has been made in introducing new guidance for service agencies, particularly in the Foreign and Commonwealth Office and Consular services, the police (FCO et al., 2002), social services (FCO et al., 2004).[17] The practice of mediation and reconciliation has been strongly discouraged by these and other initiatives, and the concessions introduced for victims subject to domestic violence and immigration control represent another major victory for women's rights advocates.[18]

However, the struggle is a difficult one, requiring a more united black and minority women's movement, with strong support from white feminists and anti-racists alike. SBS has attempted to build bridges within and outside the black and minority women's movement. In 2002, it established a loose network of black and minority women and women's groups to give a collective voice to their demands to end gender violence against black and minority women. It has also worked with white women's groups, such as Justice for Women and Women's Aid, to build alliances on common issues such as domestic violence.[19] SBS has also worked with anti-racist and anti-communal groups to fight racism, and religious and communal hatred, and focused on the problems experienced by poor and low-income groups of women subject to domestic violence, such as fighting for women with immigration problems to have access to public funds in order to prevent destitution and to enable them to break out of economic dependency on a violent partner. This approach is based on the belief that a progressive movement needs to be built which tackles all oppressions, including those based on race, gender and class, at the same time. One struggle should not be waged at the expense of another, and our common goal must be to fight for the rights of all rather than the rights of a few.

As a result, SBS has attempted to shift the debate on black and minority women and gender violence into the mainstream debates and interventions on gender violence and human rights. The idea of universal rights counters those of cultural relativists and racists alike. However, as human rights organisations are just beginning to think about gender as a human rights issue, they still have a long way to go in relation to black and minority women's rights, especially in Western countries. Nevertheless, some of the battles at the United Nations have been about the tensions between universal human rights and specific cultural rights, and feminists are increasingly looking towards international human rights instruments to assert women's rights. At the national level, despite the Human Rights Act 1998, which incorporated the European Convention on Human Rights 1958 into UK law, the state still pays too little attention to upholding women's human rights, particularly those of black and minority women.

From honour killings to domestic violence?

Having witnessed the forced marriage debate shift into one on 'honour killings', SBS now faces the immediate question of how to shift both these issues into the mainstream debate on domestic violence.

The government has recently been preoccupied with the Domestic Violence, Crime and Victims Bill (now the Domestic Violence, Crime and Victims Act), which introduces legislative changes to the way domestic violence is addressed in the criminal and civil justice systems. The bill was introduced following publication of the government consultation document on domestic violence, *Safety and Justice* (Home Office, 2003) – historically, the first significant consultation exercise on government strategy on domestic violence. However, this document was widely criticised for failing to address a number of issues affecting black and minority women, including by its narrow definition of domestic violence as concerning only intimate partners. The government failed to acknowledge domestic violence perpetrated by other family members, or culturally specific forms of harm such as forced marriage and 'honour crimes'. As a result of these criticisms, the government is now developing a separate domestic violence strategy on black and minority women and re-examining the definition.[20]

The question remains whether a separate strategy is the best way forward. The danger of separation, of course, has been the problem of differential treatment for black and minority women. There is also a debate within the feminist black and minority women's movement on how to make our demands so that the state gives the required attention to the specific needs of black and minority women as well as mainstreaming their needs by incorporating them into wider policies on violence against women without being singled out for differential or racist treatment.

This debate came into sharp focus in relation to the issue of 'honour killings' following the death of Heshu Yones in 2002. SBS allied with Middle Eastern Women's groups composed of Kurdish, Iraqi and Iranian women to fight her case and to raise the underlying political and social issues it highlighted.[21] A clear division on strategy emerged. The Middle Eastern groups wanted to separate 'honour killings' from domestic violence on the grounds that domestic violence is trivialised by the wider community and by the state and not regarded as a serious problem. However, SBS, and other predominantly South Asian groups,[22] argued that the issue had to be integrated within the framework of domestic violence (and within wider issues of violence against women and human rights) to prevent a racist reaction from the state, as witnessed, to an extent, in the case of forced marriage. Also, SBS wanted to build on the work of women's groups, which has been about ensuring that domestic violence is treated seriously and that the state should be held accountable for failing to do so.

Rukshana Naz's case, we had argued, represented three issues: forced marriage, an 'honour killing' and domestic violence. All these elements similarly existed in the case of Heshu Yones. Her father was concerned about the fact that she had a boyfriend, and wanted to control her sexual behaviour in order to improve her marriage prospects. He had also subjected her to domestic violence. Prior to her death, Heshu had planned to leave home. In her farewell note she wrote to her father, saying:

> Me and you will probably never understand each other, but I'm sorry I wasn't what you wanted, but there's some things you can't change. Hey, for an older man you have a good strong punch and kick. I hope you enjoyed testing your strength on me, it was fun being on the receiving end. Well done.[23]

The difference in perspective stemmed, in our view, from the fact that the Middle Eastern groups had been less active in the UK than in struggles in their own homelands, where 'honour killings' are treated with varying degrees of indulgence by statute and individual practice, and where the debate on domestic violence is not so well developed. On the other hand, the South Asian groups have been more active in the UK and understood the wider context of racism and the debates on domestic violence (Gupta, 2003b). In the end, although differences of emphasis remain, the two groups agreed to tackle both 'honour killings' and domestic violence. For Heshu's memorial in October 2003, we used the slogan: 'There is no "honour" in domestic violence, only shame!'

Bridging the space

In Sweden, where the debate on 'honour crimes' has raged for longer than in the UK, particularly following the death of Fadime Sahindal (a 26-year-old Kurdish woman who was killed by her father in 2002), some in government have developed a policy of linking the issue with the notion of patriarchy in order to mainstream the issue. However, at a conference organised by the Swedish government in 2003,[24] the debate still centred on whether or not the issue should be separated from violence against women and the human rights dialogue.

This dilemma has implications for social policy and practice in a context where there is a general failure to place gender violence against black and minority women within a wider framework of human rights, violence against women or even domestic violence. The result can be exoticisation of the issue and racism in dealing with victims and minority communities. The Metropolitan Police, as result of the critique by SBS and others, have responded by saying 'murder is murder', but nevertheless virtually every recent death of an Asian or Middle Eastern women is labelled as an 'honour killing' first, and a domestic homicide second. The Metropolitan Police estimate that there are around twelve honour killings per year in the UK, based on their own analysis and definitions, and are now reviewing 117 cases[25] (Bennetto and Judd, 2004; R. Cowan, 2004; BBC News Online, 22 June 2004) with the objective of improving risk assessment. The police also argue that not all 'honour killings' are linked to domestic violence or the control of women, and point to cases of men killed in so called 'honour killings' (without showing how these do not relate to the control of women). Although there are differences of opinion within the Metropolitan Police, Commander Baker has argued that honour killings are more about culture than gender – thus removing the issue from the framework of violence against women and placing it in the debate on race.[26] This approach constructs particular racial groups as 'high risk' and therefore in need of special measures and control. The scale of the Metropolitan Police Service review is, for instance, unprecedented when compared to their investigation of racial murders. This has already produced its own problems, with some accusing the police of racism. For instance, in the recent case of Shafilea Ahmed, a 17-year-old Pakistani/British woman from Cheshire, found murdered in Cumbria, her parents were arrested on suspicion of her kidnapping, but were later released without charge. There had been a history of self-harm when Shafilea was taken on a trip to Pakistan, where she was (reportedly) to marry. A family friend, speaking to the *Eastern Eye* newspaper (9 July 2004), defended Shafilea's parents and said:

A lot of people believe they are innocent ... if the family had been white, I am sure the police would not have jumped to conclusions like this. They assumed it was an honour killing, but this is just a stereotype. The police went too far.

For black and minority women's groups and survivors, the solution is simple: the state must take responsibility by providing more resources and ensuring better responses from service agencies to tackle the problem of domestic violence, forced marriage and all other forms of violence against women, regardless of their cultural or racial background. 'Honour crimes' are not so much a form of abuse, but a specific motive or excuse for the abuse. While these justifications have to be challenged, our priority is to ensure that oppressive religious and cultural values do not become extra constraining factors for any woman when escaping abuse. The Metropolitan Police have issued a memorandum to their forces informing them how to deal with the issue of 'honour killings'. While this may help to create greater awareness of pressures on black and minority women, unless the police understand and deal with all the extra obstacles these women experience, including the impact of racism, their response will be inadequate or even racist if based on stereotypical views of the community.

The police, however, are not alone in shifting the ground. The media too have played a role, and some reports, particularly those on forced marriage, have supported more immigration controls (e.g. *Newsnight*, 12 July 1999) and 'Westernisation' to resolve the 'culture clash' experienced by minority women in order to free them from oppressive norms and values in their community. In 2003, the Channel 4 documentary series *Dispatches* broadcast 'Killing for Honour', and missed the crucial aspect of gender violence,[27] examining instead the problem of killers entering the UK to commit murder and of such killers and other UK-based killers escaping justice by leaving the country for the Indian subcontinent. The documentary pointed to the lack of an extradition treaty between the UK and countries of the Indian subcontinent. However, the wider question that concerns us is how the government will react to this problem – by introducing extradition treaties or more immigration controls?

Ironically, the government's current position of advocating draconian policies on immigration and integration has forced us to defend multiculturalism, particularly as we find liberal commentators such as David Goodhart (2004) and Trevor Philips (*The Times*, 3 April 2004)[28] coming out in support of Blunkett's approach. Multiculturalism at its best aims to promote racial tolerance, and at its worst fails to address power inequalities such as sexual oppression within communities or the structural basis for racism. Blunkett's brand of integration smacks more of assimilation and the denial of minority rights altogether, at times justified in the name of protecting minority women's rights. For SBS, however, to use Mike O'Brien's language, 'mature multiculturalism' should be about taking forward the human rights agenda and bridging the space between race and gender, demanding black and minority women's rights without trampling on the rights of black and minority communities.

Notes

Hannana Siddiqui writes from the experiences of Southall Black Sisters (SBS), where she is a Joint Co-ordinator. SBS has been active on the issues of domestic violence, forced marriage and so-called 'honour crimes' against black, mainly South Asian, women in the UK since 1979. See further Gupta, 2003c.

1. Whilst the terms 'honour killings' and 'honour crimes' are problematic, SBS have used them to engage in current UK debates. Subsequent to writing there has been a palpable shift in language towards the terms 'honour-based' and 'honour-related' violence.

2. Research has shown that Asian women are two to three times more likely to commit suicide than women in the general population. The experience of SBS and Asian women's groups suggests that abusive and oppressive practices in the family are the cause.

3. For example, the Athens News Agency on 25 March 1998 reported the life sentence of Greek songwriter Akis Panou, who admitted to killing his daughter's married boyfriend, claiming it was a crime of 'honour' committed in the heat of the moment.

4. *R. v. Shabir Hussain* [1998], Newcastle Crown Court, unreported; Court of Appeal decision allowing retrial: *R. v. Shabir Hussain* [1998] Crim LR 820.

5. *R. v. Zoora Ghulman Shah*, 1998, Court of Appeal, unreported.

6. *R. v. Ahluwalia* [1992], 4 All ER 889.

7. Sahjda's cousins Tafarak Hussain and Rafaqat Hussain were found guilty of her murder – Rafaqat as the principal killer and Tafarak Hussain as an accomplice; both were sentenced to life imprisonment (BBC News Online, 20 October 2003).

8. The exception to this is a UK-sponsored joint resolution (with Turkey) on honour killings to the UN General Assembly, tabled in October 2004, an initiative led by the Foreign and Commonwealth Office.

9. Although the Metropolitan Police have undertaken this work recently, the West Yorkshire police have raised these issues in their local area, in the media and other forums for much longer.

10. For a summary of the meeting, see www.soas.ac.uk/honourcrimes 'Events'.

11. The change in Home Secretary from David Blunkett to Charles Clarke in December 2004 does not appear to have signalled a change in the government's approach to forced marriage, with continued use of immigration-based solutions; see further www.homeoffice.gov.uk/conrace/race/forcedmarriage.

12. For example, 'It is ludicrous that girls of 16 should be brought here from Pakistan as wives, not knowing where they are going and not knowing what their futures will be. A great deal is expected of them, and they often do not live up to those

expectations. It is also ludicrous that girls as young as 15 and 16 are being taken off to Pakistan for marriage in order to facilitate entry clearance. An age limit of 21 would give those girls at least a fighting chance' (*Hansard*, 19 February 2003, Column 277WH, para. 5–6).

13. Subsequent to the powerful men's lobby from such groups as Fathers For Justice, propagating the 'myth' of non-contact with children following separation, there is increasing pressure for all women, including those experiencing domestic violence, to seek mediation-based solutions in family law cases. This state response submits to men's demands and attempts to reduce legal aid costs.

14. The work of black and minority women's groups highlights the high number of cases of women/girls being forced into marriage in the UK. Also, see *Observer*, 22 February 2004, for feature on under-age 'community' marriages in the UK.

15. *Islam (AP) v. Secretary of State for the Home Department; R. v. Immigration Appeal Tribunal Ex Parte Shah (AP)* [1999], 2 WLR 1015, [1999] 2 All ER 545.

16. The Home Office has produced gender guidelines to be applied when making decisions on asylum applications. However, many of our cases involving applications for asylum on the grounds of gender-based persecution are refused or are granted – often upon appeal against refusal – discretionary or, more rarely, humanitarian leave to remain without obtaining full refugee status.

17. Following the report of the Home Office Working Group on Forced Marriage in 2000, the FCO led on forced marriage, resulting in improved FCO handling of overseas cases involving British nationals. However, there is much to be done on the UK domestic front, and whilst guidance has been issued to key public sector agencies, there are concerns around implementation and enforcement. In December 2004 the FCO and Home Office launched a joint Forced Marriage Unit (FMU), which is due to consult on the criminalisation of forced marriage during 2005. This issue has sparked divergent opinions among women's groups. For some, it will provide another weapon against forced marriage; others fear that it may deter victims from coming forward, increase the number of women being taken and held abroad, and may lead to greater police harassment of minority communities.

18. The Immigration Rules state that spouses who enter or remain in the UK on the basis of marriage to a British citizen or with settlement rights, subject to a two-year probationary period, may remain in the UK on a permanent basis if their marriage/relationship breaks down due to domestic violence. This policy was introduced as a concession in 1999 and incorporated into the Immigration Rules in 2002.

19. However, the recent 'popularity' of black and minority women's issues has also attracted the attention of some white women or white-led organisations, which have proven to be less than sympathetic allies, often holding paternalistic attitudes and engaging in a crusade to 'save' black and minority women – resulting, in some cases, in more immigration controls! Politically, this undermines black and minority womens' rights activists from leading their own struggles and making their own demands.

20. In 2004 the Home Office definition of domestic violence was extended to include abuse by family members, which, it notes, ensures that issues such as forced marriage and 'honour crimes' are properly reflected (Home Office, 2005).

21. The Middle Eastern groups included the Kurdistan Refugee Women's Organisation

and the Middle East Centre for Women's Studies (SBS held a joint seminar on honour crimes with these two groups and a memorial for Heshu Yones with a wider coalition, including Kurdish Women Action Against Honour Killing and Iranian and Kurdish Women's Rights Project).

22. Such South Asian groups included the Newham Asian Women's Project and Imkaan. In addition, the Project on Strategies to Address 'Crimes of Honour', coordinated jointly by Interights and the Centre for Islamic and Middle Eastern Law, based in the School of African and Oriental Studies, has also been active on forced marriage and 'honour crimes' in the UK and supportive of the SBS position. In recent years there have also been a wide range of organisations in the sector that have endorsed the need for greater work on 'honour crimes', including 'honour killings' and forced marriage. In particular, over thirty black, minority and other women's and community groups supported SBS's national report on forced marriage, examining the UK context one year after the Home Office report 'A Choice by Right' (SBS, 2001: 10). Some of these and more than fifteen other groups have also endorsed international reports which highlight 'honour crimes' in the UK, including the 2003 CEDAW Shadow Report published by Womankind (Sen et. al., 2003). Several of these groups, and others, have been involved in highlighting service provision issues, particularly housing, through their work with South Asian women experiencing domestic violence. See, for example, the work of Shamshad Hussain and the Manningham Housing Association (Bradford). Details of further organisations within the sector that have engaged in or contributed to UK-based work on 'honour crimes' can be found in the UK section of the CIMEL/INTERIGHTS Directory of Initiatives (www.soas. ac.uk/honourcrimes).

23. This extract from Heshu's letter was cited in many media reports; see, for example, BBC News Online, 30 September 2003.

24. Expert Meeting on Violence in the Name of Honour, Ministry of Justice, Stockholm, 4–5 November 2003; conference document available at www.regeringen. se/content/1/c6/02/38/79/5ae5baa4.pdf.

25. This figure has recently been extended to include suicides and missing persons as well as homicides. The Crown Prosecution Service (CPS) engagement with 'honour crimes' also increased during 2004 and included a well-publicised conference. A senior CPS source informed SBS that internal research showed a lack of convictions in homicide cases involving minority women, supporting our long-held view that these women are often failed by the criminal justice system.

26. In 2005 another section of the Metropolitan Police established a Forced Marriage and Honour Based Violence Working Group (Home Office funded) with governmental and non-governmental membership, led by police members who support SBS demands to mainstream the issue into gender-based violence work and are working to shift 'honour' terminology within forces.

27. For more information, see www.channel4.com/life/microsites/K/killing_honour/. This documentary covered only one case of a man who was killed in what they described as an 'honour killing'. However, even this case involved a slight against a woman's reputation as the man was killed by the woman's family when he refused to agree to the marriage of his son to a cousin in Pakistan. All the other cases centred on women subjected to 'honour killings' or crimes.

28. Chair of the Commission for Race Equality; see further www.cre.gov.uk/.

14

Of consent and contradiction:
forced marriages in Bangladesh

DINA M. SIDDIQI

This chapter considers forced marriage in law and practice in contemporary Bangladesh.[1] It examines constitutional and legal provisions as well as the limitations of such provisions in relation to the individual's right to marry. In addition, the chapter interrogates the cultural meanings of consent and coercion, and attempts to unravel the multiple interests and circumstances surrounding forced marriage.

The analysis proceeds on the premiss that the definition of forced marriage is neither fixed nor transparent, and may indeed be an inadequate descriptor for the multiple incidents glossed under the term. Among other things, the study indicates that when 'force' is exerted, the desired outcome may not be marriage. Frequently, the objective may be the forcible *separation* of a socially 'undesirable' or unapproved match. In many instances, what appears to be at stake is control over potential marital alliances as well as the regulation of sexuality, rather than the simple prevention of marriages of 'choice'.

The chapter highlights difficulties in locating a clear-cut and unambiguous definition of force. Cultural understandings of the significance of marriage complicate matters considerably. Marriage constitutes a primary rite of passage into social adulthood for men and women, and the desire to marry is, arguably, universal and rarely contested. Familial pressures to marry tend to be expressed in idioms of love, duty and filial obligation. Consequently, the lines between cultural compulsion, social realities and individual desires can be blurred. Since prevalent codes of honour and shame do not allow − or consider it shameful and immodest − for an unmarried woman to express individual desire, determining where consent ends and coercion begins can be an especially tricky task.

This chapter is based on a study carried out by Ain-o-Salish Kendra (ASK; the Law and Mediation Centre), a national human rights organisation based in Dhaka, Bangladesh. The study, conducted in 2002, was commissioned to analyse the complex legal and social practices that constitute forced marriage in Bangladesh.[2] The ASK study drew on a wide range of sources and methodologies, including case law analysis of the treatment of consent and coercion in relation to marriage, largely by the superior courts, over the past thirty-five years; scrutiny of police station (*thana*) records to gauge the understandings, recognition and responses of police personnel and their perceptions of forced marriage; and documented a number of case studies of women subjected to, or threatened with, forced marriages, and subsequently placed in the state's 'protective' custody. Interviews were also conducted with key actors, including activists from community-based and human rights organisations, lawyers, and British consular officials, whose opinions critically inform current understandings of consent, legal entitlement and marriage practices.

The chapter is divided into three sections. The first section sets out the laws that inform marriage practices in Bangladesh, including constitutional and statutory provisions, as well as the personal laws dealing with marriage as applicable to the Muslim majority and the Christian and Hindu communities, and a brief overview of the situation of Bangladesh's ethnic/indigenous minorities that do not fall under the purview of the country's personal laws.[3] Since a significant proportion of documented cases of forced marriages involve British-Bangladeshi dual citizens, concerns related to marriage in diaspora communities are touched upon. The second section offers a theoretical analysis of forced marriages, drawing on newspaper reports, interviews with key actors, and available scholarship. The final section examines legal cases to assess possible legal remedies to the problem, including consideration of the right to refuse to be forced into a marriage, the options to exit a forced marriage and the right to marry the individual of one's choice.

Legal provisions informing marriage practices in Bangladesh

The legal system inherited by Bangladesh at Independence in 1971 was shot through with contradictions (Pereira, 2002: 135–43). The parameters of the present legal system were established under British colonial rule, which decreed, among other things, a distinction between 'personal or religious' law – largely governing rights within the family and, in particular, marriage – and a 'secular' sphere of law governing the remainder of social life. This distinction was fairly arbitrary at times but had lasting implications for the rights of women and religious minorities in the post-colonial era.

Constitutional provisions

The Constitution of Bangladesh 1972 establishes a clear distinction between the public and religious/personal domains of law. This split affects the rights of all citizens, since many of the so-called personal or religious laws are inconsistent with the provisions of equality guaranteed in the Constitution. More specifically, when it comes to issues of marriage, divorce, adoption and inheritance, each individual is governed by the rules of the religious community to which he or she was born. Inevitably, the question arises of what happens when personal laws conflict with the rights of individual citizens.

Article 10 of the Constitution (one of the 'Fundamental Principles of State Policy') declares that 'steps shall be taken to ensure participation of women in all spheres of national life.' As a corollary, Article 14 provides that it 'shall be a fundamental responsibility of the state to emancipate ... the backward sections of the people from all form of exploitation'. The Fundamental Rights provisions of the Constitution are particularly relevant. Article 27 states that 'all citizens are equal before the law and are entitled to equal protection of law'; Article 28(1) declares that 'the State shall not discriminate against any citizen on grounds only of religion, race, caste, sex or place of birth'. Significantly, Articles 7(2), 26(1) and 26(2) declare void any law that is inconsistent with the Constitution. These provisions, read alongside the Preamble and Fundamental Principles of State Policy, provide a framework to ensure the equal treatment of men and women by the state in all spheres of life.

Unfortunately, the Constitution qualifies the rights of equality conferred upon female citizens. Article 28(2) states that 'women shall have equal rights with men *in all spheres of the State and of public life*' (emphasis added). Thus the state's commitment to the equal treatment of women is considered by some commentators to be circumscribed, since it may be interpreted as not automatically including the private or personal sphere. However, since Article 28(2) does not explicitly override the preceding Articles guaranteeing the equal treatment of all citizens, it could be argued that the Constitution recognises the just claim of women to be treated equally with men in all spheres of life, both personal and public, and thereby retains its initial pledge to ensure fundamental human rights and the equal protection of the law for all its citizens irrespective of religion, sex, and so forth.

In framing arguments for legislative protection against instances where a woman's consent to marriage is completely disregarded, and a unilateral

laws since the nineteenth century; thus contemporary Christian laws in Bangladesh were formulated for a specific purpose in a different era and are both inadequate and antiquated (Agnes, 1999: 144).

Two Acts passed by the British (Parashar, 1998) in the late nineteenth century continue to regulate marriage and divorce among Christians in Bangladesh today: the Indian Divorce Act 1869 and the Christian Marriage Act 1872, with the Code of Canon Law governing Catholics. Marriage in Christianity is a sacrament and not easily voided; in principle all Catholics adhere to the doctrine of sacramental indissolubility. Christians in Bangladesh may as a matter of conscience follow the laws and rules of the religious bodies to which they belong, although they are free to come before the civil courts for adjudication in matrimonial and other matters (Pereira, 2002: 47). State legislation has lent marriage the attributes of a civil contract between two parties. The consequent tension between civil and canon law frequently places Christians, especially practising Catholics, in a difficult and contradictory position.

The Christian Marriage Act provides for the solemnisation and regulation of Christian marriages. The express consent of both parties is necessary to validate a Christian marriage. However, both the Code of Canon Law and the Christian Marriage Act recognise child marriages contracted with the consent of the minor's guardian.[20] The 1872 Act recognises the father as the primary legal guardian of the child and excludes the mother's right to give or withhold consent in the marriage of her minor child, if the father or another legally appointed guardian is also present. However, the CMRA simultaneously applies in such cases, leaving a wide margin of ambiguity since no minimum age for marriage is stipulated in the civil law governing Christians.

The parameters of the Divorce Act 1869 derive from then contemporary British laws. Under section 10 of the 1869 Act, Christian men can obtain divorces on the grounds of adultery alone. In contrast, Christian women must demonstrate adultery coupled with cruelty, desertion, incest or bestiality. In Britain, subsequent enactments have liberalised divorce laws considerably, as is the case in India. However, Christian personal laws in Bangladesh remain frozen in time. Therefore, divorce or judicial separation remains an especially fraught issue for most Bangladeshi Christians, especially Catholics.[21]

Marriage practices in 'ethnic' communities

Referred to alternately as tribal, indigenous or ethnic, there are at least twenty-seven communities in Bangladesh that are linguistically and culturally distinct from the dominant Bengali-speaking population.[22] Needless to say, there are great differences in social organisation and marriage practices among these smaller communities,[23] making it inappropriate to present generalisations about marriage. Many of the communities are Buddhists and animists, an increasing number are Christians, and a few are Hindus. On the whole, especially among those that have not incorporated Hindu practices, these groups tend to have fairly flexible marriage rules. A requirement for the consent of both partners appears to be the norm in arranged marriages, and there has been a recent increase in the trend towards 'love marriages'. The largest group, the Chakmas, call such marriages *mon miloney bibaho* ('a marriage of the minds'). Dowry, child marriages and prohibition on widow remarriages are rare in such communities, although historically the payment of a bride price was common.

For the purposes of this chapter, two points should be noted. First, the 'tribes' in present-day Bangladesh were subject to a different legal regime from that applicable to the dominant religious groups living in British India. Most 'tribal' groups lived in 'protected' territories, intentionally maintained as distinct cultural environments. Their inclusion in the state of Bangladesh is a matter of historical contingency as much as anything else. Consequently, the marriage practices of these groups do not fall under the purview of the personal laws of the country.

Second, the lack of written records has had severe consequences on people's livelihoods and rights to landownership. Most groups possess no legal documentation to the land they live on and cultivate. This has helped locally dominant groups to usurp the property of ethnic minorities. Marginality in the development arena has also helped to reduce many to extreme poverty and landlessness. The resultant increased social vulnerability especially affects women, who are frequently forced to submit to the sexual advances of local powerful men. Abductions, sexual assault or forced marriages of indigenous women by Bengali settlers or army personnel, especially in militarised zones, are not uncommon in these circumstances, often justified by the misconceived Bengali stereotype that 'tribal' women are easy and lacking in virtue (ASK, 2000; Willem van Schendel and Dewan, 2001).

Theoretical analysis of forced marriage

Interpretive ambiguities

The situation we are considering is not simply of women being randomly forced into marriages against their will, although this does sometimes happen. This stereotypic and Western-biased image of arranged marriages is both crass and empirically incorrect. Instead, most marriages are negotiated within and between family groups in a variety of ways: sometimes decisions are contested, and sometimes successfully resisted; often they end in compromise. (Gardner, 1995: 186)

That a woman or girl may indicate her consent to a marriage through silence rather than speech signals a specific construction of femininity, in which modesty, passivity and 'shame' (*lojja-shorom* in the Bangladeshi context) outweigh action and speech. Needless to say, there are multiple interpretations of a woman's silence, including modesty and good conduct, active assent, resistance or resignation.[24]

Santi Rozario and others have noted that shame (or *lojja*) in the Bangladeshi context carries connotations beyond the word's English equivalent (Rozario, 2001: 85); it is seen as a positive quality, invoked to prevent transgression of social norms. As a virtue, it is inculcated in girls from an early age, embodied in gestures, behaviour, movement and clothing. In the appropriate context, a lowered gaze, modest gait and silence can be construed as markers of positive shame. It is gravely immodest for young women to discuss their marriage prospects openly. This, however, does not mean women's voices are necessarily excluded in marriage negotiations, as mothers, sisters and other female relatives are critical avenues for communicating likes and dislikes. However, it remains true that cultural expectations compel women to resist voicing their opinions too explicitly in matters of marriage, thereby encouraging the interpretation of a woman's silence as assent.

Consent in most cases is a formality, especially in a cultural environment that valorises marriage as a necessity for everyone, men and women. Marriage rituals transform the status of individuals and authorise the passage into social adulthood (Rozario, 2001: 85), the completion of the self. Girls are socialised into embracing the role of mother and wife (lullabies and nursery rhymes celebrate the coming of the groom to take the girl away); a woman's social identity and status are incomplete without the stamp of marriage. Rahnuma Ahmed and Milu Shamsun Naher, in their work on marriage in Bangladesh, state:

> A girl is socialised into believing that 'only parents know what is best for her' and *lojja* (a sense of shame) as a value operates in such a way as to make it a very exceptional case when a girl does not agree to the marriage arranged by the parents or elders. (Ahmed and Naher, 1987: 94)

Without subscribing entirely to this passive construction of female subjectivity, it remains the case nonetheless that hegemonic cultural forces and practices, reinforced by ideologies of 'purity', 'honour' and 'chastity', make it difficult for individual women or girls to resist the 'inevitability' of marriage, since it constitutes an integral part of the social identity of both men and women. In such circumstances, both 'consent' and 'coercion' are notoriously slippery terms.

The desire to marry is taken for granted to such an extent that women are frequently not asked for their consent until they are 'at the altar', so to speak, if they are asked at all. The practice of allowing a third person, usually the legal guardian, to express consent on the bride's behalf makes it easy to sideline her wishes. As Elina Khan, a practising lawyer, remarked, verbal consent in these circumstances, even if it is expressed unambiguously, remains incomplete. In her opinion, complete consent requires the bride to be consulted on, and to agree to, the various stipulations in the marriage contract, including the amount of *mehr* and the conditions for a delegated divorce. In practice, the bride's opinion on such matters is rarely solicited, whereas the bridegroom's assent is actively sought. Therefore, even if the bride consents to the marriage at the time of the actual ceremony, her equality with the groom is only superficial; she is certainly not on an equal footing in terms of decision-making power.[25]

Similarly, Habibunessa, a family lawyer, noted that in her experience most people have little understanding of what marriage actually entails. In general, neither the groom nor bride, regardless of their express consent to the wedding, understand the emotional and social consequences of marriage. In Habibunessa's view, real consent signifies a willingness to enter into a relationship keeping in mind the legal rights, social obligations and emotional aspects of marriage.[26] She added that generally women's lives were subject to the dictates of male family members, and this domination extended to matters of consent in marriage. In her words, '[I]n marriage too, women's opinions and choice coincide with those of male family members. The status of the family supersedes all other considerations.'[27]

Other lawyers and activists agree that there is a huge gap between the law, which calls for the bride's express consent to be obtained, and social practices that either marginalise or completely ignore the bride's wishes. Many interviewees associated this practice more with rural Bangladesh, where the authority of the patriarch or head of household rules in all matters, including marriage.

The conceptual boundaries between arranged and forced marriages are frequently blurred. Forced marriage refers to events that involve the exercise or application of *some form of force* on the persons contracting the marriage. As such, the definition is vague, begging the question of how to draw the line between wholly arranged and wholly coerced marriages, and between different degrees of socially acceptable and unacceptable 'force'. Most marriages would seem to fall somewhere in between, to a greater or lesser degree.

With connotations of the violent suppression of individual volition and desire, forced marriage conjures up images of female subjugation, cultural backwardness, and a need for societal evolution. When used in a predominantly Muslim context, forced marriage recalls the stereotypes of patriarchal oppression that invariably accompany discussions of Muslim women's lives. It would be useful, however, to unravel some of the legal and cultural presumptions associated with arranged marriages to seek to clarify the concept of forced marriages. Critics of arranged marriages argue that it is *always better* (read more liberating) to be able choose one's partner. Such negative evaluations, *inter alia*, assume the existence of a culturally unmarked, completely autonomous individual citizen who is the repository of rights. In practice, in all societies the individual is socially embedded; s/he is a product of cultural practices, social relations and the larger political economy. This does not exclude her/him from being an individuated member of the community/society capable of exercising agency. [28]

Sexual asymmetry and female subordination – critically mediated by class and social privilege – mark gender relations in Bangladesh. As in other societies, the subordination of women rests on the ability of dominant social groups to regulate female sexuality, mobility, labour and social identity. In the circumstances, the use of 'force' in matters of marriage is undoubtedly a commonplace occurrence. Coercion can be social and cultural as well as physical and emotional, including emotional blackmail. The degree to which a particular individual is vulnerable to arguments drawing on loss of face and 'family honour' will depend on the extent to which that person is socially and economically embedded in her life-world. Moreover, prevalent codes of honour and shame do not allow – or consider it shameful and immodest – for an unmarried woman to express individual desire.

In short, it is difficult to define 'force' neatly in this context, a point poignantly underscored by one lawyer's interview. In recollecting her ambivalence and discomfort at the time of her own marriage, she reveals how difficult it is even for highly educated, professionally oriented women to express their individual desires in the face of overwhelming but indirect family pressure. Such pressures are usually expressed in the idiom of love, concern and discharging family obligations (in this case the older brother's duty to 'settle' his sister):

My brother settled the marriage, and I was 21 then. Though I was given an option to make my own decision, *I could not avoid the decision of the family*. Of course I liked my husband, but I still have a feeling that I didn't want it the way it took place. I didn't want it to take place right at that stage. I was doing my post-graduation work, and I wanted to marry after I had completed the course. But I couldn't establish my wishes. In the marriage ceremony, I remember, somebody sitting beside me expressed consent on my behalf.[29]

Evidently, speaking out or protesting can easily be interpreted as ingratitude or disloyalty in the best of circumstances. Cultural understandings of coercion and consent do not necessarily distinguish between force (as overt intimidation) and emotional and psychological pressure (which may be quite subtle, as above). The latter is not only acceptable but also expected.[30] Nevertheless, it is worth remembering that the centrality of marriage to social coherence and female identity confers considerable cultural legitimacy even to marriages women are explicitly coerced into.

The dangers of unscripted alliances

An initial review of the case studies collected for this chapter affirms the need to rethink the category of forced marriage itself. It appears that for heuristic reasons as much as anything else, a variety of circumstances have been classified under the aegis of forced marriage. This serves to obfuscate or gloss over significant differences in our understanding of the issue and in the shaping of laws and policy interventions. In light of these case studies it would be analytically inadequate to view such marriages *only* as a clash between tradition and modernity, between the rights of the liberated individual and a static patriarchal community.

To understand the prevalence of forced marriages, one must appreciate the multiple meanings and implications of marriage as a 'social fact' in Bangladeshi society. Among other things, marriage is a public act with significant social repercussions. Socially 'appropriate' matches can be used to reinforce kinship ties, enhance social networks and status, and affirm group boundaries. By the same token, marriages that transgress accepted social or community boundaries can lead to a loss of face or 'honour' and threaten family, lineage or community identity. In short, marriages involve more than two individuals coming together; any potential match is charged with the possibility of giving rise to social conflict.

In order to open up the category of forced marriage, it is productive to situate the coercive measures used to regulate marriage practices and alliances within a much broader framework. Force is frequently exerted to prevent individuals from marrying socially 'inappropriate' partners as much as to coerce women to marry socially approved partners. The forced exclusion of marriage partners, through cultural coercion as well as legal sanctions, occurs in all societies to a greater or lesser degree, serving to reinforce racial, ethnic, religious and class boundaries.

At the same time, most communities, even those with strict codes of sexual and moral conduct, are able to absorb a certain amount of transgressive behaviour, *as long as such acts are ostensibly in the private realm*. However, when questions of marriage arise, private acts breach the public domain (Chowdhry, 1998). Marriage is an essentially public and political act, and in many places in South Asia, including Bangladesh, one that structures alliances, hierarchies and social networks. Marriages can seal or undermine existing social relations of kinship and alliance and often set a public precedent for similar future arrangements. Consequently, marriage requires the validation not only of the state but also of the community concerned. Therefore, marriages that are potentially disruptive to kinship and political alliances, community, caste and class boundaries frequently provoke opposition. The situation becomes especially volatile when existing power relations are disrupted through larger economic and political processes.[31]

Forced marriages in the media

Rights violations in Bangladesh are tracked primarily through media reports. Invariably, forced marriage items concern high-profile cases of women with dual citizenship; 'ordinary' forced marriage is presumably not newsworthy.

The ten reports collected by ASK for this chapter, published in various local and national newspapers, all originated in the greater Sylhet region of Bangladesh, which has a long history of migration to the United Kingdom. Whilst these diasporic ties lend some specific characteristics to the region, it is not clear if the problem is more accentuated in the Sylheti-Bangladeshi community or if this reflects a bias in reporting. It appears that forced marriage in greater Sylhet draws particular media attention whenever the girl is British–Bangladeshi (sometime termed *londoni koinya*). Such events initiate considerable social discussion and gossip. In contrast, local women/girls being forced into marriage with local men tends to be seen as a 'normal' or everyday event, not newsworthy unless coupled with other extraordinary developments.[32]

The press reports gloss over the complexities of individual cases, blurring the lines between unambiguously forced marriages, arranged marriages entailing disputes, and love marriages contracted without parental sanction. Notably, in several cases a pattern is discernible, whereby young British-Bangladeshi women upon returning to Sylhet became involved with local young men whom their guardians refused to accept, arranging their marriages elsewhere. Subsequently, the couples eloped and the families sought to recover the women by lodging cases of abduction under section 366 BPC against the men.

The issue in these cases is not marriage per se but the forcible separation of a socially undesirable or unapproved partnership. That abduction must be invoked to initiate legal measures, under section 366 BPC, against marriages made with the woman's consent – but without parental approval – explains the slippage between abduction and elopement. In practice, a primary effect of section 366 BPC is to reinforce familial control over female mobility and sexuality.

Surprisingly, the press clippings reveal that cultural incompatibilities (e.g. a modern woman/girl from the UK and a village man/boy from Bangladesh) are not always at issue. Rather, in these elopement cases questions of parental control and the autonomy of children are at stake; critical factors, particularly in the case of girls, are the desire to regulate sexuality and protect 'family honour' and 'face'.

Forced marriage as reflected in police station records

Interviews with police personnel in the Sylhet region revealed that whilst officers are aware of forced marriages in their locality,[33] because it is not recognised in statutory law they are powerless to intervene unless other criminal offences may be involved or the individual seeks police assistance. The officer-in-charge of one police station felt that his hands were tied where the guardians of a girl forced her into a marriage, either without consulting her or ignoring her wishes irrespective of whether it is public knowledge that she agreed to the marriage under compulsion. In cases where the girl is a dual citizen, the British High Commission can request the police to ascertain whether she was forced into marriage, thereby violating legal rights she possesses as a British citizen.[34] This particular officer-in-charge reported that, in practice, police intervention tends to stop with the girl's passage to the premises of the British High Commission.

Neither of the above types of cases are formally recorded at the sample police stations, suggesting that police records do not accurately gauge the extent or pervasiveness of the problem. The Newham Bengali Community Trust, an NGO that has assisted British-Bangladeshis subjected to forced marriage (then working in liaison with the British High Commission in Dhaka), claims to know of approximately 300 incidents, of which only 74 cases were recorded by the police.

Cases most likely to be recorded by the police involve allegations of abduction, invariably lodged by parents or others seeking custody of women/girls that have eloped. The two cases investigated, one in 2002 (in conjunction with the NBCT), turned out to be 'false'. One of these cases involved the alleged abduction of British citizen Shomia Begum, aged approximately

14 or 15 years, by a local youth, Salauddin. According to the complaint, lodged by Shomia's family, she had been abducted, after intimidation, to coerce her into marrying Salauddin, a proposal her family had previously rejected. However, a police investigation revealed that the narrative of intimidation, abduction and coercion had been fabricated. Shomia had fallen in love with Salauddin and, in the face of her family's opposition to the match, had eloped with him.

Clearly, unsanctioned or unscripted relationships not only disrupt various social expectations and financial/political considerations but also indicate the kind of female independence and unregulated sexuality that defy dominant constructions of femininity and 'family honour'. The abduction narrative therefore has a double function, allowing the woman's family to save face and, if they are successful, to prevent the unapproved match.

What happens once a case is lodged and the couple are 'recovered' depends to a great extent on the age of the girl. A sub-inspector remarked:

> Firstly, there are a huge number of cases in which the girl had an understanding or relationship with a boy of her choice, of whom the parents or guardians disapproved. When they eloped, the parents or guardians filed a case under section 366 of the Penal Code – or any other special law – alleging that the boy had kidnapped the girl with the purpose of extorting consent to marriage or of marrying her forcefully. Invariably these allegations are found to be false and the girl found to be consenting. So, if the girl is major, the investigation ends in a final report; but if she is of minor age, a charge-sheet is drawn up against the accused and the girl is either kept in protective custody, or returned to her parents' or guardian's custody.

Activist perspectives

Those lawyers and human rights activists interviewed generally agreed that forced marriage was a social rather than legal problem. Accordingly, interviewees perceived a direct relationship between forced marriage and women's education, economic independence and empowerment, thus requiring strategies of response based on raising women's consciousness. The general consensus was that illiteracy, ignorance of laws, poverty, and a certain kind of 'rural mentality' resulted in forced marriages.

However, such characterisations tend to mask the complexities of social change. Increasing prosperity and links with the outside world may actually lead to greater pressure on young women to abide by the decision of their elders.[35] A notable exception to the interviewee consensus, human rights lawyer Elina Khan, turned conventional wisdom on its head, categorically stating that forced marriages were more prevalent in urban, affluent and educated families of high social standing. Echoing the general analysis of this chapter, she noted that in cases where a young woman becomes involved with a socially unsuitable partner, her guardians simply resort to force to marry her to a partner of their choice. Furthermore, affluent and educated parents, in their quest for 'good' matches, frequently ignored their children's wishes by *imposing* arranged marriages. Khan recalled a wedding she recently attended, where a 13-year-old girl, living in Australia, was married to an 18-year-old boy, based in the USA. From Khan's perspective, the girl was incapable of appreciating the consequences of marriage due to her young age; therefore the marriage involved some degree of force. Khan's definition of force indicates the difficulties of drawing analytical boundaries between forced and arranged marriages when minors are involved.[36]

Ibrahim Ali, a lawyer and chairperson of a Sylheti human rights organisation, recognised the often problematic nature of statutory provisions which can be employed to harass rather than help women. His comments capture the problems with the legal system, as described in the next section.[37]

Analysis of legal remedies

The act of compelling someone to contract a marriage is not in itself an offence under the Penal Code, as noted previously. It can be assumed that numerous marriages take place without the consent of the bride, even if very few reach the courts, whether in civil or in criminal jurisdiction. Consequently, few reported decisions on forced marriages are available.

Civil jurisdiction

If a marriage takes place without the consent of one party, or if any force is exercised, an individual may seek redress from the Family Courts[38] to have the marriage dissolved or declared void. A review of cases before the Family Courts indicates that most cases turn on one of two issues: (1) determining the bride's consent to the marriage contract; and (2) the husband's unilateral right to forcible restitution of conjugal relations.

In general the cases support the concept of Muslim marriages as social contracts, with validity requiring a proposal of marriage by one party accompanied by an explicit acceptance by the other party (i.e. consent to the marriage). Most judges take the validity of a marriage to hinge on clear proof of the bride's consent; cohabitation does not establish validity.[39]

Since Independence, judges have, in particular cases, invoked constitutional equality provisions, providing women more flexibility in personal law cases.

In 1982 the case of *Nelly Zaman* vs. *Giasuddin Khan*[40] marked an important milestone in the laws of conjugal restitution. Invoking Articles 28(2) (guaranteeing equal rights to men and women in all spheres of public and state life) and 27 (guaranteeing equality before and the equal protection of the law for all citizens) of the Constitution, the presiding judge held that the restitution of conjugal rights against the wife's wishes violated accepted constitutional guarantees (Mansoor, 1999: 172–3). Some studies show that the *Nelly Zaman* case is being used as a precedent for similar cases in Dhaka. [41]

Using an alternative approach, in 1991 another Family Court judge observed that under Islamic law the wife had the right to refuse conjugal rights if she was treated with cruelty or if dower was not paid promptly.[42] One should not overstate the case here, however. Although in certain instances the courts have cited constitutional provisions in relation to family law issues, these have rarely been upheld by the highest court.

Criminal jurisdiction

As the preceding analysis suggests, criminal cases relating to forced marriage usually centre on violations of section 366 BPC. Most cases turn on questions of guardianship and minority, the need for custodial protection, and, significantly, questions of consent in relation to the age of the 'victim'. The legal device of the habeas corpus petition (under either Article 102 (2)(b)(i) of the Constitution or section 491 Code of Criminal Procedure (1898)) – is frequently used to determine the custody of alleged victims of forced marriage.

The response of the courts to victims of forced marriage is mixed at best. The courts rarely refer to which of the woman's rights have been violated, specifically the rights to equality and equal protection of the law, personal liberty, freedom of movement and expression and to choice of marriage. However, in a number of significant exceptions, *all relating to cases where a woman is found to be over 18*, the courts have acknowledged the right to choice of marriage, giving due weight to a woman's statement that she has married of her own volition, and have directed that she be set at liberty (into her own custody).[43] In these cases, the courts believed that the age of the woman could be determined with certainty.

However, in instances where doubts arise regarding age, questions of custody and consent can become quite complicated. Individual judges possess tremendous discretionary power. Scientifically and legally acceptable determination of age remains unresolved, and, in the absence of reliable documentation, judges frequently appoint a medical board to determine age. This process appears to be highly subjective, lending itself to contradictory outcomes – as exemplified in *Ananda Mohan Bannerjee* vs. *State* (35 DLR (1983) 315) where Priti Banerjee claimed she was 20 while her father insisted she was only 14; such ambiguity and lack of resolution leaves considerable scope for manipulation on all sides. Further, the medical practices in question are not only intrusive and sexualised; they do not necessarily offer definitive answers. It is not clear how the examination of 'private parts', as in this case, can lead to a determination of age; nor are ossification tests definitive.

Babul Miah vs. *State* (30 DLR (1978) 187) highlights other complexities. In the first place, constructions of the female subject as dependent and in need of protection informed the magistrate court's decision to send Parisha into judicial custody; the girl's will was completely elided while negotiations proceeded around determining her age. Such ideologies of protection work in multiple regressive ways. In the eyes of the law, Parisha's mother rendered herself incapable of taking care of her own daughter because she has remarried – despite the validity of divorce and remarriage in Muslim law, she has transgressed the unspoken rules of patriarchy and forfeited her right to her daughter.

Several of the cases collected by ASK involve conversion of women from minority communities to the majority religion, thus involving the transgression of religious and community boundaries. A rigorous count is beyond the scope of this chapter, but such cases seem to appear proportionally more than one might expect. It could be that interreligious marriages are more likely to result in court action given the symbolism associated with women's bodies and sexualities as markers of community identity, and the perceived threat of such marriages to minority community identities.

There are also cases where the courts have completely discounted the girl's will. In these cases not only is evidence of age disregarded, but judges draw on cultural constructions of women as minors and victims, so vulnerable to manipulation by others that they are not capable of assessing their own interests, thereby justifying being held in 'protective' custody against their will. In both the Illy Begum[44] and Ranjana Rani[45] cases, the courts were concerned primarily with the notion of 'minority' and the need to be placed 'in custody', whether with parents or neutral third parties, including, in the worst case, jail authorities.[46] In some cases, the court appears to go to great lengths to establish minority, as for example in Ranjana's case, where even though a medical board and her school certificate determined her to be well over 18, the court chose to discount the evidence proffered in favour of her parents' statement to the contrary. It did so on the presumption that parental authority and statements always override the claims and desires of their children. Had Ranjana been deemed a major, the court would likely have still justified detaining her in custody, ostensibly to 'ascertain her free will' in a neutral environment. The presumption here is that the woman, even if she is legally an adult, is not necessarily capable of independent decisions. Rather, she is likely to be easily influenced, and enticed by false promises. The agency of the woman, her subjectivity, is never quite fully formed; it is always vulnerable and open to manipulation. The woman as a subject of the law is incomplete.

The judgment in the Illy Begum case lays bare how power relations within the family, specifically between parents and children, are disregarded in favour of a patriarchal and 'harmonious' family structure. The Appellate Division, in overturning the High Court ruling to release Illy Begum, made abundantly clear that the word of the parent overrode that of the child, especially in matters such as age and marriage partner. The case turned on the young woman's age, for which, in the court's opinion, no proof is as good as the statement of the parents.

Having established minority, the judge then invoked the instability of such young minds ('the attitude of girls who are mostly guided by infatuation and the flush of youthful romanticism without caring for tomorrow') to justify his decision. Remarkably, he systematically misinterpreted the evidence before him to make his case. He read Illy Begum's letter to her mother, which expresses a desire to see her (but not changing her position that she married out of free will), as instructive of how a young girl can change her mind 'once she is freed from the trance which sometimes casts a spell on her'. Once the female subject is infantilised, even if she is of age, or if she is reduced to a minor, she seems to be completely at the mercy of the individual judgments of the courts.

Clearly, questions of minority, guardianship and protective custody are of paramount significance as such cases unfold in court. In cases involving 'straightforward' coercion, a critical factor affecting the final outcome is the young woman's knowledge of her rights, and, if she is a British citizen, her ability to contact the police or consular officials. In a 'typical" case registered in 2001 in Maulvibazar, Sadar, an 18- or 19-year-old British-Bangladeshi woman, was brought to the village of Raghunandanpur to be married to a Bangladeshi man. She refused and sought assistance from the consular section of the British High Commission, which in turn requested the local police to help her leave the country. Presumably the young woman possessed some degree of maturity, given her age, and was able to muster the resources to seek help from the British High Commission. Younger girls may find it more difficult to resist family pressures and may not be aware of the possibility or source of institutional support, especially when placed in an entirely unfamiliar environment, compounded by the confiscation of travel/identity documents.

By the same token, it is striking that in most of these reported cases the agency of women, even when they are not minors, is systematically dismissed or discounted by law enforcement personnel as well as by judges and magistrates. Women's speech seems to carry little legitimacy or weight for state functionaries. An implicit patriarchal complicity among judges, police personnel and other officials can be discerned in the action and rhetoric around 'forced marriages'. Clearly, dominant constructions of femininity, underpinned by ideologies of protection and victimhood, shape the practice and interpretation of statutory law.

Furthermore, existing statutory provisions inadequately protect the right either to marry the person of one's choice or to avoid a forced marriage. A woman who turns to the courts for help in avoiding a forced marriage cannot expect any immediate legal action, even if she finds herself facing a sympathetic and progressive judge. Moreover, women seeking court action frequently find themselves incarcerated and harassed in the name of safe custody.

Conclusion: patriarchal complicities and possible remedies

The term 'forced marriage' needs to be interrogated rather than taken for granted. Force in marriage practices can be asserted not only to compel two individuals to contract a marriage but also to prevent them from forming marital unions. Potential marital alliances involve multiple interests and stakes, subject to change from all directions, including from the forces of migration, globalisation and structural changes in the economy. Much more research is required to locate the specific reasons that lead a given community to control marital alliances in Bangladesh.

Families exert different degrees of emotional and psychological pressure on individuals to submit to 'appropriate' matches. The invocation of affective ties and familial obligations can be interpreted as coercive – from an external perspective – even if it is not perceived as such by the actors involved. These factors complicate any attempt to locate a neat definition of 'force'. Contests over parental control and individual autonomy, the regulation of female sexuality, and ideologies of 'honour' and 'shame' must be located within the social landscape that gives rise to forced marriages.

Ultimately, however, the right to marry a person of one's own choice is at the crux of the matter. Even when individuals turn to the courts for protection, they are stymied rather than helped. Antiquated and inappropriate laws, premised on highly patriarchal concepts, provide a major obstacle. Although the Constitution and the statutory laws of Bangladesh have generally helped vulnerable citizens to demand and exercise certain rights, the protection of women's rights by the legal system must be viewed with a degree of scepticism. Clearly, existing statutory provisions are often problematic and can be used to harass women rather than to help them. Moreover, individual judges (and related professionals such as doctors and police personnel) have considerable discretionary power which can influence the resolution of forced marriage cases.

Culturally dominant presumptions of appropriate sexuality, of respectability and of gendered personhood permeate the legal meanings and judicial interpretations of the law. Frequently, the notions of appropriate femininity and the place of the patriarchal family that judges draw on have the effect of reinforcing existing hegemonies of gender, class, religion and sexuality. Srimati Basu has argued in the context of Indian courts,

> The law is administered by judges whose very notions of logic, fairness and justice are embedded within their discursive universes, and hence their interpretations reinforce cultural biases in the very act of attempting to transcend them through the law. (Basu, 1999: 250)

Thus the male judge who places the 'abducted' young woman in family or protective custody – disregarding all evidence that she is able to lead an autonomous existence – may very well identify with the parents of the woman. Or he (or she, for that matter) may be convinced of the need to uphold social mores in the face of what s/he perceives to be disintegrating moral values. Broadening this argument requires close inspection of the language and judicial tropes employed in a larger body of judgments.

The situation calls for both legal and social strategies.[47] Existing statutory provisions should be restructured to help rather than harass those who seek state protection and who wish to assert their right to marry, or not. A possible measure would be to allow for the application of legal injunctions against being forced into marriage. Whatever the form, legal protection should be promptly available and easily accessible. An urgent step would be the withdrawal of using 'safe' custody without the woman's consent, accompanied by appropriate measures to prevent the abuse of protective custody practices.[48]

In addition, forcing an individual into a marriage contract should be criminalised. However, given the embeddedness of marriage in social relations, and the difficulties of pinpointing 'force' in this cultural context, criminalisation is necessary but not a panacea. It is essential to ensure women's access to the legal rights they already possess. Among other things, this calls for the sensitising and training of judges, medical personnel, police officers and magistrates on questions of consent, coercion and the individual's right to marry.

Changing entrenched patriarchal viewpoints will, unfortunately, take a long time. In the meantime, women and girls themselves must be armed with knowledge of their legal rights.

Notes

I would like to thank Sara Hossain, Faustina Pereira, Tanim Hossain Shawon and Lynn Welchman for their detailed comments on an earlier draft, and Amirul Huq Tuhin for research assistance. Thanks also to Sanchita Hosali for her help throughout the editing process.

1. This chapter does not consider one of the more publicised instances of forced marriages in Bangladesh, through *fatwas* given out at informal village courts or *shalish*. The *shalish* may proclaim *fatwas* forcing marriage on women or by refusing to recognise the validity of specific marriages. One example is the *hilla*, or 'intervening' marriage, forced on rural women through *shalish* rulings, typically following disputes over the validity of Islamic verbal divorces (Amnesty International, 2004b).

2. Tanim Hussain Shawon, S.M. Mushfiqur Rahman and Urmee Rahman carried out the research and wrote up the initial findings for the study.

3. That is, each of these ethnic groups has its own personal laws, which are enforceable in their respective jurisdictions.

4. Thanks to Sara Hossain for pointing out the need to consider that the law itself is hetero-normative, assuming that a woman's life partner is by definition male.

5. As pointed out by Sara Hossain.

6. With some limitations, anyone can be detained under section 54 of the Code of Criminal Procedure (CrPC); safe custody also extends to minors.

7. See Sonbol, 1996, which draws heavily on court records from the Ottoman Empire to demonstrate both the diversity of personal law practices and the considerable access women of various classes had to the Ottoman courts for redress.

8. In the prominent nineteenth-century case of *Abdul Kadir* vs. *Salima* ([1886] 8 All. 149), Syed Mahmood J. argued that marriage among 'Mahomedans' was not a sacrament but purely a civil contract. Thirty years later, in *Asha Bibi* vs. *Kadir* [1909 33 Mad. 22] the legal opinion was that the contract of marriage is not like other contracts, allowed by law to be for a limited period only. Similarly, in another eminent case – *Anisa Begum* vs. *Muhammad Istefa* ([1933] 55 All. 743) – marriage was held to be not only a civil contract but a religious sacrament. Several decades later, in *Khurshid Bibi* vs. *Mohd. Amin* (PLD 1967, S.C. 97), S.A. Rahman J. contended that marriage among Muslims was not a sacrament but in the nature of a civil contract, even though the nature of the contract was special, with spiritual and moral overtones.

9. The registration of a marriage contract provides women with critical legal protection as orally contracted marriages do not provide much of a basis for subsequent legal action, making it difficult to prove rights to inheritance, dower and maintenance. Proving the existence of a Muslim marriage in the absence of official documents is not impossible, however, if one can produce the original witnesses.

10. Section 5 Muslim Family Law Ordinance 1961, Muslim Marriages and Divorces Act 1974.

11. *Dr. A.L.M. Abdullah* vs. *Rokeya Khatoon* (1969) 21 DLR 213 declared that 'Unless it is established by clear, direct and specific evidence that the woman gave her consent to the marriage, anything just short of that will not prove marriage.'

12. Although the average age at marriage in Bangladesh has generally increased in recent years, the mean age at marriage for adolescents is well below the legal minimum. The national average age at first marriage for females is 18 and for males 21. However, in rural areas, a significant number of girls are married between the ages of 14 and 16. The mean age at marriage during adolescence is 12.4 years for girls and 13.4 for boys. The incidence of marriage among girls is about eighteen times higher than that of boys during adolescence; see further www.unescobkk.org/ips/arh-web/demographics/demosub 1–1.cfm.

13. Under classical Muslim law, a minor girl contracted in marriage by her father or grandfather could not exercise the option of puberty. However, the Dissolution of Muslim Marriages Act of 1939 lifted this restriction, conferring the right upon the wife only, because the husband has the inherent right to divorce the wife at any time without assigning any reason. Notably, a man married during minority has the same right to dissolve the marriage, but in his case there is no statutory provision within which he must exercise his right.

14. Opinion of a Senior Assistant Judge, Family Court, speaking off the record.

15. Paradoxically, the 1856 Act actually circumscribed some of the rights of women from communities that already sanctioned widow remarriage (see further Sen, 1998).

16. In further contrast to India, Bangladeshi Hindu men continue to be able to enter into valid polygamous marriages.

17. Thanks to Afsan Choudhury for reminding me of this 'exceptional vulnerability'.

18. For instance, of the 926 cases involving marriage taken up by ASK between July 2003 and February 2004, only 17 involved Hindu women (Sharma, 2004: 8).

19. This section draws heavily on Pereira, 2002: 46–58.

20. Christian Marriage Act 1872, Section 19.

21. Pakistani Christians, subject to the same archaic laws, can now dissolve marriages or enter into new ones by converting from Catholicism or Protestantism to small evangelical sects like the Church of God. Unfortunately, the National Council of Churches, the foremost authoritative body among Pakistani Christians, does not recognise such marriages or divorces. Consequently, women who are abducted by their families find themselves without any legal recourse (*HIMAL,* 15/08/02: 23).

22. There is some dispute over the actual number and size of ethnic groups. Members of ethnic minorities claim that their numbers are systematically underestimated in the census in order to undermine their rights (Mohsin, 2000).

23. For a description of marriage practices among specific groups, see Rahman and Shawon, 2000.

24. Cultural ideologies of 'honour', 'shame' and 'modesty' are shared fairly evenly by Bengali speakers of different religious communities. The analysis in this section applies to women in all Bengali-speaking communities.

25. Interview with Advocate Elina Khan, Investigation Director, Bangladesh Society for the Enforcement of Human Rights.

26. Interview with Advocate U.M. Habibunessa, Naripokkho, a women's rights organisation.

27. In the course of another ASK study, interviews with women revealed that in most cases the woman's consent to marriage had been sought only at the ceremony, that too as a formality, often with someone else giving consent on the bride's behalf (Kamal, 2001: 55).

28. Agency is a complex, relational term; as such, 'free choice' is an extremely problematic concept. For any socially embedded individual, multiple relations of power structure her options and 'choices'. The ability to exercise choice becomes especially fraught when questions of economic and social deprivation are involved (Asad, 2000).

29. Name withheld to protect privacy; emphasis added.

30. In their study of Pakistani and Bangladeshi migrant community perceptions of forced marriage, Samad and Eade write: 'There is a degree of ambiguity over the understanding of coercion, particularly with regard to inter-religious marriages. Force is unacceptable but emotional and psychological pressure appears to be condoned' (2001: 110).

31. Prem Chowdhry's research on inter-caste marriages in North India provides an insightful illustration in this regard. As caste and community boundaries become increasingly tenuous, codes of 'honour' are more fiercely defended. This explains some of the extreme violence met by those who infringe caste and kinship norms in marriage (Chowdhry, 1998: 333).

32. I would like to thank Tanim Hossain Shawon for underscoring this point.

33. The two sample police stations are located in the greater Sylhet region. In order to protect the confidentiality of the interviewees and of those whose cases have been reviewed, place and names have been withheld or changed.

34. This is not to imply that Bangladeshi women and girls who are forced into marriages do not have their rights violated. The difference here is that the law in Bangladesh does not recognise forced marriage as a violation of individual rights.

35. As argued by Katy Gardner in the case she studied of the *londoni gram* in Sylhet (Gardner, 1995).

36. That such practices are socially acceptable and widespread is evident from the wedding's guest list, which apparently included high dignitaries from law-enforcement agencies as well human rights activists.

37. Interview with Advocate Ibrahim Ali, Chairperson, Assistance for Human Rights, Sylhet.

38. Family Courts Ordinance of 1985. The Family Courts hear matters pertaining to matrimony, including marriage, divorce, dower and maintenance, have jurisdiction over all religious communities (excluding the indigenous populations of the Chittagong Hill Tracts) and are presided over by an Assistant Judge.

39. *Iftikhar Nazir Ahmad Khan* vs. *Ghulam Kibria* (1968) 20 DLR (WP) 176; *Khodeja Begum and others* vs. *Md. Sadeq Sarkar* 50 DLR 181; *Khurshid Bibi* vs. *Baboo Muhammad Amin* (1967) 19 DLR (SC) 59; *Most. Sardar Banu* vs. *Saifullah Khan* 21 DLR (WP) 115.

40. (1982) 34 DLR 221.

41. Ibid., p. 172.

42. *Hosne Ara Begum* vs. *Rezaul Karim* 43 DLR (1991) 543; cited in Mansoor, 1999: 173.

43. See *Monindra Kumar Malakar* vs. *State* 42 DLR (1990) 349 and *Ananda Mohan Bannerjee* vs. *State* 35 DLR (1983) 315.

44. *Khairunnessa* vs. *Illy Begum* 48 DLR (AD) (1996) 67.

45. *Sukhendra Chandra Das* vs. *Secretary, Home Ministry* 42 DLR (1990) 79.

46. As of January 2000 women and children can no longer be sent to jail in the name of safe custody.

47. This section incorporates recommendations made by the lawyers and activists interviewed for the ASK study. The suggestions of Advocate Ibrahim Ali were especially valuable.

48. In July 2003, the Nari-o-Shishu Nirjaton Domon (Shongshodhon) Ain (Suppression of Violence against Women and Children (Amendment) Act) was passed, requiring the consent of a woman/girl to be taken into account by the court before passing an order placing her in 'safe' custody.

15

From fathers to husbands:
of love, death and marriage in North India

UMA CHAKRAVARTI

Possession and control of the woman by the man to whom she belongs has nurtured in law notions of adultery, seduction, and enticement. Fathers seeking to retrieve their daughters from the men the daughters choose to live with resort to charging the other man with kidnapping, abducting and inducing the daughters to compel them into marriage. The popularity of this provision has had the court remark that it is 'unfortunately a section which comes before the court possibly more often than any other particular section in the [penal] code, except those of riot and hurt.' (Ramanathan, 1999: 50)

Prologue: a late beginning

The theme of violence surrounding marriages or relationships not arranged by the parents of the partners, particularly of the woman/girl, has caused considerable concern in India over the last few years. The violence surrounding these self-arranged marriages, often called love marriages in South Asia, have come to be (mis-)termed 'honour crimes' (and in the case of homicide 'honour killings') in a wide range of locations – including in West Asia and South Asia, and in diaspora communities from these areas. Feminists writing about and resistance groups against such violence tend to reproduce the term, though placing it within scare quotes to distance themselves from its ideological baggage. I consider that this is not enough of a distance and that, as feminists, we must discard the term in search of another that does not mask the violence in the killings and abuses, but rather describes it more aptly, acknowledging feminist understandings of violence, which do not accept the ideology under which such violence is masked.[1] The fact that the term 'honour killing' has tended to come into popular parlance from international locations only serves to increase my discomfort because the violence becomes associated with the 'uniqueness' of Asian cultures, with irrational communities and aberrant and archaic patriarchal practices refusing to modernise. This chapter examines instead the structures of power that make such violence possible by drawing on the enormous and pioneering work conducted by AALI (Association for Advocacy and Legal Initiatives), a legal support group in Lucknow, North India, and from other women's groups such as All India Democratic Women's Association (AIDWA), Vanangana, and Women's Association for Mobilisation and Action (WAMA). I will also draw on my personal fact-finding experience as a member of a democratic rights group, and on a range of feminist scholarly writings that have begun to appear in the last few years in South Asia.[2]

The social and ideological context of violence of choice marriages: the notion of *izzat* in North India

A unique and crucial basis of stratification in large parts of the Indian subcontinent is the caste system, an elaborate hierarchy of birth-based groups. Historically these status groups were also related to control over land and other productive resources; thus where caste was the dominant form of stratification this was broadly congruent with class. The entire structure of caste and its reproduction, as a system, was contingent upon endogamy, carefully controlled marriages within certain bounded groups. Reproduction everywhere has historically been a social rather than an individual act, but it is also inextricably linked to the political economy of communities and the ways these communities organise and reproduce themselves *as identifiable communities*. The marriage system in India demonstrates this point very effectively.

Violation of the marriage codes is regarded as an attack upon *izzat* ('honour' or 'prestige'), a wide-ranging masculine concept underpinning patriarchal practices in India across all castes. Action to uphold *izzat* is always a male prerogative: women can only 'incite' action; since violence is sanctioned to uphold *izzat* the use of the term masks its real meaning for those who experience the violence. As the case studies below demonstrate, the concept of 'honour' in punishing 'defilers' is essentially a means of maintaining the material structures of 'social' power and social dominance.

'Honour' is one of the most valued ideals in the subcontinental patriarchies, whether Hindu, Sikh or Muslim – with most communities seeking to gain and maintain 'honour'. In general *izzat* is measured by the degree of respect shown by others. Irrespective of how much 'honour' is ascribed to their particular caste, individual families can gain or lose 'honour' through money and power. But since all families do not have money or power, other aspects are also critical. Actions that are appropriate, or in accordance with normative codes, maintain the 'purity' and 'honour' of the family, lineage or caste, whereas actions that are inappropriate defile the 'honour' and 'purity' of the caste, family and lineage. Women are the repositories of 'family honour' – of their own family as daughter, and of their husband's family as wife and mother; as noted in the common saying, often repeated by parents to girl-children and in-laws, 'The prestige of the family is in the hands of its daughter.' The implication for women is that their 'dishonourable' conduct can irreparably ruin their family. Thus by constantly evoking the twin notions of 'honour' and 'dishonour', families either condition women into appropriate, or shame their inappropriate, behaviour.

This somewhat benign notion of *izzat*, coupled with women's own interest (and therefore their complicity) in upholding such notions and the material and social power of their communities, maintains the normative codes of their families and communities. Even those women and men at the bottom of the social hierarchy, who therefore do not necessarily derive material benefit from their socially situated position, share the cultures of their castes and communities. They too have codes to maintain, and marrying an appropriate partner, negotiated by male kinsmen, is as much an aspect of their lives as it is for other women. Endogamous marriage is ubiquitous, practised by Hindus and non-Hindus, as many such communities also practise caste and status differentiation (Chen, 2000: 22–3).

Violence surrounding 'transgressive' relationships in North India often involves bodies within the informal legal system such as *panchayats* (village-level bodies, traditionally non-elected, with policing and punitive powers, which did not include the Dalits or women; since the 1960s there are also statutory *panchayats*, which are elected bodies and, after a series of amendments, now have reservations for Dalits and women; thus there are multiple bodies in the villages).[3] There is widespread sanction for the violence that follows across castes and religious communities.[4]

'Love' marriages present a clear threat to this intricate web of social, material and cultural factors requiring specific marriage structures. Once 'love', or 'choice', is conceded, reining in the choice to suitable partners from within an acceptable circle becomes difficult. (It is not necessary that the social and material factors that underpin the marriage system in India have to function in each case to explain the opposition to choice marriages – ultimately the cultural codes can function autonomously to debar choice to individuals who are violating the norm of parental- and community-sanctioned marriages.) Elopement thus provides an avenue to realise the 'love' or 'choice' marriage that families actually prevent or are perceived as preventing. However, elopements have also provided the space for development of the 'criminality of marriage' in India (Mody, 2002), as illustrated below. The 'criminality' of a 'love' marriage is significantly enhanced where it crosses religious communities, particularly in cases of Hindu women marrying Muslim men, where the taboo nature of the union forces elopement.

The idea of women as the sexual property of their communities is deeply internalised, mobilising not merely the family but also the community, frequently accompanied by violence. While there is a long history of rumours of abduction and coercion around such relationships going back to the 1920s and 1930s in Bengal, when the lines between Hindu and Muslim religious communities began to harden politically (Datta, 1999: ch. 4), right-wing Hindu mobilisation in recent years has led to both ideological and organisational moves to counter such relationships. These organisations first track the public notices of intending marriages (as required under s.10–15 Special Marriage Act 1954) and then inform the girl's/woman's parents their daughter is planning a secret marriage in 'court'. Because of these procedures young Hindu women have no other (practical) option but to convert and then marry under the Muslim law.[5] Violence both before runaway marriages and thereafter (if the couple succeed in marriage) is the norm, with the purported threat to the breakdown of law and order being used by the police and executive to retrieve the girl/woman.

A new and particularly gruesome process was witnessed during and after the Gujarat carnage in 2002; at the height of the violence Geeta, a Hindu woman who had a relationship with a Muslim man, was dragged out of her house, stripped and killed, and then left on the street as an example to all other women of the punishment to be inflicted on women who transgressed the boundaries of community (*Times of India*, 19 April 2002). Several months later a Hindu girl who married a Christian was forcibly separated from him by right-wing goons, and forced to abort her four-month pregnancy (*Asian Age*, 7 June 2003; *Indian Express*, 8 June 2003). Self-appointed guardians of 'morality'/policers of community boundaries are thus compounding an already violent scenario in relation to inter-community marriages.[6] From a situation where the father, the family, the community, and even the state could use different degrees of violence against women, Hindutva ideology, by emphasising women as the repositories of the 'honour' of the Hindu nation, has thus expanded as well as created afresh the legitimacy for violence against young couples marrying across boundaries.[7]

Narratives of violence

An elopement and four deaths

Two Jat (traditionally dominant landholding caste in Northern Indian states of Haryana and western Uttar Pradesh) sisters, Susheela and Lalita, went missing from their parental home late one evening, and rumours spread that they had been forcibly abducted. The following day public demonstrations were held outside offices of local government officials demanding the perpetrators be found; details of the case and the demonstration appeared in news reports, many relying on the account of Rohtas, a local villager. The next day the police rounded up twelve people – all Dalits (comprising castes formerly known as the 'untouchables') – for questioning. Two of those questioned were related to Rajpal, a Dalit whom Rohtas and others had discovered was allegedly implicated in the 'abduction'. Notwithstanding the interrogations, Dalits were being placed under considerable pressure and harassment from the police and Jats, including the threat of reprisal rapes of Dalit women by Jat men. Consequently, several Dalit men and women submitted a statement to the Superintendent of Police calling for the harassment to stop and for the guilty to be punished in accordance with the law. The statement, published in a local newspaper, was signed by Poonam, a young married Dalit woman, who was both a friend of Susheela and an acquaintance of Rajpal – she had therefore become a particularly vulnerable target. Following repeated interrogation, in isolation, including by the Deputy Superintendent of Police (alleged to be a relative of the father of the missing girls), interrogation of her husband and family, and unable to bear the humiliation of the Deputy Superintendent's imputations of an illicit relationship with Rajpal, Poonam committed suicide.

The day following the media coverage, the missing girls surfaced in another town and subsequently each made a statement to the magistrate. Susheela reported she had eloped and married Rajpal of her own free will. According to Rohtas, Lalita stated that her father beat her for defending Susheela's choice of intended husband, and due to the fear of further beatings she left with her sister and Rajpal. Both sisters refused to return to the parental home, seeking instead protective state custody. However, the magistrate sent them to relatives, who returned them to their parents. That night they both died of poisoning. While the family claimed it was 'suicide', women in the neighbourhood had heard them cry out for help in the night and many people believe that the girls were forcibly poisoned because Susheela refused to retract her statement to the magistrate, thus refusing to implicate her husband in the charge of forcibly abducting her.

However, characteristically, no one would go public about what they had heard. No investigation was conducted into the deaths as the police accepted the theory of the suicide. Rajpal's house was vandalised and remained vacant five months after the incident.

The *panchayat* was very active throughout the days following the disappearance of the girls. During its first meeting, Rohtas was charged with misconduct for going to the press. Whilst Rohtas did not accept the charge, he considered it expedient to apologise to defuse the tension in the village and hoped the matter would end there. However, Rohtas was summoned several times more, severely reprimanded, fined and beaten. In the final *panchayat*, three elderly Dalits were summoned and charged with complicity in the 'abduction' of the girls. The Jats charged the Dalits with eating the food given by them only to attack the Jats' honour (*hamari roti khate ho aur hamari izzat par dhava bolte ho*). Unable to bear the continuing harassment, and fearful of the future, one older Dalit committed suicide. The strained relations and tension in the village were still palpable four months later. Five young men had been arrested, three were released on bail, and two remained in jail. Rajpal was finally bailed in April 2003 and the case of abduction was eventually closed in December 2003 – a full year after the 'elopement' and the tragedy of four deaths.[8]

'If you step out of your place you will suffer the consequences'

Radha sought to escape the humiliation she suffered by being considered a burden by her brothers (their parents had died). Having contemplated suicide, Radha instead asked Deepak, a childhood acquaintance, to marry her. Her brothers would not allow the marriage because Deepak was of a lower caste (Bania) than Radha (Thakur). Thus when the couple married and fled to another town Radha's brothers filed charges of kidnapping against two of Deepak's brothers and two of his sisters, of whom all but one sister were arrested. The brothers also forcibly took over Deepak's land knowing he was unable to return.

Radha sought assistance from the State Women's Commission (SWC), and through them the National Human Rights Commission, at whose intervention Radha recorded her statement before a magistrate (six months after the marriage), asserting she was a major and had married Deepak of her own free will. However, Radha's brother submitted a protest petition six months later alleging she was of unsound mind and had falsified her statement due to fear of Deepak and his family (he further argued that the SWC had used force against Radha). Regrettably, Radha and Deepak stopped attending the kidnapping hearings against Deepak's family because a board of doctors declared Radha to be of sound mind, which, in addition to Radha's recorded statement, led them to believe the case had concluded. However, due to legal technicalities the case continued, and in the absence of Radha and Deepak non-bailable warrants were issued against those charged with the kidnapping. One of the brothers-in-law surrendered to the court and was subsequently granted bail. In the interim Deepak's sisters had married and, as their in-laws did not know of the criminal charges against them, elaborate manoeuvres were required to ensure their attendance at court.

Radha, extremely bitter about the harassment she has faced, has appeared on television programmes on violence related to choice in marriage. Her bitterness is compounded by the length of time the legal system took to address her situation; by the time of the final court hearing she had a 2-year-old child. Further, whilst Deepak's family were generally sympathetic, following the extreme harassment they all suffered – having to leave their home and move to the city, and appear before the court repeatedly – they held Radha responsible for their situation. Radha has been victimised twice for the 'crime' of choosing a partner from a caste lower than hers. To add to her humiliation, when the High Court finally heard her case under section 482 of the CrPC (allowing the court to make any order to prevent an abuse of power) the judge declared 'If one steps out of the limits [for women] this is bound to happen.'[9]

The 'madness' of love

Megha Mathur, alias Yasmeen (her name following conversion), married Mohammed Ikram Hussain against her parents' wishes by converting to Islam and executing a *nikahnama*. When Mohammed went to collect Megha/Yasmeen from a visit with her parents, she was prevented from leaving with him. He filed a habeas corpus petition as husband and next friend of Megha/Yasmeen, seeking her release from the illegal detention of her parents. The High Court required the parents to produce Megha/Yasmeen. The parents filed a counter-affidavit, denying the facts alleged by Mohammed and the jurisdiction of the Court, alleging *inter alia* that Megha/Yasmeen had been suffering a mental illness prior to the alleged marriage (and thus was not capable of allegedly converting or consenting to marriage), and she could not be produced as she had been sent to a hospital in another town for treatment. The Court stated that it was not a court of trial and would not examine the disputed facts in detail (evidence of age and the *nikahnama* were therefore not addressed); rather, it would only accept that Megha/Yasmeen was a major and a Hindu and Mohammed was a Muslim. The Court did not accept beyond doubt that she had 'voluntarily and legally' married Mohammed, nor that she had converted to Islam, and, given the disputed nature of these 'facts', the Court found the writ petition for habeas corpus untenable. Evidence submitted by Mohammed in support of his and Megha/Yasmeen's relationship, including love letters, was taken by the Court as proof of her unsound mind, particularly as several letters were allegedly written in blood. These convinced the judge that Megha/Yasmeen had 'become a victim for the last five years to the vagaries of adolescence, and had been emotionally disturbed, and that due to this state of mind it was but natural and physically consequential that she started having attacks of mental disorder'. The letters therefore did not create the conviction that 'Megha's marriage was a result of a long-standing free volition [*sic*] and sensible decision.' The custody of her parents was therefore the most appropriate for her. There was no need for Megha/Yasmeen to be produced before the Court so long as she was not 'mentally cured' and did not become a 'normal girl'.[10]

The end of a struggle: justice without compensation

Seema (aged 25, an MBA graduate) left her parental home, following a three-month confinement, to marry Shahid by converting to Islam. The couple felt unable to marry under the cross-religious marriage (i.e. without conversion) provisions of the Special Marriage Act 1954 because such intended marriages are required to be recorded on a public notice board. They feared that Seema's family, whose disapproval of the long-established relationship with Shahid was well known, would learn of their intentions and prevent the marriage. To pre-empt any harassment related to the marriage Seema immediately recorded a statement before the magistrate that she had married of her own will. However, the statement was considered invalid because it had not been made in relation to an objection to the marriage or an FIR (First Information Report – complaint to the police). Seema's family subsequently filed an FIR alleging kidnap and wrongful confinement, upon which Shahid and members of his family were arrested.

Seema sought to (re-)record her statement and stay the arrest of her husband and in-laws; however, she was unable to do so given her sister's husband's connections with local lawyers. Thus Seema moved the State High Court, which stayed the arrests. However, the local police, having no information of this, arrested Shahid's uncle and detained him for a month. Shahid's house was attacked and police seized household goods as part of their search for the 'kidnapped' Seema. The couple approached the NHRC, who asked for a police report but were unable to offer substantial relief. Further orders granted further stays of arrest. In the interim an order to take Seema's statement was finally given, but was subsequently rejected on the ground that such an application must come only from the police and not the person seeking to record the statement. Believing the local police and administration were biased, Seema finally recorded her statement in another city, with the assistance of AIDWA. Seema was then required to make another statement in her local court to close the kidnapping case against her husband. With the help of both AIDWA and AALI, Seema attempted to make the statement. However, the Additional Chief Judicial Magistrate sent her to the state shelter, arguing that Seema had been in the custody of the 'accused' and was therefore under duress and in no mental condition to make a statement. Since Seema did not want to be placed in judicial custody, she was literally dragged out of the courtroom by a woman constable and four armed policemen. Members of AALI were unable to prevent Seema's forcible removal, having already been subjected to abusive language by the police.

Subsequently, the District Judge granted AALI's application seeking Seema's release, upon which she was able to record her statement, which led to the dismissal of charges against her husband and in-laws. The FIR against Shahid and his family was finally closed one year after the marriage, but members of Shahid's family, including his uncle, were never compensated for their losses at the hands of the police or for the loss of their freedom during the course of the case (AALI case files).

The criminal justice system in action

Immediately after a young couple 'elopes', the criminalisation of their action and the contestation of the validity of the marriage begin. The research on which this chapter is based indicates the following pattern in this criminalisation process. First, the father of the woman alleges that she is a minor, and files charges against her husband of kidnapping/abduction, wrongful confinement, and often rape.[11] Members of the man's family may also be incorrectly implicated, including womenfolk. This serves to increase both the seriousness of the offence and the potential retaliatory power of the woman's family, and may be employed to compel the couple to surface or withdraw from the marriage. It is also a way of settling scores with what Indian legalese refers to as the 'opposite party' – that is, the man's family; retaliation for their loss of izzat by attacking the izzat of the offending family.[12] Subsequently, the police vigorously search for the 'missing girl', who is actually regarded as 'kidnapped', raiding every conceivable hiding place, often arresting members of the man's/boy's family. At this point the young couple may surface (individually or jointly) due to the pressure of an 'underground', often unsustainable, existence and the humiliation of loved ones. This may mean facing violence, or even death, as in Susheela's case study above, or the arrest of the man. Where the woman does surface or is 'found', she is often sent to a state-run 'protective' home, a supposedly neutral space where she is inaccessible to the two contending parties – that is, the father/parents and the husband. In practice, however, the natural caste-based allegiances of the authorities (see interview with the Narela Superintendent of Police below) and the illicit nature of unsanctioned 'love' marriages mean that parents usually gain access to, and thus have the opportunity to pressurise, the woman. The woman should then make a statement before a court recording her choice in the matter, technically stating whether she wishes to go with her partner or parents. Only if she has clear and incontrovertible proof of her status as a major[13] – acceptable by the judge – will the court 'allow' and uphold her exercise of choice. In cases of marriage across caste or religion, the criminal justice system usually requires a bone density (ossification) test to indicate the woman's age, a test which usually has a margin of error that can be a cause of further dispute between the contending parties.[14] Finally the judge's verdict will grant custody either to the parents – who are regarded as the 'natural' guardians and the woman/girl's real 'well wishers' – or on occasion to the husband.

This process to ascertain both the woman's/girl's capacity to consent and its actual acceptance in court is never straightforward or uncomplicated, as indicated by the above case studies. The reality is long-drawn-out proceedings, often lasting years – in Radha's, case she had a 2-year-old child by the final hearing. In some cases couples remain 'underground' for years, living a fugitive-like existence, facing enormous hardships, physical and mental stress, and the possibility of physical violence and the end of their attempt to create a viable relationship should they surface or be found. Thus, the state's capacity to criminalise choice restricts other fundamental rights of the runaway couple, including of movement and expression. Clearly the police and the lower levels of the judicial hierarchy play a significant role through their capacity to act as extensions of the father's authority over the 'errant' woman/girl, the grounds for seeking to 'retrieve' and return her to the 'custody' of the father.

The involvement of the administration and the police is predicated on the penal clauses of kidnapping, abduction and rape – especially if the 'abducted/kidnapped' woman/girl is (allegedly) a minor and therefore cannot consent to sexual relations with anyone but the man her father has chosen as her husband. There is, however, a technical legal variance here; while women cannot choose to marry before the age of 18 (because the notion of guardianship applies until this age), they can be legally married before that age under both Hindu and Muslim customary practice. Further, while organising an 'under age' marriage is punishable under the Child Marriage Restraint Act 1929, the marriage, regardless of whether contracted without the consent of the partners, is not void. In contrast, if the 'child' marries of his/her own choice and against the wishes of the parents, the lack of parental consent would render the marriage void.[15] The law itself thus permits the use of force in marriage. Under civil law, applicable to all, a woman must be 18 to be party to any contract.[16] Further, criminal law, also applicable to all, requires a woman to be 16 to 'consent' to sexual relations (but if she is married by parental choice her husband can have sexual access to her at 15). These anomalies between various laws are created by the first link in the chain of criminalising self-choice marriages: the penal clauses on kidnapping, abduction and rape. From the real need to have criminal clauses in place (to prevent trafficking and sexual abuse of women, including sale into prostitution and rape[17] – very real fears for the family, community and the state), the slide to every man being regarded as a predator and every woman being in danger is very easy, especially when the parents of the woman in question contest what they know to be an assertion of choice by the daughter. Since the strength of the ideology of handing over a daughter in marriage is pervasive in all sections of the community, including those who staff the administration, the criminalising of the marriage follows almost naturally, as the responses of the civil and criminal administration to the 'love' marriages clearly illustrate. While investigating the harassment following an inter-caste marriage between a Jat girl and Dalit boy in Narela, the Station House Officer/Superintendent of Police, a Jat himself,[18] made the following statement in an interview for this chapter:

> Many of the cases of reports of missing girls are not kidnappings at all although the FIRs are registered as such; they are cases of elopement, but we have to proceed with the investigations on the basis of the kidnapping charges. When I get a case like this I often know that they are elopements—from the photographs of the girls [sic] it becomes clear that they are involved in love affairs and would have gone on their own. Later when we investigate the case we find clues in the notebooks such as the drawings of hearts and arrows, and names of boys, or code words, and so on…. But we have to treat these cases as kidnappings because of social pressure. Also you must understand that the police are not above society; they live in and reflect its values, and they reflect its vibrations…. I cannot finish off Jat domination can I? I do not believe in the hierarchy of castes but I do consider that there should be separation between castes and that each should have their autonomy. Marriage is an important institution, it is an important part of Hindu society, and we must respect it in all its variations; taking pride in one's community is natural. I am conservative in matters of marriage and believe that the arranged marriage is best for our society. Let me say that I have given my daughter all freedom of choice, she can marry whomever she likes, but he should be Jat.

The interviewee's position that policemen were part of society and reflected its values was forcefully expressed by an Assistant Commissioner of Police in Lucknow, who said to women activists pressing for the recording of a girl's statement about her choice of partner:

> You are talking to me about rights! What shall I tell this poor father, who had complete control of his daughter for 17 years, 11 months and 29 days? What magic happened on the 30th day that he has to watch helplessly as she dishonours him? (AALI, 2004: 35)

Without such forthrightness, the Deputy Commissioner of Jhajjhar said that although 'love' marriages are a matter of individual choice and are legal, and while the Constitution grants freedom of choice as well as recognising inter-caste and inter-community marriages, the region did not share these values or regard them as acceptable; therefore there is both opposition and violence in response to these marriages. On matters of custom, the administration has to work with the community – which likes to govern itself – so as to defuse any threat to the breakdown of law and order. He had no difficulty in accepting the police theory of suicide in the case of Susheela and Lalita, above, supporting the theory with the probability that the girls could not cope with the social stigma they faced. The 'social stigma' was naturalised and regarded as sufficient reason for young girls – who had actually tried to escape the clutches of their parents – to kill themselves.

The Deputy Superintendent of Police of Jhajjhar, a distant kinsman of the girls, on the other hand, had no dilemmas, constitutional or otherwise. His personal investigations, he related with obvious enjoyment, presenting himself as a local version of Sherlock Holmes, had revealed a relationship between Susheela and Rajpal; he was therefore fully aware that the case was one of elopement and not kidnapping/abduction, but he proceeded with the abduction charges because that was the way for the father to retrieve the girls. Consequently, four people died and Rajpal spent a year in jail, without any subsequent official recognition of his suffering.

In sum, even the judges have been forced to recognise that in the fight between the '"two sides", the state [does] throw in its weight in on the side of the father'.[19]

The law in action: making sense of the judicial 'mind'

It is against the backdrop of fear of the 'taking' of women/girls that 'choice' marriages are dealt with by the police, and later by the judges who may hear the case. At the heart of choice marriages is the contest between two sets of men for the custody of a woman. It is not surprising, therefore, that questions of 'custody', and the authority of 'natural' guardians, are central issues for the judges to settle.[20] The judge's decision will determine whether the woman is 'returned' to the 'custody' of the father or can be allowed *legally* to move to the 'custody' of the husband in a self-choice marriage.

There are a number of striking features in this contest between these two sets of men. First, the 'party' that does not have custody of the woman often has to move the court through a habeas corpus writ to seek her production in court to ascertain her will. Data collected in Lucknow reveal that the largest number of habeas corpus writ petitions are about contests over women. Second, such habeas corpus petitions are between two civil society parties, sometimes between two communities,[21] or where one party believes that the woman in question is 'in danger to her life'[22] from the other because she is in what the Supreme Court recognises as 'private detention'.[23] By contrast, habeas corpus petitions for the production of men are usually against the police, or another arm of the state, which has breached a freedom and presents potential danger to the detained person. In *Mohd. Ikram Hussain* vs. *State of UP and Others*[24] the Supreme Court highlighted an important dimension to this contest over custody, namely that a habeas corpus petition for such a purpose is not available for a man charged with kidnapping. Rather, the only remedy available to such a person is to establish the 'factum' marriage and then seek retrieval through restitution of conjugal rights.

Third, phrases apprehending danger, which lace judicial discourse, sit uneasily with other oft-used phrases such as 'free will', 'sweet will', 'consent', all suggesting the women's agency. Technically therefore the court will set free a woman (from protective custody), or her partner from arrest, because she declares her choice in favour of her husband, against whom the charges of kidnapping then must fail. However, where this occurs there is the risk that the parents could still physically seize, confine and coerce her into stating that she was earlier acting under duress, or was a victim of fraud. The husband then may have to file for restitution of conjugal rights, while the parents will file for the annulment of the marriage. Thus there is a huge grey area in the notion of choice even when asserted in a court, with little possibility of a woman actually acting on her own, and being allowed to do so.

The actual arguments of the judges, lawyers, parents and husbands also indicate fuzziness around 'choice' marriages, and notions of 'consent', or 'soundness of mind', in exercising choice. Again there is no clear pattern discernible in the actions of the judges. There is a tendency to create a hierarchy of values in defining custody with some judgments referring to the most 'appropriate' custody, when deciding in favour of the father – especially where there are no technical reasons, such as the disputed age of the girl, to counter the father's (or brother's) natural right over her. There is also evidence of notions of 'soundness of mind', capacity to make a sensible decision, mental disease/disorder being pressed into judicial service when the choice of a woman is across religious boundaries, where the most appropriate custody is invariably held to be with the parents, the woman's 'natural'[25] or 'real' well-wishers, rather than a predatory man taking advantage of a helpless woman. A woman's choices are attributed to the vagaries of adolescence, a hormonal flush,[26] a kind of madness, or an irresponsible expression of dangerous desire as in Megha Mathur's case study above.

Another line of reasoning naturalised in judicial discourse is the idea that a woman who has been in the custody of her chosen partner is under coercion and not in a position to make an independent decision; therefore before determining the case she must first be put into the supposedly neutral protective custody of the state. Conversely a woman in the custody of her parents is not recognised as subject to any form of coercion or pressure: there is a natural bias in favour of the parents, who, as far as the judicial system is concerned, could never be acting against her interests.

The implicit undercurrents of judicial disapproval relate to a peculiar ambivalence about women and the expression of desire: judges often not only accept but even cast women as consenting partners in cases of rape, dismissing the charges (Dhagamwar, 1992; PUDR, 2003: 19). The courts also recognise that men can be falsely charged with abduction and rape to escape the ignominy of an 'illicit' (but consensual) relationship if the couple are suddenly discovered. Yet, when a woman 'elopes' the argument of consent is not accepted. It appears that choice – or desire – as expressed by a woman is somehow intrinsically illicit when it is against parental diktat and caste or community norms, and therefore needs to be disrupted. Thus in situations that could actually be licit sexual relations within marriage, women are not regarded as being able to be consenting partners; according to the courts these women must have been forced under threat to life, or some form of irrationality, to become consenting partners – or else they must simply be incapable of consenting through their status as minors, intrinsically incapable of discretion on account of their age. It is as if women have no capacity for rational judgement or discretion in any case.

Significantly the courts can also be inconsistent when confronted with a situation of a woman who claims to have married according to choice but is a minor. For example, in *Gian Devi* vs. *Superintendent, Nari Niketan and Others* (1976 SSC 234) the fact of the girl's status as a minor (she had married her husband of her own choice) created a hurdle in her being allowed to go with her husband, who sought her release from the wrongful confinement of her parents. Since she was unwilling to go with her parents, she was placed in state protective custody and sent to the Nari Niketan. When she attained majority the husband appealed on her behalf for her release. As the woman made it clear that she wished to go with her husband, the authorities were instructed to let her go forthwith as, in the words of the court, 'she could not be "detained" against her wishes'. In a similar case when the minor girl made a statement under section 164 of the CrPC of having married of her own will she was sent to the Nari Niketan. Later her age as a major was accepted and the husband was released from custody. However, the woman remained in the Nari Niketan and her husband had to file on her behalf for release from such 'illegal detention'.[27] In contrast, in another similar case a Muslim girl married a Muslim man before she was 18; the husband claimed that marriages among Muslims were legal after the puberty of the girl. The court did not accept this argument, struck down the validity of the marriage, and returned her to the custody of the father as her natural guardian. She was never produced in court to ascertain her opinion—'the sweet will' of the girl was not relevant since she was not yet in a position to make an informed choice.[28]

Notwithstanding the above discussion, there are a number of cases to demonstrate the way the law can actually work to uphold women's right to choice. Such judgments function as a benchmark for the liberal interpretation of constitutional law on equality and individual freedom, and also restrain the police and magisterial administration from performing arbitrary actions such as forcing women into 'protective custody'. One judgment has even recognised the possibility of danger to the woman's life where she is 'restored' to the custody of her family and community.[29]

In Gulshan Jahan's case[30] she had married Jamshed in the presence of witnesses, and claimed to be a major. However, her father filed an FIR stating that she was a minor (14) and had been kidnapped by Jamshed, on the basis of which Jamshed was arrested. The High Court had to consider Gulshan's disputed marriage and thereafter establish whether she was with Jamshed of her own 'sweet will'. Medical examination established she was over 18 at the time of the event,[31] and the Court found that the detention order was 'wholly invalid' and deserved to be quashed. Accordingly the Court held that since Gulshan Jahan stated she had married Jamshed of her own choice, and that the *guardianship of her father had ceased on the day she became a major*, and since both Gulshan and Jamshed were majors, the law did not 'prohibit them from loving each other'. They had a right to 'live with dignity and honour and make their life meaningful'. The Court also noted the couple's right to privacy, to protection of life and personal liberty under Article 21 of the Constitution.

According to the AALI report, the Supreme Court and the High Courts have played a central role in recognising women's right to autonomy and choice in matters of marriage, once there is indisputable proof that the woman is a major. As explicitly stated by the Court in *Jyoti alias Jannat and Another* vs. *State of UP and Others*:

> According to the Indian Majority Act 1875, a person who is 18 years of age is a major vide section 3 of the Act. The law deems that a major understands his/her welfare. Hence a major can go wherever he/she likes and live with anybody. India is a free, democratic, secular country. Hence if a person is a major, even parents cannot interfere with that individual.... Once a person becomes a major that person cannot be restrained from going anywhere or living with anybody. Individual liberty under Article 21 has the highest place in the Constitution.[32]

There are also instances where the Supreme Court has taken issue with police and administrative harassment of couples choosing to marry across caste/community lines. In the Arvinder Singh Bagga case, where many members of the husband's family were arrested, the wife held in police custody and threatened by the Superintendent of Police, the Court came down heavily on the police. It sought prosecution of the police officers involved, as well as payment of compensation, holding that torture was not just physical, but also mental and psychological, and was calculated to frighten and make a woman submit to the demands of the police. Such things, the judges held, should not happen in a country 'still governed by the rule of law'. In a second round of action the judges in this case awarded a compensation of Rs.10,000 each to the woman involved and to her husband's uncle and Rs.5,000 each to all the others who were 'illegally detained and humiliated for no fault of theirs'. The judges also ordered the state government to prosecute all the offending police officers involved in 'this sordid affair'.[33]

In 1999 an important issue came up before the Allahabad High Court, Uttar Pradesh: Rani Gupta moved the court, claiming her father was forcing her into a marriage to a boy she disliked. Of her own 'free will' she entered into a marriage with another person of her choice. The court accepted that she was a major – 'going by her appearance' – and Rani was given the opportunity of making a voluntary statement to the court on her choice. The court stayed the arrest of her husband, stating that the personal liberty of Rani Gupta should not be interfered with.[34]

In this case the couple had married within their caste and community, but in another case, also heard by the Allahabad High Court, six months later, there was the same outcome in a case involving a Hindu woman converting to Islam to marry a Muslim.[35] As pointed out earlier, a Hindu–Muslim marriage is among the most strongly opposed of relationships and the courts have found ways of dismantling them under various guises. In an extraordinary move the court in this case argued that since Renu had gone to the extent of converting for the sake of her love, placing her with the parents would create unforeseen complications for both the partners, who 'initially belonged to different communities'. The Court held that 'caste and community barriers in our country play their own role'. The Court also found:

> We may observe here that efforts should be [made] to preserve the marriage rather than to destroy the same. In the social background of our country, if Renu is married to someone else, and the husband comes to know of her previous affair with the petitioner at least the lives of Renu and her husband may be ruined. While emphasising the need to preserve the marriage, in a somewhat similar case … the Supreme Court had observed, that 'nothing should be allowed to happen to affect that position.' [This] is not a case of enticing away a minor girl from the lawful guardianship of her parents. From the circumstances [it] is clear, and we cannot shut our eyes to her statement, *that if she is sent back to her father she may be killed* [emphasis added].

The court dismissed further proceedings on the FIR on kidnapping as a sheer waste of public time and money, recognising the potential for harassment of the petitioner and his wife.

In a final case (following the classic pattern — a young woman makes a choice, which the parents deny; the stage is reached where she is put into state protective custody) the Allahabad High Court accepted the woman's status as a major, declaring that she could go 'wherever she wanted, and live with whomever she liked'. The court found:

> [Since] she is a major she has a right to go anywhere and live with anyone. In our opinion a man and a woman, even without getting married can live together, if they wish. This can be regarded immoral by society but it is not illegal. There is a difference between law and morality.[36]

Since the petitioner had stated that her life was in danger, the court also ordered the police to ensure her security.

Making a difference: the importance of support

The Hindustani saying *der aye, durust aye* — 'started late but good nevertheless' — aptly captures the contemporary moment in addressing denial of choices in marriage. The increasing attention in the press, although problematic, has helped to draw attention to these violations of constitutional and human rights, including the right of women to dignity within families and communities. Whereas previous civil society work has centred on handling each case individually, women's groups, civil and democratic rights groups, and even some political parties are now recognising the need to mobilise opinion against these gross forms of violence and exert pressure on the administration to take action to support the exercise of constitutional rights. In particular the campaign for choice in marriage needs to address and counter the sanction, support and participation in the killings by large sections of the communities to which the victims belong and in doing so to reject the perception that this violence is a peculiar phenomenon relating to the world of women without relevance to the public-political domain.[37] Unfortunately the role of the National Commission for Women has recently been limited to the actions of individual members,[38] rather than engaged in active and sustained Commission-based work. Civil rights groups such as the People's Union for Civil Liberties (PUCL) in Rajasthan and PUDR in Delhi have also supported young couples being hounded by the law and/or their families. The PUDR report *Courting Disaster* was a consequence of the organisation's attempt to support Dalit families being harassed by the administration in cases of self-choice marriages.

The legal work of AALI and its participation in a wider discussion at national and international levels has been mutually enriching. AALI's legal work on violations of choice marriages demonstrates that legal support groups/women's groups, or collaboration between the two, can make a real difference to endangered young women and help to secure their constitutional rights. AALI has successfully worked with other women's groups such as AIDWA, Vanángana and WAMA, all of which also work independently. AIDWA, due to its wide national membership, has been the only organisation able to take up the issue in states other than Uttar Pradesh, notably in Haryana, notorious for such violence and where there is no other organisation ready to tackle the political power of the dominant castes. AALI has also sought to work with the Muzzafarnagar administration in establishing an effective Adult Rights Cell to assist young people choosing to marry against family diktat.

In March 2003 AALI convened a National Consultation on 'Women's Right to Choose If, When and Whom to Marry', bringing together representatives of women's organisations, lawyers and academics from various Indian states, Indian government officials as well as members of international organisations. In July of 2003 Dalit and left groups convened a meeting in Delhi to focus on violations of rights of marginalised groups, including the constitutional right to choice in marriage. In December of that year AIDWA held a national convention centred on violations against women and men in inter-caste and inter-community marriages, which enabled people who had suffered attacks and violations to present their own accounts. These interventions by various groups have been an example of feminist politics in action.

Through these conventions and on the basis of casework experience, a number of relevant suggestions have been identified. First, couples 'on the run' could be legally permitted/entitled to record a sec.164 CrPC statement regarding choice in the presence of any magistrate anywhere in the country rather than being limited to the jurisdiction where the kidnapping or other criminal charges have been filed. The AIDWA convention has suggested that all suicides of women be investigated by conducting a post-mortem. The process of civil marriages under the Special Marriages Act also needs to be made simpler and quicker, given that the current system is rarely an option for couples marrying across religious boundaries.[39] The cruel irony of government cash rewards to inter-caste marriages in the face of the enormous violence that the administration and the legal system actually inflicts upon individuals choosing their own partners needs to be countered, with the administration establishing mechanisms that actually uphold constitutional guarantees. A team of women activists suggested to the Superintendent of Police in Muzzafarnagar in August 2004 that they should obtain a guarantee of safe custody of the girl before she is handed over to the parents in cases of the disputed age of the girl and/or her decision to make a choice marriage that is contested by her father/parents. This would make them responsible for the safety of the girl until the courts can adjudicate the disputed question of legal 'custody' or the autonomy of the woman.

By way of an interim conclusion

Where choice marriages are being obstructed and facing violence, the conflict essentially emanates from the contradiction between constitutionally guaranteed freedoms and certain penal clauses routinely used by families seeking to regain control of their 'errant' daughters. Thus we find that the defence of culture/community and notions of 'honour' are rarely a factor in the judgment.[40] Rather the biases of the court against the daughters seeking to assert their rights to choice and the corollary sympathy for the parent[41] have to be couched in terms of technicalities of age of discretion, capacity to make rational judgements and similar legal grounds. The moral and legal ambivalences of the court are therefore pegged on technicalities or deductive reasoning that favours the parents over the daughter's choices. On occasion the police may use the community argument to explain why they prevented a woman from going with her husband and held her in illegal detention.[42] What is significant is the lack of courage among the judiciary to follow openly the sentiment of a Pakistan Supreme Court judgment, which, although it upheld a woman's right in Islamic law to marry on the basis of choice, expressed strong disapproval of 'husband shopping' by women (Ahmad, 1988: 22).[43] What they have stated quite directly is the reverse, which is that in India consent would include the consent of parents and other relatives; they thereby give legal recognition to a widely shared norm in Indian society and curtail the notion of adult consent (Uberoi, 1996: 331).[44]

A serious concern is that the courts are the ultimate recourse for deciding the fate of the couple. Along the way the couple can be traced, brought back, separated, or, far too often, even physically eliminated. All this is possible not only because of the widespread sanction of violence in many communities but also because of the survival of institutional mechanisms within these communities for internally policing dissenters and nonconformists. There have been occasions where this 'informal legal system' has taken the extreme step of awarding the 'death penalty'. The existence of these parallel and unconstitutional 'legal' bodies is a direct threat to the possibilities of asserting choice in marriage and they therefore need to be kept under control by the administration. Currently, however, a particular strand of opinion in the social sciences has taken to valorising the 'community' and its traditions as well as community institutions as a counter to the intrinsically repressive modern state, without any recognition that there is a repressive, casteist and patriarchal dimension to communities too. It is important to recognise that in the context of choice marriages men and women who cross family and community boundaries are subject to the violations of their rights as citizens: for the upper-caste woman and the lower-caste man, in particular, *the right to live is conditional upon denying choice* and accepting the control of the dominant patriarchal, caste-based family on the one hand and caste power of the dominant castes (who have the power to punish both the upper-caste woman and the lower-caste man) on the other. The death penalty is regarded by the dominant as a valid form of the retrieval of their social power, passing under the name of *izzat*. As feminists we need to understand the relationship between structures and ideologies in order to work towards expanding the arena of women's fundamental rights.

Notes

This chapter is the outcome of an enormous amount of collaborative work with Tulika Srivastava, Saarika Kalia, Jasveen, Shahira and others from AALI (the Association for Advocacy and Legal Initiatives, Lucknow, India), who have lived and breathed 'choice' marriages ever since I have known them. It has been a very rewarding and enriching experience working with all of them. I would like formally to acknowledge the work with AALI and in particular their very detailed report on which this chapter is based: AALI, *Choosing a Life... 'Crimes of Honour' in India: the Right to If, When and Whom to Marry, a View from Uttar Pradesh and Rajasthan* (2004), available at www.soas.ac.uk/honourcrimes. I have also drawn much from discussions with the following friends: Prem Chowdhry, who pioneered scholarship in this field, Usha Ramanathan and Pratiksha Baxi, and from many others whose works I have cited. Special thanks also to Deepika Tandon, Harish Dhawan, Shahana and Prem Chowdhry from the PUDR team that produced *Courting Disaster: A Report on Inter-Caste Marriages, Society and State* (Delhi, 2003), who have also contributed to my understanding of violence around choice marriages, as well as to our many informants during the course of the PUDR investigations, particularly Rohtas, Jaikishan and others in Narela and Talav. Note that some names have been changed to protect the identitites of those included.

1. Potential terms could include 'crimes of denial of choice in marriage' or 'denials of choice in marriage killings', or other phrases which focus on the violence being a consequence of the *assertion* of choice.

2. See, for example, Chowdhry, 1998, 2004a, 2004b, and the works cited in the notes below.

3. A notorious incident occurred in Kandravali (Muzzafarnagar district, 100 km from Delhi). A young couple, distant relations belonging to the same Dalit caste and village, eloped and married. Six months later they returned and were summoned to the village *chaupal* (central meeting spot) by the villagers (including members of the girls' family). Upon arrival the couple were beheaded by an uncle of the girl. There was no regret among the villagers, who had collectively watched the killing, which was regarded as a punishment for the 'grave social violation'. *Pioneer*, 11 August 1993.

4. Ibid.

5. In a North Indian city the corporators and President of the BJP, along with the Bajrang Dal (the stormtroopers of the right-wing Hindutva formation), organised a four-hour street action, burning tyres and causing disruption to the traffic on a busy road in an affluent area of the city, demanding the retrieval of a Hindu girl (N), who had been allegedly kidnapped by a Muslim man (A). The violent action continued until N appeared before the magistrate's office to make a statement under sec.164 CrPC stating she had married A of her own choice (AALI case files).

6. In July 2001 Bharti, a Hindu woman who legally married a Muslim man in Ahmedabad after conversion (advised and supported by a lawyer), was hounded by a right-wing organisation seeking to retrieve and reconvert her, supported by the right-wing administration. When Bharti's lawyer moved the courts for her production by the police, who had her in their custody, but had allowed 200 Hindu activists to storm the police station and then removed her to a government-run home, they pleaded their inability to do so as she had killed herself. She had died of burns under extremely suspicious conditions in the Hindu Mahasabha office (Malekar, 2001).

7. It is significant that the new National Council of Educational Research and Training class XI sociology textbook, introduced by the BJP government in

2002, reiterates the popular notion that matrimony norms require endogamous and intra-religious marriage.

8. Information compiled by PUDR fact-finding team, 2002–03, for *Courting Disaster.*

9. 'Aukat se bahar kaam karenge to yehi hoga' (AALI case files).

10. *Yasmeen alias Megha Mathur* vs. *Ramesh Chand Mathur and Suneeta Mathur* Writ Petition no. 319 (High Court) of 1993.

11. AALI Report, 2004: 59 per cent of the sample cases seeking court intervention in denial of choice in marriage saw the husband/lover also facing charges of kidnapping and abduction, which are cognisable (arrestable without a warrant) and non-bailable (bail can only be granted by a judge).

12. See the account of Radha cited above and the case of Satish and Babita in *Courting Disaster*, pp. 5–8.

13. AALI Report, 2004: in 62 per cent of the sample cases both partners were adults; in 4 per cent the man was an adult and the woman a minor; in 19 per cent both were minors; and in only 2 per cent the woman was a major and the man a minor.

14. See *Smt. Suneeta through her husband Tulsi* vs. *State of UP and Others* 2003 (1) JIC 1927 (All); and *Jamshed & Another* vs. *State of UP and Others* Cr. Misc. application No. 4522 of 2000 (All).

15. *Takabul Jahan* vs. *Rizwan and Others* 2003 (2) JIC (All).

16. Under Hindu law there is an uneasy relationship between marriage as a sacrament and marriage as a contract; while the age for *contracting* a valid marriage is 18 for a girl, the sacramental tie of a marriage before that age is valid because of the anomalies of the law.

17. *Mohd. Ikram Hussain* vs. *State of UP and Others* AIR 1964, SC 1625.

18. The Superintendent of Police of Narela has an M.A. in political science, is a law graduate and is very conscious of human rights discourses; his statements to the PUDR team were made in April 2003 with great camaraderie; he made only one statement that he did not want quoted.

19. *K. Belal alias S.K. Raja and Others* vs. *State of Orissa and Others* 11 (1994) DMC 327.

20. *Kiran Singh* vs. *Anand Pratap Singh and Others* AIR 1980, SC 1749.

21. *Arvinder Singh Bagga* vs. *State of UP and Others* AIR 1994, SUPP (1) SCC 500, where there was a fear that people of one community would forcibly take away the girl of another.

22. *Kiran* vs. *Anand Pratap Singh.*

23. *Mohd. Ikram Hussain* vs. *State of UP and Others.*

24. Ibid.

25. *Takabul Jahan* vs. *Rizwan and Others* 2003 (2) JIC 209 [All].

26. The attitude that 'love' is a phase of hormonal madness in girls is crudely dealt with in a current television advertisement: the ad begins with an irate father dragging his daughter and dumping her on a bed and locking her up to prevent her meeting her 'boyfriend'. The maddened girl then scrawls her boyfriend's name all over the walls; the smart mother then has the room painted with Asian Paints – the girl is thrilled at the appearance of the room and when the boyfriend next calls she hangs up on him, saying 'wrong number'. The violence of immobilising women and infringing their rights is naturalised with a neat solution provided by

the market. The lasting image is that of being facetious about a 'deadly' serious issue that is evoking little concern.

27. *Smt. Suneeta through her husband Tulsi* vs. *State of UP and Others* 2003 [1] JIC 1027 (All).

28. *Takabul Jahan* vs. *Rizwan and Others.*

29. *Mohd. Kallo alias Mohd. Jubeel* vs. *State and Others*, Writ petition No. 979 (M/B) of 1999.

30. *Jamshed and Another* vs. *State of UP and Others* 2003(2) Lucknow Criminal Reports 26.

31. A range of medical tests have been used by the courts to establish age in such cases, including bone ossification tests. Documentary evidence of age is often lacking or conflicting and witness evidence is usually not sufficiently reliable as parents or other witnesses who can testify to age may have a vested interest in the person's age (for example, if the person is deemed to be a minor, under the law she would fall within parental control).

32. *Jyoti alias Jannat & Another* vs. *State of UP and Others* 2003[2] JIC 468 (All).

33. *Arvinder Singh Bagga* vs. *State of UP and Others.*

34. *Shiv Kumar Gupta alias Raju* vs. *State of UP and Others* 1999 Lucknow Law Journal 254.

35. *Mohd. Kallo alias Mohd. Jubeel.*

36. *Payal Sharma alias Kamla Sharma* vs. *Superintendent, Nari Niketan, Agra and Others* 2001 (3) AWC 1778.

37. For example, the article written by Syeda Hameed on the brutal killing of two sisters was published under the column 'Women's World' in *Mainstream* (1999).

38. Syeda Hameed's interventions as member of the National Commission for Women.

39. In Muzzafarnagar, where violence over inter-caste marriages has been extreme, the data on the applications to marry under the Special Marriage Act are very revealing: of the thirty-seven applications made in 2002 only 18 per cent ended in actual marriage. A very large number of applications lapsed because either one or other of the applicants did not make it to present themselves before the magistrate, and then even after they had done so did not make it to the actual marriage ceremony within the stipulated period, so their applications lapsed. This could be because they were prevented from appearing on the said date or were afraid of the consequences of their marriage without parental approval (AALI Report, 2004).

40. This dimension of judgments, reflecting the compulsions of adhering to con-stitutional requirements that makes it possible for the Government of India to deny to international bodies that there are aspects of culture and tradition that are responsible for violations of the rights of women. The government specifically denied the incidence of 'honour killings', claiming that the report of the UN Rapporteur on violence against women was based on 'hearsay' (*Indian Express*, 12 October 2002). Women's and human rights groups have countered this government position; e.g. AIDWA issued a statement carried in *People's Democracy*, 27 October 2002, offering to provide evidence to the government and rebutting the charge of lack of credibility in the UN Rapporteur's report with the counter-charge that the government suffered a loss of credibility with its denial.

41. In *S.K. Belal alias S.K. Raja and Others* vs. *State of Orissa* 11 (1994) DMC 327

the judge expressed great sympathy for the parents of a girl who had married a Muslim. 'I am conscious of the pangs suffered by the parents of petitioner No. 3 for the way she has spurned the parental care and home and chosen a boy of another community as her life partner, much to their embarrassment and humiliation in their own society. But then some events are irreversible and one had better reconcile with it than take a journey against the current.' He had been forced to accept the legal position, which was that 'when two persons competent for the purpose decide to lead life together as husband and wife, the law of the country does not permit [the] throwing of spanners in their lives.'

42. Thus in *S.K. Belal alias S.K. Raja and Others* vs. *State of Orissa* the police claimed that they detained the woman overnight due to the threat to law and order being posed by the congregation of a large number of members of the husband's community (Sikh); and there were delays in arranging both the medical test (age determination) and recording of her statement before the magistrate.

43. Many judges in India would heartily subscribe to the sentiments of Justice Khalil–ur-Rahman, who suggested the elders of the family should be an important part of the process of the selection of a spouse. He said, 'let the elders of the family do the search and even the research, and then whatever is available be put before the boy or the girl as the case maybe, who should have the final choice in the matter': *Hafiz Abdul Waheed* vs. *Asma Jahangir*, PLD 1997 Lahore 301.

44. It is interesting that the norm of the arranged marriage is perfectly melded into the world of global capital, the market and consumerism in the Indian advertisement industry. An advertisement for diamonds Indianises the diamond ring to fit the arranged marriage: the couple have an arranged marriage, and then the diamond ring seals the birth of the first baby. The voice-over expresses the woman's sentiments, acknowledging that the couple were tied together by others, but that other ties then were created between the couple – it is those ties that are perhaps the mark of a love marriage!

16

Tackling forced marriages in the Nordic countries: between women's rights and immigration control

ANJA BREDAL

Forced marriage became the subject of public concern in Norway and Denmark in the 1990s; at that time forced marriage was less visible in Sweden, though the front pages of newspapers there carried dramatic stories about 'immigrant girls' and their families. The Norwegian government prepared a Plan of Action in 1998, the Danish turned to immigration laws, and the Swedish government was silent – until the murder of Fadime Sahindal in 2002.

In this chapter, I describe the development of public awareness of, and policy measures against, forced marriages in the Scandinavian countries, with the main focus on governmental initiatives in Norway. I also discuss key elements of Danish policies. I have chosen to omit Sweden, mainly for reasons of priority, but also because Swedish policies have been more concerned with 'honour related' violence in general rather than the specific manifestation of forced marriage.[1] The format of this article is mainly descriptive, but I will make some evaluative comments.[2]

Norway

The first depiction of forced marriage in Norway to gain mass public attention was a feature article in 1992 written by freelance journalist Hege Storhaug based on an interview with 'Sima', a Norwegian-Pakistani girl who had been forced by her parents to marry a second cousin whilst on holiday in Pakistan (*Dagbladet*, 8 November 1992).[3] Sima had been beaten and locked up, but managed to escape and, with the assistance of the

Norwegian Embassy in Islamabad, return to Norway. The newspaper story attracted considerable attention, but no broader debate was generated at this stage. Throughout the 1990s, more cases appeared in the media, and several organisations took the first initiatives to help young people at risk, pioneered by the Oslo Red Cross.

From the outset, in the mid-1990s, the debate on forced marriage, and consequently on arranged marriages, was located within the already polarised 'immigrant debate' (Eide, 2002; Gullestad, 2000a, 2002b, 2004; Hagelund, 2003). One side claimed that there were only a few incidents of forced marriage, charging media generalisations with contributing to stigmas already attached to certain ethnic minority groups. Others argued that the known cases were only the tip of the iceberg, accusing the critics of not daring to admit that severe abuse was going on for fear of being labelled racist or contributing to racism (Wikan, 2002).

It was not until the autumn of 1997 and media coverage of the case of 'Nadia' that the debate was lifted to a political level. According to newspaper reports, 18-year-old Nadia had been abducted by her parents, who took her to their country of origin, Morocco. She managed to telephone her employer and several friends in Norway informing them of her situation. Following substantial pressure from the Norwegian embassy and other Norwegian authorities,[4] her parents agreed to send her back to Norway. Nadia was convinced that her parents planned to marry her by force, but since this could not be proved they were charged only with abduction ('forcibly holding someone against her will [frihetsberøvelse] with the stipulation that the offence had exceeded one month'; Wikan, 2002: 185). In November 1998 they were found guilty.[5]

The 'Nadia' case was, along with NGO and media pressure in general, the impetus behind a parliamentary request to the government (tabled by MP Erna Solberg of the Conservative Party)[6] to develop an Action Plan on forced marriages. The government Action Plan, published in December 1998, focuses on both prevention and remedy. It discusses at length the complexities of the ongoing debate over the distinction between forced and arranged marriage, noting that while the individual's perception of having a real choice is pertinent, it is difficult to draw the line between coercion and pressure. Nevertheless, it firmly states:

> This action plan does not apply to arranged marriages provided that these are entered into in accordance with Norwegian law, and the international conventions to which Norway is a party. The aim of the action plan is to contribute towards ensuring that no coercion, either physical or mental, is used to persuade either or both parties concerned to enter into marriage.

The Plan is vague about the size of the problem it seeks to address. It does, however, highlight the need to engage in dialogue with relevant minority groups, as well as secure assistance for those who fear, or have been victims of, forced marriage. Several 'action points' focus on the need to strengthen capacity and procedures within mainstream services. Although the Plan raises the issue of a specific national support institution, it argues against centralising, stating: 'We believe … that it is useful to retain diversity, and in fact to strengthen it, rather than to try to create something that aims to be all things to all people.' However, the Plan does announce the establishment of a national telephone helpline to rationalise the information work. The Ministry for Children and Family Affairs subsequently decided that such a helpline would be administered by the Oslo Red Cross as the organisation with the longest experience in the area. The helpline was opened in April 2000, evaluated after its first three-year period (Oslo Red Cross, 2003) and continues to operate on a project basis.

In view of the events to follow, perhaps the most striking aspect of this pioneering action plan is its remarkably short section on legal changes. In particular, no mention is made of using stricter immigration laws to fight forced transnational marriages. Rather, the only law-based action appears to suggest *liberalisation* of immigration practice, as Action Plan para 8.1 states that the authorities will 'investigate the possibilities for continued residence in Norway after the marriage annulment'.[7]

A rather sudden change of climate and interest in the debate on forced marriages and related issues occurred in January 2002, with the dramatic and tragic murder in Sweden of Fadime Sahindal, a young Swedish woman of Kurdish origin.[8] This incident dominated Nordic media in the following months, and led to two significant changes. First, 'a new openness' was created, and greeted by some as a positive step towards a free and open-minded debate on the more problematic aspects of immigration, in particular by Muslims (Wikan, 2002). Others were critical, seeing this turn as legitimising stigmatisation of ethnic minorities, who were already victims of racial discrimination (Gullestad, 2002b). This latter critique was also linked to the second change: more politicians, and not only the right-wing populist Progress Party, known for its tough stance on immigration control, turned to the immigration laws as a way of curtailing forced marriage and other types of violence against minority women, to a large extent seeing this as an 'immigrant problem'.

The proposed introduction of an age limit of 24 for family reunification on the basis of marriage as a measure to combat forced marriage had already been advocated by the freelance journalist-cum-activist Hege Storhaug in 1998. However, it was not until the murder of Fadime Sahindal that this and other similar proposals gained political support. In addition to the age rule, a ban on cousin marriages – in general or at least as a basis for reunification – was suggested by politicians from several parties in spring 2002.[9] During the same period, the Norwegian government issued their 'Renewed Initiative against Forced Marriage', a collection of thirty new measures compiled in a short leaflet. The first measure highlights the government's continued prioritisation of support for organisations working with young people in crisis situations. Of the thirty measures contained in the initiative, ten are law-related actions, covering criminal, civil and immigration law.

Before discussing the most relevant of these and 'older' applicable legislation, it is useful to outline briefly the legislative system in Norway. When introducing new legislation, the relevant ministry writes a consultation paper explaining the background and the relevant alternatives, which is widely distributed to different government agencies, NGOs and other interested parties in a consultation process called *høring*. The written submissions from the consultation are commented on in the ministry's proposition/Green Paper submitted to the Norwegian parliament (*Stortinget*).[10]

Civil law

The inclusion of a special provision for the annulment of forced marriages in the Norwegian Marriage Act (Act No. 47 of July 1991)[11] is directly related to the struggle against forced marriages. During a total revision of the Marriage Act in the late 1980s, the right to annul a marriage, including a forced marriage, was removed, as it was considered obsolete and superfluous in light of new effective divorce regulations.[12] However, just before the new Act entered into force (1 January 1993), the old Marriage Act provision was used to annul the forced marriage of 'Sima', which thus came to have a historic impact on Norwegian law. Occurring at a time when there was a growing awareness around the problem itself, the case reopened the question of annulment. As of 1 January 1995, section 16(3) and (4) of the Marriage Act allows

> either of the spouses to bring civil action against the other in order to have their marriage annulled, if he or she has been forced into the marriage by unlawful conduct. Action should be taken within six months after the spouse has been set free from the coercion, and can in no event be taken later than five years after the marriage has been contracted. (author's translation)

Annulment, unlike divorce, is retroactive, and involves declaring a marriage null and void – that is, as if it had never existed.[13] Aside from Karim's case, official registers only show one other case of annulment of a forced marriage

– in Fredrikstad City Court (*byrett*) in 1998 – also concerning a marriage contracted in the parents' country of origin.[14]

The Renewed Initiative signalled several potential civil law changes.[15] As of 1 March 2004, section 16(a) of the Marriage Act grants *Fylkesmannen* (the chief administrative officer of a county) the right to institute legal proceedings to establish the validity of a marriage, including, where forced marriage is suspected, within a five-year limitation period. A circular from the Ministry of Children and Family Affairs (26 February 2004) notes that such action can be of assistance to a spouse who is reluctant to take legal action herself/himself. Whilst it cautions that the provision should be practised with care, and only applied in clear cases, it is possible to bring a case where neither of the spouses agrees, on the grounds that one or both may be too afraid to express their true preferences. At the time of writing this new provision has not, to the knowledge of the author, been used.

Further, given that children/young people under the age of majority may be the victims of forced marriage, the Children's Act was amended to invalidate child-marriages contracted by parents. Thus section 30(4) reads: 'An agreement to marry made by parents on behalf of the child is not binding.'

Criminal law[16]

Until recently forced marriage has been illegal according to the general provisions of the General Civil Penal Code (PC) on illegal use of force.[17] In the 'Renewed Initiative', the government indicated the possibility of inserting a special provision on forced marriages into the PC. In 2003, s.222 PC regulating compulsion/coercion was amended to include a specific subsection on forced marriage, a change supported by the Ministry for Justice, the police and many of those involved in the consultation process preceding the amendment.[18] According to this provision, both the spouse and/or the family members involved in organising the forced marriage can be charged. Force in the case of marriage is also considered an aggravating factor and incurs an increased penalty, which can be imprisonment for up to six years, and is applicable to all those taking part in the coercion.

Section 222(3) provides that if the felony is committed by the victim's next of kin,[19] public prosecution will be instituted only at the request of the aggrieved person unless required in the public interest. As from 2003 a mandatory prosecution clause was introduced in cases of forced marriage so that the perpetrators may be prosecuted without the victim's consent. This mirrored the mandatory public prosecution provision regarding domestic violence cases, instituted in 1988.[20] The ministry's rationale for this amendment was to relieve the young person of having to initiate legal action against her own family. In the consultation process, several agencies, such as the Women's Shelter in Oslo and Oslo Crisis Centre, raised the concern that some young people may want to escape forced marriages without criminalising their parents or other close kin, and that this provision may deny them the right to choose that option. Others assumed that the police would in practice pay attention to the victim's wishes. The Red Cross and others warned that minority youth still hesitate to contact assistance agencies and that this provision would work against the fragile trust established between them, making some young people even more reluctant to report their grievances if they risked sparking off a prosecution. Also, NGOs would have to consider this possibility when deciding whether to request police assistance in connection with meetings with parents, applying for violence alarm protection kits for the young person or a protected address, and would have to inform their 'client' accordingly.

Pursuant to measure 9 of the 'Renewed Initiative', section 220(1) PC was passed, making it an indictable offence to enter into or contribute to a marriage with a person below the age of 16. The punishment for entering, or taking part in, such a child marriage is imprisonment for up to four years, although the contributors (family members) may be subject to harsher punishment than the perpetrator (the minor's spouse).

As of mid-2004, there has been only one known criminal case of forced marriage in Norway. In April 2002, a man of Pakistani origin was found guilty of having forced his daughter to marry against her will, in accordance with s.222(1) PC, as well as having committed extensive and sustained violence against his wife and two daughters. The court found that this crime had been committed under serious aggravating circumstances due to the extent of the violence and sentenced the defendant to three years' imprisonment, of which one year was unsuspended with a probation period of four years; he thus served one year in prison.[21]

Immigration law

A new provision in the Immigration Rules passed by the legislature in autumn 2003 now provides that a Norwegian citizen who wishes to bring her or his spouse to live in the country must prove that she can provide for the spouse where one of them is under the age of 23. The general rationale for this measure is 'an assumption that the younger a person is, the less able is she to withstand pressure from her parents'.[22] Another justification was the prevention of 'surprise marriages', as for example when a young woman is hurriedly married off during a holiday to the parents' country of origin.

It was also rationalised that this age bar would motivate parents to increase their daughters' educational status in order to secure a level of income that would meet the family reunification requirements. However, according to the ministry's consultation document, it could also have the opposite effect, motivating the early withdrawal of girls from education to allow enough time to earn the requisite amount of money to facilitate her husband's entry. This was, however, rejected as an insufficiently weighty counter-argument.

Security and housing

The lack of housing for victims of actual or potential forced marriage has long been a problem raised by the NGOs. Several young women have turned to women's shelters, but these are only available for short-term stays, and may not be appropriate for this group.[23] Young men have no similar alternative. As from 2003, and as part of the follow-up of the Renewed Initiative, ten special flats have been made available by Husbanken (the Norwegian State Housing Bank)[24] for the use of young people or couples who need housing in a crisis situation connected to forced marriage. The Bank cooperates with certain local authorities and the equipped flats are available on short notice for young people throughout the country. The flats can be used for up to one year. All enquiries are directed through the two NGOs, SEIF and ORKIS (see below).

'Bokollektivet' is a special safe house for young women from one of two categories: (1) women recently arrived in Norway as spouses who have experienced violence from their husbands and/or in-laws; (2) women who have grown up in Norway and have been or are in danger of being forced into marriage. These are women who live under serious threats to their mental and/or physical health and/or their life, and who need special security measures as well as individual follow-up and counselling on psychological and/or practical matters. Bokollektivet was established in 2000 by the Oslo Crisis Centre. Since opening, Bokollektivet has had forty women residents from South Asian, Middle Eastern and African backgrounds. Average live-in time for 'newly arrived' women has been seven to eight months, and four months for victims of forced marriages (Oslo Red Cross, 2003; Paust, 2002). An independent evaluation (Paust, 2002) and the shelter's own reports show that there is a clear need for supportive housing such as this, but that the collective has been run on a minimum (non-sustainable level) of funds. In June 2004, the Oslo Crisis Centre announced that it will close the shelter if more funds are not secured (*Aftenposten*, 1 July 2004).

As with other victims of violence, several young men and women have changed their names and live in secret addresses to avoid being forced to marry or face sanctions after having run away from home to avoid or escape a forced marriage, and many of them have some kind of alarm protection.[25] According to section 37 of the National Register Regulation of 4 March 1994 (Folkeregisterforskriften),[26] a person can obtain a blocked address in one of two possible categories: Code 7 is 'confidential' and blocks the address from private persons but not from public officials; and Code 6, 'strictly confidential', which makes the address available only to the National Register personnel in the municipality of residence and specially authorised officials in the Tax Inspectorate. Most forced marriage victims live in Code 7 addresses. There have been several cases of breaches of confidentiality, where public offices have revealed the young people's addresses (SEIF, 2003).

Lack of statistics

Support centres and NGOs produce statistics from their own caseloads, but the registration criteria are vague and inevitably vary between organisations. The Red Cross's suggestions for a coordinated system of registration have evinced little interest, possibly due to the lack of resources and methodological problems that would be involved in establishing this. Yet one cannot disregard the possibility that organisations may have an interest in being unclear on the size of their caseloads as there is a considerable competition for funds.

As an indication of the order of numbers we are talking about, it can be noted that SEIF reported in June 2004 that it has been involved in 39 emergency cases of forced marriage so far this year; 65 per cent of cases concerning girls, the remainder involving boys and young couples. In 2003 they had 57 cases, and 45 in 2002. The women's shelters' secretariat (covering 33 of the 55 shelters in Norway) reports that during 2003 they had 45 occupants who had experienced forced marriage issues, and 47 in 2002 (*Dagsavisen*, 8 June 2004).

The NGO sector

As already mentioned, Oslo Red Cross (ORKIS) was the first organisation to address the problem of forced marriages in the media and to target their counselling and support services towards the young women and men affected. Selvhjelp/SEIF (literally: 'self help for immigrants and refugees'),[27] who began their work later, are, together with ORKIS, the main recipient of government funds for casework on forced marriages. The MIRA Resource Centre, the only national networking organisation for minority women, engages in advocacy and has included forced marriage in its legal and social assistance portfolio to immigrant and refugee women as well as to young girls from ethnic minorities.[28] MIRA is known for criticising the government for not acknowledging its status as an NGO that not only fights for minority women's rights but also organises and empowers those women on an anti-racist and feminist platform (Predelli, 2003).

Although they are united by the need to fight forced marriages, there are significant differences between the NGOs both in ideology and in working methods. While ORKIS tends to distinguish between arranged marriages and (different forms and degrees of) forced marriages in much the same way as the Action Plan, SEIF tends to regard all arranged marriages as 'contracted under larger or lesser degrees of force' (Storhaug, 2003). And whereas ORKIS tends to be in favour of trying to facilitate dialogue between the young person and her/his family, if the young person so wishes and provided her/his security is not at risk, SEIF appears more focused on the individual and helping her/him to escape the family. There has been some discussion around the possibilities and desirability of any kind of 'mediation' or 'conflict management', but this has so far been quite rudimentary and antagonistic, and – symptomatic of this problem area in general – has not been linked to mainstream debates on conflict resolution in families.

Writing on forced marriages in Norway, and the influence of NGOs in particular, one cannot avoid commenting on the private foundation Human Rights Service (HRS), established in 2001 by Hege Storhaug and Rita Karlsen. Through the years the organisation has presented itself in different ways, but now calls itself a think-tank on integration issues with a particular focus on 'the rights of women and children – and on such violations of those rights as forced marriage, female genital mutilation, and honour killings'.[29] Shortly before the murder of Fadime Sahindal, the previously mentioned Nadia and another young women with a personal history of having been forced to marry, Jeanette, joined the organisation. The two young women's legitimacy as 'authentic victims' and Storhaug's experience and network as a journalist ensured the efficiency and effectiveness of the organisation's lobbying. It is fair to say that Storhaug and HRS have been central in both bringing forced marriages to the attention of the public, and – increasingly – in influencing state policies to combat the practice.[30] In particular HRS has fiercely campaigned for the tightening of immigration controls as a main strategy to fight this violation of women and children's human rights. Their proposals have in particular been taken up and presented in parliament by the Progress Party, but have often had the support of many and sometimes all parties.[31] The Progress Party has also been instrumental in securing funds directly from the state budget to HRS, whereas other NGOs are obliged to apply to the ministries.[32] Outside Norway, HRS is perhaps best known as one of the main advisers on women's issues to the Danish Integration Minister, Bertel Haarder (see below), and in 2003 presented Haarder with an award for being the leading European politician on integration issues (Storhaug, 2003).

The organisation has been controversial, and several critical voices have been raised against its policy of linking feminist concerns with immigration control. Also, in two separate cases, some young women who previously had contacted HRS for assistance or otherwise been in contact with the organisation have accused HRS of using unethical methods in their contact with victims of forced marriages and in contributing to severe family conflicts. (*Dagsavisen*, 1 December 2004 and 7 June 2004; VG, 28 June 2004).

A note on mainstreaming

These and other NGOs have criticised the social services and other mainstream institutions, such as schools, for not taking the problem of forced marriages seriously,[33] which they attribute both to civil servants not daring or wanting to take action due to some more or less well defined 'respect for minority culture' and to a lack of knowledge and competence. The critique is similar to that voiced by Southall Black Sisters (SBS) in the UK (see Siddiqui in this volume), although Norwegian state policies are generally less influenced than the British by what SBS calls a 'multiculturalist ideology'. Another important difference between the two countries is an apparent lack of discourse on racism in Norway, partly due to a national identity which constructs Norway as an 'innocent' humanitarian state with no colonial account to settle (see Andersson, 2003; Gullestad, 2002a, 2002b, 2004; Hagelund, 2003). Acknowledging that this is a complex issue beyond the scope of this chapter, it is fair to note that the problem in Norway is caused partly by a lack of knowledge and competence in regard to forced marriage in particular, and partly by a lack of expertise and willingness to deal with race relations in general.

Furthermore, as funds were eventually made available, following a 1999 television documentary[34] that renewed the political pressure, they went to special projects run by NGOs to address forced marriages.[35] This is reasonable since this is the sector where awareness and competence building started, but it may also be argued that the support work should have been more actively pushed towards mainstream state services such as social services, housing, education and health at an earlier stage. In any case, it can be asked whether these NGOs, depending on project funds, had or have the competence *and* resources to deal with people in severe crisis (concerning both their psychological health and their security). From the government's perspective there has been a slight shift towards building competence and accountability into mainstream institutions, in particular with a substantial number of courses being run for employees in different services, and at the same time recognising the need for specialised services – both in the NGO sector and in the public sector. However, service provision related to forced marriage remains an NGO area.

The absence of forced marriage issues within the list of activities of the Government Working Group on Violence Against Women and in its December 2003 report (Norwegian Ministry of Justice and the Police, 2003: 31) is a significant missed opportunity for mainstreaming. The Working Group's primary task was to document the situation of women exposed to violence from a present or former male partner, and make recommendations on policies and measures to improve the situation of victims, prevent violence, and so on. However, the mandate provided the possibility of including violence committed by other 'close' perpetrators, which could include (although not explicitly stated) parents and siblings, as in cases of forced marriages. The Working Group chose to distinguish and differentiate its work explicitly from forced marriage and also FGM, finding that they fell outside the mandate and were in any case already comprehensively dealt with in separate action plans.

Denmark

The 1990s in Denmark, as in Norway, saw the media carry stories on individual cases of forced marriage. In Denmark, however, the dominant policy strategy from the start was to restrict the right to family unification with a spouse from abroad. Over the years this has been linked to a more general development towards what is now referred to as one of the strictest immigration policies in Europe (Grøndahl, 2003; Fenger-Grøn et al., 2003; Siim, 2003).

In 1998, under the former coalition government of the Social Democratic and Social Liberal parties, the Aliens Act was amended to allow denial of a residence permit on the basis of marriage if it was established that the marriage was based on 'an agreement entered into by parties other than the spouses themselves' (author's translation; see also Bredal, 1999). In 2000, the legal claim to family reunion on the grounds of marriage was abolished for people aged between 18 and 25 years of age, resulting in permits being granted only if an individual enquiry establishes that the marriage was entered into voluntarily. Provisional figures for 2001 show that the Danish Immigration Service refused reunification of spouses under this provision in nine cases (whereas 1,778 permissions were granted; Marthin, 2002). These low figures were interpreted as a sign that the legislation had failed to prevent many forced marriages. According to the Ministry of Refugee, Immigration and Integration Affairs, 'The previous rules applicable for family reunification had been used for immigration purposes through marriages of convenience and arranged marriages, resulting in frequent tragedies for young families' (Marthin, 2002).

Consequently, after the election of a new Liberal–Conservative government in the autumn of 2001, with the support of the right-wing populist Danish People's Party, the amended Aliens Act came into force on 1 July 2002.[36] The explicit primary aim of the Act was to reduce the number of immigrants (Siim, 2003: 6); secondary goals included the prevention of forced marriages and to ensure 'the best possible base for a successful integration'. Under the new law, there is no longer any statutory right of family reunification. In all cases, family reunification will only be granted upon a specific and individual assessment on the basis of the conditions set out. As a rule, reunification of spouses is not permitted if one of the spouses is below 24 years of age. According to the Ministry for Refugees, Immigration and Integration Affairs (Marthin, 2002):

> The age limit was set at 24 years because young people between the age of 18 and 24 normally experience a personal development – among other things through education, training or work – that will help them resist possible pressure from parents or others so they can avoid marrying against their will. The older a person is, the better she or he can resist pressure from her or his family or others, to contract marriage against her or his own will.

Other changes have since followed. The most recent provision exempts relatives, in particular cousins, who have married from the possibility of claiming family reunification at any age. The government primarily explained this as a measure against force, but health concerns have also been mentioned.[37] As of August 2004, all the following requirements must be met for family reunification in Denmark:[38]

1. Both spouses must be aged 24 years and over (age requirement).[39]
2. The marriage must be contracted voluntarily, and the spouses must not, as a rule, belong to the same family; for example, they must not be cousins.
3. The spouse residing in Denmark must have his/her own accommodation, which must be of a certain size (housing requirement).[40]
4. The spouse who resides in Denmark must earn enough money to be able to support his/her spouse and must not have received any kind of financial aid from his/her local authority within the last year. He/she must also arrange a bank guarantee of DKK 53,096 (support requirement).[41]
5. Both spouses must have ties with Denmark which are closer than with any other country (affiliation requirement).[42]

Point 2 refers to the fact that unification will not be granted if it is considered 'doubtful' that the marriage is contracted according to both parties' free will.[43] Since this provision was included in 1998, the immigration authorities have gradually relaxed the relevant evidence required; whereas the first amendment required it be *established* that the marriage was not voluntary, it now suffices to establish doubt (Liisberg, 2004). Furthermore, this rule also now applies to those over 25 years of age. In addition, two so-called rules of presumption (*formodningsregler*) have been added, implying that it is generally assumed that a marriage is not voluntary where the spouses are close kin and/or where there is a history of previous family unifications based on marriage in the individual's close family. As Liisberg (forthcoming) argues, in these cases the burden of proof is reversed, and it is the duty of the spouses to prove that their marriage is contracted according to their own free will.

These are general rules that also pertain to the majority population, much to their surprise as it turned out. In particular, there was considerable protest against the affiliation requirement, when it emerged that Danish citizens who had lived abroad for extended periods wanted to return with a spouse, but were refused permission to do so. As a consequence, the Act was amended to exempt from the requirement those with a 28-year-long citizenship, as well as those who are born in Denmark or who arrived as a small child and have lived there continuously for twenty-eight years.[44]

An important ambiguity that has arisen concerns the extent to which the new family reunification provisions are motivated foremost by a concern for potential and actual victims of forced marriages, or by a concern for failure of integration, or by a wish to curtail immigration in general and from certain countries in particular. In any case, there should be no doubt that these changes have meant a tightening of borders in the name of women's rights.

Officially it is the age requirement that most often is presented as a measure against force per se, but in order to assess the impact and efficiency of this measure it should be considered in connection with the others, and in particular with the affiliation requirement. It becomes apparent that the reforms are at best based on simplistic analyses and premises that are not always in place, and at worst are really about restricting immigration rather than protecting women's rights. In either case the result may be that the reforms exacerbate the situation for some individuals.

Arguments have been made that the Danish authorities overestimate the immigration motive behind forced marriages and underestimate some minority parents' urge to control their daughters.[45] It is assumed that the parents' motive in choosing a spouse is only or primarily to obtain a residence permit for the partner (typically a relative 'at home') and therefore the law will have a preventive effect. When a visa is out of the question until the spouses are 24, it is assumed that parents will wait for the marriage (or find a local partner). And when the woman is 24, she will be mature enough to make a truly independent choice. But could it not also happen that girls will simply be sent to the country of origin and married there, to return when aged 24? This may very well be the case, and it is here that the affiliation requirement becomes important. Since a future permit is dependent on both spouses' ties to Denmark, this could prevent parents sending their daughter out of the country, and instead seeking a husband for her in Denmark. This logic, however, ignores or underestimates the fact that parents have *other* motives that are well known – for example, that some parents are afraid their children may become too 'Danish' or too 'liberal'. If this is the case, there is a serious danger that some young girls will still be married off abroad at an early age and forced to stay there or that they will suffer from an even longer period of control whilst waiting to get married. It seems probable that if these rules do not work preventively, they will not protect, but may *exacerbate* that control – precisely because the control in some cases is so multifaceted, all-embracing and severe.

Action Plan 2003

As an afterthought to the measures taken in immigration law a comprehensive governmental plan of action was presented in 2003. Titled 'Action Plan on Forced, Quasi-Forced and Arranged Marriages', the document confirms in no uncertain terms the terminology that has dominated and instructed the Danish debate from the start – for example, the first proposals for amending the Aliens Act used the terms 'arranged marriage' and 'forced marriage' interchangeably. Starting with the use of ambiguous language, the tendency has been towards a clear position that arranged marriages are considered a serious problem, if not specifically because they are (all) forced, in the legal sense of the word,[46] but also because they are thought to counter integration, and – not least – because they have traditionally been contracted transnationally and therefore result in increased immigration. The impression that arranged marriages in general are under direct attack from Danish authorities is confirmed in Denmark's National Action Plan to Combat Poverty and Social Exclusion (2003), which introduced the overall objective of the then forthcoming Action Plan thus: 'to prevent forced marriages and forced-like marriages *and to combat arranged marriage*' (emphasis added).[47]

National and international criticism

The restrictions have been criticised and contested by politicians, scholars and human rights activists.[48] So far, however, this criticism has not resulted in any change in the thrust or content of the government's hard-line policy.

In its report, published October 2004, the Danish Institute for Human Rights (2004) looks into different aspects of the Danish family reunification policy from a human rights perspective. The report concludes that the age requirement, together with the affiliation requirement, will result in violations of the right to family life (European Convention of Human Rights, Article 8). More generally it is argued that the new provisions shift decision-making power from a strictly law-based right to family unification to a considerable amount of administrative discretion, weakening security under the law.

Denmark's policies have also met with international criticism. For example, the UN Committee on the Elimination of All Forms of Discrimination Against Women, when considering Denmark's report in 2002, regretted the increased age requirement and 'urged Denmark to consider revoking this legislation', and to 'explore other ways of combating forced marriages' (CEDAW, 2002: para. 345)'. The report of the visit of the Council of Europe's Commissioner of Human Rights (Alvaro Gil-Robles) to Denmark on 13–16 April 2004 criticises the state for not living up to its international obligations. The report caused considerable debate in Denmark during the summer of 2004. Among other things, Gil-Robles urged the Danish government to reconsider the age requirement. The Head of the National Department at the Danish Institute of Human Rights, Birgitte Kofod Olsen, welcomed the report, confirming that 'the laws on family reunification are problematic from a human rights perspective'.[49] The government issued a memorandum dismissing the critique.

Conclusion

At the centre of the Danish, and increasingly also the Norwegian, policies is the generalisation from individual cases of forced marriage to the marriage practices of whole minority groups, along with a strong focus on seeing marriage as a strategy for immigration. These core aspects have been instrumental in the legitimisation of stricter immigration regulations, including policies that are questionable from a human rights perspective. But they are also problematic for other reasons. First, this approach disregards the complexities of the problem of violence against women. Second, it disregards women's agencies and subjectivities. To argue that all arranged marriages are actually forced marriages effectively collapses very different categories of experiences into one. Those who, more or less openly, resist and fight against their parents' plans and impositions are put in the same category as those who uncritically accept the tradition, as well as those who have struggled in their own mind as to what is the right thing to do and who end up accepting an arranged marriage. In short, minority women *as a group* are constructed as immature subjects with no capacity for autonomy. Those who claim that they have not been forced into marriage are written off as what Narayan has coined as either 'victims' or 'dupes' of 'their culture' (Narayan, 2001: 418).

On the other hand, those who criticise state interventions tend to make a clear-cut distinction between free-choice arranged marriages and clear-cut cases of force. According to Gullestad, for instance, '"Forced marriage" is the term for a deviation from arranged marriage, a custom practised in large parts of the world' (Gullestad, 2002b, author's translation).[50] Although this concern to avoid and resist the racism inherent in much of the discourse on, and some policies against, arranged marriages is important, a definition of forced marriage as a deviation from an otherwise seemingly unproblematic 'custom' is flawed. Gullestad's definition implies more than a distinction in principle.

The increased knowledge available on psychological violence, emotional blackmail (SBS, 2001; Siddiqui, 2001) and family loyalties necessitates a much more complex analysis of force than is brought forward by multiculturalist or anti-racist critics of state intervention. These insights should be carried over into the legal discussions and definitions of force. Furthermore, although it is important to recognise concerns surrounding so-called 'adapted prefer-ences' (Moller-Okin, 1999; Nussbaum, 2000) and the dangers of individuals monopolising the right to define their (her) capacity for choice, it is highly problematic to insist that a whole group of people need to be saved from their own choices.

This analysis, in part, supports the often mentioned claim that the distinc-tion between arranged and forced marriages is blurred, and is an important point to be made on an individual level, but it remains more problematic on a group level. When used as the rationale for general measures, as in the Danish Action Plan, it is easy to construct all arranged marriages as forced per se, regardless of the individual's perception and subjective will. The Danish government's rhetoric in itself contributes to the blur, and restrictionists have an interest in upholding and strengthening this blur. What is an important insight in the fight against forced marriages and strengthening women's position within the relevant groups is misused to tighten the borders.

A policy combining a simplified rhetoric of free choice with a seemingly paradoxical disregard for the subjective wills of the individual members of whole groups of people is *not* a woman-friendly policy. Even if one accepts the argument, which is occasionally presented, that some individuals' rights (the right to love and family life in those cases where the marriage is freely contracted) must be sacrificed in order to protect others from a much graver rights violation (having a foreign, and potentially violent and abusive, spouse forced on them), alternative strategies should be discussed – not only to avoid racial discrimination and human rights violations but to develop truly feminist strategies against forced marriages and other 'honour violence', as a specific manifestation of violence against women in general. Implicit in the immigration approach is a logic that the state should save the individual from her parents, and sometimes from herself, instead of empowering her to become stronger in her own resistance and develop a greater sense of direction in life and determination vis-à-vis her family and community. Let us consider an example. When the first restrictions were introduced in Denmark, the following comment was made by UNG-sam, an NGO which was at the time in the forefront of the struggle against forced marriages: 'The government want the young people to inform them when they want to say no. They want to take responsibility over our lives. It is much better that the young people learn to say no to their parents' (Bredal, 1999: 79, author's translation).[51] UNG-sam was not advocating a hands-off policy, leaving young people to find their own way out of forced marriage situations, as other community representatives have done. On the contrary, this was the first organisation to seek state funds towards a support service, assisting young people both in protesting and in fleeing from forced marriages. But they were nevertheless sceptical about a policy that tended to construct such young people as victims incapable of resistance, and thereby to perpetuate their dependency on others.

This is, however, not to argue against state intervention in cases where an individual is not capable of seeing her own best interest, as is more likely the more victimised and the younger a person is. Nor is it to underestimate the fact that some individuals face such grave sanctions that their lack of protest and their total conformity should be taken as a warning sign in itself. Rather, first and foremost, there is a need for complexity and to treat each individual case as part of that complexity. There is both a tendency, in particular within communities and among multiculturalists advocating a 'respect for other cultures', to underestimate the psychological pressure and violence that young women and men face within the context of arranged marriage, and – among some politicians, governments *and* feminists – a tendency to oversimplify and overestimate the compulsion involved in the same context. The latter tendency is clearly motivated by several factors, of which the need to legitimise a general desire for stricter immigration control is one.

Both the Danish and the Norwegian governments present their policies and measures as 'packages' against forced marriage. Correspondingly, critics concerned with the racist and discriminatory effects of (at least some of) these policies tend to lump all measures together in broadbrush allegations of stigmatisation – representing, or playing into the hands of, those community leaders and others who resist state intervention in 'private matters' such as violence against women and who fight to preserve patriarchal practices and 'traditions'.

There is a need for policies and measures, as well as research, sensitive to the complex and varied practice and perception of what are often called (cultural) customs or traditions. The time has come to be less concerned with defining force on a general level and more with responding to the various concerns of the individuals involved, and *their* definition of *their* situations – which may well prove that the same actions taken by parents are interpreted and perceived in quite different ways by different young people. A sharper distinction must be made between those legal and social policy measures that are taken to strengthen individuals' right to self-determination and facilitate the empowerment of those individuals, and those that are designed to regulate or police group behaviour. Similarly there is a need to distinguish between measures and strategies that allow for individual assessments of a criminal act or otherwise oppressive actions and those that rest on a predefined categorisation of a tradition or practice such as – typically – veiling or arranged marriage. In general, what is needed is a more sophisticated and discriminating analysis of ethnic minorities' patriarchal practices, the state interventions designed to combat them, and women's responses to both.

For Nordic and other European feminists fighting forced marriage and other forms of violence against all women, there is clearly a need to be aware of the use by some parties of the women's rights discourse for racist and discriminatory purposes. The challenge is not to let this danger lead us into apologetics or paralysis. What feminists in Norway and Denmark need to develop is an anti-racist feminism that empowers them to fight forced marriages without resorting to the immigration laws and alliances with anti-feminist political parties.

Notes

I am indebted to the CIMEL/INTERIGHTS 'Honour Crimes' Project for their extensive editorial input and enthusiastic support, and in particular to Sanchita Hosali. Thanks also to Maria Ventegodt Liisberg, Birte Siim and Sherene Razack for sharing their forthcoming/unpublished papers with me. In particular, Kaja Moe Winther's thesis has been an invaluable source for the legal sections and should be consulted for in-depth discussions on legal and human rights aspects.

1. See *Government initiatives to help young people at risk of honour-related violence.*

2. For a critique of Norwegian and Danish policies as culturalist and racist, see Razack, 2004.

3. 'Sima's' story is also documented in Karim, 1996; Wikan, 2002.

4. Measures included, *inter alia*, the freezing of all social benefits to the family for a period.

5. The father received a suspended sentence of one year and three months and the mother a one-year suspended sentence. The father was also fined 15,000 kroner and ordered to pay 60,000 kroner in court costs. The verdict was in accordance with the counsel/prosecution's submission for leniency referring to Nadia's plea that her parents not be imprisoned. Both sentences were appealed and after the death of Nadia's father the case was dropped. See Wikan, 2002, who was an expert witness duing the trial, for further details.

6. 25 November 1997. Stortingsforhandlinger Nr. 5, 14–25 November, Sesjonen 1997–98, sak nr. 343. Mrs Solberg is now Minister of Local Government and Regional Development, and her portfolio includes Immigration and Ethnic Minority Affairs.

7. Under Immigration Regulation s.37(6) there is currently a three-year trial period before the spouse is granted a residence permit on an independent basis.

8. Fadime Sahindal was well known in Sweden because of her father's and brother's previous violence against her, and her own public appearances. The father was convicted of murder (and received a life sentence). It should also be noted that this murder occurred less than six months after 11 September 2001, both events being central in the explanation of what followed. The debate in Norway is known to have been more focused on forced marriages and Muslims than in the Swedish context.

9. Among the proposers were MPs from the Labour Party, the Socialist Left Party and the Progress Party, as well as the Human Rights Service.

10. For more information about the legislative system, see www.stortinget.no/english/legislation.html (English).

11. Available at www.lovdata.no/all/nl-19910704–047.html (Norwegian). For an unauthorised English translation, see www.lovdata.no/info/uenga.html.

12. In Norway, as in the other Nordic countries, divorce has become increasingly easy, and today the right to a civil divorce is unconditional, following a one-year compulsory separation period: s.21 Act no. 47 of 1991.

13. Accordingly, any child born inside an annulled marriage is legally considered born out of marriage. Questions regarding paternity are regulated by the Children's Act (Act no. 7 of 1981), available at www.lovdata.no/all/nl-19810408–007.html (Norwegian). For an unauthorised English translation, see www.lovdata.no/info/uenga.html.

14. Both cases are available in Norwegian from the respective courts.

15. Ot.prp. nr. 103 (2002–2003) Om lov om endringar i lov 4. juli 1991 nr. 47 om ekteskap(ekteskapslova) m.m. Other relevant documents: Besl.O.nr.24 (2003–2004); Innst.O.nr.17 (2003–2004).

16. Obviously forced marriage should be considered within the framework of violence

against women, particularly within families (natal and conjugal). It is beyond the scope of this chapter to include all policy measures and legislative changes made in Norway in this broad area, as this has been a particularly prolific area of policy development. For a comprehensive discussion on violence against women, including recommendations, see the Governmental Committee on Violence against Women Report *Retten til et liv uten vold* (The Right to a Life without Violence) and the Government's Action Plan on Violence in close relations (2004–2007).

17. For an unofficial English translation by the Norwegian Ministry of Justice, see www.ub.uio.no/ujur/ulovdata/lov-19020522-010-eng.doc.

18. As outlined in the Green Paper on amendments in the Norwegian Civil Penal Code (Ot.prp. nr.51 (2002/2003). The other documents (legislative history) are: Innst.O.nr.17 (2003–2004); Innst.O.nr.106 (2002–2003). For a discussion on the legal specifications and boundaries of 'unlawful conduct' etc., see Winther, 2003.

19. The term 'next of kin' is defined in s.5 PC thus: 'Wherever this code uses the term a person's next of kin, it thereby includes his spouse, ascendants and descendants, siblings and equally close relatives by marriage, foster parents and foster children, and his fiancée. If the marriage is dissolved, the said provisions shall continue to apply to events occurring before the dissolution. The spouse of a relative by marriage is also regarded as a relative by marriage' (Winther, 2003).

20. It should be noted that the mandatory prosecution in cases of violence against women would also apply to many or most cases of forced marriages, as physical or other forms of violence are often involved.

21. The judgment was given by Indre Follo Municipal Court (*tingrett*) and is available in Norwegian as case no. 02–00292 M/0 of 4 April 2002. For information about the Norwegian Court System, see www.domstol.no/Domstolene/index.asp.

22. In Norwegian: 'en antakelse om at jo yngre partene er, dess vanskeligere er det å motstå press fra familien': Rundskriv, 2004 available at http://odin.dep.no/krd/norsk/regelverk/rundskriv/016081-250015/dok-bn.html.

23. See Paul, 1998, for a presentation of the Norwegian women's shelters.

24. Husbanken is a state building fund for financing the building of small private houses. For information in English, see www.husbanken.no/portaler/iPortEnglish.nsf. A leaflet in Norwegian on the housing project can be ordered from the same web address.

25. The kit consists of a safety telephone directly connected to the police, a cell-phone, an answering machine, an acoustic alarm; see further www.likestilling.no/english/alarm.pdf.

26. See www.lovdata.no/for/sf/fd/xd-19940304-0161.html.

27. See further www.seif.no/publikasjoner/en/.

28. See further www.mirasenteret.no.

29. See further www.rights.no.

30. In a study on ethnic minority women's NGOs and NGOs fighting for such women's rights, Line Nyhagen Predelli (2003) finds that HRS stands out as the organisation that has the broadest and closest contact with policymakers, in particular the parliament. She also finds that minority women's influence is generally informal and limited to typical areas such as forced marriage and FGM.

31. For example, the proposal to introduce a provision in the Marriage Act requiring all religious marriage contracts to include a mutual agreement between the spouses to grant each other equal rights to divorce. Another proposal suggested the Immigration Act should include provisions addressing foreign marriage contracts, to avoid so-called 'limping marriages', which have been reported as a problem for some Muslim women who have had a civil divorce that is not recognised by the husband. Forced marriages were also mentioned in this context but with no apparent connection to the topic. The first part of the proposal was adopted overnight by parliament in 2003, as a more or less direct quote from HRS's book *Human Visas* (2003). Parliament also asked government to consider the feasibility of the inclusion in the Immigration Act. On the basis of two commissioned studies the Ministry for Local Government and Regional Development advised against both provisions, and MPs are reported to regret their first vote on the grounds that the question turned out to be far more complex than they first thought, particularly in terms of human rights in general and specifically freedom of religion (Thorbjørnsrud, 2003; Emberland, 2003; *Aftenposten*, 3 April 2004).

32. In 2002 HRS received 1.6 million Norwegian kroner in project support; and in 2004, 2 million kroner in core funding.

33. See, for example, annual reports at www.seif.no; Wikan, 2002.

34. TV2 Rikets tilstand 7 Oct 1999 'Tvangsekteskap' (Forced marriage). See further http://www2.tv2.no/riketstilstand/n2i.vis?par=13033 (Norwegian).

35. ORKIS, SEIF and, to a lesser extent, MIRA engage in casework. Several other organisations have received funds toward educational and other activities (Fangen, 2002).

36. L152 af 2002 (lov nr. 365).

37. Forslag nr. L 6 til lov om ændring af udlændingeloven (Ændring af reglerne om tilknytningskrav ved ægtefællesammenføring m.v.) fremsat for Folketinget den 8. oktober 2003.

38. See further www.udlst.dk

39. Aliens Act § 9, s.1(1).

40. Ibid., s.6.

41. Ibid., s.4(1).

42. Ibid., s.7.

43. Ibid., s.8

44. Aliens Act 2002, amended by Law No. 1204 of 27 December 2003.

45. This point was made by Hannana Siddiqui (SBS) and the author (Bredal, 2002) in a workshop on Nordic policies against forced marriages at the Metropolis Conference in Oslo, October 2002.

46. Often the rhetoric is that the young people who are content to marry in this way are incapable of knowing their own best interests.

47. See also the Government's Memorandum with comments to Council of Europe Commisioner on Human Rights Gil-Robles' report (see below): www.inm.dk/imagesUpload/dokument/Memorandum_of_the_report_of_8_July_2004.pdf.

48. For a collection of critical essays on the general tendency toward stricter immigration control, see Fenger-Grøn et al., 2003, in particular Grøndahl on family reunification.

49. See www.humanrights.dk/news/Commissioner_report/(English).

50. In a footnote, Gullestad adds: 'The media panic around these issues seems to have

led to considerable confusion. Many, including central politicians, have a problem distinguishing between forced marriage (deviation from established norms) and arranged marriage (following established norms). The fact that there is a sliding scale between mild pressure and force (Bredal, 1997, 1999) does not make it any less important to maintain a distinction in principle' (Gullestad, 2002b, note 33).

51. The Danish NGO scene has been in flux recently; thus the UNG-sam referred to here existed only for a short period in the late 1990s. They were a group of young ethnic minority people who rallied around the issue of forced marriage and helped other young people on an idealist basis.

References

AALI (2004) *Choosing a Life... 'Crimes of Honour' in India: the Right to If, When and Whom to Marry, a View from Uttar Pradesh and Rajasthan*, available at www.soas.ac.uk/honourcrimes.

Abdo, N. (1999) 'Gender and Politics under the Palestinian Authority', *Journal of Palestine Studies*, vol. 28, no. 2: 110, 38.

'Abdu, J. (1999) *Jarimat 'sharaf al-'a'ila fi mujtami' 'arab 1948 fi filastin*, Cairo Institute for Human Rights Studies, Cairo.

Abdul Salam, S., and A. Sulaiman (2003) *Dalil tadribi: al'unf dudd al-nisa'* [Training Manual: Violence against Women], CEWLA, Cairo.

Abu Odeh, L. (2000) 'Crimes of Honour and the Construction of Gender in Arab Societies', in P. Ilkkaracan (ed.), *Women and Secuality in Muslim Societies*, Women for Women's Human Rights, Istanbul.

———— (1997) 'Comparatively Speaking: The "Honor" of the "East" and the "Passion" of the "West"', *Utah Law Review* 2: 287.

———— (1996) 'Crimes of Honour and the Construct of Gender in Arab Societies', in M. Yamani (ed.), *Feminism and Islam*, Ithaca Press, Reading.

Abu-Lughod, L. (1986) *Veiled Sentiments: Honor and Poetry in a Bedouin Society*, University of California Press, Berkeley.

Acker, J., K. Barry and J. Esseveld (1983) 'Objectivity and Truth: Problems in Doing Feminist Research', *Women's Studies International Forum*, vol. 6, no. 4: 423.

Afshar, H. (ed.) (1993) *Women in the Middle East: Perceptions, Realities and Struggles for Liberation*, Macmillan, London.

Agnes, F. (1999) *Law and Gender Inequality: The Politics of Women's Rights in India*, Oxford University Press, Delhi.

Ahmad, N. (1998) 'The Superior Judiciary: Implementation of the Law and Impact on Women', in F. Shaheed et al. (eds), *Shaping Women's Lives: Laws Practices, and Strategies*, Shirkat Gah, Lahore.

Ahmed, L. (1992), *Women and Gender in Islam: Historical Roots of a Modern Debate*, Yale University Press, Yale.

Ahmed, R., and M. Shamsun Naher (1987) *Brides and the Demand System in Bangladesh: A Study*, Centre for Social Studies, Dhaka.

Al-Abadi, M. (1986) *Al jaraem al kubra fi al ashaer al urdunia* [The Great Crimes in Jordanian Tribes], Manshorat Dar Majdalawi, Amman.

Al-Anbari, S.S. (ed) (2000) *Qanun al-'uqubat raqm 111 1969 wa ta'dilathu* [Penal Code no. 111 of 1969 and Amendments], Al-maktaba al-qanuniya, Baghdad.

Al-Haq (1989) *Punishing a Nation*, Al-Haq, West Bank.

Al-Khouri, Fu'ad Ishaq (1993) *Al-dhihniyya al-'arabiyya: al'unf sayyid al-ahkam*, Dar al-saqi, Beirut.

Al-Rais, N. (2000) *Al qada'a fi falastin wama'uqat tataworeh* [The Justice System in Palestine and Obstacles to Its Development], Al-Haq, West Bank.

Ali, R. (2001) *The Dark Side of 'Honour': Women Victims in Pakistan*, Arqam, Lahore.

Ali, S., and K. Arif (1998) 'Parallel Judicial System in Pakistan and Consequences for Human Rights'. in F. Shaheed et al. (eds), *Shaping Women's Lives: Laws, Practices and Strategies in Pakistan*, Shirkat Gah, Lahore.

Amnesty International (2004a), Making Rights a Reality: The Duty of States to Address Violence against Women, Amnesty International, London.

—— (2004b) *Fundamental Rights of Women Violated with Impunity*, Amnesty International, London.

—— (2002) *Pakistan: Insufficient Protection of Women*, AI Index: ASA 33/006/2002, Amnesty International, London.

—— (2001a) *Broken Bodies, Shattered Minds: Torture and Ill-treatment of Women*, AI Index: ACT 40/001/2001, Amnesty International, London.

—— (2001b) *Iraqi Kurdistan: Torture and Ill-treatment of Women in the Name of 'Honour'*, AI Index: ACT 77/001/20012001, Amnesty International, London.

—— (1999a) *Pakistan: Violence against Women in the Name of Honour*, Amnesty International, AI Index: ASA 33/17/99, London.

—— (1999b) *Pakistan: Honour Killings of Girls and Women*, AI Index: ASA 33/18/1999, Amnesty International, London.

Andersson, M. (2003) 'Immigrant Youth and the Dynamics of Marginalisation', *Young*, vol. 11, no. 1.

An-Na'im, A. (2001) 'Human Rights in the Arab World: A Regional Perspective', *Human Rights Quarterly*, vol. 23, no. 3: 701.

—— (1995) 'The Dichotomy between Religious and Secular Discourse in Islamic Societies', in M. Afkhami (ed.), *Faith and Freedom: Women's Human Rights in the Muslim World*, I.B. Tauris, London.

—— (1994) 'State Responsibility under International Human Rights Law to Change Religious and Customary Laws', in R. Cook (ed.), *Human Rights of Women*, University of Pennsylvania Press, Philadelphia.

—— (1993) *Human Rights in Cross-Cultural Perspective* University of Pennsylvania Press, Philadelphia.

Antolisei, F. (1991), *Manuale di diritto penale. Parte Generale*, Giuffrè, Milan.

Araji, S.K. (2000), 'Crimes of Honor and Shame: Violence against Women in Non-Western and Western Societies', *Red Feather Journal of Postmodern Criminology*, http://critcrim.org/redfeather/journal-pomocrim/pomocrimindex.html.

—— and J. Carlson (2001) 'Family Violence Including Crimes of Honour in Jordan', *Violence Against Women*, vol. 7, no. 5: 586.

Aref Al-Aref (1933) *Al qada'a ind al badu* [Justice among the Bedouins], n.p.

Arnold, K.C. (2001) 'Are the Perpetrators of Honor Killings Getting Away with Murder? Article 340 of the Jordanian Penal Code Analyzed under the Convention on the Elimination of all Forms of Discrimination against Women', *American University Journal International Law Review* 16: 1343.

Asad, T. (2000) 'Agency and Pain: An Exploration', *Culture and Religion*, vol. 1, no. 1, May.

Asghar, R. (2004) 'Religious Fervour Blocking Moves against Gender Discrimination', *Dawn*, 31 March 2004.

ASK (Ain-o-Salish Kendra) (2000) *Human Rights in Bangladesh, 1999*, ASK, Dhaka.

Athens News Agency (1998) 'Songwriter Akis Panou Sentenced to Life', 25 March.

Baker, N.V., P.R. Gregward and M.A. Cassidy (1999) 'Family Killing Fields: Honour Rationales in the Murder of Women', *Violence Against Women*, vol. 5, no. 2: 1.

Barakat, H. (1985) 'The Arab Family and the Challenge of Social Transformation', in E.W. Fernea (ed.), *Women and the Family in the Middle East: New Voices of Change*, University of Texas Press, Austin.

Bardakoğlu, A. (2004) President of the Directorate of Religious Affairs, Press Release, 8 March 2004, World Women's Day, available at www.diyanet.gov.tr/english/default.asp.

Barthi, A., et al. (n.d.), '*al-wathiqa al-lubnaniyya li-ilgha' jami' ashkal al-tamyiz dudd al-mar'a* [The Lebanese Covenant for the Repeal of All Forms of Discrimination against Women], Joint Committee of the Civil Committee on Women's Affairs and the Advocates' Union, Beirut.

Basu, A. (1999) *She Comes to Take Her Rights: Indian Women, Property and Propriety*, SUNY Press, New York.

—————— (ed.) (1995) *The Challenge of Local Feminisms: Women's Movements in Global Perspective*, Westview Press, Boulder CO.

BBC News Online (2004a) 'Cousins Jailed for Bride's Murder', 20 October.

—————— (2004b) 'Europe Tackles "Honour Killings"', 22 June.

—————— (2003a) 'Honour Killing Father Begins Sentence', 30 August.

—————— (2003b) 'Police Delve into "Honour Killings"', 30 September.

—————— (2001) 'Blair Backs Blunkett on Race', 10 December.

—————— (1999) 'Forced Marriage Clampdown Welcomed', 5 August.

Bedell, G. (1992) 'Fighting for Women's Honour without Shame', *Independent*, 15 March.

Begikhani, N. (2004a) 'Honour-based Violence among the Kurds', paper for *When Human Rights and Culture Clashes*, organised by CHANGE, London, 7 January.

—————— (2004b), 'Honour-based Violence in the Kurdish Context', paper for Metropolitan Police conference on Honour Crimes, London, 18 June.

—————— (2004c) 'Honour-based Violence in the European Context: The Case of Heshu Yunis', paper for the European Conference 'Honour Related Violence within a Global Perspective: Mitigation and Prevention in Europe', Stockholm, 7–8 October.

—————— (2003a) 'Les meurtres d'honneurs dans le Diaspora kurde', paper for 'Devenir' seminar organised by Foundation France–Libertés and l'Envol d'Alcyone, Paris, 10–11 October.

—————— (2003b), 'Socio-cultural Dimension of Honour Killings: The Kurdish Case', paper for 'Time of Silence Has Gone', conference organised by Koerdische Vrouwen-vereniging (KVV) and Kontakt der Kontinenten (KDK), Soesterberg (Netherlands), November 29 (Kurdish), available at www.Kurdistannet.org and www.jinname.org.

———— (2001) 'Kurdish Women and National Identity', paper for Exeter University Department of Middle Eastern Studies, April, and Middle East Studies Association of North America, October, available at www.kurdishmedia.com.

———— (1997a) 'La femme kurde dans les littérature Européannes principalement Française et anglaise du XIXème et du début du XXème siècle', Ph.D. thesis, Sorbonne, Paris.

———— (1997b) 'La femme Kurde face à la montée islamiste', *Cahiers de l'Orient* 47.

Beltrami, S., and R. Petrucci (2001), *Codice Penale annotato con la gurisprudenza*, Simone, Naples.

Bennetto, J., and T. Judd (2004) 'Murder Cases under Review to Identify "Honour Killings"', *Independent*, 23 June.

Bettiol (1982), *Diritto Penal*, Padua, cited in F.S. Fortuna, *Il delitto d'onore nel Codice Penale Italiano del 1930* ['*Honour* Crimes' in the Italian Penal Code of 1930], paper presented at the International Meeting on Strategies to Address 'Crimes of Honour', London, February 2002.

Birmingham Post (2003) 'Islam Opposes Marriage by Force Says Muslim Leader', 16 January.

Bishara, A. (2003), *Turuhat 'an al-nahda al-mu'aqa* [Essays on the Disabled Renaissance], Riyad al-ra'is li'l-kutub wa'l-nashar, Beirut.

Bisharat, G. (1989) *Palestinian Lawyers and Israeli Rule: Law and Disorder in the West Bank*, University of Texas Press, Austin.

Blood and Honour/Combat 18 (n.d.), 'Code of Honour', available at www.skrewdriver. net/honourcode.html.

Boddy, J. (1998) 'Violence Embodied? Circumcision, Gender Politics, and Cultural Aesthetics', in R.E. Dobash and R.P. Dobash (eds), *Rethinking Violence against Women*, Sage, Thousand Oaks CA.

Bourdieu, P. (1966) 'The Sentiment of Honour in Kabyle Society', in J.G. Peristiany (ed.), *Honour and Shame: The Values of Mediterranean Society*, University of Chicago Press, Chicago.

Boyer, R. (1995) *Lives of the Bigamists: Family, Marriage and Community in Colonial Mexico*, University of New Mexico Press, Albuquerque.

Brandes, S.H. (1980) *Metaphors of Masculinity: Sex and Status in Andalusian Folklore*, University of Pennsylvania Press, Philadelphia.

Bravo, A. (2001) 'Madri fra oppressione ed emancipazione' [Mothers Between Oppression and Emancipation], in A. Bravo, M. Pelaja, A. Pescarolo and L. Scaraffia (eds), *Storia sociale delle donne nell'Italia contemporanea* [Social History of Women in Contemporary Italy], Laterza, Bari.

Bredal, A. (2004): 'Blind Slaves of Our Prejudices: Debating "Culture" and "Race" in Norway', *Ethnos* 2.

———— (2002a) 'Invisible Fences: Egalitarianism, Nationalism and Racism', *Journal of the Royal Anthropological Institute*, 8 March: 45–63.

———— (2002b) *Det norske sett med nye øyne. Kritisk analyse av norsk innvandringsdebatt* [Looking at Norwegian's with New Eyes: A Critical Analysis of the Norwegian Immigration Debate], Universitetsforlaget, Oslo.

———— (2002c) Paper on the Nordic Ministries, for workshop, 'Combating Forced Marriages in Scandinavia: Three Different Policy Approaches in a Comparative Perspective', at Seventh International Metropolis Conference, 'Togetherness in Difference', 9–13 September, Oslo.

——— (1999) 'Arrangerte ekteskap og tvangsekteskap i Norden' ['Arranged Marriages and Forced Marriages in the Nordic Countries], *TemaNord*, 604, Nordisk Ministerråd, Copenhagen.

Bruner, E.M. (1993) 'Introduction: The Ethnographic Self and the Personal Self', in P. Benson (ed.), *Anthropology and Literature*, University of Illinois Press, Urbana.

Bullough, Vern L. (1997) 'Medieval Concepts of Adultery', *Arthuriana*, vol. 7, no. 4.

Campbell, J.K. (1964) *Honour, Family, and Patronage: A Study of Institutions and Moral Values in a Greek Mountain Community*, Clarendon Press, Oxford.

Campbell, J.K. (1987), 'Honour and the Devil', in D. Gilmore (ed.), *Honour and Shame and the Unity of the Mediterranean*, American Anthropological Association, Washington DC.

CEDAW (2002) *Report of the Committee on the Elimination of Discriminationa Against Women*, 27th Session, UN Doc. A/57/38, Part II.

CEWLA (2002), *Jara'im al-sharaf: nazhra tahliliyya wa ru'ya mustaqbiliyya* [Crimes of Honour: Analysis and Prospects], CEWLA, Cairo.

Chen, M. (2000), *Perpetual Mourning: Widows in Rural India*, Oxford University Press, Delhi.

Chohan, S. (1999), 'Oh Yes You Do', *Guardian*, 16 August 1999.

Chowdhry, P. (2004a) 'Private Lives, State Intervention: Cases of Runaway Marriage in Rural North India', *Modern Asian Studies*, vol. 38, no. 1: 55.

——— (2004b) 'Caste Panchayats and the Policing of Marriage in Haryana: Enforcing Kinship and Territorial Exogamy', *Contribution to Indian Sociology*, January–August: 1.

——— (1998) 'Enforcing Cultural Codes: Gender and Violence in Northern India', in J. Nair and M. John (eds), *A Question of Silence? The Sexual Economies of Modern India*, Kali for Women, Delhi.

CIMAC (n.d.), Comunicación y Información de la Mujer, *La ley contra la violencia intrafamiliar, logro de las oaxaqueñas y el IMO*, CIMAC, Mexico.

CLADEM (2002), *Declaração Universal dos Direitos Humanos desde uma perspectiva de gênero*, CLADEM, Lima.

——— (2002/2004) *Balances nacionales. Esfuerzos y actividades dirigidas a erradicar la violencia contra las mujeres* (16 countries), CLADEM/UNIFEM, Lima.

CLADEM and Equality Now (2004) *Call for Action 'Beijing + 10'*, CLADEM/Equality Now, Lima/New York.

Connors, J.F. (1989) *Violence against Women in the Family*, United Nations, Vienna.

Conso, G., and V. Grevi (1992), *Profili del nuovo Codice di Procedira Penale*, CEDAM, Padua.

Coomaraswamy, R., and L.M. Kois (1999) 'Violence against Women', in K.D. Askin and D.M. Koening (eds), *Women and International Human Rights Law*, Vol. 1, Transnational Publishers, New York.

Cotes, P. (2004) 'JUSTIÇA, Defesa Ilegítima: em pleno século XXI, assassinos ainda lavam a honra com sangue e são absolvidos por júris populares', *Revista Época*, Globo, São Paulo.

Cowan, J.M. (1980) *Hans Wehr: A Dictionary of Modern Written Arabic*, Libraire du Liban, Beirut.

Cowan, M. (2004) 'New Probe on Murders' *Birmingham Evening Mail*, 22 June.

Cowan, R. (2004) 'Most "Honour Crimes" Hidden by Fear, Police Look to Europe in Battle Against Cultural Taboos', *Guardian*, 23 June.

Crenshaw, K. (1991) 'Mapping the Margins: Intersectionality, Identity Politics and Violence against Women of Color', *Stanford Law Review* 43: 1241.

Dajani, S. (1994) 'Between National and Social Liberation: The Palestinian Women's Movement in the Israeli Occupied West Bank and Gaza Strip', in M. Tamar (ed.), *Women and the Israeli Occupation: The Politics of Change*, Routledge, London.

Dajjani, M. (1998) 'The Palestinian Authority and Citizenship in the Palestinian Territories', available at www.pna.org/.

Danish Institute for Human Rights (2004) *Ægtefællesammenføring i et menneskeretligt perspektiv* [Spousal Unification in a Human Rights Perspective], Danish Institute for Human Rights, Copenhagen.

Dara'awi, D. and M. Zhaika (2000) *Mahkamat amn al-dawla: bayn al-darura wa'l-mashru'iyyah* [The State Security Court: Between Necessity and Legality], Al Damir, Ramallah.

Das, V. (1993), 'Masks and Faces: An Essay on Punjabi Kinship', in P. Uberoi (ed.), *Family Kinship and Marriage in India*, Oxford University Press, Oxford.

Datta, P.K. (1999) *Carving Blocs: Communal Ideology in Twentieth Century Bengal*, Oxford University Press, Delhi.

De Mello, S.V. (2003) 'Violence against Women – What Next?' Opening Statement by Mr Sergio Vieira de Mello, UN High Commissioner for Human Rights at event co-organised by OHCHR and the NGO Committee on the Status of Women, Palais des Nations, Salle XXI, 8 April.

Delaney, C. (1987) 'Seeds of Honour, Fields of Shame', in D. Gilmore (ed.), *Honour and Shame and the Unity of the Mediterranean*, American Anthropological Association, Washington DC.

Dhagamwar, V. (1992), *Law, Power and State*, Sage, Delhi.

Dirks, N. (1992) 'Introduction: Colonialism and Culture', in N. Dirks (ed.), *Colonialism and Culture*, University of Michigan Press, Ann Arbor.

Dobash, R.E., and R.P. Dobash (1998) 'Cross-Border Encounters: Challenges and Opportunities', in R.E. Dobash and R.P. Dobash (eds), *Rethinking Violence against Women*, Sage, Thousand Oaks.

Dupret, B. (2001) 'Normality, Responsibility, Morality: Virginity and Rape in an Egyptian Legal Context', in A. Salvatore (ed.), *Muslim Traditions and Modern Techniques of Power*, Yearbook of the Sociology of Islam, vol. 3, Lit Verlag, Hamburg; Transaction Publishers, New Brunswick and London.

Duzkan, A., and F. Kocali (2000) 'She Fled, Her Throat Was Cut', in P. Ilkkaracan (ed.), *Women and Sexuality in Muslim Societies*, Women for Women's Human Rights, Istanbul.

Eide, E. (2002) '"Down There" and "Up Here:" "Europe's Others" in Norwegian Feature Stories', Ph.D. thesis, Institutt for Medier og Kommunikasjon, HiO, Norway.

el-Dessouki, A. (1997) 'Egyptian Press Coverage of Sexual Violence against Females', master's thesis, American University of Cairo, Cairo.

el-Jesri, Manal (2004), 'In the Name of Honour', *Egypt Today*, April: 80.

el-Morr, Awad (2002) 'Nazhra tahliliyya li 'ahkam jara'im al-sharaf' [Analytical Consideration of Crimes of Honour Rulings], in *Jara'im al-sharaf: nazhra tahliliyya wa ru'ya mustaqbiliyya* [Crimes of Honour: Analysis and Prospects], CEWLA, Cairo.

Eluf, L.N. (2000) 'Homens que matam', *Folha de São Paulo*, 30 August, A3.

Emberland, M. (2003) 'Menneskerettslige aspekter ved lovforslag', Dok 8, 122.

Fangen, K. (2002) 'Tvangsekteskap. En evaluering av mottiltakene' ['Forced Marriage: An Evaluation of Measures Taken Against It'] *Fafo-rapport* 373.

Faqir, F. (2001) 'Intrafamily Femicide in Defence of Honour: The Case of Jordan', *Third World Quarterly*, vol. 22, no. 1: 65.

Faraj, R.R. (2003) 'The Individual in Kurdish Society: A General Reading of the Place of the Individual in Society', *Rahand* 14–15: 376, Rahand Centre for Kurdish Researchers, Sulaimaniya.

Faraj, R.R., and Shwan H. (2003a) *A Study Into Patriarchal Culture and its Effects on Certain Forms of Marriage in the Erbil Governorate* (Kurdish), carried out by Khatu Zin Centre for Social Action, under the supervision of Dr Karim Sharif Qarachatani.

—— (2003b) *A Study in the Statistics on Violence against Women* (Kurdish), Women Information and Cultural Centre, Sulaimaniya.

—— (2001) *Tragically Committed Crimes against Women* (Kurdish), Series 3, Women's Information and Cultural Centre, Sulaimaniya.

Fawzi, A. (2004), 'Hakayat sharah al-mar'a wa'l-qanun' [The Story of Women's Honour and the Law] *Sabah el Kheir*, 22 June.

FCO et al. (2004) *Young People and Vulnerable Adults Facing Forced Marriage: Practice Guidance for Social Workers*, FCO, London.

—— (2002) *Dealing with Cases of Forced Marriage: Guidelines for the Police*, FCO and ACPO, London.

Fenger-Grøn, C., K. Qureshi and T. Seidenfraden (eds) (2003) *Når du strammer garnet. Et opgør med mobning af mindretal og ansvarsløs asylpolitik*, [When You Tighten the Net: Settling Accounts with the Persecution of Minorities and Irresponsible Asylum Policies], Århus Universitetsforlag, Århus.

Fiandaca, G., and E. Musco (1995) *Diritto Penale, Parte Generale*, Zanichelli, Bologna.

Fickling, D. (2004) 'Bestseller on Honour Killing "is a Fake" in Sydney', *Guardian*, 26 July.

Fleischmann, E. (2003) *The Nation and its 'New' Woman: The Palestinian Women's Movement 1920–1948*, University of California Press, Berkley.

Fortuna, F.S. (2002) *Il delitto d'onore nel Codice Penale Italiano del 1930* ['Honour Crimes' in the Italian Penal Code of 1930], paper presented at the International Meeting on Strategies to Address 'Crimes of Honour', London, February (unpublished).

Foster, A.M. (2001) *Sexuality in the Middle East: Conference Report* Middle East Centre, St Anthony's College, Oxford.

Gardner, K. (1995) *Global Migrants, Local Lives: Travel and Transformation in Rural Bangladesh*, Clarendon Press, Oxford.

Gaudiano, R. (2000) 'Una nuova dignita' per le donne del sud', *Incontri* 63, Arbe Editoriale Pubblicitaria S.r.l., Modena.

Geetha, V. (1998) 'On Bodily Love and Hurt', in M.E. John and J. Nair (eds), *A Question of Silence? The Sexual Economies of Modern India*, Kali for Women, Delhi.

Gender Equality Centre (2002), 'Human Rights Service utnytter jenter i nød' [Human Rights Service Exploits Girls in Distress], *Dagsavisen*, 1 December.

Gilmore, D. (1987) *Honor and Shame and the Unity of the Mediterranean*, American Anthropological Association, Washington DC.

Giovannini, M.J. (1987) '*Female Chastity Codes in the Circum-Mediterranean: Comparative Perspectives*, in D. Gilmore (ed.), *Honour and Shame and the Unity of the Mediterranean*, American Anthropological Association, Washington DC.

Glaser B.G., and A.L. Straus (1967) *The Discovery of Grounded Theory: Strategy for Qualitative Research*, Aldine, Chicago.

Gonzáles, R. (n.d.) *Vetusto el Codigo Civil vigente que regula las relaciones familiares: perspectiva machista justifica la violencia de género en Edomex*, CIMAC, Mexico.

Goodhart, D. (2004) 'Too Diverse?', *Prospect*, February.

Griswold, E. (2001) 'This Man's Sister Was Raped so He Killed Her. It Was a Matter of Honour', *Sunday Times Magazine*, 8 July.

Grøndahl, M. (2003) 'Familiesammenføring – fra verdensrekord til verdensrekord', in C. Fenger-Gørn, K. Qureshi and T. Seidenfraden (eds), *Når du strammer garnet. Et opgør med mobning af mindretal og ansvarsløs asylpolitik*, Århus Universitetsforlag, Århus.

Guerrero Caviedes, E. (2002) *Violencia contra las mujeres en América Latina y el Caribe español, 1990–2000: Balance de una década*, ISIS International/UNIFEM, Chile.

Gullestad, M. (2004) 'Blind Slaves of Our Prejudices: Debating "Culture" and "Race" in Norway', *Ethnos*, vol. 69, no. 2: 177.

———— (2002a) 'Invisible Fences: Egalitarianism, Nationalism and Racism', *Journal of the Royal Anthropological Institute*, March: 45.

———— (2002b) 'Det Norske sett med nye øyne, Kritisk analyse Norsk innvandrihgsodebatt' [Looking at Norwegians with New Eyes: A Critical Analysis of the Norwegian Immigrant Debate], Universitetsforlaget, Oslo.

Gupta, R. (2003a) 'Legal Hijacking', *Guardian*, 13 June.

———— (2003b) 'A Veil Drawn over Brutal Crimes', *Observer*, 3 October.

———— (ed.) (2003c) *From Homebreakers to Jailbreakers: Southall Black Sisters*, Zed Books, London.

Habib, F. (2003) 'Disallowing Debate on Honor Killings', *Daily Dawn* (Karachi) 17 November.

Hagelund, A. (2003) 'The Importance of Being Decent: Political Discourse on Immigration in Norway 1970–2002', Ph.D. thesis, Unipax, Oslo.

Haj, S. (1992) 'Palestinian Women and Patriarchal Relations', *Signs*, vol. 17, no. 4: 761.

Haj-Yahia, M. (2000) 'Wife Abuse and Battering in the Sociocultural Context of the Arab Society', *Family Process*, vol. 39, no. 2: 237.

Hall, S. (1999) 'Life for "Honour" Killing of Pregnant Teenager by Mother and Brother', *Guardian*, 26 May.

Hameed, S.S. (1999),'Haria Ki Garhi', *Mainstream*, 6 March.

Hansard (2003) 'Debate on Immigration', HC Deb, 19 March, vol. 401 cd 277 WH para. 5–6.

Hassan, M. (1999) *Sex, Gender, Politics: Women in Israel*, Hakibbutz, Tel Aviv.

Hassan, Y. (1995) *The Heaven Becomes Hell: A Study of Domestic Violence in Pakistan*, Shirkat Gah Special Bulletin, Lahore.

Hijazi, Mustafa (1998) *Al-takhalluf al-ijtima'i* [Social Backwardness], Ma'had al-inma' al-'arabi, Beirut.

Hill, A. (2004) 'Runaways Stalked by Bounty Thugs: Asian Families Pay Violent Hunters Thousands to Track Down Daughters', *Observer*, 18 April.

Home Office (2005) *Domestic Violence: A National Report*, March 2005 Home Office, London.

———— (2003) *Justice and Safety: The Government's Proposals on Domestic Violence*, Consultation Paper, Home Office, London.

———— (2000) *A Choice By Right: Report of the Working Group on Forced Marriage*, Home Office, London.

Human Rights Commission of Pakistan (1999 and subsequent annual reports) *State of Human Rights*, Lahore.

Human Rights Watch (2004) *Honoring the Killers: Justice Denied for 'Honor' Crimes in Jordan*, Human Rights Watch, New York.

———— (1999) *Crime or Custom? Violence against Women in Pakistan*, Human Rights Watch, New York.

———— (1991) *Criminal Injustice: Violence against Women in Brazil*, Human Rights Watch Women's Project, New York.

Hungria, N. (1956) *Comentários ao Código Penal*, vol. VIII, 3rd review and updated edition, Forense, Rio de Janeiro.

Huntington S.P. (1993) 'The Clash of Civilisations', *Foreign Affairs*, vol. 72, no. 3: 22.

Ilkkaracan, P. (2000) 'Exploring the Context of Women's Sexuality in Eastern Turkey', in P. Ilkkaracan (ed.), *Women and Sexuality in Muslim Societies*, Women for Women's Human Rights/KIHP, Istanbul.

Independent Centre for Strategic Studies and Analysis (ICSSA) (n.d.), 'Don't let our honour die', ICSSA, Pakistan, http://icssa.org/ICSS%20-%20themes_moral_honour_killing.htm.

Jayawardena, K. (1995) *The White Woman's Other Burden: Western Women and South Asia During British Colonial Rule*, Routledge, London.

Jehl, D. (1999) 'Arab Honor's Price: A Woman's Blood', *New York Times*, special report, 20 June.

John, M.E. (1998) 'Globalisation, Sexuality and the Visual Field: Global Issues and Non-Issues for Cultural Critique', in M.E. John and J. Nair (eds), *A Question of Silence? The Sexual Economies of Modern India*, Kali for Women, Delhi.

———— (1996) *Discrepant Dislocations: Feminism, Theory, and Postcolonial Histories*, University of California Press, Berkeley.

Joseph, S. (2000) 'Gendering Citizenship in the Middle East', in S. Joseph (ed.), *Gender and Citizenship in the Middle East*, Syracuse University Press, Syracuse.

———— (1999) 'Theories and Dynamics of Gender, Self and Identity in Arab Families', in S. Joseph (ed.), *Intimate Selving in Arab Families: Gender, Self and Identity*, Syracuse University Press, Syracuse.

———— (1994) 'Gender, Culture and Human Rights', *Al-Raida* 65–66: 8.

Joshi, P. (2003) 'Jumping through Hoops: Immigration and Domestic Violence', in R. Gupta (ed.), *From Homebreakers to Jailbreakers: Southall Black Sisters*, Zed Books, London.

Kamal, K. (2002) 'Jara'im al-sharaf fi al-sahafa al-misriyya' [Honour Crimes in the Egyptian Press], in *Jara'im al-sharaf: nazhra tahliliyya wa ru'ya mustaqbiliyya* [Crimes of Honour: Analysis and Prospects], CEWLA, Cairo.

Kamal, S. (2001) *Her Unfearing Mind: Women and Muslim Laws in Bangladesh*, ASK, Dhaka.

Kandiyoti, D. (2000) Foreword, in S. Joseph (ed.), *Gender and Citizenship in the Middle East*, Syracuse University Press, Syracuse.

———— (1996) *Gendering the Middle East: Emerging Perspectives,* I.B. Tauris, London.

———— (1988) 'Bargaining with Patriarchy' *Gender and Society*, vol. 2, no. 3: 1.

Kar, M., and H. Hoodfar (1996) *Personal Status Law as Defined by the Islamic Republic of Iran: An Appraisal*, Special Dossier, Women Living under Muslim Laws, London.

Karim, N. (1996) *Izzat: For ærens skyld* [Izzat: For the Sake of Honour], Cappelen, Norway.

Kelly, L. (1988) *Surviving Sexual Violence*, Polity Press, Cambridge.

Khabarain (2004) 'Karokari Kay Maslay Par Hukumati Arkaan Larparay Spiker Ne Ejlaas Multvi Kar Diya', *Khabarain* (Urdu daily), 20 July.

Khadr, A. (1998) *Al-Qanoun Wa Mustaqbal Al-Mar'a Al-Filistinyyeh* [Law and the Future of the Palestinian Woman], Women's Center for Legal Aid and Counseling, Jerusalem.

Khan, H. (1995) *Eighth Amendment: Constitutional and Political Crises in Pakistan*, Maktaba Jadeed Press, Lahore

Kinneir, J.M. (1818), *Journey through Asia Minor, Armenia, and Koordistan, in the Years 1813 and 1814 with Remarks on the Marches of Alexander, and Retreat of the Ten Thousand*, John Murray, London.

Krishnamurty, J. (ed.) (1989) *Women in Colonial India: Essays on Survival, Work and the State*, Oxford University Press, Delhi.

Kulwicki, A.D. (2002) 'The Practice of Honor Crimes: A Glimpse of Domestic Violence in the Arab World', *Issues in Mental Health Nursing* 23: 77.

KWAHK (2003) 'Women's Lives, Artists' Views', La Pluie d'Oiseaux and Women Information and Cultural Centre, Paris.

Lattanzi, G. (1972) *I Codici Penali*, Milan.

Law Commission (2003) *Partial Defences to Murder*, Consultation Paper No. 173, Law Commission, London.

Leader-Elliott, I. (1997) 'Passion and Insurrection in the Law of Provocation', in N. Naffisen and R.J. Owens (eds), *Sexing the Subject of the Law*, Sweet & Maxwell, Sydney.

Liisberg, M.V. (2004) 'Regler og administrative praksis for ægtefællesammenføring' [Rules and Adminstrative Practice for Spousal Reunification), in in Danish Institute for Human Rights (ed.), *Ægtefaelles-amenføring i Danmark*, Report 1, Spousal Reunification in Denmark.

Lindisfarne, N. (1993) 'Variant Masculinities, Variant Virginities: Rethinking "Honour and Shame", in N. Lindisfarne and A. Cornwall (eds), *Dislocating Masculinity: Comparative Ethnographies*, Routledge, London.

Lipsett-Rivera, S., and L.L. Johnson (eds) (1998) *The Faces of Honor: Sex, Shame and Violence in Colonial Latin America*, University of New Mexico Press, Albuquerque.

Lovett, M. (1989) 'Gender Relations, Class Formation and the Colonial State in Africa', in J. Parpart and K. Staudt (eds), *Women and the State in Africa*, Lynne Rienner, Boulder CO.

Malekar, Anosh (2001), 'Knot of Death', *The Week*, 26 August.

Manfredini, M.G. (1979) *La Posizione della Donna Nell'ordinamento Costituzionale Iitaliano*, CEDAM, Padua.

Manfredini, M. (1931) *Manuale di diritto penale: commento al nuovo codice*, Athaenaeum, Rome.

———— (1921) *Delitti contro il buon costume e ordine della famiglia*, Book 9, Milan.

Manna, A., and E. Infante (2000) *The Criminal Justice Systems in Europe and North America: Italy*, European Institute for Crime Prevention and Control, Helsinki.

Mansoor, T. (1999) *From Patriarchy to Gender Equality: Family Law and its Impact in Bangladesh*, University Press, Dhaka.

Manzini, M. (1964) *Tratto di Penale*, vol. 3, Turin; cited in F.S. Fortuna, *Il delitto d'onore nel Codice Penale Italiano del 1930* ['Honour Crimes' in the Italian Penal Code of 1930], paper presented at the International Meeting on Strategies to Address 'Crimes of Honour', London, February 2002.

Marthin, S. (2002) Presentation on behalf of the Ministry of Refugees, Immigration and Integration Affairs, for workshop 'Combating Forced Marriages in Scandinavia. Three Different Policy Approaches in a Comparative Perspective', at Seventh International Metropolis Conference, *Togetherness in Difference*, 9–13 September, Oslo.

Mayell, H. (2002) 'Thousands of Women Killed for Family "Honor"', *National Geographic News*, 12 February.

McClintock, A. (1995) *Imperial Leather: Race, Gender and Sexuality in the Colonial Contest*, Routledge, New York.

McFadyean, M. (1992) 'Sticking Out Their Necks in Southall', *Independent*, 10 December.

Mernissi, F. (1982) 'Virginity and Patriarchy', *Women's Studies International Forum*, vol. 5, no. 2: 183.

Ministry of Social Affairs (Lebanon) (1996) *Dirasat al-sukkan wa'l-masakin* [Population and Housing Study], Ministry of Social Affairs, Beirut.

Mody, P. (2002), 'Love and Law: Love Marriage in Delhi', *Modern Asian Studies* 36, 1 February.

Moghaizel, F., and M. Abd Al-Sater (1999) *Crimes of Honour: A Legal Study*, Moghaizel Institution, Beirut (Arabic).

Moghaizel, L. (1986) 'The Arab and Mediterranean World: Legislation towards Crimes of Honour', in M. Schuler (ed.), *Empowerment and the Law, Strategies of Third World Women*, OEF International, Washington DC.

Mohanty, C. (1997) 'Women Workers and Capitalist Scripts: Ideologies of Domination, Common Interests and the Politics of Solidarity', in L. Alexander and C. Mohanty (eds), *Feminist Genealogies, Colonial Legacies, Democratic Futures*, Routledge, London.

———— et al. (eds) (1991) *Third World Women and the Politics of Feminism*, Indiana University Press, Bloomington.

Mohsin, A. (2000) 'The Rights of Minorities', in Ain-o-Salish Kendra (ed.), *Human Rights in Bangladesh, 1999*, ASK, Dhaka.

Mojab, S., and N. Abdo (2004) *Violence in the Name of Honour: Theoretical and Political Challenges*, Bilgi University Press, Istanbul.

Moller-Okin, S. (1999) 'Is Multiculturalism Bad for Women', in J. Cohen et al. (eds), *Is Multiculturalism Bad for Women? Susan Moller-Okin with Respondents*, Princeton University Press, Princeton NJ.

Molyneux, M., and E. Dore (eds) (2000) *The Hidden Histories of Gender and the State in Latin America*, Duke University Press, Durham NC and London.

Moore, H. (1994) *A Passion for Difference*, Polity Press, Cambridge.

Morris, P. (1993) *Literature and Feminism*, Blackwell, Oxford.

Mortati, L. *Stati emotive e passionali e responsabilita' penale*, available at www.eurom. it/medicina/sm/sm19_2_17.html.

Moscon, G. (1961) *Pietro Germi's 'Divorce Italian Style'*, FM Editions.

Motta, C., and M. Rodríguez (2000) *Mujer y justicia: el caso argentine*, World Bank Project Publication, Buenos Aires.

Mulla (n.d.) *Principle of Hindu Law*, 5th edn, n.p.

Nandy, A. (1997) 'Colonization of the Mind', in M. Rahmena and V. Bawtree (eds), *The Post-Development Reader*, Zed Books, London: 168–78.

Nanes, S.E. (2003) 'Fighting Honour Crimes: Evidence of Civil Society in Jordan', *Middle East Journal*, vol. 57, no. 1: 112.

Narayan, U. (2001) 'Minds of Their Own: Women, Veiling and State Intervention into "Cultural Practices"', in L.M. Antony and C.E. Witt (eds), *A Mind of One's Own: Feminist Essays on Reason and Objectivity*, Westview Press, Boulder CO.

Nasim, K. (1996): *Izzat: For ærens skyld* [Izzat: For the Sake of Honour], Cappelen.

Negus, S. (1999) 'Rape and Marriage', *Middle East International*, 21 May.

Noronha, M. (1998) *Direito Penal*, vol. 3. 23 ed. rev. e atual. por Adalberto de Camargo Aranha, Saraiva, São Paulo.

Norwegian Ministry of Justice and the Police (2003) *Retten til et liv uten veld* [The Right to a Life with Violence]: Report from a Governmental Committe on Violence Against Women, NOU, Oslo.

Nourse, V. (1997) 'Passions Progress: Modern Law Reform and the Provocation Defense', *Yale Law Journal* 5: 1331.

Nussbaum, M. (2000) *Women and Human Development: The Capabilities Approach*, Cambridge University Press, Cambridge.

Organisation of the Islamic Conference (2000) Letter to the UN Secretary-General, UN Doc. A/C.3/55/4 and annex, 2 October.

Oslo Crisis Centre (2002) 'Bokollektivet. Prosjektrapport for Bokollektivet, et botilbud for unge minoritetskvinner utsatt for tvangsekteskap eller vold i ekteskap 2000–2002', Oslo Krisesenter, Oslo.

Oslo Red Cross (2003) *Informisjonstelfon om tvangsekteskap: Evalueringsrapport 2000–2002*, Oslo Red Cross, Oslo.

Pallotta, G. (1983), *Nel Palazzo del Potere*, SEI, Turin.

Pannain, R. (1957) *Manuale di Diritto Penale*, Book 2, *Parte Speciale 1*, Unione tipografica, Torrese.

Parashar, A. (1998) 'Do Changing Perceptions of Gender Justice Have a Place in Indian Women's Lives? A Study of Some Aspects of Christian Law', in M. Anderson and Sumit Guha (eds), *Changing Concepts of Rights and Justice in South Asia*, Oxford University Press, Delhi.

Paul, R. E. (1998) 'Shelters for Battered Women and the Needs of Immigrant Women', *Temanord* 507.

Paust, Malin (2002) 'Evaluering av Bokollektiv for kvinner med minoritetsbakgrunn – et prosjekt ved Oslo Krisesenter 2000 – 2002', [An Evaluation of the Safe House for Ethnic Minority Women – A Project Run by Oslo Crisis Centre 2000–2002] *Forskning/2001/2/0322*, Oslo Krisesenter, Oslo.

Pelaja, M. (2001) 'Il cambiamento dei comportamenti sessuali' [The Change of Sexual Behaviours], in A. Bravo, M. Pelaja, A. Pescarolo and L. Scaraffia (eds), *Storia Sociale delle Donne Nell'Italia Contemporanea* [Social History of Women in Contemporary Italy], Laterza, Bari.

People's Union for Democratic Rights (2003) *Courting Disaster: A Report on Inter-Caste Marriages, Society and State*, PUDR, Delhi.

Pereira, F. (2002) *The Fractured Scales: The Search for a Uniform Personal Code,* University Press, Dhaka.

Peristiany, J.G. (1966), *Honour and Shame: The Values of Mediterranean Society,* Chicago University Press, Chicago.

Peristiany, J.G., and J. Pitt-Rivers (eds) (1992) *Honor and Grace in Anthropology*, Cambridge University Press, Cambridge.

Peteet, J. (1991) *Gender in Crisis: Women and the Palestinian Resistance Movement*, Columbia University Press, New York.

Pimentel, S. (1978) *Evolução dos direitos da mulher: norma, fato, valor*, Editora Revista dos Tribunais, São Paulo.

Pimentel, S., and V. Pandjiarjian (2000) 'Defesa da honra: tese superada?', *Folha de S. Paulo*, 12 September: A3.

Pimentel, S., V. Pandjiarjian and A.L. Schiritzmeyer (1998) *Estupro: crime ou cortesia? Abordagem sóciojurídica de gênero*, Sergio Antonio Fabris Editor, Porto Alegre.

Pitt-Rivers, J. (1968) 'Honor', in D.L. Sills (ed.), *International Encyclopaedia of the Social Sciences*, vol. 17, Macmillan, New York.

——— (1963) *Mediterranean Countrymen: Essays in the Social Anthropology of the Mediterranean*, Mouton, Paris.

Predelli, L.N. (2003) 'Uformelle veier til makt: Om minoritetskvinners politiske innflytelse' [Informal Avenues to Power: On Minority Women's Political Power], *Makt- og demokratiutredningen 1998–2003, Rapportserien 60*, Norway.

Radford, J. (1992) 'Introduction', in J. Radford and D.E.H. Russell (eds), *Femicide: The Politics of Women Killing*, Open University Press, Buckingham.

Rahman, M., and T.H. Shawon (eds) (2000) *Tying the Knot: Community Law Reform and Confidence Building in the Chitagong Hill Tracts*, Human Rights Summer School and Community Law Reform, University Press, Dhaka.

Ramanathan, U. (1999) 'Images (1920–1950): Reasonable Man, Reasonable Woman and Reasonable Expectations', in A. Dhanda and A. Parasher (eds), *Essays in Honour of Lotika Sarkar*, Eastern Book Co., Lucknow.

Razack, S. (2004) 'Imperilled Muslim Women, Dangerous Muslim Men and Civilized Europeans: Legal and Social Responses to Forced Marriages', *Feminist Legal Studies* 2.

Rehof, L.A. (1993) *Guide to the Travaux Preparatoires of the United Nations Convention on the Elimination of All Forms of Discrimination Against Women*, Martinus Nijhoff, Dordrecht.

Roman, M. Anwar (1988) *Groosha-i-Adab*, Jinnah Road, Quetta.

Riziq, H. (2000) 'Sakin al-sharaf yadhbah al-banat!' [Girls Slaughtered by the Knife of Honour!], *al-Musawwair*, 7 July.

Rouse, S. (1999) 'Feminist Representations: Interrogating Religious Difference', in M. Sinha, D. Guy and A. Woollacott (eds), *Feminisms and Internationalisms*, Blackwell, Oxford.

Rozario, S. (2001) *Purity and Communal Boundaries: Women and Social Change in a Bangladeshi Village*, University Press, Dhaka.

Ruane, R.A. (2000) 'Murder in the Name of Honour: Violence against Women in Jordan and Pakistan', *Emory International Law Review* 14: 1523.

Rundskriv (2004) 'Ekteskapsloven iba om fylesmannes adgang til & reise sak om et ekteskap består eller ikte består, 26 June, available at http://odin.dep.no/krd/norsk/regal/rundskriv/016081-250015/dok-bn.html.

Said, E. (1978) *Orientalism*, Routledge & Kegan Paul, London.

Saidawi, R.R. (2001) *Jawari: Dirasa haul al-'unf dudd al-mar'a fi'l-'a'ila* [A Study of Violence against Women in the Family], Lebanese Council to Eliminate Violence against Women/Dar al-Kutb, Beirut.

Samad, Y., and J. Eade (2001) *Community Perceptions of Forced Marriage: A Report for the Community Liaison Unit*, Foreign and Commonwealth Office, London.

Sayigh, R. (1992) 'Palestinian Women: A Case of Neglect', in O.A. Najjar and K. Warnock (eds), *Portraits of Palestinian Women,* University of Utah Press, Salt Lake City.

SBS (Southall Black Sisters) (2001) *Forced Marriage: An Abuse of Human Rights One Year after 'A Choice by Right': An Interim Report*, SBS, London.

Seed, P. (1988) *To Love, Honour and Obey in Colonial Mexico: Conflicts over Marriage Choice, 1574–1821*, Stanford University Press, Stanford.

SEIF (2003), 'Veien videre. På flukt fra tvangsekteskap – hvordan har det gått med de unge?' [The Road Ahead: On the Run from Forced Marriages – What Has Happened to the Young People?], available at www.seif.no/tvangsekteskap/VeienVidere/.

Sen, P. (2003a) 'Successes and Challenges: Understanding the Global Movement to End Violence against Women', in H.K. Anheier, M. Glasius and M. Kaldor (eds), *Global Civil Society*, Centre for Civil Society/Centre for Study of Global Governance, London: 119–47.

———— (2003b) '"Honour Crimes" and Human Rights', presentation for CIMEL/ INTERIGHTS 'Crimes of Honour' Project at Expert Meeting on Violence in the Name of Honour, Ministry of Justice, Stockholm, 4–5 November, available at www.soas.ac.uk/honourcrimes/Events_Sweden_Sen.htm.

Sen, P., C. Humphreys and L. Kelly, with Womankind Worldwide (2004) *CEDAW Thematic Shadow Report 2003: Violence against Women in the UK*, Womankind Worldwide, London.

Sen, S. (1998) 'Offences against Marriage: Negotiating Custom in Colonial Bengal', in M. John and J. Nair (eds), *A Question of Silence: The Sexual Economies of Modern India*, Kali for Women, Delhi.

Sev'er, A., and G. Yurdakul (1999) 'Culture of Honour, Culture of Change: A Feminist Analysis of Honour Killings in Rural Turkey', *Violence against Women: An International and Interdisciplinary Journal*, vol. 7, no. 9: 964–99.

Shah, Hassam Q. (2002) *Don't Let Them Get Away with Murder*, Shirkat Gah, Lahore.

Shah, N. (1998a) '*Faislo*: The Information Settlement System and Crimes Against Women in Sindh', in F. Shaheed, S. Warraich, C. Balchin and A. Gazdar (eds), *Shaping Women's Lives. Laws, Practices and Strategies in Pakistan*, Shirkat Gah, Lahore.

———— (1998b) *A Story in Black: Karo-kari Killings in Upper Sindh*, Reuter Foundation Paper 100, Oxford.

Shalhoub-Kevorkian, N. (2003) 'Re-examining Femicide: Breaking the Silence, Crossing "Scientific" Borders', *Signs: Journal of Women in Culture and Society*, vol. 28, no. 2: 581.

———— (2002) 'Femicide and the Palestinian Criminal Justice System: Seeds of Change in the Context of State Building?', *Law & Society Review*, vol. 36, no. 3: 577.

———— (2000a) 'Mapping and Analysing the Landscape of Femicide in Palestine', research report submitted by the Women's Center for Legal Aid and Counseling, Jerusalem (UNIFEM submission).

———— (2000b) 'The Efficacy of Israeli Law in Preventing Violence within Palestinian Families Living in Israel', *International Review of Victimology*, vol. 7, nos 1–3: 47.

———— (1999a) 'The Politics of Disclosing Female Sexual Abuse: A Case Study of Palestinian Society', *Child Abuse & Neglect* 23: 1275.

———— (1999b) 'Towards a Cultural Definition of Rape: Dilemmas in Dealing with Rape Victims in Palestinian Society', *Women Studies International Forum*, vol. 22, no. 2: 157.

———— (1999c) 'Law, Politics and Violence against Women: A Case Study of Palestinians in Israel', *Law and Policy*, vol. 21, no. 2: 189.

——— (1997a) 'Tolerating Battering: Invisible Way of Social Control', *International Review of Victimology* 5: 1.

——— (1997b) 'Wife Abuse: A Method of Social Control', *Israel Social Science Research*, vol. 12, no. 1: 59.

Sharma, S. (2004) 'Hindu Women in Bangladesh', *Daily Star*, 27 June.

Shirkat Gah (1996) *Women, Law and Society: An Action Manual*, Shirkat Gah, Lahore.

——— (2002) *There is No 'Honour' in Killing: Seminar Report*, Shirkat Gah, Lahore.

Siddiqui, A. (1999) 'A Vote for the "Honour" Killers', *Dawn*, 8 August.

Siddiqui, H. (2001) Conference Paper, Metropolis Conference, Oslo, October.

Siim, B. (2003) 'Gender Equality and Recognition of Ethnic Minorities in Denmark', unpublished conference paper for 'Gender and Cultural Diversity: European Perspectives', London School of Economics and Political Science, 17 October.

Sircar, N. (2003) 'Sikh Woman Killed for Refusing Arranged Marriage', *Hindustan Times*, 5 May.

Smart, C. (1995) *Law, Crime and Sexuality: Essays in Feminism*, Sage, London.

Socialisti Democrati Italiani Donna (n.d.) 'La Nostra Storia', available at http://195.94.177.122/newsdi/sdi_new/donne/storia.php.

Sonbol, A. (ed.) (1996) *Women, the Family and Divorce Laws in Islamic History*, Syracuse University Press, Syracuse.

Spatz, M. (1991) 'A "Lesser" Crime: A Comparative Study of Legal Defences for Men Who Kill Their Wives', *Columbia Journal of Law and Social Problems* 24: 597.

Spierenburg, P. (1998) 'Knife Fighting and Popular Codes of Honor in Early Modern Amsterdam', in P. Spierenburg (ed.), *Men and Violence: Gender, Honor and Rituals in Modern Europe and America*, Ohio State University Press, Columbus: 103–27.

Spivak, G. (1988) 'Can the Subaltern Speak?', in C. Nelson and L. Grossberg (eds), *Marxism and the Interpretation of Culture*, University of Illinois Press, Chicago.

Storhaug, Hege, for SEIF (2003) 'Tvangsekteskap. En kriseguide' [Forced Marriage: A Guide in Case of Crisis], available at www.seif.no/tvangsekteskap/kriseguide/.

Storhaug, H., and Human Rights Services (2003) *Human Visas: A Report from the Front Lines of Europe's Integration Crisis*, Kolofon forlag.

Stowasser B. (1998) 'Gender Issues and Contemporary Quran Interpretation', in Y.Y. Haddad and J. Esposito (eds), *Islam, Gender and Social Change*, Oxford University Press, Oxford.

Strauss, A. (1987) *Qualitative Analysis for Social Scientists*, Cambridge University Press, New York.

Tamayo, G.L. (2000) *Questão de vida: balanço regional e desafios sobre o direito das mulheres a uma vida livre de violência*, CLADEM/Oxfam, Lima (Spanish); CLADEM/Oxfam, 2001, São Paulo (Portuguese).

Taraki, L. (1997) 'Contemporary Realities and Trends', *Birzeit University Women's Studies Program Report* 12.

Teubner, G. (1992) 'Regulatory Law: Chronicle of a Death Foretold', *Social and Legal Studies*, vol. 1 no. 4: 451.

Thorbjørnsrud, B. (2003) 'Det muliges kunst. En utredning om mulige tiltak for å sikre alle "like, religiøse som lovmessige retter til skilsmisse"' [The Art of the Possible: A Study on Possible Measures to Secure All Individuals 'Equal, Religious and Legal, Rights to Divorce'], available at http://odin.dep.no/archive/krdvedlegg/01/23/Thorb007.pdf.

Uberoi, P. (1996) 'When is Marriage Not a Marriage? Sex, Sacrament and Contract in Hindu Marriage', in Patricia Uberoi (ed.), *Social Reform, Sexuality and the State*, Sage, New Delhi.

United Nations (2002) *Women, Peace and Security*, United Nations, New York.

Van Bruinessen, M. (1992), *Agha, Sheikh and State: The Social and Political Structure of Kurdistan*, Zed Books, London.

Volta R. (1989) *'L'applicabilita' dell'attenuante di cui all'art.62 n.1 del codice penale ai cosiddetti delitti d'onore'*, La Tribuna, Piacenza.

Walker, C. (1995) 'Conceptualising Motherhood in Twentieth Century South Africa', *Journal of Southern African Studies*, vol. 21, no. 3: 417.

Welchman, L. (2005) 'Crimes of "Honour": Problematising a Project', in S. Joseph (ed.), *Women and Human Rights in Muslim Communities*, forthcoming.

———— (2000) (ed.), 'Summary Report – CIMEL/INTERIGHTS Roundtable on "Crimes of Honour"', *Yearbook of Islamic and Middle Eastern Law*, vol. 6, 1999–2000: 439.

Wieringa, S. (ed.) (1995), *Subversive Women: Women's Movements in Africa, Asia, Latin America and the Caribbean*, Zed Books, London.

Wikan, Unni (2002) *Generous Betrayal: Politics of Culture in the New Europe*, University of Chicago Press, Chicago.

Willem van Schendel, W.M., and A.K. Dewan (2001) *The Chittagong Hill Tracts: Living in a Borderland*, University Press, Dhaka.

Winther, K.M. (2003) 'Forced Marriage in a Human Rights and Women's Right Perspective Exemplified through Norwegian and Pakistani Legislation', unpublished thesis, Department of Law, University of Oslo.

Youssef, N. (1973) 'Cultural Ideals, Feminine Behaviour and Family Control', *Comparative Studies in Society and History*, vol. 15, no. 3: 326.

Zahil, M. (1968) *Jara'im al-sharaf fi lubnan* [Honour Crimes in Lebanon], Centre of Research, Beirut.

Zanaty, Muhammad Salam (1995) *Nizham al-'arab al-qabaliyya al-mu'asira*, vol. 3, Maktabat al-nahda al-misriyya, Cairo.

———— (1994) *Nizham al-'arab fi al-jahiliyya*, Maktabat al-nahda al-misriyya, Cairo.

About the contributors

Abdullahi Ahmed An-Na`im is Charles Howard Candler Professor of Law at Emory Law School, Atlanta, USA. An internationally recognised scholar of Islam and human rights, and human rights in cross-cultural perspectives, he teaches courses in human rights, religion and human rights, Islamic law, and criminal law. Additional research interests include constitutionalism and politics in Islamic and African countries. Professor An-Na'im directs several projects, including the Religion and Human Rights Program of the Law and Religion Program at Emory University School of Law.

Dr Nazand Begikhani is an active advocate of women's human rights with particular focus on the rights of Kurdish women. She has written and campaigned extensively on the issue of 'crimes of honour' both in Kurdistan and in Kurdish diaspora communities and is a founding member of the NGO Kurdish Women Action against Honour Killing (KWAHK). She is currently a freelance researcher and expert report writer on gender-based discrimination with regard to asylum and refugee status, and is a sub-editor at the BBC.

Juliana Belloque is a lawyer working with the Latin American and Caribbean Committee for the Defence of Woman's Rights–Brazil (CLADEM). She holds a Master of Law and is currently pursuing a doctoral degree in the Criminal Process of Law at the University of São Paulo. She is Professor of Law at the University of United Metropolitan Faculties and a member of CLADEM–Brazil and the Institute for the Promotion of Equality.

Maria Gabriella Bettiga–Boukerbout is an Italian lawyer currently practising immigration in London. She holds a Master of Law from the School of Oriental and African Studies, focusing on Islamic Law, Immigration and Human Rights. She has previously worked with the CIMEL/INTERIGHTS 'Honour Crimes' Project and intends to carry out doctoral research in this area in the future.

Dr Anja Bredal is a researcher at the Institute of Social Research in Oslo, having recently completed her Ph.D. on negotiations and conflicts between young people of South Asian backgrounds and their parents around the issue of arranged marriage. She has worked on marriage-related issues, including research on forced and arranged marriage, and has published a report on this topic for the Nordic Council.

The Centre for Egyptian Women's Legal Assistance (CEWLA) is a non-governmental organisation which campaigns for women's rights, with an emphasis on legal equality and the amendment of discriminatory laws, including working on the issue of 'honour crimes'. **His Honour Counsellor Awad al-Morr** was formerly Chief Justice of the Supreme Constitutional Court of Egypt. **Azza Sulaiman**, a lawyer and co-founder of CEWLA, is the organisation's General Director and works actively in the field of human rights and development. **Dr Siham Abdul Salam**, an anthropological researcher and human rights activist, is a consultant to CEWLA.

Dr Uma Chakravarti has been teaching history at Miranda House, University of Delhi, India, since 1966. She has been associated with the Indian women's movement and the movement for democratic rights, and has been part of a number of initiatives to document erosions of civil rights since the 1980s. She has written widely on gender, caste and labour.

Dr Jane Connors is currently a senior human rights officer in the Treaties and Commission Branch of the Office of the High Commissioner for Human Rights (Geneva). Prior to this she was the Chief of the Women's Rights Section in the Department of Economic and Social and Affairs of the United Nations (New York). She has taught law at several UK and Australian universities and has written widely on the work of the UN human rights treaty bodies, violence against women and the human rights of women.

Dr Radhika Coomaraswamy is the former United Nations Special Rapporteur on violence against women, its causes and consequences (1994–2003). She is currently the Director of the International Centre for Ethnic Studies in Colombo, Sri Lanka, and holds a variety of academic and non-governmental appointments. She has published widely on issues of constitutionalism, ethnic studies and the status of women and has won many awards, including the Human Rights Award of the International Human Rights Law Group.

Reem Abu Hassan is a Jordanian lawyer specialising in human rights, child rights and women's rights. She is a member of the legal firm Obdeidat & Freihat, Attorneys at Law in Amman, Jordan, and is an active member of a number of rights-focused committees and groups. She has worked on the subject of 'crimes of honour' for a number of years.

Sara Hossain is a barrister practising at the High Court Division of the Supreme Court of Bangladesh, and with Dr Lynn Welchman is Co-Director of the CIMEL/INTERIGHTS 'Honour Crimes' Project. She has been involved in a number of cases of abduction of British/Bangladeshi women by their parents for the purposes of forced marriage and has written and spoken widely on forced marriage. From 1997 to 2003, she was the Legal Officer for South Asia at the International Centre for the Legal Protection of Human Rights (INTERIGHTS), London.

The Lebanese Council to Resist Violence Against Women works on the range of manifestations of violence against women in Lebanon, including 'honour crimes' and 'honour killings'. **Danielle Hoyek**, an attorney at law (member of the Beirut Bar), is vice-president of LCRVAW and a member of its Research Committee. **Dr Rafif Rida Sidawi** holds a Ph.D. in sociology and is a member of the General Assembly of LCRVAW and its Research Committee. **Dr Amira Abou Mrad** holds a Ph.D. in Criminal Law and is a consultant to the LCRVAW Research Committee.

Valéria Pandjiarjian is a feminist lawyer with a history of working on women's rights. She is currently coordinator of the regional violence area of the Latin American and Caribbean Committee for the Defence of Woman's Rights (CLADEM), a member of IPÊ/CLADEM–Brazil and the Institute Patrícia Galvão–Communication and Media, and is Director Council Member of Citizenship Advocacy for Human Rights and Feminist Collective Sexuality and Health, as well as a consultant for AGENDE Actions in Gender Citizenship and Development.

Silvia Pimentel is Professor of Philosophy of Law at the Catholic University of São Paulo. She is a prolific women's rights activist, holding positions such as National Coordinator of the Latin American and Caribbean Committee for the Defense of Woman's Rights (CLADEM–Brazil), President of the Institute for the Promotion of Equity (IPÊ) and Director Council Member of the Commission of Citizenship and Reproduction and other non-governmental organisations. Her most recent appointment is to the UN Committee on the Elimination of All Forms of Discrimination Against Women.

Dr Purna Sen is Programme Director of the Asia region at Amnesty International. She was formerly a lecturer in Gender and Development at the Development Studies Institute and a Visiting Fellow at the Centre for the Study of Global Governance (both at the London School of Economics). She has been involved in research, policy development, activism and advisory work at the international level and in relation to activities relating to violence against women in India, Jordan, Morocco and the UK. She recently co-authored the CEDAW Thematic Shadow Report on Violence Against Women in the UK. She has worked with a number of women's groups and is currently involved with the refugee Women's Resource Project.

Nadera Shalhoub-Kevorkian is Professor of Social Work and Criminology, Hebrew University, Jerusalem. She has written extensively on issues of gender, violence and Arab/Palestinian women. She is a prominent activist and is the Director of the 'Femicide Project' at the Women's Centre for Legal Aid and Counselling (WCLAC), which seeks to document the legal, social and psychological factors contributing to the killing of women.

Dr Dina Siddiqi is Senior Associate at the Alice Paul Center for the Study of Women and Gender, University of Pennsylvania, USA. A cultural anthropologist, Dr Siddiqi is a South Asia specialist who has written extensively on globalisation and gender, sexual harassment, violence against women and the cultural politics of Islamisation in Bangladesh. She has worked as a research consultant for Nagorik Uddyog, the Centre for Policy Dialogue, Bangladesh Legal Aid and Services Trust and Ain-o-Salish Kendra in Dhaka, Bangladesh.

Hannana Siddiqui is joint Coordinator of Southall Black Sisters, where she has worked since 1988. Her work includes campaigning and casework with women and children experiencing domestic violence. She is currently working on the issue of forced marriage and served as a member of the Home Office Working Group on Forced Marriage until her resignation in April 2000. She has written extensively on the work of Southall Black Sisters and black/Asian women experiencing violence.

Aida Touma-Sliman is co-founder and General Director of Women Against Violence (WAV), a Palestinian women's organisation in Israel, which provides services to women experiencing violence as well as campaigning on relevant issues. She was a founding member of al-Badeel, the coalition for struggle against 'family honour' crimes, established in 1994, by women's and human rights organisations from the Palestinian community in Israel.

Sohail Akbar Warraich is the Law Coordinator for Shirkat Gah Women's Resource Centre, Pakistan. He holds a Master's in Law in Development (University of Warwick), focusing on Constitutional Law and Development, and Gender, Law and Development. He brings to the field of law a strong interest in the interrelationship between the principles of law and the realities of people's lives. He has developed paralegal training and legal consciousness courses for community-based organisations and has contributed to several international and national publications related to women's legal rights.

Dr Lynn Welchman is a Senior Lecturer in Islamic Law at the Law Department of the School of Oriental and African Studies, and with Sara Hossain is Co-Director of the CIMEL/INTERIGHTS 'Crimes of Honour' Project. She was formerly the Director of the Centre of Islamic and Middle Eastern Law (CIMEL) at the School of Oriental and African Studies. Prior to her academic appointment, she worked with the Palestinian NGO human rights movement, and has also undertaken work for international human rights organisations.

Index